EDITED BY EDWARD W. ERICKSON

AND LEONARD WAVERMAN

The energy question
An international
failure of policy

VOLUME 2 NORTH AMERICA

UNIVERSITY OF TORONTO PRESS

© University of Toronto Press 1974
Toronto and Buffalo

Volume 1
ISBN 0-8020-2134-4 (cloth)
ISBN 0-8020-6238-5 (paper)

Volume 2
ISBN 0-8020-2140-9 (cloth)
ISBN 0-8020-6240-7 (paper)

LC 73-91565

Printed in the United States of America

Contents

EDWARD W. ERICKSON AND LEONARD WAVERMAN
Introduction   vii

Part One: The United States   1

EDWARD W. ERICKSON AND ROBERT M. SPANN
The US petroleum industry   5

PATRICIA E. STARRATT AND ROBERT M. SPANN
Alternative strategies for dealing with the
natural gas shortage in the United States   27

RICHARD L. GORDON
Coal: our limited vast fuel resource   49

DUANE CHAPMAN
Electricity in the United States   77

STEPHEN W. MILLSAPS, ROBERT M. SPANN, AND EDWARD W. ERICKSON
Tax incentives in the US petroleum industry   99

Part Two: Canada   123

J.G. DEBANNÉ
Oil and Canadian policy   125

Contents

RICHARD E. HAMILTON
Natural gas and Canadian policy   149

LARRETT HIGGINS
Electricity and Canadian policy   171

R.M. HYNDMAN AND M.W. BUCOVETSKY
Rents, rentiers, and royalties:
government revenue from Canadian oil and gas   191

Part Three: Policy Overlaps   215

LEONARD WAVERMAN
The reluctant bride: Canadian and American energy relations   217

H.S. HOUTHAKKER
The energy problem   239

FRANKLIN M. FISHER
Technological change and the drilling cost-depth relationship 1960-6   255

JOHN HELLIWELL
Economic consequences of developing Canada's Arctic gas   267

DONALD N. DEWEES
Transportation energy demand   293

G.D. QUIRIN
Non-conventional energy sources   315

STEPHEN L. McDONALD
Conservation regulation and the elements of a national energy policy   331

TOM STOEL AND LEONARD WAVERMAN
Protection of the environment   357

PAUL W. MacAVOY
Policy disharmonies: problems created by
the organizations that control energy markets   377

CONTRIBUTORS   391

EDWARD W. ERICKSON AND LEONARD WAVERMAN

Introduction

Both Canada and the United States are primarily fossil-fuel energy economies. In electrical generation, there is some use of hydro and nuclear power. But the electrical generation sector accounts for only about one-quarter of primary energy consumption (the other three sectors are transportation, residential, and commercial and industrial consumption); hydro and nuclear sources account in turn for varying fractions of the energy used in electrical generation, approximately 35 per cent in Canada and 25 per cent in the US; and potential new hydro sources are limited. Even if nuclear power begins to fulfill the promise that its advocates anticipate, atomic energy is apt to be a very junior partner in the overall North American energy supply and demand balance at the turn into the 21st century. At least for the lifetimes of most of the readers of these volumes, the North American energy economy is apt to remain based on fossil fuel.

Are we running out of fossil fuel? Of course, the world is running out of fossil fuel. The world is finite. But this does not mean that the world's economy is going to grind to a halt any time soon because we have used the last lump of coal, the last drop of oil, and the last whiff of natural gas.

Scare reports often assert that the US, Canada, North America, or the world only has x years of oil or gas reserves at current production rates (x is usually a relatively small number of years, say, 10 or 15). To put this into perspective, one must realize that, since we began to keep reserve statistics, the reserves-to-production ratio has always been a relatively small number of years. This is because proved reserves are like a grocer's shelf inventory. This inventory costs money to acquire. Just as a grocer does not carry unnecessary shelf inventory, the oil and gas industry does not intentionally engage in the premature develop-

Edward W. Erickson and Leonard Waverman

ment of reserves. Production is a flow out of this inventory and discoveries are a flow into the inventory. Worldwide discoveries have been more than keeping pace with worldwide consumption. (See volume I of *The Energy Question*.)

For example, the real cost (what we have to give up in terms of labor and other resources to discover and develop oil) of oil has not sharply increased on a worldwide average. This may seem strange to say at this time when the world price of oil has been rising rapidly. But the world price increases have not been the result of real resource cost increases. They have been the result of the producer nations finding a way to combine their efforts and exercise substantial monopoly power.

For perspective, a comparison to flue-cured tobacco is appropriate here. For a long time the US enjoyed a monopoly on flue-cured tobacco. The basic power of monopoly is the power to withhold. The US monopoly on flue-cured tobacco has been enforced by production controls; had the US allowed unrestricted production of tobacco and free market sales, the price and cost of tobacco (net of rents) would have been lower. The same is true for oil. The recent worldwide price increases are a result of monopoly power exercised by the producing *countries* (not the companies) rather than real cost changes.

A similar proposition holds with respect to the political aspects of the Arab oil embargo. For years the United States has prohibited trade with Cuba because of US disagreements with Cuban foreign policy. Now, in the world oil market, the shoe is on the other foot.

The exercise of monopoly power by the major oil-exporting countries will have effects, however, on real costs in North America. Because the price of imported oil will be artificially high and its reliability doubtful, it will appear worthwhile to develop higher-cost US and Canadian reserves. The most prominent examples of these reserves are shale oil and tar sands oil. The shale oil is in the western United States; the tar sands are in Canada. At current world oil prices, development of these reserves is economically feasible. There are environmental problems which must be overcome, but the magnitudes of these reserves are stupendous. Together they total hundreds of billions, perhaps over a trillion, of barrels of oil. Together, with yet to be discovered and developed conventional oil and gas from Alaskan, Canadian, and US onshore and offshore sources, these reserves will last well into the 21st century. Coal reserves are also enormous.

LONG-RUN NORTH AMERICAN SUPPLIES OF CONVENTIONAL OIL AND NATURAL GAS

The most widely accepted estimates of the price elasticity of supply of North American crude oil discoveries is that it is about unity – a 1 per cent increase in the price of oil results in about a 1 per cent increase in new discoveries. The price elasticity of supply of new natural gas discoveries may be higher than that for oil. In the long run, the elasticities of supply for discoveries are an approximation of the long-run supply elasticities for production. Before oil or gas can be produced, they must be discovered.

There are problems, however, with using such elasticity estimates for forecasting future discoveries and production. First, the level of future expected prices is apt to be far outside the range of prices which underlie the estimated elasticities. It is always dangerous to extrapolate functional relationships far beyond the data from which they were estimated. If the long-run price of oil stabilizes at, say, over $8 per barrel in the US, forecasts of discovery response based upon supply elasticities estimated from price data in the $2 to $4 range will be at best quite chancy. The same caveat applies to natural gas if deregulation is accomplished, ceilings are abolished, and field markets for production and reserves are allowed to clear at approximately double the wellhead price of recent years. Both prudence and cowardice cause us to be very reluctant to predict how much greater than 12 million barrels a day North American (combined US and Canadian) crude oil production will be in 1980.

This caution applies to both supply response at alternative prices and the level of prices themselves. There is no meaningful way to discuss the question of how much oil and gas we can ultimately expect to recover from the North American continent and its surrounding outer continental shelf except in the context of also specifying the price (and tax) climate in which drilling and production take place. The US real prices for crude oil and natural gas will be the North American reference prices against which the economics of other fuels and technologies must be evaluated. And, as in the past, the US prices will be policy variables. The higher are real prices, the larger will be the volumes of discoveries, proved reserves, production, and ultimate recovery. Also, the more rapid are any price rises and the more certain are oil and gas operators about their permanence, the larger and more rapid will be the supply responses. Beyond this, the policy uncertainties prevent us from being much more specific.

The second complicating factor is that existing onshore oil and gas production in the lower forty-eight states of the United States and in western Canada is typically in older petroleum areas. These areas have been relatively thoroughly drilled. The most attractive prospects have been tested. There is evidence that the exhaustion of potential drilling sites may shift the supply curve of discoveries back to the left at a rate of about 2 to 4 per cent or so per year. In the context of North America as a whole, this effect may be offset by activity in Alaska; the Canadian Arctic; the eastern, western and deeper areas of the Gulf of Mexico; the Alberta foot hills and northern British Columbia regions; offshore Newfoundland and Nova Scotia; offshore California; and the US Atlantic outer continental shelf. But there is no sure proof of oil and gas other than the drillbit. Until there is an additional accumulation of operating experience, it would be foolhardy to hazard an exact adjustment based on speculation about these areas.

The third complicating factor involves the relationship between discoveries and production. There are four aspects of this problem which must be considered. They are all related to price. (1) At higher prices, it is economically worthwhile to shift production from the future to the present and perhaps to sacrifice some ultimate recovery. Thus, from a given discovery, there may be higher earlier production of shorter duration. This effect may be more than offset by three opposing forces. These are: (2) the incentives to be more aggressive in terms of extensions of existing and newly discovered reservoirs; (3) the incentives to use existing technology more intensively to increase the fraction of oil in place that is recovered through secondary and tertiary production techniques; and (4) the continuing development of new and improved recovery technology and reservoir engineering techniques. It is our judgment that the combined net effect of all four of the factors which affect the relation between discoveries and ultimate recovery will be to continue to shift the supply of ultimate recovery in year $(t + n)$ to the right for any discovery made in year t. But it is impossible to specify even an approximate magnitude for such an effect.

These three general areas of complicating factors are the reasons for our profound uneasiness with regard to forecasting future North American production. Our readers, however, deserve at least a guess. If the current world level of prices persists and the US and Canadian prices of crude oil are allowed to rise to that level, it is our judgment that North American conventional crude oil output in the 1980-85 period could be as much as 50 to 100 per cent higher than present levels. The elements of the lower end of this prediction are two million additional barrels a day from Alaska, two million additional barrels a day from extensive and intensive operations in new and existing offshore areas, two million additional barrels a day from onshore areas, and maintenance of the existing level of production. Even at the level of prices postulated, continued regulatory failures and their attendant uncertainties – together with a run of dry holes – could result in not achieving even the lower end of the range. Alternatively, major finds in Alaska and offshore areas alone could push total North American crude oil production through the top of the upper end of the range.

With regard to natural gas, Professors MacAvoy and Pindyck estimate that under a scenario of deregulation of US wellhead prices for natural gas, 1980 US natural gas production could equal approximately 33 trillion cubic feet at a real new contract field price of 65.5 cents per mcf. This is approximately a 50 per cent increase over current levels and is roughly consistent with alternative estimates by Professors Spann and Erickson. It would appear likely under a similar scenario that annual Canadian natural gas production in the early 1980s might approximate 12 trillion cubic feet if it were freely competing in an integrated North American energy market at prices consistent with a netback from a real US price in the 65 cents per mcf or greater range and an optimal transportation network. These volumes might in turn be augmented by Alaskan gas reaching US and Canadian markets through a Mackenzie Valley pipeline.

The prospects for conventional North American oil and natural gas supplies for North American markets are not dim. They critically depend upon price and regulatory policy, but if the current level of world prices persists and is readily translated into incentives for US and Canadian production, supply response from conventional sources can be expected to be substantial.

PROSPECTS FOR TAR SANDS AND OIL SHALE

The largest known reserves of oil in the world are in the Canadian Athabasca tar sands and the US Rocky Mountain oil shales. This is not conventional oil in terms of the necessary means of production. Production is essentially a mining operation. Pilot plants have been built and used, but substantial operating experience is lacking. As with conventional oil, the volume of oil shale and tar sands reserves that is economically recoverable depends upon the price. The ultimate potential of these reserves of oil will depend upon the price and availability of alternative substitute sources of conventional crude oil – whether indigenous to the North American continent or from other areas.

Various trade press reports indicate that the capital costs for Canadian Athabascan tar sand oil are on the order of one billion dollars per 100,00 to 125,000 barrels per day of capacity. At a 15 per cent cost of capital and assuming a ten-year producing life for each increment of installed capacity, this works out to a capital cost of $4 to $5 per barrel of production. A 10 per cent cost of capital reduces the capital cost to about $3.50 to $4.25 per barrel of production. If operating and transportation costs are approximately equal to capital costs per barrel, tar sands oil is economically feasible at prices in the $8 to $10 per barrel range. (Based on current price expectations, lease bonuses in excess of $200 million have recently been paid for 5000 acre tracts of oil shale deposits.) These cost estimates are highly tentative and dependent over time on learning-curve experience, technological developments, environmental considerations, and the oil content and homogeneity of the deposits.

If the combined recoverable reserves of the tar sands and oil shale deposits total one trillion barrels of oil, and if the rate of growth of North American oil demand proceeds at 6 per cent per year, then these deposits alone would be sufficient to supply *all* North American oil requirements until the year 2010. This calculation includes no oil from conventional sources and no imports from other areas. We have already discussed the potential of oil from conventional sources. The industry's interest in building superports suggests that an assumption of no available imports is unrealistic. Moreover, production from tar sands and oil shale is not now on stream and the start-up lead times would be substantial and in turn would extend the life of these reserves. Nevertheless, it is the availability of these reserves that makes the talk surrounding 'Project Independence' more than idle conversation.

In fact, there is a possibility for more than oil autarky. If the world price of oil holds, if aggressive development of oil shale and tar sands oil is undertaken, and if the more optimistic expectations for Alaska, Nova Scotia, Newfoundland, and the US Atlantic outer continental shelf are realized, it is possible that North America could become a net oil exporter to Japan and Europe in the 1980s. The law of joint probabilities, of course, makes such a development unlikely.

ENERGY AND THE ENVIRONMENT

The most critical long-run dimension of the 'energy crisis' is the intersection of energy and environmental policies. Both the production and consumption of energy have important environmental effects. Energy production problems are associated with strip mining, offshore drilling, refinery wastes, and tanker spills. Environmental problems associated with primary energy consumption include thermal and air pollution from electric power generation, automobile emissions, and industrial, residential, and commercial residual energy wastes.

The distinction between the long and the short run in the friction between environmental/economic/energy policies is important. In order to facilitate adjustment to the immediate dimensions of the energy crisis, environmental policy will have to accommodate energy policy. In the long run, energy policy can accommodate to environmental policy. Examples are air pollution standards for electrical generation, offshore drilling in the Atlantic, or superports. In the short run, it may be necessary temporarily to relax or postpone more stringent air pollution standards. This would allow coal to be burned (to the extent it is available in the short run) in many uses. In setting environmental standards for offshore drilling or superports, however, we are not dealing with such an immediate problem. This is not to say that decisions in these areas can be indefinitely delayed with no adverse effects on the energy situation. But the time horizons for these longer-term projects are such that if standards are determined and imposed, the energy companies can adjust to them in their planning.

Environmental protection will raise long-run costs. These increased costs must be borne ultimately by consumers of energy. But we use so much energy that, when the total environmental investment costs are spread over total energy use, the result will not be a skyhigh increase in unit energy costs from this reason alone. We are not facing a dramatic shift in the energy intensity of our society as a result of the costs of environmental safeguards. Proper planning must be done, but the focus of that planning will not be to gird ourselves for the apocalypse. Rather, it will be to solve in an orderly way the more mundane question of how much increases in the quality of the environment are worth in terms of increased cost in energy production and use.

LONG-RUN NORTH AMERICAN DEMAND FOR OIL AND NATURAL GAS

Recent growth in North American oil and natural gas demand has taken everyone by surprise. This especially is true of US oil demand. In 1968, US domestic oil demand (including exports, residual fuel oil, and petrochemical feedstocks) was 13.1 million barrels per day. In 1974, it is likely that US oil demand in the absence of supply restrictions would have been 18.7 million barrels per day (see Table 1). This is an increase of 43 per cent in six years, or a compound annual growth rate of over 6 per cent.

As a point of reference for comparative purposes, consider the demand estimates reported in *The Oil Import Question*.[1] The staff of the Cabinet Task Force on Oil Import Control reviewed all the demand forecasts and projections submitted to the task force by various companies and government agencies. The purpose was to arrive at a consensus estimate of what prospective US consumption experience was apt to be. No new and original estimations were conducted. The consensus compound growth rate was 3.1 per cent; projection of this rate implies 1974 consumption of 15.7 million barrels per day. The difference between projected 1974 consumption and actual 1974 consumption (unconstrained by embargo or other supply restrictions) is 3.0 million barrels per day – a difference of about 20 per cent. This difference goes a long way toward explaining the present shortage of US refining capacity and the pressure put on world oil prices by unanticipated US demand for refined products in the world market (see Table 2).

The consensus estimate of US demand in 1980 derived from submissions to the Cabinet Task Force was 18.6 million barrels per day. The 1980 estimates of Mobil and Exxon, for example, were 17.7 and 19.3 million barrels per day respectively. In 1973, US demand passed through 17.7 million barrels per day. In the absence

Edward W. Erickson and Leonard Waverman

TABLE 1

US supply and demand for oil (millions of barrels per day)

	1973 Preliminary	1974 Preliminary pre-embargo	1974 Demand limited by supply
SUPPLY			
Domestic production			
Crude oil	9.2	9.0	9.2
Gas liquids	1.7	1.7	1.8
Total	10.9	10.7	11.0
Imports			
Crude oil	3.2	3.9	2.5
Residual	1.8	2.2	1.6
Other products	1.1	1.3	1.0
Total	6.3	7.4	5.1
Processing gain	.3	.5	.4
Total supply	17.4	18.7	16.4
DEMAND			
Gasoline	6.6	7.0	5.6
Aviation fuel	1.1	1.1	1.1
Distillate	3.2	3.6	4.0
Residual	2.7	3.2	2.9
Other products	3.4	3.7	2.4
Total domestic demand	17.1	18.5	16.0
Exports	.2	.2	.2
Total demand	17.3	18.7	16.2

SOURCE: *Oil and Gas Journal,* 'Review and Forecast Issue,' 28 January 1974, p. 109

of supply restrictions, US consumption would pass through 19.3 million barrels per day in 1975. The general underestimation of US demand growth should not be viewed as evidence of a conspiracy to mislead the Cabinet Task Force and other government policy-makers. The growth in US consumption over the decade prior to 1968 averaged only about 3 per cent per year. Government and non-industry analysts also underestimated the post-1968 growth in demand for oil.

What were the sources of the errors in the projections which led to such significant underestimation of US demand? Three major problem areas stand out.

TABLE 2

US imports

Crude imports by origin 1973 preliminary (thousand barrels per day)			Product imports, origin not traced 1964-73 (thousand barrels per day)	
Canada		998	1964	1060
Middle East			1965	1229
Saudi Arabia	445		1966	1348
Iran	191		1967	1409
Other	133	769	1968	1549
Africa			1969	1757
Nigeria	461		1970	2095
Algeria	140		1971	2245
Libya	148		1972	2532
Other	67	816	1973	2923
Latin America		428		
Far East		201		
TOTAL		3212		

SOURCE: *Oil and Gas Journal,* 'Review and Forecast Issue,' 28 January 1974, p. 118

First, and most important, the severity of the regulation-induced shortage of natural gas production and reserves has been greater than anticipated. The need for deregulation of the wellhead price of natural gas was apparent long before 1968. Nothing has as yet been accomplished. The resulting shortages of natural gas were translated into new demands for fuel oils.

Second, environmental restrictions shifted oil demand beyond its long-run growth curve. In response to clean air standards, many electric power generation facilities abandoned coal and shifted to fuel oil. The same shift occurred for some industrial energy uses. Automotive emission controls caused a substantial decrease in the gasoline mileage yielded by new autos. This decrease, while modest in each year, when accumulated over several model years of new automobiles caused a non-trivial change in the gasoline consumption characteristics of the automobile stock and a corresponding increase in oil demand.

Third, the US has been moving down the long-run demand curve for oil. This was a result of a secular trend of decreasing real oil prices. For example, the nominal price of gasoline in 1951 was 27.2 cents per gallon. In mid-1973, it was 40 cents per gallon. However, the consumer price index has increased from 77.8 to 135 over the 1951-73 period. Thus, the real price of gasoline has actually *de-*

Edward W. Erickson and Leonard Waverman

creased by over 25 per cent. The price trends of fuel oils also involved real price declines. The result was that the growth in demand represented both a shift to the right in the demand curve and a movement down along the demand curve. Most analysts considered the price elasticity of demand for oil to be quite low. For example, estimates of the price elasticity of demand for oil contained in submissions to the Cabinet Task Force were on the order of -0.1.[2] That is, for an elasticity of -0.1, a 10 per cent decrease in price would result in a 1 per cent increase in consumption.

Long- and short-run fuel use decisions (for example, the trend toward heavier automobiles) were made on the basis of the real price behavior actually experienced. Recent evidence with regard to the switch to smaller cars, fuel conversion of electrical generating facilities, and decreased consumption of gasoline and fuel oil for space heating suggest three things. First, the long-run price elasticity of demand for oil is higher than had previously been believed. Second, the length of calendar time which distinguishes the long- from the short-run may be shorter than many had thought. And third, the cross-elasticity of demand between fuels may be higher than simple projections based on constant relative prices had anticipated.[3] The combined effect of these demand factors was to contribute to the acceleration of demand growth in the 1970s beyond the rate anticipated in projections based upon the experience up through 1968.

In addition to acceleration in the rate of growth of oil demand due to regulation-induced natural gas shortages, environmental factors and direct and cross price effects, other factors also played a part in increased US oil consumption. The most important other factor is the uncertainty with which the industry viewed the future. Because of indecision over an effective oil import policy, environmental pressures which limited some refinery capacity (see Table 3), and domestic price controls, the oil industry did not expand 'enough' in all areas – production, storage, and refining. Other important causes of the crisis include the failure of nuclear electrical generating equipment to be delivered on time or to perform at advertised efficiency levels, which resulted in reliance upon oil-fueled internal combustion turbines for baseload demand as well as peak-shaving service. In our opinion, the basic causes of the recent rapid US demand growth for oil have been the three major factors detailed above.

The crisis was not felt so strongly in Canada, even though imported oil is as important as in the US. Canada relies for some 10 per cent of its consumption on Mid East imports. In Table 4 we detail supply and demand balances for 1973 and a forecast for 1974. Canada, unlike the US, is self-sufficient in oil. The volume of oil exports exceeds the volume of oil imports. The embargo (which was or was not levied against Canada, depending on which producer was asked) affected mainly the area of Canada east of the Ottawa Valley (Quebec and the Maritimes).

TABLE 3

Preliminary list of refineries that have either been prevented
or are being held up currently because of environmental considerations

Company	Site	bd
Shell Oil Company	Delaware Bay	150,000
Northeast Petroleum	Tiverton, RI	65,000
Steuart Petroleum Company	Piney Point, Md	100,000
Hampton Road Energy Co.	Norfolk, Va	180,000
Atlantic Richfield	Machiasport, Me	200,000
Metropolitan Petroleum		
Company (Pittston)	Eastport, Me	250,000
Fuels Desulfurization, Inc.	Riverhead, LI	200,000
Maine Clean Fuels	Searsport, Me	200,000
(Main Clean Fuels is a subsidiary of Fuels Desulfurization, Inc., and the refinery proposal at Searsport is the same proposal which was turned down at Riverhead, Long Island)		
Supermarine, Inc.	Hoboken, NJ	100,000

SOURCE: Office of Energy Advisor, Department of Treasury, memorandum by
Douglas L. McCullough, Senior Staff Advisor, 27 August 1973; based on data from
US Department of the Interior, Office of Oil and Gas.

In 1961, the federal Canadian government had decided that no oil imports be
allowed west of the Ottawa Valley. Until 1973, Quebec and the Maritimes
(which imported all their oil requirements) had the advantage of cheaper oil
than Ontario, the province at the end of the domestic pipeline. The role is now
reversed – a domestic price freeze west of the Ottawa Valley (at $4.10 per barrel
of crude) has kept prices well below the levels in Quebec and the Maritimes. In
order to lessen the impact on eastern Canada, the federal government has subsidized tanker shipments to the east coast via both the Panama Canal and the
Great Lakes (volumes forecast to be 100,000 bd in 1974). The federal authorities have also proposed an extension of the domestic pipeline through Quebec
and a subsidy to oil users in the east. Not wishing to extend the domestic price
freeze to American purchasers of Canadian oil, the Canadian federal officials
levied an export tax on crude oil, now amounting to $6.40 per barrel.

This combination of moves outraged the provinces with energy reserves and
angered American officials. The resulting furor and one-up-manship games in
Canada between the western provinces and Ottawa has no counterpart in the US.
It would be difficult for an American to understand the underlying schisms in
Canadian federalism, which oil and oil policy have brought into the open. The

TABLE 4

Canadian oil demand and supply balance (thousand barrels per day)

	Domestic production[1]	
	1973	1974
Alberta	1795	1823
Saskatchewan	237	232
British Columbia	64	64
Manitoba	14	14
Other	5	5
Total	2118	2137

	Exports	
	1973	1974
US Dist I-IV	872	805
US Dist V	255	225
Total	1127	1030

	Domestic consumption	
	1973	1974
British Columbia	163	175
Prairies	242	250
Ontario	507	520
Eastern Canada	756[2]	780[3]
Total	1668	1725

Oil is defined as crude plus liquefied petroleum gases
1 includes 50,000 bd of synthetic crude from the tar sands
2 includes 14,000 bd of domestic crude
3 includes 100,000 bd of domestic crude

SOURCES: *Oilweek*, 18 February 1974; last column is authors' estimate.

basic question that Canadians are unable to resolve is to what extent the various parts of the country will share in oil profits.

There are both good and bad elements in Canadian policy, elements which should be of some lesson to Americans. First, Canadian governments did not introduce the formal allocation systems and restrictions on refinery outputs which characterize American policy. The absence of shortages of gasoline in eastern Canada show the overwhelming costs of US policies. We feel that the domestic price freeze in Canada is not of long-term benefit to Canadians – it encourages energy use and involves a subsidy to oil users, a subsidy which is not necessarily progressive. The decision to extend the domestic pipeline through Quebec and guarantee that market to western Canada will prove exceedingly costly, if, as we feel, world prices will fall. Ten dollars per barrel domestic oil in Quebec will not be a bargain if the world price is $5.

Canada did not have the environmental pressures to limit refinery capacity as was evident in the US. At the present time, projects adding one million bd to domestic refining capacity are currently under construction or planned. The Alyeska pipeline project which will involve supertankers passing close to the Canadian west coast stirs many visions of a *Torrey Canyon* type of spill, despoiling the fjords of British Columbia.

When the underlying economic situation is changing, projections of long-run demand can be seriously in error. Recent experience is ample evidence of this simple principle. Depending upon what assumptions are made with regard to direct and cross-price elasticities for various fuels, income elasticities, and trends in prices and incomes, nearly any projected time path of fuels demand can be generated. Our knowledge with regard to both the various elasticity coefficients and the exact (or even approximate) magnitudes of the likely time coefficients of the price trends is now very imprecise. It is a complicated and interrelated system that involves the supply and demand balances among alternative fuels and the effects of various regulatory and other public policies. One thing can, however, be said with certainty. If the long-run trend of North American real oil prices reverses itself and begins to rise, projections of North American oil demand based upon the experience of recent years will be much too high.

A NORTH AMERICAN ENERGY ECONOMY?

After the submission (and ultimately the rejection) of the Cabinet Task Force Report, one of the informal recommendations of the majority of the task force was that steps be taken to further coordinate and integrate US and Canadian energy policies. Some US steps were taken in this direction, but they were neither very vigorous nor pursued at a high enough level to be fruitful. US energy policy-makers were too involved in pursuing the courses of action necessary to ensure the development of the trans-Alaska pipeline and the rise in Mid East oil prices to negotiate a common North American energy policy. But even had substantial efforts been made in this direction, it is not clear that success would have been easily achieved. Canadian energy policy is moving away from continentalism. There is moreover great fear of Americans. No evidence of this fear is more appropriate than present Canadian discussions of the route of the oil pipeline extension to Quebec. Canadians are reluctant to use the cheapest route, which runs through the US, because of fears, real or imaginary, of American takeover.

A simple but apt observation has been that the US would like access to Canadian resources on US terms and that Canada would like access to US markets on Canadian terms. This observation, of course, applies to any trade situation. Presumably the terms of trade can be worked out. The existence of substantial trade certainly suggests so. The new world oil market certainly creates ample incentives to do so. But in the process of negotiating the terms of trade for a North American energy economy, coherent domestic energy policies for both the US and Canada must be formulated. At the moment, Canadian and US friction with regard to energy policy between the two countries is only overshadowed by the discord within each country with regard to their respective domestic energy policies.

The catalogue of internal policy conflict within each country is strikingly similar. The items which are generating political heat (not to be confused with useful energy) include:

domestic price freezes,

tax policy,

formation of national energy companies,

tar sands and oil shale development,

pipeline policy,

the role of the federal government in energy policy vis-à-vis state and provincial governments,

the over-all level of energy prices,

access to foreign markets, and

the degree to which increased interdependence between the Canadian and US energy economies is desired.

The list is formidable. If each country must successfully resolve each policy problem in a mutually consistent manner, the prospect for an efficient allocation of North American energy resources does not appear bright. Successful policy formulation, however, is often a triumph of substance over form. Whatever institutional idiosyncrasies are pursued and adopted in each country, the laws of supply and demand will still hold. The separate benefits of a more closely integrated

North American energy economy will make policy coordination mutually advantageous. In our opinion, the game is worth the candle. North American coordination of energy policy may be the vehicle for internal rationalization of both Canadian and US policies.

AN IMPENDING SENSE OF 'DÉJÀ VU'

There is, however, one stumbling block to the formulation of separate domestic and mutually coordinated North American policies. This is the relation between the North American energy economy and the world oil market. This juxtaposition has been a source of policy problems before. The Ottawa Valley Line and Mandatory Oil Import Controls are witness to that. In the light of recent high world oil prices and the Arab oil embargo, both of these 'solutions' to the problem of the relation between the world oil market and the North American energy market have been abandoned – at least temporarily. But, in the longer run there is little reason to believe that world oil prices are likely to remain higher than North American oil prices. This is particularly true if the United States actively pursues 'Project Independence' and if that policy involves coordination with Canada on a North American energy policy which involves substantial reliance upon oil shale and tar sands as crude oil sources.[4]

The trade news is full of evidence which suggests that the current situation is a transitory phenomenon. The *Wall Street Journal*, 22 February 1973, reports that Kuwait rejected as too low all 32 bids in its first oil auction. Part of the reason for the low bids may have been the absence of US demand at the auction.[5] Another reason may have been the short-run availability of other oil at lower prices from alternative sources. The long-run world oil supply situation looks optimistic (from a consuming-country point of view). A sample of recent news reports indicates substantial worldwide successful exploration activity, some evidence of a preference for auction sales of host country royalty oil, increased participation of governments in the oil trade, and an expanding legion of national oil companies such as the National Iranian Oil Company, Petromin, Kuwait National Petroleum Company, Iraq National Oil Company, Nigerian National Oil Company, Pertamina, and Venezuelan Petroleum Corporation. The prospect is for substantial downward pressure upon the world price of oil. Even Henry Kissinger may be unable to prevent the forces of the marketplace from operating.

If the United States pursues Project Independence, if the final version of Project Independence is a coordinated North American policy, and if Project Independence involves establishing North American real oil prices in a range whose upper end approaches approximately double the current levels – whether conventional crude oil or shale oil and tar sands oil are the marginal North American supplies – then the most likely prospect is that some time before 1980 the world price of oil will begin to be below the North American price of oil by an increasingly large margin. The early 1980s would then produce a repeat performance of the late 1960s. The Cabinet Task Force on Oil Import Control will be replaced by a North American Energy Sufficiency Commission. Economic integration of the world energy market may assume a role in the world order of the late 20th and early 21st centuries similar to the role that political integration of the Balkans played in the late 18th and early 19th centuries. The challenge is to learn from our mistakes.

We hope that the eighteen papers presented in this volume will present sufficient data, history, and opinions for readers to pinpoint past mistakes and to see future policy options. Together with the papers in Volume I, sufficient information is provided, we trust, on the true nature of the crises: shortages of appropriate policies, not shortages of energy.

NOTES

1 The Report of the US Cabinet Task Force on Oil Import Control (Washington: GPO, 1970)
2 The distinction between long-run and short-run elasticities were not clearly established in the submissions. Nor were the bases indicated upon which the elasticity estimates were made.
3 For some preliminary econometric work on the problem of direct and cross-price elasticities, see E.W. Erickson, R.M. Spann, and R. Ciliano, *Fossil Fuel Demand* (Philadelphia: Decision Sciences, 1973), a report for the now disbanded Office of Science and Technology of the Executive Office of President, US Government.
4 Because of their high cost relative to inframarginal North American energy supplies, such as Alaskan oil or various natural gas sources, it may be appropriate to think of oil shale and tar sands oil as peak-shaving rather than base-load supplies.
5 See the editors' introduction to Volume I of *The Energy Question* for a discussion of the role of the US contribution to incremental world oil demand. The absence of demand for the US market by buying companies may have been a result of the US allocation system. Under the allocation system, crude oil supplies must be shared. There is no incentive to acquire additional crude oil which must be shared on the basis of the average price of all oil if the marginal price of the additional oil exceeds the average price. Although the evidence is limited and clouded by the special circumstances surrounding this

particular sale, the Arab-Israeli war, the oil embargo, and poor policy planning in the United States, it may be that the United States does have some elements of monopsony power in world oil markets.

PART ONE

The United States

EDWARD W. ERICKSON AND ROBERT M. SPANN

Energy policy involves a great many interactions with other policy areas. Some examples include the balance of payments, priorities with regard to social support of long-run research and development, environmental protection, foreign policy, and antitrust. These interactions can be very complex and it is desirable not to have, for example, the R&D policy tail wag the energy policy dog – or vice versa. This holds for all other policy combinations and formulations as well.

A particular example is antitrust. Many people realize that the energy crisis is a policy failure. It then becomes incumbent to find the policy that failed. If a single policy failure can be found that alone is sufficient, in the eye of the beholder, to explain our current unfortunate situation, then that relieves him of the necessity of examining all the perplexing policy interactions.

Perhaps because of the persistent strain of populism in the American psyche, an enduring single-barreled explanation is the classic charge of monopoly. Charges of effective collusion and conspiracy can be bent to fit any set of facts. And the evils of monopoly explain all ills.

Professors Erickson and Spann examine the US petroleum industry and conclude that it is effectively competitive. Their analysis centers on two recent charges of anti-competitiveness: excessive long-run profitability and collusion in offshore joint-bidding ventures. Professors Erickson and Spann do not here examine the structural characteristics of the industry. This is because of the large number of firms. By many counts, there are at least twenty major petroleum companies. In how many other industries is it possible to talk of the twenty major firms? Even if one adopts the Federal Trade Commission's

3

definition of eight major petroleum companies (as Professors Erickson and Spann do to simplify their analysis), in how many industries are eight major firms so approximately evenly matched and surrounded by so vigorous a competitive 'fringe'?

Erickson and Spann focus on long-run profitability. In 1973, the short-run profitability of the industry improved dramatically. This was primarily a result of the shortages resulting from the policy-induced energy crisis. For example, the profits of Exxon, the largest firm, increased nearly 100 per cent. But this did not lead the financial community to bid up the price of Exxon's common stock on the expectation that this increased profitability was an indication of a permanent change in the earnings capacity of the company based upon successful exploitation of newly found private monopoly power. Rather, by the end of 1973, the price of Exxon common stock had declined by about 20 per cent from its 1973 high. This response is consistent with expectations that the increasing earnings are transitory, not permanent. In fact, the price behavior of Exxon's common stock roughly parallels the overall performance of the general market for equities.

Professors Erickson and Spann do not take the issue of competition versus monopoly lightly. Since so many people attach so much importance to it, it must be taken seriously – particularly as a constraint on policy initiatives. But in their opinion, there is considerable danger that the formal and informal antitrust tail will wag the energy policy dog.

EDWARD W. ERICKSON AND ROBERT M. SPANN

The US petroleum industry

The United States has traditionally relied on free market forces and decentralized decision-making for solutions to resource allocation problems. The free market may not always solve resource allocation problems in a socially acceptable way: (*a*) when all costs and benefits are not internalized for the decentralized decision-makers responsible for production and consumption decisions; and/or (*b*) when the markets in question are not effectively competitive. Environmental questions are discussed elsewhere in these volumes. We focus here on some of the evidence regarding competition in the US petroleum industry.

COMPETITION IN THE US PETROLEUM INDUSTRY

Competition in the United States petroleum industry is an important topic in the policy discussions surrounding the current energy crisis. Concern over this subject runs the gamut from the marketing of gasoline through refining, pipelines, oil production, the field markets for natural gas, and the activities of traditional petroleum companies in other energy areas such as coal and nuclear power.

In our view, bigness is unfortunately confused with monopoly power. This confusion clouds the consideration of rational policy responses to the current energy crisis. The discussion of the competition issue generates a great deal of emotion on both sides of the question. It is too much to expect that we will be able to settle the issue here; it seems to be a permanent feature of political economics. We do, however, hope that we can illustrate convincingly with hard facts some of the reasons why, in our analytical judgment, the US petroleum industry is effectively competitive.

5

Edward W. Erickson and Robert M. Spann

Our analysis centers upon two main areas. The first is the record of long-run profitability in the US petroleum industry. Profitability is an important index of the existence and exercise of market power. The petroleum industry is a large industry, and the firms within it are also large. Effective monopoly results in a divergence between long-run marginal costs and prices. Prices in excess of long-run marginal costs (including a competitive return on invested capital) result in excessive earnings. These excessive earnings are reflected in higher than normal, above average rates of return on stockholders' equity capital. Thus, the rate of return on corporate stockholders' equity capital is one measure of the presence or absence of market power in the petroleum industry.

The record of long-run profitability in the US petroleum industry indicates that the firms in this industry do not enjoy substantial, systematic market power. This index of effective competition yields positive results whether the comparison is to all US manufacturing, Moody's 125 Industrials, Moody's 24 Public Utilities, or a group of industrial firms known to possess market power, or the cost of equity capital for the petroleum industry.

The second area is the record of bidding for offshore acreage. This second area is particularly important for a number of reasons. First, a common practice in offshore bidding is for firms to enter joint bidding partnerships for particular tracts. It has been alleged that this practice is motivated by attempts at collusion rather than pooling of risks in a competitive economic environment. Second, offshore areas represent a very important component of new natural gas and crude oil supplies. It is important that we be satisfied that this significant portion of the industry is, in fact, effectively competitive. Third, a major cause of the current energy crisis is the cumulative effect of Federal Power Commission ceilings on the wellhead price of natural gas. This is a striking example of regulatory failure and regulation induced shortage. It appears that the only permanent solution to this problem is congressional action to deregulate the field markets for natural gas. [Editors' note: See the chapter on natural gas by Starratt and Spann.] But before this can be done, it must be demonstrated to Congress that these markets are effectively competitive. The offshore market is a prominent illustrative case. Our analysis indicates that the markets for offshore acreage and the output from productive offshore leases are effectively competitive.

INDUSTRY PROFITABILITY

Market power shows up as economic profits. The US petroleum industry has not earned the kind of long-run returns on stockholders' equity which are to be expected for firms that enjoy substantial, systematic market power. Recent profits of the petroleum industry have been much higher than the long-run average. This

TABLE 1

A comparison of rates of return on stockholders' equity between ten selected
large firms in concentrated industries and the eight major petroleum companies[1]

Firm	Rate of return on stock-holders' equity, 1972
General Motors	17.8
Xerox	23.4
IBM	18.7
Burroughs	15.4
Bristol-Myers	17.8
Eastman Kodak	20.4
Kellog	22.3
Proctor and Gamble	19.1
Pfizer	17.7
Eli Lilly	29.8
Ten company average	20.2
Average for eight major petroleum companies (1971)	11.1

is partly a result of the energy crisis and its attendant shortages. The energy crisis
has been policy induced and is not a result of market power. Long-run profitability
is the appropriate measure of competitiveness. Petroleum firms have had dramatic
increases in profits in recent quarters. Two points must be made with regard to
these profit increases. First, a substantial portion of petroleum firms' profit increases are the result of regulatory failures. The chief contributing factors were:
(1) failure to relax mandatory oil import quotas in an orderly and expeditious
fashion; (2) the regulation induced shortage of natural gas production and reserves; and (3) the subsequent effect of environmental controls to shift fuel demands to natural gas and to prolong the shortages of refinery capacity and refined
products. Second, the recent percentage increases in profit performance of the industry have to be gauged against a normal base year, adjusted for inflation and
compared to the profit performance of the general US economy. Even when these
adjustments are made, there may still remain a transitory component which is the
result of the energy crisis itself. In a well-functioning economy, these earnings
would be the signals that would cause resources to flow into this industry and ultimately return profits to their long-run levels. For purposes of discussion of long-
run policy responses, the appropriate measure of profitability is a long-run measure.

Table 1 compares the overall average profitability of the eight major petroleum
companies named in the FTC complaint (see Table 3 for a listing of the companies)

Edward W. Erickson and Robert M. Spann

TABLE 2

Comparison of rates of return

Year	Moody's 125 industrials	Eight largest petroleum firms
1971	11.2	11.1
1970	10.2	10.8
1969	12.2	10.8
1968	13.0	12.4
1967	12.4	12.4
1966	14.2	11.6
1965	13.7	12.1
1964	13.3	10.5
1963	12.4	11.5
1962	11.6	10.7
1961	10.5	10.4
1960	10.8	10.2
1959	11.6	9.8
1958	10.2	· 9.6
1957	13.2	13.1
1956	14.3	14.1
1955	15.4	13.7
1954	13.2	12.8
1953	13.4	13.9
1952	13.2	13.6
1951	14.6	15.3

with ten large industrial concerns generally conceded to possess some market power. The comparison indicates that each of the nonpetroleum firms earns more than the average for the eight major petroleum companies. The average for the ten nonpetroleum firms is 20.2 per cent. The average for the eight major petroleum companies is 11.1 per cent. The ten-company nonpetroleum average exceeds the average for the eight major petroleum companies by 9.1 percentage points, or 82 per cent.

Table 2 compares the rate of return on stockholders' equity for the eight major petroleum companies with the average for Moody's 125 industrials on a year-by-year basis from 1951 to 1971. In 16 of 21 years, the average for the eight major petroleum companies is less than that for the firms that make up Moody's 125 industrials. Moreover, in eight of the ten years covering 1962-71, the rate of return for the eight major petroleum companies was less than the return for Moody's 125 industrials. In one year, 1967, they were equal. In only one year, 1970, did the return for the eight major petroleum companies exceed that of Moody's 125 industrials – and then by only six-tenths of one percentage point, or 5.8 per cent.

In the eleven years prior to 1962, the rate of return for the eight major petroleum companies exceeded the rate of return for Moody's 125 in only three years. These were the consecutive years 1951, 1952, and 1953. On average then, the long-run trend over this period in the return on stockholders' equity for the eight major petroleum companies has been down relative to Moody's 125 industrials. This points up an interesting anomaly with regard to the use of concentration ratios. On the basis of concentration ratios and other data, the FTC has charged the eight major firms to be anti-competitive. Assuming that there are no errors in the FTC data, the concentration ratios do show an increase in concentration in the 1960s. But this is inconsistent with the profitability data. This highlights the difficulty of drawing inferences from gross concentration data alone and underlines the necessity of appropriately defining markets and the conditions of entry for those markets.

In the FTC complaint, rate-of-return data for the eight major petroleum companies are compared with rate-of-return data for all manufacturing. Table v-1 of the FTC Report is reproduced here as Table 3. Rate-of-return data are relevant to a discussion of whether or not the earnings of companies contain evidence of the exercise of monopoly power. In our judgment, a careful examination of the rates of return for the major oil companies does not indicate evidence of monopoly earnings. Instead, rate-of-return data indicate that the major oil companies earn a competitive rate of return. In addition, rate-of-return data indicate that the petroleum industry has been getting more competitive in recent years.

For the period 1961-71, on average, four of the eight major petroleum companies earned a lower rate of return on stockholders' equity than the average for all manufacturing industry. Four of the eight major petroleum companies earned more than the average for all manufacturing. Thus, the rate-of-return experience for the eight major petroleum companies has not been atypical with respect to all manufacturing. As with any average, some earn above the average and some earn below the average.

For the period 1961-71, on average, six of the eight major petroleum companies earned less on stockholders' equity than the average of Moody's 125 industrials. Two of the eight major petroleum companies earned more than the average for Moody's 125 industrials.

If the period is expanded to include the years 1951-71, there is evidence that the profits of the eight major petroleum companies were higher (relative to all manufacturing industry and Moody's 125 industrials) in the earlier years of 1951-60 than they were in the later years of 1961-71. For the years 1951-71, five of the eight major petroleum companies earned more on stockholders' equity

9

TABLE 3

Net income after taxes as a per cent of stockholders' equity for the eight largest integrated petroleum firms, 1951–71[1]

	1971	1970	1969	1968	1967	1966	1965	1964	1963	1962
Exxon	12.6	12.0	10.4	13.0	13.0	12.1	11.9	12.6	12.8	11.1
Mobil	11.2	10.6	10.1	10.5	10.0	9.7	9.2	8.8	8.6	8.2
Texaco	13.4	13.1	13.1	15.4	15.3	15.9	15.5	15.2	15.5	14.8
Gulf	10.2	10.4	12.1	13.2	13.1	12.3	11.2	11.0	10.9	10.6
Shell	8.7	8.7	10.9	12.3	13.8	13.4	13.4	12.3	12.0	11.2
Standard (Indiana)	9.6	9.3	10.0	10.1	9.5	9.1	8.1	7.5	7.3	6.6
ARCO	6.9	7.4	8.4	11.0	10.2	9.4	8.1	7.3	7.0	7.7
SOCAL	10.4	9.8	10.2	10.7	10.8	12.1	11.9	11.3	11.2	11.6
Weighted average	11.1	10.8	10.8	12.4	12.4	12.1	11.6	11.5	11.5	10.7
Return on equity in all manufacturing[2]	9.7	9.3	11.5	12.1	11.7	13.4	13.0	11.6	10.3	9.8
Net difference[3]	1.4	1.5	-0.7	0.3	0.7	-1.3	-1.4	-0.1	1.2	0.9

	1961	1960	1959	1958	1957	1956	1955	1954	1953	1952	1951
Exxon	10.4	10.1	9.4	8.7	14.0	15.8	15.2	13.6	16.2	16.6	18.4
Mobil	7.8	7.0	6.5	6.4	9.3	12.0	11.2	10.7	11.6	11.3	12.4
Texaco	14.4	14.3	14.1	13.6	16.2	16.3	15.7	14.8	13.7	13.6	14.6
Gulf	10.9	11.6	11.0	13.5	16.2	14.8	14.3	13.4	14.4	13.0	14.1
Shell	9.5	10.3	11.1	8.8	13.8	15.0	15.4	16.3	17.2	15.2	17.8
Standard (Indiana)	6.5	6.4	6.5	5.7	7.5	7.9	9.2	7.4	8.7	8.8	11.7
ARCO	8.1	8.6	5.8	6.8	7.4	10.1	9.0	9.6	12.2	10.7	12.6
SOCAL	11.7	11.8	12.0	13.0	15.5	15.8	15.1	15.3	15.0	15.0	16.2
Weighted average	10.4	10.2	9.8	9.6	13.1	14.1	13.7	12.8	13.9	13.6	15.3
Return on equity in all manufacturing[2]	8.9	9.2	10.4	8.6	10.9	12.3	12.6	9.9	10.5	10.3	12.1
Net difference[3]	1.5	1.0	-0.6	1.0	2.2	1.8	1.1	2.9	3.4	3.3	3.2

1 Based on 'Moody's Industrial Manual'

2 'Economic Report of the President,' January 1973, p. 280. The Federal Trade Commission is cited as the source.

3 Weighted average return for the 8 companies less that of all manufacturing

SOURCE: Table V-1 of the Federal Trade Commission Report, *Investigation of the Petroleum Industry* (Washington: Government Printing Office for the Permanent Subcommittee on Investigations of Committee on Government Operations of the US Senate, 1973).

than the average for all manufacturing industry. Two earned less. For these same 1951-71 years, five of the eight major petroleum companies earned less on stockholders' equity than the average for Moody's 125 industrials. Three earned more.

Relative to the average for both all manufacturing and Moody's 125 industrials, the eight major petroleum companies were more profitable for the 1951-71 period than for the 1961-71 period. This could only occur if they were more profitable in the years 1951-60 than in the years 1961-71. Profitability has been decreasing. To the extent that decreased long-run profitability is an index of increased competition, the profitability indices indicate that the petroleum industry has been becoming more rather than less competitive. (This indication is consistent with, for example, the record of entry into offshore activity.)

Comparison to averages such as Moody's 125 industrials and all manufacturing industry may be misleading. This is because some of the nonpetroleum firms in these averages may possess market power (see, for example, Table 1). This makes the averages themselves higher than the normal, long-run, competitive rate of return. There is a way to correct for this.[2] A standard procedure in regulatory proceedings is to calculate the cost of equity capital for the particular firm(s) in question. Earnings on equity capital are then compared to the cost of equity capital.

Modern analysts typically calculate a range for the cost of equity capital. This is because a range is more reliable than a point estimate. Using standard techniques for the years 1967-71, the range for the cost of equity capital for the eight major petroleum companies is 10.3 to 12.3 per cent.[3] The midpoint of this range is 11.3 per cent.

For this same 1967-71 period, the average earnings on stockholders' equity for the eight major petroleum companies were 11.5 per cent. Within the limits of the precision of such calculations, the earnings on stockholders' equity (11.5 per cent) and the cost of equity capital (11.3 per cent) are approximately equal. This is what we would expect in an effectively competitive industry operating in an economy with well-functioning capital markets. The rate-of-return data indicate that the eight major petroleum companies are part of a competitive industry and are themselves earning the competitive rate of return. If simple monopoly power or more complex collusive behavior were an important feature for the petroleum industry, one would expect it to show up in the rate-of-return data. It does not.

The rate-of-return data examined here do not indicate that the petroleum industry has been competitive in all times or in all places. It is well known that some of the classic American antitrust cases involve the petroleum industry. One of the costs of maintaining a competitive economy is constant surveillance by the antitrust agencies. But the recent rate-of-return data do indicate that this surveillance has paid off – at least with respect to the petroleum industry.

11

Edward W. Erickson and Robert M. Spann

There is another possible difficulty with regard to rate-of-return analysis when it is applied to large, integrated companies operating in several distinct markets. This possible difficulty is that the companies may have monopoly power in some markets, but not in others. In such a case, monpoly earnings in some markets may be used to subsidize less than competitive earnings in other markets. The effect could then be an overall rate of return on equity capital equal to the cost of equity capital with monopoly earnings in some markets submerged in the overall average. (Such a situation leaves unanswered the question of why a company not regulated on a rate base, fair rate-of-return standard would persist in operating in a market in which it was earning less than the competitive rate of return. We pose this question, but do not consider it further.) A market in question is the offshore Gulf of Mexico area. An important component of domestic oil and gas supplies is the offshore area in the Gulf of Mexico. Nearly 20 per cent of US total natural gas and crude oil production comes from this offshore area, which will be even more important in the future. Fortunately, a good deal of data exist which allow the application of rate-of-return analysis to the offshore area in the Gulf of Mexico.

OFFSHORE LEASE SALES

It has been charged that joint bidding ventures in offshore lease sales are evidence of a collusive pattern in the petroleum industry which escapes the surveillance of the antitrust authorities. This charge is inconsistent with the record of profitability for the industry (both on offshore activity and in aggregate) and the actual pattern of bidding behavior. The evidence is consistent with the proposition that the industry is in general effectively competitive – and particularly so with regard to offshore activity.

In our opinion, joint bidding is a vehicle for pooling risks involved in offshore operations and serves as a vehicle which enhances entry into offshore activity by relatively smaller firms. This opinion is consistent with an analysis of offshore lease sales by Professor Jesse W. Markham.[4] Markham found that there was no statistical evidence that joint bidding reduces the number of bidders and that joint bidding is not inconsistent with an increase in the number of bidders and the average bid.

This evidence is also consistent with a more detailed analysis of the actual bidding patterns and the rate of return on assets committed to offshore activity. We have analysed the record of bid patterns for joint ventures.

The patterns for winning bids are summarized in Tables 4, 5, and 6. These tables show percentage bids in each category that were made by firms or groups of firms which contained no representatives of the eight major petroleum companies.

TABLE 4

Joint venture bidding patterns for winning bids, 1954-73 sales

Number of firms in combine	Number of bids	Per cent nonmajors
1	1121	49
2	356	24
3	145	43
4	206	46
5 and over	69	77
Overall	1897	44

TABLE 5

Joint venture bidding patterns for winning bids, 1973 sale

Number of firms in combine	Number of bids	Per cent nonmajors
1	11	36
2	14	71
3	10	80
4	38	87
5 and over	31	74
Overall	104	75

TABLE 6

Joint venture bidding patterns for winning bids, 1972 sales

Number of firms in combine	Number of bids	Per cent nonmajors
1	63	60
2	52	27
3	39	41
4	24	25
5 and over	14	50
Overall	192	42

13

Edward W. Erickson and Robert M. Spann

As Table 4 indicates, approximately half of the winning bids were made by single firms or combinations of firms which included no representative of the eight majors. In addition, almost half of the single-firm winning bids were made by nonmajor firms. This evidence is not consistent with a situation in which the major firms are able to enforce collusive bidding arrangements as a result of their participation in joint bidding ventures.

Tables 5 and 6 confirm the results of Table 4. In 1972, 42 per cent of all winning bids were made by nonmajor firms and 60 per cent of winning single-firm bids were made by nonmajor firms. In 1973, 75 per cent of all winning bids were made by nonmajor firms and 36 per cent of all winning single-firm bids were made by nonmajors. This is not evidence of collusive bidding patterns.

When Tables 5 and 6 are combined and compared with Table 4, an interesting result emerges. In the combined 1972 and 1973 lease sales, 54 per cent of all winning bids were made by single firms or combines which included no majors. This compares to the equivalent figure for all 1954-73 lease sales of 44 per cent. Also, in the combined 1972-3 lease sales, 57 per cent of all single-firm winning bids were made by nonmajor firms. This compares to the equivalent figure for 1954-73 lease sales of 49 per cent.

These comparisons indicate that for a large number of firms entry is possible into offshore activity, that joint bidding is not always necessary for such entry but that it is a facilitating factor, and that entry has occurred over the 1954-73 period. (These conclusions are also supported by a similar analysis of second and third place bids.)

Out of a total of 776 joint ventures which submitted winning bids, only 91 (or 12 per cent) consisted of majors alone. But 295 (or 38 per cent) consisted of non-majors only. One-half of all joint ventures consisted of both majors and nonmajors, but the turnover in bidding partnerships was significant. There were no winning combines in excess of three firms which consisted only of majors. These data are a very strong indication that offshore activity is undertaken in a very competitive economic environment.

THE RATE OF RETURN
TO OFFSHORE ACTIVITY

If the lines of argument developed in the two previous sections are correct, the rate of return to resources committed to offshore activity should be equal to the competitive rate of return. This can be tested. In order to determine if the rates of return in the Gulf of Mexico offshore area are competitive and typical of the competitive rate of return earned by the petroleum industry, we analysed the available data. This financial and economic analysis included lease bonuses, so it is also relevant to the question of 'collusive joint bidding combines.' There is one methodological difference between the offshore rate-of-return analysis and the eight major company average analysis reported above. First, the rates of return are computed on total assets. This is because it is impossible to break out the equity capital components on a disaggregated basis. This difference is adjusted for and does not affect the conclusions. Second, in addition to discussing retrospective rates of return, we analysed prospective rates of return of the three very recent lease sales. This analysis involved computing competitive lease bids on the basis of a discounted cash flow model. These results are discussed below. The prospective analysis also required estimating future oil and gas prices. These price assumptions are also discussed below.

There have been a number of studies of the rate of return on investment expenditures for offshore exploration, development, and production. These studies conclude that the rate of return for offshore activity is approximately equal to the competitive rate of return on investment in the American economy. These findings are consistent with the conclusions of staff studies for the Cabinet Task Force on Oil Import Control.

One of the recent studies was done by L.K. Weaver and associates of the Bureau of Mines.[5] This was a very detailed engineering-economics study of a typical, successful 5000 acre offshore tract in the Gulf of Mexico. The Weaver study indicated that the rate of return on total assets committed varied between 14 and 17 per cent – depending on the rate of withdrawal of the oil and gas. The Weaver study, however, was for a successful tract. Not all tracts are successful. For example, only 40 per cent of the tracts leased in 1970 have resulted in commercially feasible production. Some of the currently unproductive tracts may yet become producers, but the effect of unproductive acreage is to reduce the rate of return toward the competitive rate.

An estimate of prospective profitability at the time of a lease sale is of more interest for the problem at hand than a study of retrospective profitability. The data underlying the Weaver study are very complete and amenable to adjustment to reflect economic conditions at the time of the 1972 and 1973 lease sales. We have adjusted the Weaver data on the basis of the 1972-3 economic situation. Investment decisions are based on forecasts of future prices and costs. Our adjustments included: (i) increasing geophysical, platform, and drilling costs to current rates, and (ii) assuming oil prices of $5 a barrel and gas prices of 65 cents per mcf. These prices, particularly the oil price, would not be relevant for a lease sale to be held now. This is because there has been a revolution in expected prices. Prices for new oil are in the over $6 a barrel range. Controls, embargos, and regulatory paralysis have so muddied the water that it is very difficult to quantify price expectations at this time. For oil, they are certainly higher than $5 a barrel.

Edward W. Erickson and Robert M. Spann

For natural gas from the federal offshore areas, there is no telling. Overall, realized average hydrocarbon prices will likely be higher than the expected prices upon which lease bids were made. This will create windfall profits. [Editors' note: See the Millsaps, Spann, and Erickson chapter on tax policy for a more complete discussion of this problem. An excess profits tax for the petroleum industry has recently been proposed. Not only is such a tax complicated to administer, but it does not provide a permanent solution to the fundamental problems discussed by Millsaps, *et al.*] But the existence of possible windfall profits does not change the relevance of the calculations reported here.[6] For the purposes of these calculations, the relevant prices are the expected prices at the time the bids were made. Reasonable estimates of expected prices for the 1972 and 1973 lease sales are $5 a barrel and 65 cents per mcf. These are the prices used here.

The expected price and adjusted cost data were combined with the relevant tax parameters, a rate of return on total assets of eight per cent, and Weaver's estimated reserve data to build a discounted cash flow model which takes into account the fact that in an overall offshore exploration campaign not all tracts are successful. This model was then used to predict bonus bids per acre for the 1972 and 1973 lease sales. The predicted bids were then compared with actual bids as an indicator of the competitiveness of both offshore production activity and the bidding process.

The test of competitiveness is the relation between predicted and observed bids. If predicted bids exceed observed bids, then this is an indication that the Federal Treasury is not capturing all the rents from offshore tracts. If observed bids are approximately equal to or exceed predicted bids, then this is an indication that a competitive bidding process is at work. This is a straightforward test, but it must be applied to a number of lease sales. Just as is the case of a computation of the cost of equity capital, a range of data which includes some of the variation from lease sale to lease sale is more reliable. Also, this is a single test and its results must be considered jointly with other available evidence. The bidding process actually generated winning bids per acre for the 1972 and 1973 lease sales as follows: 19 December 1972, $4,108 per acre; 12 September 1972, $2,017 per acre; and 19 June 1973, $2,908 per acre. The average predicted bid for the three lease sales equaled roughly $2500 per acre. The observed bid for the three lease sales equaled roughly $2700 per acre. The observed average bid slightly exceeds the predicted average bid.

The bidding evidence suggests that the offshore leasing process is highly competitive and that rents resulting from the unit cost advantages of offshore areas are captured by society at large in the form of payments to the Federal Treasury. This behavioral evidence is consistent with the structural evidence from concentration ratios and the performance evidence from the analysis of overall industry profitability.

The evidence indicates that oil and gas companies earn no more than a competitive rate of return on offshore activity. Lease bids for individual 5000 acre tracts may be as high as $100 million. In the Alaskan lease sale, the total bonus payments approximated one billion dollars. These aggressive bids occur regardless of whether firms are bidding in joint ventures to pool risks or bidding individually. Presumably the companies are not indifferent to sums of this order of magnitude.

If the companies could be sure to be successful in the acquisition of acreage by bidding smaller amounts, they would do so. But competition makes this impossible. Joint bidding ventures are unsuccessful as a mechanism for obtaining an essential, specialized resource on noncompetitive terms. This evidence, together with the long-run profit performance of the industry, and the patterns of lease bidding combinations, indicates that joint bidding ventures are similarly ineffective in creating noncompetitive conditions in the sale of oil and gas.

The evidence from the offshore bidding data is especially important for public policy formation with regard to natural gas field markets. It indicates that higher supply prices for new natural gas supplies are the result of the higher costs of securing those supplies. It is true that offshore areas are quite important in current production, and even more important in terms of prospective production. But offshore areas still account for a minority fraction of total production (relative to onshore areas) and will do so for the balance of this decade. It is also true that offshore areas have lower unit costs (net of bonus payments) than do onshore areas. In light of this, two questions may be asked, 'What do offshore costs, including bonuses, have to do with onshore costs?; and, with respect especially to natural gas, why should we allow prices to rise on offshore natural gas if those price increases will simply be captured by the Federal Treasury as increased bonus payments?'

There are several points which should be made with regard to these questions.

(a) Offshore costs including bonuses are a reasonable proxy for onshore costs. If the companies could discover and produce onshore gas at lower costs than the costs (including bonuses) for offshore gas, and sell it in intrastate markets, they would do so. The basic economics of maximizing profits by equating at the margin indicates that the unit costs of incremental onshore new gas supplies must be in the neighborhood of those for offshore gas.

(b) Not all offshore tracts are successful and commercially feasible. Higher prices for offshore gas will make some tracts that are not now productive commercially feasible and will also stimulate more intensive drilling. The net effect of this will be to increase offshore areas' gas supplies that will be available to the interstate market. We need all the gas we can get.

Edward W. Erickson and Robert M. Spann

(c) Artifically holding offshore gas prices down to a level below that of the best substitute – onshore gas – will encourage waste in consumption. Prices will lag further behind opportunity costs and aggravate the existing shortage. A significant part of the current shortage is demand induced. In addition to finding ways to stimulate supply, public policy should also cause available supplies to be rationed among the highest valued uses. The price system is the most efficient rationing system we know. A way to both stimulate new supply and conserve our scarce gas resources by allocating them to their highest valued use is to allow market clearing prices to operate.

Thus the data from offshore bidding are instructive on two counts. First they are consistent with the overall picture of the domestic petroleum industry as an effectively competitive industry. In this connection, setting maximum prices in the field markets for natural gas cannot be justified on the basis of protecting consumers from monopoly power. Rather, maximum prices merely deprive consumers of gas that they desire and result in willy-nilly income redistribution among various users of alternative fuels. Second, the offshore bidding data indicate that a *prospective*, cost-based, regulated wellhead price in the field markets for natural gas in 1972 and 1973 would have been on the order of 65 cents per mcf. Since the actual ceiling price on new gas was only about one-half of that, it is not surprising that the shortage of production and reserves began to take hold with a vengeance. The lesson is clear. *Ad hoc* tampering with competitive markets eventually results in serious dislocations. The same is apt to be true for other segments of the industry.

COMPETITION, MONOPOLY,
AND POLITICAL POWER

Although we believe that the petroleum industry is in general effectively competitive, this does not mean that it is not without substantial political power. Political power is different from market power. This is as true in petroleum as it is in agriculture. Industry political power may change the economic environment in which the whole industry operates, but not the long-run profitability of individual firms. Evidence of the political power of the industry can be found in the historical record of market demand prorationing, mandatory import quotas, and other federal policy (the Connally 'Hot Oil' Act, for example) which supported the prorationing system and the depletion allowance and related tax provisions. But the industry is not omnipotent. Witness the continued ceiling price on natural gas and the reduction in percentage depletion. Moreover, even when the industry is successful at creating some advantage, resources flow and the benefits are competed away. The result is that in the long run – which is often

18

a relatively short period of calendar time – the benefits are capitalized into the cost structures of the competing firms and earnings are at a competitive rate. This phenomenon, together with the large size of the firms, explains some of the special intransigence of the industry with regard to adverse policy changes. Monopolists could also be expected to resist adverse policy changes. But the competitive nature of the industry helps explain the Bismarckian sincerity with which industry representatives argue their case. Moreover, because of the large size of the leading firms, small changes in profitability result in opportunity losses which must be measured in billions of dollars. This makes such arguments even more compelling. Public policy formulation which fails to recommend changes on a prospective and/or compensatory basis is apt to result in policy failures.

Some examples are illustrative. The Cabinet Task Force on Oil Import Control recommended replacing the quota system with a tariff. This in itself is unremarkable. But the recommendation was also widely interpreted to include a rollback of the domestic price of oil toward the then prevailing world price level. Such a rollback would have imposed substantial capital losses on the industry. (It would also have definitely ended the pernicious market demand prorationing system, but substantial progress in this direction could have been made by simply replacing the quota with a tariff at the then existing domestic price level.) It is not surprising that the industry resisted strenuously. The Cabinet Task Force cannot be wholly blamed for the current situation in world petroleum markets, but it certainly helped to set the stage for the events that have come to pass.

Another example is the Alaskan pipeline. As a result of the Alaskan lease sale, the industry was induced to pay nearly a billion dollars in lease bonuses for North Slope acreage. This money was expended on the basis of the expectation that the Alaskan pipeline would be constructed rapidly. Until oil is marketed from the North Slope, these expenditures represent a deadweight on the earnings of the companies involved. It is not surprising that the companies resisted delays in the construction of the pipeline and recommendations for consideration of an alternative Canadian route, which would have further stretched out the period before revenues were forthcoming and a return began to be earned. [Editors' note: See the chapter by Helliwell for a discussion of the Canadian pipeline.]

Environmental policy is another case in point, particularly with regard to offshore drilling. This is another situation where 'up front' lease bonus costs are substantial. If lease bids are made on the basis of one set of costs derived from a particular set of environmental safeguards, and then if it is proposed to make these safeguards more restrictive, it is no wonder the companies may object. Retroactive rulings affecting leases on which the companies are locked in as a result of large lease bonuses or established production can have the effect of confiscating stockholders' capital. This is unlikely to be the case in the current climate

19

of substantial price increases. But it must be remembered that at times the industry has experienced long periods of constant or declining real prices. It is not impossible that such periods may reoccur. If environmental protection is to have the cooperation of the industry, it should not be advocated on a naive assumption that 'the companies can be made to pay.'

The purpose of these examples is not to depict the industry in angelic terms. Rather, they are intended to make a simple point. Determined, and sometimes successful, political lobbying by the industry is evidence neither for nor against monopoly or competition. In the context of a long-run competitive earnings situation, such lobbying can take on a special sense of urgency to preserve the retrospective institutional arrangements upon which cost and profit structures are based. Prospectively, special opportunities may be created. But if the past is any guide to the future, resource flows will rapidly erode any supranormal benefits and the results will be a new set of policy-created, institutionalized, sunk costs which will obstinately refuse to become bygones.

CONCLUSIONS

On the basis of the evidence examined here, we conclude that in general the US petroleum industry is effectively competitive. This evidence will not convince everyone. Those with eyes to see a special vision of monopoly find support in the fact that the directors of Big Oil form insidious 'interlocks' with, among others, the Metropolitan Opera, the Los Angeles Rams, the Boy Scouts, the University of Texas, the Mayo Foundation, the New York Zoo, and the H.J. Heinz Company.[7]

As a result of the persistent belief that the industry enjoys monopoly market power, various public policy remedies in addition to specific antitrust action are often proposed. These include nationalization of the industry; disintegration of the industry into hermetic modules which separate gas and oil, and production, transportation, refining, and marketing; and creation of a federal energy company to search for, produce, and process oil and gas. The first two proposals ought to be evaluated primarily in terms of their costs, the last proposal in terms of its benefits. Proponents of a federal energy company see two major benefits. First, they believe that such a company would make a significant contribution to the US energy supply. Second, they believe that such a company would provide a benchmark and source of information now denied federal and state policy makers.

There is an example of such a venture in another energy area. This is TVA. The total assets of TVA are about $4,000,000,000. The total assets of Amerada-Hess are $1,378,000,000. Thus, if we were to create a TVA-sized national energy company devoted to oil and gas production, it would only be about three times as large as Amerada-Hess. Even if all the resources of such a venture were committed to oil and gas exploration and production, the contribution of such a venture to the long-run oil and gas supply problem would be marginal. It would be noticeable, but it alone would not usher in a new era of abundance. Moreover, we could not create such a national energy company overnight. The energy problem is here and now.

With regard to an information benchmark and increased flows of standardized information, there is a better alternative way to achieve this than through creation of a national energy company.[8] A frequent complaint is that federal public policy makers receive oil and gas related information only from the 'industry' (implicit in this complaint is the assumption that state agencies in producer states – the Texas Railroad Commission, for example – are indistinguishable from the private industry), and that the industry provides only that information in only those forms which make hard answers to hard questions of public policy difficult or ambiguous to determine.

A national energy company would do little to resolve this problem. Even if funded at maximum feasible levels, it would not be large enough to provide more than a very limited sample. Moreover, the data it would provide would be point estimates generated under particular sets of circumstances. Most useful for policy determination are ranges of data generated under diverse situations. A way exists simultaneously to mollify those who believe that the industry is denying public policy-makers extensive and consistent data and to improve the data actually available as inputs to the policy determination process.

The United States is creating a Federal Energy Administration. The FEA could be empowered both to collect data from the industry and to audit the tabulations in a much more systematic way than is now done. Amendments have been offered to legislation and language has been proposed for committee reports that specify and clarify these powers. For example:

By and large, it is the giant vertically (and often horizontally) integrated energy companies who have heretofore been suspected of shielding or shading vital information from governmental access and scrutiny. The Committee expects the Administrator to create a sufficient inspection capability to monitor and verify the information supplied by such enterprises, and to induce – just as with the Internal Revenue Service or the Securities and Exchange Commission – maximum voluntary full disclosure ... (and) ... to establish categorical groupings of energy information, of sufficient comprehensiveness and particularity to permit fully informed program monitoring and policy guidance by both the Administrator and the Congress. What the Committee has in mind is the kind of information categories de-

21

Edward W. Erickson and Robert M. Spann

veloped in 1970 under the direction and with the approval of Secretary Shultz for petroleum data collection,[9] including such matters as (1) petroleum and natural and liquified gas reserves, production, transportation and refining cost and capacities, both domestic and international, and the utilization thereof; (2) storage location, capacities, cost, and utilization for both crude oil and products by type; (3) actual transfer (as opposed to 'posted') prices in both integrated and non-integrated transactions; and (4) structural information relevant to petroleum industry competition, including location and ownership of reserves and facilities throughout the chain of activity from production through marketing, and joint and collaborative arrangements among companies with respect thereto. The Administrator would be expected to develop similarly comprehensive and particularized categories of energy information for all other forms of fossil and nonfossil fuels.[10]

Where serious questions exist, it is ultimately for the courts to decide issues of anti-competitiveness. The existence and exercise of information gathering powers by the Federal Energy Administrator such as those outlined above would be useful both in the enforcement of the antitrust laws and to neutralize the argument that one of the indicators of anti-competitiveness with respect to the petroleum industry is the process through which technical and economic information is gathered and distributed.

NOTES

1 These companies are Exxon, Mobil, Texaco, Gulf, Shell, Standard of Indiana, ARCO, and Socal.
2 Another correction would involve accounting procedures. Unless accounting conventions are standardized across industries, ambiguities may result. Unfortunately, the most general thing that may be said about standard accounting conventions is that they are not standard. For example, if proved oil, gas, and coal reserves and domestic real estate are undervalued on energy company balance sheets with respect to similar items on the balance sheets of companies in other industries, the effect may be to overstate the profitability of energy companies. But problems with the balance sheet valuation of assets are not limited to the energy companies. Were one to make a one-time adjustment for energy companies, one would also have to do so for such companies as, for example, IBM, etc. Although there would be some changes in absolute magnitudes, it is not clear that the pattern of comparison would change. In addition, it is likely that the FTC is correct with respect to the profitability of the majors

as a group versus the profitability of the independents as a group. There is likely to be some real economic advantage to integration.

3 The discounted cash flow method was used to calculate both of these estimates. The 10.3 per cent calculation is the sum of the average 1971 dividend yield for the eight companies plus the average five-year growth rate in earnings per share. The 12.3 per cent estimate was derived by substituting the average beta factor for the eight major petroleum companies (0.95) into a regression equation which related DCF estimates of the cost of equity capital for electric utilities to their beta factors.

4 Jesse W. Markham, 'The Competitive Effect of Joint Bidding by Oil Companies for Offshore Lease Sales,' in *Industrial Organization and Economic Development* (Boston: Houghton Mifflin, 1970), Jesse W. Markham and Gustav F. Papanek, editors, pp. 116-35

5 L.K. Weaver, H.F. Pierce and C.J. Jirik, *Composition of the Offshore U.S. Petroleum Industry and Estimated Costs of Producing Petroleum in the Gulf of Mexico*, United States Department of the Interior Information Circular 8557 (Washington: GPO, 1972)

6 The other side of the windfall profits coin is windfall losses. Some firms in the industry have at times experienced negative windfalls. For example, in the early and middle 1950s some firms acquired already existing production capacity. The price at which this capacity was acquired reflected a forecast of tax policy, ultimate recovery, operating costs, prices and market demand factors (allowable production rates). Over the next several years, Texas market demand factors fell from an average of about 70 per cent to a low of 28 per cent. The results were stretched out payout periods and implicit capital losses on the acquired properties.

7 In the 'Washington Merry-Go-Round' column published in *The News and Observer*, 22 December 1973, Raleigh, North Carolina, Jack Anderson refers to an unpublished study of interlocking directorships by the Center for Science in the Public Interest. According to the Anderson column, the study shows that directors of the 18 largest oil companies have 460 'interlocks,' including 132 at banks, 31 with insurance companies, 12 with utilities, 46 with schools, 15 in transportation, and 224 with large manufacturing and distribution companies.

8 With regard to TVA, the same benchmark argument was used at the time of its creation. We know of no widespread use of TVA as a benchmark in rate-of-return hearings before state utilities commissions.

9 Cabinet Task Force on Oil Import Control, *The Oil Import Question*, paragraph 345b (Government Printing Office, 1970)

10 Excerpt from a proposal by Representative John Culver for the House of Representatives Committee on Government Report on H.R. 11793, 'Federal Energy Administration Act of 1973.' Representative Culver offered amendments to strengthen the information gathering power of the FEA as follows:
'(a) The Administrator shall, for purposes of Section 5(8) of this Act, have authority to collect energy information from all persons owning or operating facilities or business premises who are engaged in any phase of energy supply or major energy consumption, and to require full identification of all data and projections as to source, time, and methodology of development ...
(b) The Administrator shall collect, assemble, evaluate, and analyze energy information pursuant to categorical groupings, established by the Administrator, of sufficient comprehensiveness and particularity to permit fully informed monitoring and policy guidance with respect to the exercise of each of the advisory and program responsibilities vested in the Administrator under Section 5 of this Act or otherwise.'

PATRICIA E. STARRATT AND ROBERT M. SPANN

The natural gas shortage in the United States is a dramatic example of regulatory failure and inadequate policy response. The shortage has been regulation-induced. Following the 1954 Phillips decision of the Supreme Court, the Federal Power Commission embarked upon an ill-fated set of policies which amounted to imposing a ceiling price on natural gas field prices. This occurred at a time when natural gas demand was rapidly increasing. A shortage of reserves began to develop in the 1960s, but because of the then existing large reserve stocks and the leads and lags involved, an actual production shortage did not develop until recent years. We now have a full-blown shortage of both reserves and production.

This shortage has been aggravated because of further regulatory failures. The inability of the United States to settle on an appropriate oil import policy resulted in uncertainty about the economics of expanding domestic refining capacity. In addition, the effects of more stringent environmental standards on natural gas demands were not adequately anticipated. The effects were to increase dramatically the demands for natural gas at a time when new natural gas supplies were dramatically decreasing and when price was not allowed to function either to stimulate new supplies or ration scarce existing supplies to their highest valued end uses. Tight domestic refining capacity meant that domestic fuel oil was not available to take up the slack, and product imports markedly increased.

Ms Starratt and Professor Spann believe that an appropriate solution would be to deregulate the wellhead prices of natural gas and allow field prices to find their market clearing levels. We agree. Such a policy would go a long way toward rationalizing US energy policy.

This chapter should be compared to the Erickson & Spann chapter, especially with regard to competition in the US petroleum industry, and should also be read along with the Hamilton chapter on Canadian natural gas, the Grennes & Winokur chapter on the balance of payments, the Homet chapter on self-sufficiency, the McDonald chapter on the US coal industry, and the MacAvoy chapter on policy interconnections.

PATRICIA E. STARRATT AND ROBERT M. SPANN

Alternative strategies for dealing with the natural gas shortage in the United States

The United States faces an extensive shortage of natural gas at regulated prices. This shortage is becoming increasingly severe as time passes. Use of natural gas in the United States has more than doubled in the past fifteen years, rising from 10.5 trillion cubic feet (Tcf) in 1957 to 23.0 Tcf in 1972. In 1971, natural gas accounted for 36.4 per cent of domestic energy consumption and was delivered to 42 million customers in the fifty states. Yet, over the years, drilling and reserves added per foot drilled have generally declined.

New customers are denied service in many areas. Present customers cannot always purchase the volumes for which they have contracts. Pipelines are curtailing (reducing or cutting off) some customers' deliveries under both firm and interruptible contracts due to insufficient reserves to meet contract commitments. Some service abandonments are in sight. Interstate pipelines reported supply deficiencies of 453 billion cubic feet (Bcf) for the April 1971-March 1972 period. The next year (and for the same period) deficiencies of about one trillion cubic feet were reported to the Federal Power Commission (FPC). There are also shortages in some areas in the producing states.

In our opinion, no responsible commentators on the natural gas industry would disagree with the fact that a shortage of natural gas does exist and will grow worse if present policies are not altered. There is now considerable discussion of what policy changes are appropriate for natural gas. This discussion should be taking place in a larger framework of concern about national energy shortages and the need to develop a coherent, coordinated national energy policy.

Several alternative policies have been proposed to help alleviate the current natural gas shortage. These policies are not necessarily mutually exclusive. The

27

three policy proposals which have received the most attention are:
1 Deregulation of the wellhead price of natural gas;
2 Direct end-use controls on natural gas including reallocation of supplies away from the intrastate market to the interstate market;
3 Development of synthetic natural gas (SNG) and use of imported liquefied natural gas (LNG).

In what follows, the likely effects of alternative policies for dealing with the natural gas shortage are discussed in the light of what past policies have or have not achieved.

ORIGINS AND EXTENT OF THE NATURAL GAS SHORTAGE

There are several different types of shortages that can occur in the natural gas market.[1] First, there can be a shortage in the sense that, during the winter season (when gas is in higher demand), distributors may find that the quantities of gas being delivered are insufficient to meet peak (highest level) demand on very cold days. When such shortages occur, pipelines and distributors are expected to cut off certain large industrial and electric utility customers. These 'interruptible' customers are supposed to have alternate fuel capacity to use in such circumstances.

Another kind of shortage would preclude gas pipelines and/or distributors from expanding sales due to insufficient new incremental supplies. In this situation a particular pipeline may not have contracted for sufficient reserves of natural gas for a future increased level of output.

The third kind of shortage exists when pipelines are unable to obtain enough supplies from producers to maintain current deliveries to gas customers at previously contracted-for volumes. This type of shortage could be due either to a drilling and/or discovery rate lower than required to meet demand. In this situation, the required gas volumes are simply not available for sale.

All three forms of natural gas shortages currently exist. The first type has become more common in recent years; in the past few winters, gas supplies have been cut off with more frequency and for longer periods of time. Companies with interruptible contracts (or schools, as at Denver in January 1973) whose gas supplies were never interrupted before are now experiencing frequent and longer interruption in deliveries. The problem of interruptibility and priority of use is becoming more important as the shortage worsens – entailing potential conflicts within the federal bureaucracy which were not resolved at the beginning of 1974.

The symptom of the deeper shortage is the continuation and rising level of natural gas curtailments (reductions in contracted-for deliveries) by pipelines to their customers. These do not relate simply to weather conditions but rather to the low level of gas supplies being discovered and produced. In 1971, there was a waiting list of potential customers in Chicago as follows: 14,000 residences, 2000 businesses, and 800 industrial users. By 1972, some potential gas customers were denied service in twenty-one states. Because of this shortage, moreover, the FPC proposes to cut off supplies to certain large-scale interruptible users as long as demand exceeds supply. Early in November of 1973 the Transcontinental Gas Pipeline system told about 180 North Carolina industrial and institutional gas users not to expect any natural gas over the period from November 16 to April 15. Similar situations have occurred in other states. Should the shortage become more severe, contracts to firm (as opposed to interruptible) customers may be voided by the FPC on the basis of priority uses of natural gas. *All* industrial sales could be made on an interruptible basis, moreover, should the FPC's proposed rules be issued as orders.

The problem underlying the deeper shortage is that the nation is using twice as much gas as producers are finding. Proved reserves increased by 63 per cent between 1946 and 1970, while annual production increased by 344 per cent. From 1968 to 1970, reserve additions replaced only 51 per cent of the gas that was produced.[2] This trend continued in 1971 and 1972.[3] As of 17 May 1973, the reserves to production (R/P) ratio for 1970, the year-end proven recoverable reserves divided by production, was 11.9 years, when computed on the basis of the FPC National Gas Survey.[4]

The result is that pipeline curtailments are deepening beyond spot cut-offs on cold days and are projected to become substantial in the future. During the winter of 1971-72, seven major interstate pipelines curtailed service to existing customers. As reported by the FPC in hearings on fuel shortages in January 1973, the gas shortage is far more pervasive this year and will continue to deepen unless there is a long-term reversal of the finding trends since 1956.[5]

On 10 April 1973, the FPC chairman, John N. Nassikas, reported: 'Direct industrial sales declined 7.4 per cent in 1972. For the April 1972-March 1973 period, fifteen major pipelines have projected deficiencies of almost one trillion cubic feet or about 10 percent of the annual sales of those pipelines representing almost five percent of total annual domestic gas production. This represents a sharp increase from reported deficiencies of 453 billion cubic feet for the April 1971-March 1972 period.' Other commentators on the natural gas market have reached similar conclusions. Breyer and MacAvoy concluded that for the years 1964-68 'the total demand for reserves was 1.5 to 2.2 times higher than the

Patricia E. Starratt and Robert M. Spann

actual reserves acquired under FPC price ceilings; therefore, *excess* demand for reserves was 50 to 120 percent of realized levels of commitments.'[6]

THE CAUSE OF THE NATURAL GAS SHORTAGE

The current shortage of natural gas is a direct result of Federal Power Commission ceilings imposed on the price producers are allowed to charge for natural gas sold in the interstate market. FPC price ceilings were instituted in 1960 as a result of the Supreme Court's 1954 Phillips Decision[7] which extended the coverage of the Natural Gas Act[8] to natural gas producers.

The price ceilings had two effects which have resulted in the current shortage of natural gas. Demand for natural gas was stimulated by artifically low prices, whereas supply was reduced by lower-than-free-market prices.

This is best illustrated in the standard supply-demand framework. In the absence of controls, the price and output of natural gas is determined by the simultaneous solution of the supply and demand functions for natural gas. In the absence of regulatory intervention, this leads to a natural gas price which clears the market at the established, ruling, equilibrium price. Quantity supplied is equal to quantity demanded. If a ceiling price which is less than the market-clearing equilibrium price is imposed on the natural gas market, the quantity demanded increases because of the reduced price of natural gas relative to other fuels. The quantity supplied falls as natural gas supplies (with costs in the range below the equilibrium market-clearing price, but above the regulated ceiling price) are no longer economically feasible. The amount of the shortage is the excess of quantity demanded over quantity supplied. In 1972 in the United States, the regulation-induced shortage of natural gas (excess demand at the ceiling price) was of the order of 20 per cent of actual production.

The shortage in the natural gas market is mainly due to price ceilings, not technological conditions. If the price of natural gas were raised, supply would increase as prospects were drilled which may be profitable at higher prices but are unprofitable at artifically low ceiling prices.[9] Demand for natural gas would decrease as some current natural gas users shifted towards alternative fuels.[10]

That the shortage did not appear immediately after the introduction of ceiling prices was due to the nature of the natural gas sales contract. Natural gas is sold under long-term contracts (usually twenty years) in which a producer commits reservoirs to a specific pipeline. The only part of current production which is affected by price controls is that part of current production which is the result of contracts signed after price controls were instituted. The immediate effect of the price ceiling is to lower the rate at which natural gas is discovered and to create an excess demand for reserves. The full extent of the shortage is not felt

TABLE 1

New non-associated natural gas discoveries
and new contract prices in the United States, 1953-69

Year	New non-associated discoveries (Tcf)	New interstate contract price (cents per mcf)	New contract price in 1958 dollars
1953	8.5	13.3	15.1
1954	11.0	11.7	13.1
1955	6.8	14.4	15.8
1956	13.5	14.8	15.7
1957	13.8	16.9	17.3
1958	12.3	18.6	18.6
1959	10.3	18.4	18.1
1960	9.3	18.2	17.6
1961	7.0	17.9	17.1
1962	6.8	17.5	16.5
1963	9.4	17.0	15.9
1964	5.4	16.2	14.9
1965	7.1	17.4	15.7
1966	5.4	17.4	15.3
1967	3.4	18.6	15.8
1968	1.2	19.0	15.5
1969	1.7	19.7	15.4

SOURCES: Foster Associates and American Gas Association

in the market for natural gas production until the fraction of total production resulting from contracts signed after the institution of price controls is a substantial share of the market.

Currently a substantial fraction of natural gas production is from contracts signed after the FPC price ceilings were effective. The current shortage is a direct result of the reduction in the rate of new natural gas discoveries during the 1960s, and this low level of natural gas exploration and discovery was due to FPC price ceilings.

Table 1 illustrates the pattern of natural gas prices, discoveries, and new contract commitments. Real new contract prices rose during the 1950s and began to decline about the time price ceilings were introduced. The real wellhead price of natural gas fell 15 per cent in the first nine years of field price regulation. Discoveries of natural gas peaked at approximately the same time as did real new contract prices. New contract production in the interstate market remained approximately constant during the 1960s even though the demand for natural gas was growing at a rapid rate.[11]

31

The data in Table 1 are not a perfect indication of the price-quantity supply relationship in natural gas supply. It is possible that changes in other relevant variables have influenced natural gas supply as well. Interest rates rose during the 1960s, and so may have increased the cost of capital to gas exploration firms. Discoveries might decrease over time at constant prices since good gas prospects are always drilled before poor prospects. Over time, the distribution of prospects available for drilling shifts toward higher-cost discoveries. It takes higher real prices to bring forth the same volume of discoveries as time passes. Technological advances, however, may serve to mitigate or even eliminate this effect. Finally, changes in the oil market affect the gas market since these two products are substitutes in fuel consumption and joint products in production.

Many of these factors are taken into account in econometric models which will be discussed below. But the conclusions gleaned from econometric models are the same as those indicated by Table 1. The decline in natural gas discoveries which led to the natural gas shortage is a direct result of FPC price controls. Substantial additions to natural gas supplies would result from increases in the field market prices to market clearing levels.

COMPETITION, MONOPOLY, AND CONTRIVED SHORTAGES

The production of natural gas is neither a pure monopoly nor a purely competitive industry. There are many independent sellers and buyers, but in particular markets for limited periods at least, some monopoly power exists on the part of producers. In other markets, pipelines have exercised 'monopsony' power and depressed field prices. Examples of both horizontal affiliations (joint bidding, farm-outs, exchange agreements) and vertical integration (pipeline and distribution interests in production and producer interests in pipelines) are not difficult to demonstrate.

The conclusion reached in most recent studies by professional economists not associated with either the industry or regulatory agencies is, however, that natural gas field markets are workably competitive in most places for most of the time (apart from the constraints of regulation itself).[12] Supply may not have been forthcoming simply because individual producers compared drilling prospects with expected prices and decided to invest elsewhere. The American Gas Association definition of 'proved reserves' includes the phrase 'recoverable ... under existing economic and operating conditions.' It is likely, as is alleged by industry adversaries, that some producers are in fact 'sitting on' reserves or prime exploration acreage until the price is right; but this behavior is just as consistent with the hypothesis that regulation is holding prices below *competitive* levels, as with the existence of collusion or monopoly.

There are, however, a variety of indicators that the shortage of natural gas is not simply the contrivance of producers. Some of these indicators do not depend upon published estimates of proved reserves. One such indicator is the increasingly frequent curtailments and shortages even in unregulated intrastate markets. It is worth noting too that local gas-distributing companies which have historically been fierce opponents of field price increases and deregulation are now largely convinced that there is, in fact, a shortage and that the shortage is regulation-induced. Some of these distributors now go so far as to advocate decontrol of field prices for new gas.

The liquidation of the natural gas surplus that undoubtedly existed in the 1940s and 1950s, and an eventual excess of demand over supply can, moreover, be predicted as the inexorable outcome of (1) natural gas prices that remain significantly lower than those of other fuels; (2) the 'topping out' of domestic oil production (and thereby the supply of dissolved and associated natural gas); and (3) the progressive discovery and depletion of the best onshore reserves and prospects.

Even if the current reserve and producibility estimates were deliberately biased by the producers to create an illusion of shortage today, the continuation of the foregoing trends guarantees that there will soon be a real and growing shortage that need not be invented. This trend of increasing shortages can only be prevented by altering the policies which have led to the shortage.

POLICIES FOR ELIMINATING
THE NATURAL GAS SHORTAGE

In review, the policy alternatives which have been proposed to eliminate the natural gas shortages are:
1 Deregulation of the wellhead price of natural gas;
2 Use of synthetic natural gas (SNG) and imported natural gas (LNG); and
3 End-use controls on natural gas including forced diversion of intrastate sales to the interstate market.

Each of these policies is analyzed in the succeeding sections of this paper. The result of that analysis is that price deregulation is the most efficient and least costly method of eliminating the shortage of natural gas. Synthetic natural gas and imported liquefied natural gas could be utilized to eliminate the natural gas shortage; but this option would result in higher purchase costs for natural gas to the consumer and in higher real resource costs to society. Direct end-use controls will do nothing to alleviate the shortage of natural gas; the only result of this policy option is a reallocation of the natural gas shortage.

Patricia E. Starratt and Robert M. Spann

Effects of field price deregulation
Two econometric models have been developed to analyze the effects of natural gas price deregulation. One is the Spann-Erickson model of oil and natural gas supply.[13] A more detailed model of the natural gas industry has been developed by Paul W. MacAvoy and Robert S. Pindyke.[14]

Both models yield similar policy implications. The supply of new natural gas discoveries is extremely sensitive to the wellhead price of natural gas. The predicted equilibrium price of natural gas at the wellhead is roughly double the regulated wellhead price of natural gas.

Implications of the Spann-Erickson model
The Spann-Erickson model has been used to estimate the market-clearing price for natural gas.[15] Prices need to increase on the order of 100 per cent in order to eliminate the shortage of natural gas. Had such a price been in effect for the past several years so that the industry was completely adjusted to it, the effect would have been a significant increase in natural gas supply. A significant effect, reducing the shortage of natural gas, would result from the fact that natural gas would become a less attractive fuel, its prices being higher than before.[16]

The best estimate of the market-clearing price for recent years obtained by Spann and Erickson is a range. For 1972, this range was 37 to 50 cents per thousand cubic feet (mcf) at the wellhead in South Louisiana. The point estimate equilibrium price for 1972 was 43.5 cents per mcf.[17] According to Spann and Erickson's estimates, if such a price actually described the incentives facing the industry, US discoveries in 1972 would have been approximately 13.0 Tcf. Compared to recent years' discoveries, this is an enormous volume of gas, but it is less than the 14.2 Tcf discovered in 1959. Point estimates of market-clearing prices and discoveries volumes are reported in Table 2. These estimates are already out of date, because of the sudden shifts in the demand for natural gas as a result of environmental factors and the shortages of fuel oil caused by shortages of refinery capacity and crude oil input.[18] As a result of these effects, the projected prices and volumes for the later 1970s were already required in the summer of 1973. There were a number of transactions in the 1973 intrastate markets at 65 cents or better per mcf.

The projections reported in Table 2 were made upon assumptions that the US natural gas market was in equilibrium in 1972 at a price within the estimated range. Additional assumptions include a 10 per cent per year increase in natural gas demand; a -7.0 per cent per year shift in gas supply; a perfectly inelastic demand curve for natural gas; and a supply elasticity in non-associated natural gas discoveries of +3.0. The underlying assumptions imply that the real wellhead price of natural gas must increase at 6 per cent a year.

TABLE 2

Projections of non-associated natural gas prices and required discoveries, 1972-85

Year	Real price (cents per mcf)	Nominal price (5% a year inflation)	Required annual discoveries of ultimately recoverable non-associated natural gas (Tcf)
1972	43.5	43.5	13.0
1973	46.1	48.4	14.3
1974	48.9	53.8	15.7
1975	51.8	59.9	17.3
1976	54.9	66.6	19.0
1977	58.2	74.1	20.9
1978	61.7	82.5	23.0
1979	65.4	91.8	25.3
1980	69.3	102.2	27.8
1981	73.5	113.7	30.6
1982	77.9	126.5	33.7
1983	82.6	140.8	37.1
1984	87.6	156.7	40.8
1985	92.9	157.8	44.9

SOURCE: Calculations from the Spann-Erickson model.

There are two important things to be learned from the numbers in Table 2. First, on the basis of price alone, overseas imported gas in volume will not be on the same competitive footing as deregulated domestic gas in many markets by the early 1980s.[19] To the extent that the estimate of the current equilibrium price is too low, or that US discoveries cannot keep pace, the date at which imported gas will be fully competitive with domestic gas is pushed forward into the late 1970s.[20] However, international political events in 1973 affecting Middle Eastern and North African LNG cloud this prospect.

The second important thing, indicated by the magnitudes of the discovery requirements in Table 2, is that in order for domestic discoveries to meet requirements, policy-makers must permit, encourage, and support extensive offshore exploration campaigns. The Potential Gas Committee and the United States Geological Service have estimated the US potential discoverable natural gas resources at somewhere from about 1000 to 2000 Tcf. About half of these potential reserves are in Alaska and about half are in the lower contiguous states; and about half of the potential reserves in the latter area are offshore. Sufficient reserve potential exists to make deregulation successful in eliminating the natural gas shortage. It is possible to generate ultimate recovery from US non-associated

35

Patricia E. Starratt and Robert M. Spann

TABLE 3

Econometric model simulation results for policy alternatives

Year	New discoveries (Continental US) Tcf	Total additions to reserves (Continental US) Tcf	Total reserves (Continental US) Tcf	Supply of production (Continental US) Tcf
DEREGULATION				
1972	5.7	9.8	237.7	19.3
1973	6.1	12.7	229.0	22.1
1974	7.1	13.8	218.5	25.0
1975	9.1	15.4	208.8	26.0
1976	11.4	18.3	201.3	27.1
1977	14.1	22.2	196.5	28.2
1978	16.4	25.9	194.5	29.5
1979	19.1	29.9	195.3	31.0
1980	22.4	34.6	199.7	32.8
COST-OF-SERVICE REGULATION				
1972	5.7	9.8	237.7	19.3
1973	6.0	12.7	229.0	22.0
1974	7.1	13.8	220.8	22.8
1975	8.1	15.2	213.6	23.4
1976	9.2	16.8	207.5	24.0
1977	10.4	18.7	202.7	24.7
1978	11.9	20.8	199.3	25.7
1979	13.6	23.2	197.6	26.7
1980	15.7	26.3	197.5	28.0
REGULATORY STATUS QUO				
1972	5.7	9.8	237.7	19.2
1973	6.0	12.7	228.9	22.1
1974	7.0	13.8	220.5	23.0
1975	8.3	15.2	212.8	23.9
1976	9.7	17.1	206.1	24.9
1977	11.3	19.4	200.8	26.0
1978	13.2	22.1	197.3	27.2
1979	15.5	25.4	195.8	28.6
1980	18.3	29.2	196.8	30.2

SOURCE: P.W. MacAvoy and R.S. Pindyck, 'Regulatory Policies for Dealing with the Natural 4, 5, 6.

Demands for production (Continental US) Tcf	Excess demand for production (Continental US) Tcf	New contract field price (Continental US) (cents per mcf)	Average wholesale sale price (Continental US) (cents per mcf)
23.3	4.1	26.3	33.6
24.4	2.3	29.6	36.7
25.4	0.3	44.1	42.0
26.4	0.3	47.7	45.8
27.4	8.3	51.3	49.5
28.5	0.3	54.9	53.3
29.7	0.2	58.4	57.1
31.0	0.0	62.0	61.0
32.4	−0.3	65.5	64.9
23.3	4.0	26.3	33.5
24.3	2.3	29.6	36.6
25.6	2.8	30.5	38.4
26.9	3.6	31.3	40.1
28.5	4.5	32.1	41.7
30.3	5.5	33.0	43.3
32.2	6.6	33.8	44.8
34.4	7.7	34.6	46.4
36.9	8.9	35.5	48.0
23.3	4.0	26.3	33.6
24.3	2.3	29.6	36.7
25.6	2.5	32.4	38.9
26.9	2.9	35.1	41.2
28.3	3.4	37.8	43.7
29.9	3.9	40.6	46.2
31.6	4.4	43.3	48.9
33.4	4.8	45.9	51.7
35.5	5.3	48.5	54.6

Gas Shortage,' *Bell Journal of Economics and Management Science* (Autumn 1973), Tables

Patricia E. Starratt and Robert M. Spann

discoveries in the 20-30 Tcf range.[21] But results of that order of magnitude will require drilling off the coasts. This drilling can probably be accomplished within appropriate environmental constraints. But if the market is to clear at the projected volumes, environmental policy must be established so that the drilling can be begun. The environmental successes and failures must then be feedback for the formulation of subsequent policy.

The MacAvoy-Pindyke model
The econometric model of the natural gas industry developed by MacAvoy and Pindyke is considerably more detailed than the Spann-Erickson model. The MacAvoy-Pindyke model contains detailed specifications of the supply and demand relationships in the natural gas industry. Owing to its complexity, only the results of the model are discussed here.[22]

This model, much the same as the Spann-Erickson model, indicates that the primary cause of the current shortage of natural gas has been due to field price regulation. Increases in the price of natural gas at the wellhead would stimulate natural gas discoveries and reduce the demand for natural gas.

MacAvoy and Pindyke used their econometric model to stimulate the effects of three regulatory alternatives. The three policy alternatives considered were
1 deregulation of the wellhead price of natural gas,
2 cost-of-service regulation, and
3 a continuation of the regulatory status quo.
The authors assumed that a policy of deregulation would allow new natural gas prices to climb to market clearing levels, subject to the constraint that wholesale prices for natural gas do not increase by more than 50 per cent over the next five years. The authors also assumed prices for 'old' gas (natural gas under existing contracts) would not increase and the new gas price increases would be 'rolled in' with old gas.

The predicted results of such a policy are listed in Table 3. As can be seen, the policy option of deregulation would lead to a more than doubling of both new contract and average wholesale natural gas prices over the next five years.[23] Price increases of this magnitude would be sufficient to eliminate the shortage of natural gas by 1979. This result is in direct contrast to the implication of cost-of-service regulation or a maintenance of the status quo. The effects of these two policies are also shown in Table 3.

Cost-of-service regulation would lead to price increases averaging less than 1 ¢ per mcf per year. Such a policy would lead to increasing demands for natural gas, a decline in natural gas reserves, and an ever increasing shortage (measured by excess demand) of natural gas.

Maintenance of the regulatory status quo assumes that wellhead prices are allowed to increase about 2¢-4¢ per mcf per year.[24] Such a policy would tend to stabilize the shortage at its present level, but not eliminate it.

Both models indicate the present policies toward the field price of natural gas must be changed if the shortage of natural gas is to be eliminated. If natural gas prices are not allowed to rise, or are not allowed to reach the levels necessary to clear natural gas markets, shortages will continue or grow more severe.

OTHER SUPPLY STRATEGIES

One alternative to natural gas price deregulation is new types of natural gas supplies. The two new sources of supply most frequently mentioned are synthetic natural gas and the importation of liquefied natural gas. While both of these policies could lead to increased natural gas supplies, the cost of such supplies is in excess of the market-clearing price of domestic natural gas.

Foreign liquefied natural gas imports
Liquefied natural gas (LNG) imports are a relatively recent development. In order to import natural gas (methane) from overseas, it must be cooled to an extremely low temperature (-260°F) whereupon its density is increased and its volume reduced to 1/600th of its original volume so that it can be transported as a liquid. In addition to the highly specialized tankers required for transport, LNG imports require special port facilities, liquefaction plants, and facilities for re-gasification once the LNG is delivered. The lead time involved ranges up to five or more years.

There are many sources from which LNG could be imported by tankers. Companies are already investigating the possibilities of importing it from, in the Western Hemisphere, Canada, Alaska, Venezuela, Trinidad, and Ecuador, and in the Eastern Hemisphere, from Algeria, Nigeria, Australia, Indonesia, eastern and western Siberia. The volumes expected to be delivered between 1971 and the end of 1985 are: (1) North America, 29.4 Tcf; (2) Western Hemisphere, 5.0 Tcf; and (3) Eastern Hemisphere, 25.06 Tcf. The largest volume to be imported from a single country is 8.56 Tcf (Algeria); second in projected volume is 6.57 Tcf, from the USSR. At the end of 1973, there were 71 proposed LNG and SNG projects on file at the SPC.

These volumes of incremental supplies are impressive, but they will not eliminate the natural gas shortage. They are only economically feasible in the near and middle future under current regulatory practices. City Gate cost estimates for LNG are in the range of $1.00 to $1.50 centering on $1.35 per mcf.[25] As a result of international tension, these prices and the availability of gas at these prices are both subject to considerable uncertainty. This is equivalent to a domestic wellhead price of $0.80-.90 per mcf. The volume of new discoveries in the United States at these prices would considerably exceed the level of projected LNG imports.

In a deregulated setting, such imports would not be economically feasible until the domestic wellhead price of interstate natural gas rose to about three times its current level. Such imports are being considered at present because regulatory policies have not allowed domestic wellhead prices to rise sufficiently to equate the supply and demand for natural gas reserves. The substitution of imported LNG for the deregulation of the wellhead price of natural gas would lead to significantly higher burner tip prices to consumers.[26] In addition, the real resource costs of LNG are higher than those for deregulation. Even at equivalent prices for LNG and domestic conventional natural gas, some of the price of domestic gas would be composed of rents which would be captured by the federal and state treasuries in the form of bonus payments for offshore drilling rights and severance and income taxes.

A less expensive method of eliminating the shortage of natural gas is deregulation of the wellhead price of natural gas.[27] Moreover, there are no balance of payments problems or exchange rate problems as a result of deregulation.

Synthetic natural gas
There are two basic types of synthetic natural gas processes. The first would convert liquid hydrocarbons into synthetic natural gas. Synthetic (also called 'substitute' or 'artificial') gas derived from liquid hydrocarbons can be given the calorific value and heat content of natural gas, as well as the performance qualities of natural gas. Although a variety of methods for conversion have evolved, and a number of liquid hydrocarbons could be used, the British catalytic rich gas process appears most popular, with naphtha for feedstocks. SNG can also be made directly from crude in a more complicated process.

The availability of feedstocks for SNG is not limited so much by location but rather by the cost of importing naphtha for SNG. Under the new import program authorized in the President's Energy Message, a fee is imposed when naphtha is imported for an SNG plant. (The fee is not imposed when naphtha is imported for use by petrochemical companies.)

The lead time between authorization and initial production is approximately two years. The FPC has ruled that it does not have jurisdiction over SNG (in that it is not 'natural' gas as defined by the Natural Gas Act) until the SNG becomes comingled with natural gas in a pipeline. Processing applications should thus involve less time than that required for LNG projects which are submitted to the FPC for approval.

There are two options available to increase synthetic gas production from crude oil and products such as naphtha.

1 Permit the fee-free importation of petroleum products for the production of SNG, just as they are permitted for use in petrochemical plants.

2 Encourage refinery construction through legislation designed to facilitate the siting of energy plants so that more naphtha could be refined domestically.

The second major type of process for the manufacture of synthetic gas is coal gasification. In the long term, gas manufactured from domestic coal reserves also offers a solution to gas users currently unable to obtain sufficient quantities of gas. Not all types of coal could be used, however, and transportation costs could limit the areas where such gas could be priced competitively. Four processes to produce pipeline gas from coal are in the pilot plant stage, but a commercial coal gasification technique will probably not be available until 1980. Between 1980 and 1990, then, a number of coal gasification plants could probably be operating commercially, but gasified coal is not seen as a near-term solution to the shortage of natural gas.

The primary drawback to SNG options is cost. Estimated SNG costs are in the same range as estimated LNG costs – $1.00–$1.50 per mcf. To these conversion costs must be added pipeline costs. In addition, there are environmental factors associated with the mining of coal in sufficient volume to meet gas demands. In the shorter run, there are problems of crude oil supply. SNG does not appear to be as immediate, as cost-effective, or as environmentally attractive a solution to the natural gas dimension of the energy crisis as deregulation of the wellhead price.

A DEMAND STRATEGY:
END-USE CONTROLS

Several plans for end-use controls on natural gas have been proposed. Most of these plans involve some type of priority system. Top priority customers are generally defined as home-owners and small business concerns. Two reasons are given for this order of priorities. First, residential and small commercial users would find the cost of converting from gas-burning equipment to alternate fuels prohibitive; the cost burden to large industrial users would be less, because of the economies of scale achieved when larger units are converted. Second, the 'best' use of natural gas is generally thought to be in small applications (i.e., in the burner of a stove) as opposed to under boilers for the generation of electricity (where it takes generally 3 BTUs of gas to make 1 BTU of electricity).

Several factors make allocation – especially nation-wide allocation – a very complicated proposition, however. Natural gas is the cleanest burning of fossil fuels and its use is especially desirable in metropolitan areas with air pollution problems. Prohibiting its use in those areas, therefore, presents serious problems through the lowering of air quality. The costs of converting to alternate fuel capacity are very high. These costs include the purchase of alternative fuels, and the prices for alternative fuels have been rapidly increasing. To the extent that higher prices for natural gas do not exceed the cost of conversion and the use of alternate fuels or penalties for air pollution, many bulk users of natural gas would rather use natural gas than convert their facilities.

Another complicating factor to be considered is alternate fuel availability. Different fuels are available at different prices in different parts of the nation. To the extent that current and potential users of natural gas are denied service, other fuels will be required. In some areas, 'dirty' fuels are not acceptable because of air pollution problems, yet alternate sources of clean energy are in short supply. Recent spot prices for imported low-sulfur fuel oil indicate a rising demand for that fuel. Furthermore, low-sulfur steam coal is avilable in large quantities only in the Rocky Mountain area. Problems of alternate fuel availability may be especially serious in some areas owing to price or distribution problems. Coal or low-sulfur oil may be too expensive to use in areas far from supply sources.

End-use controls present difficult legal problems as well. A federal agency such as the FPC, prescribing who in producing and consuming states would continue to get natural gas and who would not, may raise constitutional issues including that of state's rights. Other legal problems raised by end-use controls include the powers of a federal agency to invalidate private contracts.

The principal fault of end-use controls is that it does nothing to eliminate the shortage of natural gas. Such controls would not increase the supply of natural gas; nor do they change the demand for natural gas. The only effect of such controls is to reallocate the shortage of natural gas. This policy would involve a low price of natural gas vis-à-vis deregulation, but we question the value of a low price of natural gas to consumers who are not allowed to purchase any natural gas at all.

CONCLUSIONS

There is a large body of evidence that the current shortage of natural gas is a direct result of Federal Power Commission price ceilings on the new contract price of natural gas. Recent econometric studies confirm that large increases in the price of natural gas at the wellhead are necessary and sufficient in order to eliminate the current and prospective shortages of natural gas. The resulting prices to consumers under deregulation would be lower than the costs of alternative supplies such as synthetic or imported liquefied natural gas. This information does not in itself say whether prices should be deregulated and allowed to find their natural level right away, or whether the deregulation should be a long drawn-out process. It is our view that a deregulation is necessary and in the public interest on economic, environmental, and national security grounds. In order for the market to work effectively to allocate our scarce natural gas supplies to the highest competing end-uses, deregulation should permit (to the extent contract renegotiation allows) the price to rise equally for 'old' gas covered under current contracts and new gas discoveries. But, to us, it seems better to pay this cost now rather than draw out the process of deregulation, continue to extend the shortage into the future, and run the risk of further administratively-induced misallocations of resources and the potential inequities of an arbitrary non-price rationing system.

NOTES

The authors are a professional staff member, United States Senate Committee on Interior and Insular Affairs, and an assistant professor of economics at Virginia Polytechnic Institute and State University. Some of the research on which this paper is based was supported by a Resources for the Future fellowship granted to Robert M. Spann. Much of the research by Patricia E. Starratt was conducted pursuant to Senate Resolution 45, authorizing a National Fuels and Energy Policy Study for the US Senate. The opinions expressed in this paper are those of the authors and do not necessarily represent the opinions or positions of the organizations with which they are affiliated.

1 Statement of Dr Bruce C. Netschert (National Economic Research Associates) before Senate Committee on Interior and Insular Affairs (Subcommittee on Minerals, Materials, and Fuels), *Natural Gas Supply Study*, 13 Nov. 1969 (37-792), pp. 84-85.

2 *National Gas Supply and Demand*, 1971-1990, Staff Report no. 2, Federal Power Commission, 1972, p. 7.

3 The optimum economic production rate of developed gas reserves may lie in the range of 8-14 per cent per year (equivalent to (R/P) ratios of 7 to 12), depending upon reservoir characteristics and the cost of capital. Without substantial new reserve additions, however, the R/P ratio will fall below the optimum rate and problems of delivery will continue to worsen. The fall in the US domestic R/P ratio for natural gas from 20.1 in 1960 to 10.5 in 1972 reflects other factors than declining gas availability. It also stems from a growing efficiency in the use of producing capacity, completion of a national gas transportation network, authorization by the FPC of shorter-term sales contracts, and the revision of restraints on the production of associated gas by state (oil) conservation authorities.

4 This FPC National Gas Survey study, conducted with staff si
  federal and state agencies, and by an independent accountir
  that AGA reserve estimates for 1970 were nearly 9 per cent
  ingly, the R/P ratio was reduced from 13.1 years to 11.9 ye

5 A survey by the Joint Board on Fuel Supply and Fuel Trar
  that 564.5 Bcf of gas was curtailed from November 1972 t
  almost 140 per cent above the 236.5 Bcf of curtailed volu
  period a year earlier. See a statement by Thomas J. Joyce,
  Natural Gas, FPC, in hearings before the Senate Interior ar
  Committee, 1 February 1973; listing the companies suffe
  ments as of February 1971.

6 Stephen Breyer and Paul MacAvoy, 'The Natural Gas Shc
  lation of Natural Gas Producers,' *Harvard Law Review,* 1*

7 Phillips Petroleum Company *v.* Wisconsin, 347 US, 672.

8 *The Natural Gas Act,* 15 USC 717(a) *et seq.*

9 For evidence of the responsiveness of quantity supplied to price incentives,
  see below or Paul A. MacAvoy and Robert S. Pindyck, 'Alternative Regulatory Policies for Dealing with the Natural Gas Shortage,' *Bell Journal of
  Economics and Management Sciences* (Autumn 1973) or Robert M. Spann
  and Edward W. Erickson, 'Joint Costs and Separability in Oil and Gas Exploration,' in Milton Searle, ed., *Energy Modeling: Art, Science, Practice* (Washington DC: Resources for the Future, 1973).

10 For an analysis of price-induced substitution possibilities in energy usage, see
  Edward W. Erickson, Robert M. Spann, and Robert Ciliano, *Fossil Fuel Demand* (Philadelphia: Decision Sciences, 1973).

11 Currently, the discovery rate is accelerating as new contract prices are being
  increased. This recent development is discussed in more detail below.

12 For example, see Clark Hawkins, 'Structure of the Natural Gas Producing
  Industry,' in Keith Brown, ed., *Regulation of the Natural Gas Producing
  Industry* (Washington, DC: Resources for the Future, 1972).

13 Spann and Erickson, 'Joint Costs and Separability.'

14 MacAvoy and Pindyke, 'Alternative Regulatory Policies.'

15 The Spann-Erickson model is a six-equation model. The estimating equations
  are the demand curves for crude oil and natural gas, the current supply functions for crude oil and natural gas, and the supply functions for new crude
  oil and natural gas discoveries. The supply side of the model was based on
  the theory of joint costs with variable proportions. The estimated responsiveness of the supply of natural gas discoveries is quite sensitive to the wellhead
  price of natural gas. For a detailed description of this model, see Spann and
  Erickson, 'Joint Costs and Separability.'

16 For a preliminary estimate of the long-run effect of higher gas prices to ration natural gas demand, see Erickson, Spann, and Ciliano, 'Econometric Analysis of Substitution Effects in Industrial Sector Energy Demands,' presented at the Operations Research Society of America meetings, 13 Nov. 1973, San Diego CA.

17 The calculated point estimate is quite close to at least one independent piece of evidence on the 1972 equilibrium price. In the early summer of 1972, under the newly announced FPC policy of allowing the wellhead price of new gas reserves to 'float,' Tenneco filed for a price of 45 cents per mcf. Also, for at least the near future, the price predictions track what evidence is available quite well. In private conversation, an independent operator reported that he had contracted to begin 1974 deliveries in the intrastate market at a price of 52 cents per mcf. The predicted 1974 price is 53.8 cents per mcf.

18 Because the economic environment has changed since the projections in Table 1 were made, they should not be regarded as point forecasts. Rather, they are illustrative of the order of magnitude of results which could be expected under a policy of deregulation.

19 Cost estimates for LNG are detailed below. Prior to the cut-off in late 1973 due to the Arab-Israeli war, some Algerian gas was reaching US markets. This was essentially peak-shaving gas. There are three other possible reasons for some current imports. These are: (1) to get on the learning curve of LNG tanker technology; (2) to establish ourselves as buyers in foreign markets; and (3) to demonstrate to the FPC the costs of their current policies. Analysis and experience both indicate, however, that if obtaining substantial and reliable additional gas supplies at the least cost is the policy objective, LNG imports are not the efficient solution for the current shortage.

20 The possible availability of Alaskan or Canadian Arctic gas supplies is not incorporated into the estimations. If such gas is available in quantity, and if environmental and political problems of pipelining can be solved, then it is likely that full competitiveness of overseas gas in the US markets will be postponed.

21 The volumes of discoveries reported in Table 2 were not calculated subject to the constraint of a constant reserves/production ratio. The required 1972 initial discoveries of non-associated natural gas are less than 1972 total gas production. This is for two reasons. First, the estimations deal only with non-associated discoveries, not total discoveries (including associated natural gas). And second, for later years in the period our data cover, they are dealing with initial reported discoveries. The ultimate recovery from such discoveries is likely to grow over time as a result of extensions and revisions. Extensions and revisions are themselves subject to economic incentives, and the reserves/

45

production ratio is in part an economic variable. The required discovery results reported in Table 2 are, however, illustrative of the order of magnitude
of new reserves necessary to clear the field market.

22 For more on this model, see MacAvoy and Pindyke, 'Alternative Regulatory
Policies.

23 The price increases in Table 3 are somewhat higher than those listed in Table
2. They are of the same order of magnitude, however. This consistency between
the two models should be taken as an indicator of robustness of properly specified econometric models for policy analysis. The two models were estimated
on different sets of data and employ different estimating equations. The fact
that both models yield similar results is an indication of their validity.

24 This is consistent with the actual behavior of prices in recent years.

25 For example, a local distributor in Boston was recently authorized by the
FPC to import liquefied natural gas (LNG) overland from Montreal during the
fall and winter seasons at prices equivalent to $1.13 and $1.58 per mcf; the
delivered price to Boston for conventional domestic supplies is 69 cents per
mcf.

26 The primary beneficiaries of LNG without deregulation would be tanker
owners and large interstate pipelines. The pipelines would benefit because
LNG would increase their rate base considerably and raise their allowed revenues under current forms of rate of return regulation. These groups support
LNG and oppose deregulation.

27 There are significant risks to the environment associated with LNG as well.
For more on this point, see 'Hazards of Spillage of LNG into Water,' prepared
for Department of Transportation, US Coast Guard, Hazardous Materials Division, by US Department of the Interior, Bureau of Mines, Sept. 1972.

RICHARD L. GORDON

In a previous era, coal was king. That era is increasingly behind us, but coal has not abdicated completely. Moreover, there is considerable discussion of a resurgence in the use of coal – as a short-term expedient in the face of dramatic changes in the costs and availabilities of oil and gas and the operating and siting problems associated with nuclear power; and in the long term, coal gasification and liquefaction are looked on by many as attractive energy supply sources.

Professor Gordon reviews the coal situation and concludes that in the long term, in economic terms, coal is neither as low-cost nor as abundant as some coal proponents seem to believe. Coal will continue to be an important energy source, but the extent to which it captures or retains electrical generation markets is critically dependent upon the assumptions made with regard to oil, gas, and (especially) nuclear costs. In this last regard, see the chapters by Kneese and Carnesale & Elleman. The nuclear power cost comparisons used by Professor Gordon do not include the costs of socially sponsored research and development for nuclear power. To the extent that these costs are sunk, this is appropriate; but future public expenditures to develop nuclear technology are just as real a cost as those incurred to mine and transport coal.

Professor Gordon's analysis should be compared to the chapters by Starratt and Spann on natural gas, Barnett on energy and growth, Adelman on the world oil market, and Erickson and Spann on the US oil market, and Dewees and Stoel on environmental factors. Gordon's discussions of the combined cycle technology and continuous improvements in coking efficiency are very apt specific examples of the general trends discussed by Barnett. In addition, the relations between the United States and Canada in the North American energy market will depend in a not insignificant way upon the ability of coal at least to hold its own in electrical generation in the United States. Alternatively, coal's role in the United States will depend upon the availability and cost of oil and gas from Canada (and from Alaska through Canada). On this, see the chapter by Waverman.

RICHARD L. GORDON

Coal: our limited vast fuel resource

Popular mythology has long held that the world must eventually return to primary reliance on coal for its energy. The argument holds that oil and gas soon will be exhausted and only coal can fill the void. This contention has attained greatly increased currency in the early 1970s because of rising energy supply problems. It is asserted that we must continue to use coal to generate electricity and also convert it to synthetic gas and crude oil. At the same time, the coal industry is complaining that stringent regulation of its activities and those of its consumers is threatening the industry's health. Fears are considerable that the coal industry will contract, at least in the states in which it has traditionally been concentrated.

Since coal competes with other fuels, these arguments necessarily involve forecasts of coal's relationship with its rivals. The implicit assumption of the return-to-coal model is that oil and gas supplies will become prohibitively expensive long before any alternatives but coal are economically viable. To a large extent, the counterargument can be developed without extensive examination of coal. The critical point is that the supplies of oil and gas are probably much greater than believed. Therefore, the prospects are quite good that, until such alternatives as nuclear fusion and solar energy develop into competitive energy sources, oil and gas will remain cheap enough to limit severely the use of coal. As oil and gas potentials are reviewed elsewhere in this volume, this paper will stress the considerations relating to coal itself. The objectives are to describe the main characteristics of the coal industry and evaluate the critical forces affecting future coal use.

49

Richard L. Gordon

PATTERNS OF COAL PRODUCTION IN THE US[1]

A central proposition in the discussion is that the United States has at least two different coal industries and much confusion arises from failure to distinguish between them. Briefly, we have the long-existing coal industry operating east of the Mississippi, which traditionally has accounted for the vast majority of US output, and an emerging coal industry in the West. At least in the East, further subdivisions are possible. A distinction can be made between the coals with the requisite properties for production of metallurgical coke – for pig iron manufacture – and those suited only for steam raising. Moreover, two great Eastern coal belts exist. The first, the Appalachian, stretches from Pennsylvania to Alabama. The second, the Eastern Interior or Middle Western, encompasses Illinois, Indiana, and western Kentucky.

Two basic considerations – the ability to strip mine and the sulfur contents of coal – affect the attractiveness of the two halves of the country. Strip mining involves removing the covering earth and then the coal with heavy earthmoving equipment in contrast to digging underground and extracting the coal in confined spaces with special mining equipment. The surface method is a much cheaper way to move materials and, therefore, produces lower mining costs when the volume of cover is sufficiently limited relative to the volume of the underlying coal deposit. Sulfur content has become critical because of growing concern over the air pollution impacts of burning high sulfur fuels. Combustion turns the sulfur into sulfur oxides whose emission creates damage to human health, plants, and materials. Therefore, stringent air pollution regulations have been designed to restrict such sulfur emissions.

These two influences combine to increase greatly the attractiveness of Western coal relative to Eastern coal. Uncommitted low-cost strippable reserves apparently are much more widely available in the West and these coals are generally low enough in sulfur content to permit compliance with federal emission standards. As shown below, there are differences in degree. To be sure, strippable coals that are low in sulfur content are scarce in the East. However, large amounts of low sulfur coals do exist and strippable resources still remain. In the West, it is not clear what portion of the vast reserves about which much is written is actually strippable at low costs.

In any case, the problems of the industry at present are concentrated in the East. Difficulties in meeting sulfur regulations combined with a variety of pressures on underground mining costs may make Eastern coal use in many of its traditional markets prohibitively expensive. Western coal is considered ready to become a major new source of energy. A variety of coal prospects, therefore, exists. At one extreme, coal could be limited to the few markets in which it has very strong competitive positions. Alternatively, a vast expansion could arise throughout the country.

The evaluation is complicated because while the two regions have different supply problems, they could both potentially serve the same demands. We must distinguish between national issues and those primarily relevant to one region or the other. Further difficulties arise in keeping the proper time perspective. As shown below, many of the developments depend critically upon the availability of new technologies for producing and using coal. Analysis must consider when each of these techniques will become commercially available since they differ markedly in their maturity. All major projects involving coal and its rivals require several years for completion even after the technology is established. It can take as long as five years to build a coal-fired electric plant and up to twice as long for a nuclear plant.

COAL MARKETS: HISTORY AND PROSPECTS[2]

We can distinguish between those markets coal presently serves and potential new ones. By the late 1960s coal use had been concentrated in three major markets – electric power generation, metallurgical coke manufacture, and exports. Most of the remaining use was scattered among different industries. As already noted, the new markets considered most likely to develop are in gasification and liquefaction.

Actually, two types of synthetic fuels from coal are being considered. The first goal is a close substitute for oil and gas and the second, a simpler, cheaper gas or liquid for electric power plant use. This difference reflects the difficulty in producing a close substitute. The chemical nature of coal is such that an expensive step in which hydrogen is introduced from external sources is required to produce a true synthetic alternative to crude oil or natural gas. Unless this upgrading occurs, the product will not be competitive in most markets. Power plants, however, would find the special properties less essential and prefer a less expensive fuel.

The present study discusses these cheaper alternatives during the examination of electric power industry fuel demands. The review of high quality synthetics is limited to an extremely cursory comment at the end. Enthusiasts of the subject may complain that this is inadequate treatment of a market that could absorb hundreds of millions of tons of coal per year. However, the critical consideration is the amount of pertinent information available and this is limited because the technology does not yet exist.

The complex process by which coal markets took the form prevailing in the early 1970s need not be reviewed in detail here. The dominant consideration is that coal is inherently a much less attractive fuel than oil or gas. Its solid state

Richard L. Gordon

and higher waste content create problems at every stage from mining to post-combustion waste disposal. In the manufacture of coke for pig-iron production alone does coal possess essential properties lacking in other fuels.[3] Otherwise, coal will be consumed only when its costs are sufficiently below those of other fuels to outweigh these disadvantages. Fortunately for the coal industry, this situation prevailed for electric utilities in a substantial portion of the United States, where coal is not only the leading electric utility fuel but has enjoyed substantial relative and absolute growth in sales to the electric power industry. Electric utilities have since the late sixties absorbed over half of domestic coal output (59 per cent in 1971). Coke manufacture, predominantly for pig-iron production, has become the second largest market for coal. This market, however, is but 25 to 30 per cent the size of the electric power sector and has been at best stagnant throughout the period since World War II. To be more precise, coke use in iron-making has fluctuated with steel output but shown no growth. Technical progress has steadily reduced the requirement of coke per ton of pig iron produced; this has almost exactly offset the impacts of iron output growth. This trend has been aggravated by steady declines in other uses of coke.

The next largest coal 'market' reported in energy statistics consists of many miscellaneous industrial demands. These uses have been trending rather irregularly downwards but as recently as 1968 had remained larger *in toto* than coking demands. A similar catch-all of retail sales has shown even more persistent declines and accounted for only 2 per cent of 1971 coal sales.

Significant export sales, predominantly for coke for iron-making, have also been maintained but they too exhibited much variation and no obvious overall trends. The main markets are Canada, Japan, and Western Europe. Canadian imports of US coal steadily declined from 1946 to 1961 and subsequently the trend was reversed. However, 1972 coal exports to Canada remained below the levels of the late forties and early fifties. Japan steadily increased its coal purchases from the US up through 1970 and from 1969 to 1971 was the largest single foreign buyer. Slowdowns in steel output and growing purchases from other countries caused drops in Japanese coal imports from the US in 1971 and 1972.

Western Europe's efforts to protect its own high-cost coal industries have long inhibited the growth of US sales to that region. Purchases have gyrated wildly in response both to economic conditions and the degree of assistance being provided the coal industry of Western Europe.[4]

For several reasons, evaluation of future prospects in old markets should stress predominantly electric power generation. Its size and potential for growth (again whether relative or absolute levels are considered) remain critical. Steel-industry views suggest that technical progress will continue to hold down the growth of

demand for coking coal; the growth would be modest even if technological progress slowed down because pig-iron production itself is not likely to grow rapidly.

Export prospects are less certain. European protectionism may lessen in the
1970s and beyond, but at the same time vigorous new competition is arising
from Australia and elsewhere. This has already cut into sales to Japan and could
affect European sales as well. Other industrial users face roughly the same problems as the electric power industry but the smaller scale of the 'other-industry'
sector's fuel use preclude adoption of techniques best utilized in large facilities.
These size limitations are problems both in installing air pollution control devices
and shifting to nuclear power.

THE PROSPECTS FOR COAL
IN ELECTRIC POWER GENERATION[5]

Before viewing the problems of coal demand in electric power generation, the
method of costing employed here should be noted. The available data are quite
rough and therefore similarly rough evaluation techniques seem the most appropriate to use. The technique employed here is 'levelizing' which converts all costs
into the equivalent required income per million British thermal units (BTUs) employed.[6] (This technique is outlined in a short appendix, not printed here, but
available from the author on request.)

Technological influences
A hierarchy of choices exists for the electric power industry. Fundamentally, the
lead times on fossil plant construction imply that fuel use capabilities are largely
predetermined five years in advance. Only the alterations feasible with existing
plants can be made.[7] The critical consideration is that it is technically feasible to
convert a coal-fired plant to oil or gas and the capital investment is fairly low
(see below). Conversion from other fuels to coal is technically feasible only if
the plant has been designed with a large enough boiler; the conversion costs (involving adding complex coal-handling equipment) could easily prove equivalent
to a 20-cent rise in coal prices.[8] For that matter, difficulties can arise in converting from one type of coal to another. Subsequently, new coal-fired plants, nuclear plants, and plants employing advanced technologies for using nuclear power
or fossil fuels can be added.

The fuel-choice situation existing in 1973, therefore, is that until about 1978
an upper limit to coal use is set by the existing and planned coal-burning capacity.
From 1978 on, coal use capability could be augmented by construction of new
plants. In both cases these plants could, if the proper circumstances developed,

53

Richard L. Gordon

be converted to oil or gas. By the early 1980s nuclear capacity also could be increased beyond the levels already programed.

By their nature, most technical advances are difficult to predict. Numerous concepts have been studied at various levels of intensity. Most remain in an indefinite status with observers disagreeing widely about the economic prospects. The main exception seems to be the advanced 'combined-cycle'; a large number of observers believe that this approach could become competitive by the early eighties. Its special status arises because its development only involves what appear to be quite feasible improvements in an existing technology.

The essence of a combined cycle is that electricity is first generated using a gas turbine – a stationary adaptation of a jet engine – and the waste heat then is collected in a recovery boiler that permits further electric power production. Gas turbines are already widely used in electric power generation and some combined cycle plants also exist. These combined cycles have much lower capital costs than conventional plants. However, thus far the system has several limitations – slightly lower thermal efficiencies, lesser reliability, and requirement of more expensive fuels than conventional fossil plants. It is felt that these problems can be overcome. The combined cycle reportedly requires around 9200 BTUs to generate a kilowatt hour of electricity but the best conventional fossil plants need less than 9000 BTUs. It is hoped combined-cycle fuel needs will fall below 8000 BTUs/ kilowatt hour by the 1990s.[9] Anticipated improvements in turbine technology are expected to permit reliable operation at higher thermal efficiencies than present-day conventional fossil plants (and it is widely argued that future conventional plants are unlikely to improve their thermal efficiencies significantly). This leaves the problem of high fuel costs. An initial suggestion was that conversion of coal or oil into a low BTU gas might solve the difficulties, but more recently attention has been directed at enabling the combined cycle directly to use heavier fuels such as residual fuel oil.[10] A low BTU gas means one with lower heat content than natural gas and, as noted above, is much cheaper to synthesize than a high BTU gas. Low BTU gas manufactured at the power plant could prove an economic fuel under certain circumstances (see below). While the combined cycle need not prove the major new technical advance in power generating, it can at least serve as an example of what such advances could imply.

Environmental problems[11]

Before evaluating prospective fuel-use patterns, it is necessary to consider the critical influence of environmental regulations on the choice. Air pollution control problems are particularly crucial. Three pollutants are generated in significant amounts by electric power plants – particulates, sulfur oxides, and nitrogen oxides. Power plants account for about half the sulfur oxides emitted nationally and a bit less than a fifth each of the other two pollutants. Coal contributes more than its share in generation to this pollution. Coal contains a much larger amount of particulates than oil and gas; the grades of coal used for power generation are higher in sulfur than is gas and much of the oil; coal also tends to generate more nitrogen oxides than other fuels. Particulate-emission control is an old problem; abatement methods, moreover, are well developed and generally do not greatly increase costs. Compliance with even stringent regulations on particulates is likely to have modest impacts on the position of coal. Quite the opposite situation prevails with nitrogen oxides; it is not clear how control will be effected in coal-burning plants.[12] However, the pressures to control emissions have remained moderate. Sulfur oxides, in contrast, create severe control problems for coal users. While fairly simple processes are available to remove sulfur from oil and gas, this is not true for coal. At best, intensive cleaning of coal can remove the portion of the sulfur that is physically separate from the coal. More complex chemical processes must be used to remove the remaining sulfur chemically bound to the coal. The most straightforward routes are to transform the coal into forms more amenable to treatment; the key alternatives are gasification or using what is called the solvent refining process that produces either a de-ashed solid or a heavy liquid fuel. Sulfur can be removed during this processing.

When plans to develop sulfur-emission controls were emerging, it was thought that such precombustion treatment would take too long to develop and be uneconomic. Low-sulfur coal was also considered too expensive to use. The alternative of scrubbing the sulfur from the power plant's stack gases was considered more promising. It quickly became apparent that the optimism was excessive. Scrubbing proved far less simple to develop or as cheap as was initially claimed. Controversy now abounds on the subject: views range from near dismissal of the concept as a complete failure to claims that solutions are close at hand.

The objective status is quite clear. By early 1973 only one *coal-fired* plant in the world – a Japanese plant using US technology – has managed successfully to scrub sulfur from stack gases on a sustained basis. Another plant in the US was allegedly close to resolving the final barriers to viability. It is agreed that the earliest estimates of costs were too low.

Many different interpretations of these basic conclusions are possible. The very government reports that treat the two scrubber ventures as proof that success is near suggest that the Japanese plant is both smaller and works under more favorable conditions than the typical US power plant and fail to explain why the US plant's scrubber problems seem so easy to solve. The company operating the plant is far less optimistic.

Similarly, the cost of such scrubbing is the subject of heated controversy. Data in various US government reports suggest that the cost per million BTUs treated could run from 12 to 17 cents for scrubbers used in new plants and 23 to 33 cents for units retrofitted to old plants.[13] Retrofitting – the addition of new facilities – often involves this type of cost disadvantage. Extra investment outlays are usually required to add such facilities to an existing plant not designed to accommodate them. Moreover, the required income per unit of output is usually higher. The expected remaining life of an existing plant normally is less than that of a new one so that fewer years remain to pay off the investment; thus, in each year, a larger income must be secured. Moreover, plants tend to produce at lower rates as they become older; thus, each unit of the smaller total output must make a larger contribution to repayment of the investment.

Discussions with electric utility industry sources suggest that government figures are too optimistic and that the true costs would be much higher. The most detailed available presentation of this view is a memorandum issued by the Commonwealth Edison Company of Chicago – the firm whose experience with scrubbers was cited by the government as evidence that success was near.[14] Commonwealth provided cost data based upon its efforts to secure a scrubber for a proposed new plant. It indicated that actual scrubber capital costs range from $51 to $63 a kilowatt in contrast to the $27 to $41 levels reported by the government. However, when such indirect costs as capitalization of interest during construction and capacity losses were considered, the true costs became $73-$87 a kilowatt. This ignores the added costs associated with the disposal of the substantial amounts of solid waste produced by scrubbing.

Commonwealth's figures imply that in using levelizing assumptions of 18 per cent capital charges and 75 per cent plant utilization, total scrubber cost including waste disposal would be from 45 to 57 cents a million BTUs. Commonwealth asserts that it is more realistic to assume a 64 per cent utilization for the first four or five years of a plant's life and a sharply lower rate in later years. While the data presented indicate a possible cost range in the first years of operation of 50-63 cents, Commonwealth's summary view is that the most probable value will lie between 53 and 57 cents. This rises to 75-85 cents in later years – a range considered applicable also to retrofitting.

Whatever the truth of these different conjectures, a sizable group of observers now believe that a synthesis process such as low BTU gas manufacture will be a preferable long-run solution. This attitude may have been stimulated by the expected availability of the advanced combined cycle, as this system would be unable to consume coal in its solid form.

Since nuclear power is being considered as an alternative to generation using fossil fuels, the issues related to nuclear side-effects must be noted here. Many concerns relate to the release of radioactive material at the nuclear plant and other facilities. A rough distinction can be made between releases associated with regular operation of the plants and discharges due to accidents. Despite well-publicized contrary arguments, the evidence suggests that routine releases will not produce measurable damages. The critical question is what damages might arise accidentally. Two typical examples of potential problems are the loss-of-coolant accident, in which a major pipe breaks off the reactor causing the coolant to evaporate, and release of stored radioactive wastes. In both cases, the Atomic Energy Commission (AEC) regulations provide both for facilities designed to reduce greatly the danger of accident and for controls to limit the impact. However, many critics of the AEC fear that its desire to promote nuclear power has produced inadequate implementation of these principles. The debate unfortunately defies neat analytic treatment because the evidence is by no means sufficiently clear-cut to resolve the debate. While the AEC has produced many documents outlining what appears to be an impressive effort to prevent disaster, the critics have shown weaknesses in the argument. Both sides rely heavily on speculations so that neither provides a conclusive proof.[15]

Potential public policy decisions
The choices can be further influenced by policy developments. As presently formulated, regulations will preclude the uncontrolled burning of coal containing more than .7 per cent sulfur but allow construction of nuclear plants.[16] Changes in these rules are quite conceivable. For example, while the available evidence suggests that many of the attacks on nuclear power are exaggerated, enough unresolved problems remain and, therefore, a markedly less favorable attitude to nuclear power conceivably could develop. Conversely, some question arises about whether rapid imposition of so stringent a set of sulfur emission standards on power plants is justified. In many parts of the country, such standards are unnecessary to meet over-all air pollution goals. For present purposes, it will be assumed that by 1980 the proposed standards will indeed be adopted or even be exceeded in places and that nuclear power will not be banned. While this is my forecast of the most probable development, it should be considered here mainly as a convenient base case whose conclusions the reader can readily modify to cover other assumptions.

ALTERNATIVES IN ELECTRIC POWER GENERATION

Before relating the points made above about coal and oil price predictions, the assumptions about capital and nuclear fuel costs may be summarized for each of the basic situations. Table 1 presents these data. First, in the shortest run in which shifts can only be made by adapting existing plants, the critical influences are the

Richard L. Gordon

TABLE 1

Capital and nuclear fuel cost assumptions for electric power fuel use analysis
(cents/million BTUs except as noted, 1973 dollars)

Case 1: Western coal compared to oil and Eastern coal in existing plant

	Greatest advantage to Western coal	Least advantage to Western coal
1 Scrubber costs = premium allowed for Western coal over Eastern coal	85	23
2 Oil capability installation costs = premium allowed for Western coal over oil	10	5

Case 2: Oil compared to Eastern coal in existing plant

	Greatest advantage to oil	Least advantage to oil
3 Oil capability installation costs	5	10
4 Premium allowed for oil over Eastern coal (1–3)	80	13

Case 3: Oil compared to Eastern and Western coal in new plant

	Greatest advantage to oil	Least advantage to oil
5 Capital cost saving of oil plant = premium allowed for oil over Western coal	16	8
6 Scrubber cost = premium allowed for Western coal over Eastern coal	63	12
7 Premium allowed for oil over Eastern coal (5+6)	79	20

Case 4: Nuclear compared to fossil fuels

	Greatest advantage to nuclear	Least advantage to nuclear
8 Excess of nuclear capital costs over coal plant without scrubber (dollars/kilowatt)	40	100
9 Excess of nuclear capital costs over coal plant without scrubbers (cents/million BTUs)	11	31
10 Nuclear fuel costs	20	20
11 Allowable delivered price of Western coal (9+10)	31	51

58

TABLE 1 continued

	Greatest advantage to nuclear	Least advantage to nuclear
12 Capital saving on oil compared to Western coal	8	16
13 Allowable delivered price of oil (11+12)	39	67
14 Scrubber costs	63	12
15 Allowable price of Eastern coal (11–14)	–32	39

Case 5: Allowable excess of nuclear capital cost over capital cost
of coal plants without scrubbers for selected coal prices and scrubber costs

Allowable nuclear excess capital costs with scrubber costs of	Coal price							
	25	30	35	40	45	50	55	60
63 cents								
16 cents/million BTUs	68	73	78	83	88	93	98	103
17 dollars/kilowatts	227	243	260	277	293	310	327	343
40 cents								
18 cents/million BTUs	45	50	55	60	65	70	75	80
19 dollars/kilowatts	150	167	183	200	217	233	250	267
20 cents								
20 cents/million BTUs	25	30	35	40	45	50	55	60
21 dollars/kilowatts	83	100	117	133	150	167	183	200
12 cents								
22 cents/million BTUs	17	22	27	32	37	42	47	52
23 dollars/kilowatts	57	73	90	107	123	140	157	173

NOTE: Allowable capital cost in cents per million BTUs is coal price plus scrubber costs less 20 cent nuclear fuel cost converted to dollars per kilowatts by division by 0.3; the 18 per cent is levelizing factor.

costs of retrofitting any additional equipment required and the limits to conversion possibilities (see cases 1 and 2 in the table). The simplest case is a plant already using Eastern coal but capable also of burning Western coal. A requirement to reduce sulfur emissions could be met by switching to Western coal or low sulfur oil or installing a scrubber. Western coal could command a premium over oil amounting to the cost of retrofitting oil-use facilities – about five to ten cents per million BTUs – and over Eastern coal by the cost of backfitting scrubbers – 23 to 85 cents.[17] The premium for oil over Eastern coal is the scrubbing cost less oil facility cost or 13 to 80 cents. Clearly, the premium for Western coal declines and at least in the case of oil competition could conceivably disappear if problems arose in adapting the plant to Western coal.

In new fossil plants (case 3 in the table), however, it is oil that can enjoy the largest premium. Available data suggest that the elimination of coal-handling facilities investment could allow an 8 to 16 cent premium for oil compared to Western coal.[18] Western coal, in turn, could command a premium of 12 to 63 cents over Eastern coals because scrubbers were not required. The possible premium of oil over Eastern coal is the sum of the handling facility and scrubber cost savings – from 20 to 79 cents per million BTUs.

In turning to nuclear power (case 4 in the table), it should first be noted that not only do longer construction lead times prevail but plants must be large and maintain high operating rates. Large size is necessary to take advantage of substantial economies of scale for the plant. The high operating rate is required because normally nuclear power involves a higher capital cost and lower fuel cost than a fossil-fired plant. The only exceptions to this rule that might arise are that some Western coals might be cheaper than nuclear fuel and it is conceivable that scrubbers could be so expensive that a coal plant equipped with scrubbers could have higher capital costs than a nuclear plant. When high capital and low fuel costs do prevail, the plant must operate at high enough rates so that the cumulative present worth of the fuel cost saving repays the extra investment.

Nuclear plant construction costs have been rising sharply since the late sixties. Much of the rise has been due to inflationary pressures that have affected all types of power plants; nuclear plants also have suffered from special problems resulting both from the normal problems of introducing a new technology and from steadily increasing regulatory restraints.

A series of cost estimates provided by the Atomic Energy Commission and, during the 1960s, by Philip Sporn, formerly president of the American Electric Power Company, and appearing in various publications of the Congressional Joint Committee on Atomic Energy, constitute one of the most systematic tabulations of these cost trends. The figures indicate that the most favorable nuclear situation was reached in 1966. Sporn showed that nuclear costs had fallen to $123 a kilowatt – only $11 a kilowatt more than in coal-fired plants. Subsequently, prices have risen sharply. By 1973 data compiled at the Oak Ridge National Laboratories for AEC use indicated that a nuclear plant started in 1973 would cost $435 a kilowatt. A coal-fired plant with scrubbers completed at the same time as the nuclear plant would cost $409, including $54 for scrubbers.

Without going into a full discussion of all the figures for recent years, it may be noted that the data suggest that a nuclear plant costs $40 to $100 per kilowatt more than a coal-fired plant without scrubbers. Some scattered newspaper stories and conversations with a few utilities suggest a possible widening of this differential but this is by no means yet a unanimous view. In any case, a $40 differential levelized at 16 per cent amounts to 11 cents a million BTUs; $100 at 18 per cent translates to 31 cents a million BTUs. This 11 to 31 cent range is used here, and modifications, such as for higher cost differentials, are one of the exercises left to the reader.[19]

Nuclear fuel cost estimates have, in contrast, been fairly stable at roughly 20 cents per million BTUs displaced. Nuclear fuel costs involve many factors other than uranium mining costs since the ore must be processed, the content of the reactive fuel – uranium 235 – must be increased, the uranium fabricated into fuel rods, and the spent fuel handled. Fuel costs are subject to forces pushing in both directions. Economies of scale and technical progress can lower many of the processing costs but these are also affected by inflation. Fears have long been expressed that exhaustion of the cheapest-to-use ore will force up mining costs, but this remains a controversial argument.

Moreover, it is possible that new technologies could lower fuel requirements enough to offset the price rises should they occur. In 1974 the first reasonably large (330 megawatts) gas-cooled reactor was scheduled for operation and orders have already been placed for 1000 megawatt gas-cooled reactors for completion around 1980. Such reactors would have lower fuel requirements and apparently similar capital costs compared to the water-cooled reactors now used in the United States. By the late 1980s a breeder reactor might be available. It would have about the same fuel requirements as a gas-cooled reactor but also would breed – that is, convert so much more of the non-reactive uranium in the fuel rods into plutonium than do present reactors that it actually produces more fuel than it uses. Thus, primarily through the ability to resell the plutonium to other reactors, the net fuel costs would be significantly lowered.

Since it may not be more costly than a water-cooled reactor, the position of a gas-cooled reactor might not depend upon rising fuel prices, but this is not true of the breeder. It may have such high capital costs that only a sharp rise in fuel costs will justify its use.[20] Thus, the breeder can be thought of as something that would offset a fuel-cost rise if it occurred. However, since this rise is much less than highly probable, the need for the breeder is not yet established. In any case, it is assumed here reactor fuel costs are unlikely to rise.

Returning to the implications for interfuel competition, the simplest case is nuclear fuel versus Western coal. Here, Western coal can receive a premium over the 20 cent cost of nuclear fuel equal to the levelized capital costs of 11 to 31 cents. Thus, a 31 to 51 cent price could be paid for Western coal. Oil would be able to bear a further premium equal to the 8 to 16 cent saving in its costs compared to a coal-fired plant, so its price could range from 39 to 67 cents. In contrast, scrubbing costs reduce the permissible payment for Eastern coal to 12 to

Richard L. Gordon

63 cents below the price of Western coal. A lowering of permissible costs by 63 cents, however, implies that Eastern coal could not compete given the nuclear costs assumed here. The assumptions most favorable to coal, that the 51 cent allowable price only is reduced 12 cents, imply that 39-cent Eastern coal would be competitive.

This argument can be reversed to show the permissible level of nuclear plant costs given various levels of coal and scrubber costs. For example, 30-cent coal and 63-cent scrubbing imply 93 cents available to pay for 20-cent nuclear fuel and the extra capital costs of a nuclear plant. Thus, there would be 73 cents per million BTUs to pay for the extra capital costs of a nuclear plant; at an 18 per cent capital charge this is roughly the levelized cost of an excess of $243 per kilowatt of nuclear over fossil plant capital costs. Each 5-cent rise in coal costs increases the allowable capital expenditures on nuclear plants to rise about $17 (see case 5 in table 1).

Even greater difficulties arise in dealing with the economics of a combined cycle using synthetic gas.[21] The analysis is complicated both by the existence of a conversion step and the higher efficiencies of the combined cycle. Thus, it was estimated that advanced coal gasification processes would use 1.15 BTUs of coal to produce a BTU of gas but that advanced combined cycles of the 1990s would need only 66 per cent as much fuel as a conventional fossil fuel plant. The net effect is a reduction of coal input requirements to 76 per cent of those in fossil fuel plants. Since oil gasification involves only 1.1 BTUs input per BTU of gas, its use in the combined cycle puts oil use at 71 per cent of conventional plant levels. To this consideration must be added the significantly lower capital costs of a combined cycle compared to a coal plant without scrubbers, the elimination of the need for further sulfur emission controls, the slightly higher operating costs of combined cycles, and the costs of gasification. Unfortunately, the capital cost estimates provided were even more speculative than those cited above for other types of equipment and have been outmoded by inflation. A rough adjustment of all the data using the assumption that inflation has doubled capital costs implies that the cost of coal could slightly exceed $1 per million BTUs and still remain competitive with nuclear power. High sulfur oil, because of higher conversion efficiencies and lower conversion costs, could survive at even higher costs of as much as $1.18. Of course, to the extent that the original estimates were over-optimistic, the true allowable prices would be correspondingly lower. Success with the combined cycle would, therefore, greatly reduce the pressures of nuclear competition on fossil fuels. Given the advantages of oil gasification and the possibility for direct use of residual fuel oil, it is conceivable, however, that oil could prove more economic than coal.

TABLE 2

Fuel price assumptions for electric power plants in Chicago
(cents/million BTUs, 1973 dollars)

	Low fuel cost models	High fuel cost models
1 FOB mine cost Western coal	25	25
2 Freight Western coal to Chicago	35	60
3 Delivered price Western coal in Chicago (1+2)	60	85
4 FOB mine price Eastern coal	40	50
5 Freight Eastern coal to Chicago	10	10
6 Delivered price of Eastern coal in Chicago (4+5)	50	60
7 Price of high sulfur oil delivered to coastal destination	50	50
8 Desulfurization expense	17	17
9 Price of low sulfur oil delivered to coastal destination (7+8)	67	67
10 Inland transportation of oil to Chicago	13	13
11 Delivered price of high sulfur oil in Chicago (7+10)	63	63
12 Delivered price of low sulfur oil in Chicago (9+10)	80	80
13 Nuclear fuel costs in Chicago	20	20

Coal and oil prices

To complete the analysis, it is necessary to appraise future coal and oil prices.
Table 2 summarizes the data. For coal, stress may be placed on strip mining of
low-sulfur Western coals and underground mining of high-sulfur Eastern coals.
The reason for the emphasis chosen in the West should be clear – these are the
most attractive resources. The choice of stress in the East reflects a forecast that
the cost of high-sulfur underground mined coal represents the best indicator of
future marginal costs and prices. Such information as could be obtained about
Eastern low-sulfur coals suggests that they are unlikely to represent a satisfactory alternative.[22] Should low-sulfur coal output be expanded to levels high
enough to meet electric utility coal needs, the marginal costs are likely to exceed those of high-sulfur coal by more than the cost of scrubbing. The neglect
of strip mining in the East is based on analogous reasoning. The evidence again
suggests that the marginal costs of high levels of strip-mined output would exceed

Richard L. Gordon

the costs estimated here for underground mines. Ample low-cost stripping reserves historically were available only in a few of the states east of the Mississippi and the evidence suggests that even in these states such reserves have already, for the most part, been put into production.

Western coal prospects
A typical vision of Western coal is that vast amounts of coal are available to be strip mined at low costs. While this view may prove correct, it is not substantiated by the data on strippable reserves. Some 868 billion tons of coal reserves exist in the Western states but only 27 billion tons are presently believed strippable at low costs. This would be ample to meet current electric power industry coal demands for perhaps seventy-five years, but it hardly provides the basis for a sustained massive dependence on coal for both the growth in electric power generation and the synthetic oil and gas prospects discussed below. For example, if the known strippable coal reserves were devoted entirely to production of synthetic gas, they could produce 9.5 trillion cubic feet of gas a year for thirty years.[23] Annual US natural gas output in the early seventies exceeded 20 trillion cubic feet. Of course, further exploration might identify additional sources of easily stripped coal so that it would prove capable of supporting more substantial outputs. An alternative view is that the Western industry might quickly be forced to shift to underground mining and the cost penalties that it involves. To the extent that this is true, Western coal is even less attractive than its supporters attempt to suggest. Its potential becomes more of providing a modest supplement than of replacing conventional oil and gas or for nuclear power.

The best Western coals can be mined for 15 cents a million BTUs but expectations are widespread that these costs will have risen to at least 25 cents by 1980. These forecasts encompass inflation and less favorable economics. The earlier ventures used the very best reserves and were developed at a slower pace that made start-up costs lower than are likely for newer ventures.

This analysis must be qualified for the impacts of desires to limit the environmental impact of the mining. The evidence is clear that the coal veins are so rich that even the most expensive reclamation conceivable will have negligible cost impacts. A wide range of reclamation cost estimates has appeared in the literature; the differences reflect both alternative assumptions about the degree of reclamation and variations in requirements from site to site. Estimates as low as a few hundred dollars and as high as $3000 an acre have appeared. One private source, for example, indicated that a particularly thorough job for Western lands could be done for $2500 per acre mined.

Clearly, the effect on cost per million BTU depends on the tons mined per acre and BTUs per ton. Here too, considerable variation is possible; coal contents as high as 66,000 tons an acre have been reported in the West and heat contents range from 5500 to 10,400 BTUs per pound in the West.[24] However, most coals run 8000 BTUs or higher. Assuming a $3000 per acre reclamation cost and a seam only containing 10,000 tons of 8000 BTU per pound coal per acre, reclamation costs less than two cents per million BTUs. This cost probably was built into the prior estimates. A more critical question is how much land disturbance residents of the West are willing to tolerate at any given time. Sentiment is growing to limit such expansion and this may be a major brake on Western coal use.

Another main drawback of Western coal is that the regions in which it is available are sparsely populated. Substantial expenses must be incurred in making the coal available to major markets. Several possibilities exist. The electricity could be generated at the mine and transmitted to major markets or the coal could be shipped by various methods.

The most substantial established effort to develop Western coal use for power generation essentially adopted the former route (although some of the generating plants are between the mine and the market). A series of plants was proposed to serve electric utilities from west Texas to southern California. The resulting air pollution and land disturbance from those plants already operating has created considerable opposition and the Interior Department decided in 1973 not to allow construction of the last and largest proposed plant in this plan.[25]

In contrast, Western coal presumably would be welcome as a source of air pollution abatement in the East. Clearly, the situation in the East cannot be easily characterized since the logistics of supply differ so much from point to point. Chicago, however, conveniently serves as a focus of analysis. It is a particularly critical market since failure of Western coal to compete in Chicago implies severe limitations on the expansion potential. Few major markets are more favorably located than Chicago to receive Western coal and many are significantly worse situated. At least under present institutional arrangements, the effect of greater distances is aggravated by sharp cost increases that would arise if it became necessary to transfer the coal between railroads. With this in mind, we may note that estimates of long-run rail shipment costs to Chicago range from 35 to 60 cents a million BTUs. Given 25 cent FOB mine costs, delivered prices would lie between 60 and 85 cents.

Eastern coal prospects
Turning now to Eastern coal, the critical consideration is that its cost began rising sharply in 1969 after long years of stability. Steam coal prices FOB mine have gone from about 18 cents a million BTUs to 30–35 cents in early 1973. The rise reflects the effects of corresponding sharp increases in input costs - particularly for labor - and a decline in output per worker since 1969 that had exceeded

Richard L. Gordon

21 per cent by 1971 and continued into 1973. These developments can be attributed to the broad problem of labor's dissatisfaction with conditions of employment in coal mining. This discontent has taken many different forms. A stringent new mine health and safety act was passed in 1969. Workers have negotiated contracts providing for sharp rises in wages and fringe benefits; wildcat strikes have proliferated; inexperienced workers had to be added; workers have been aggressively pursuing their seniority rights to change jobs. With so much turmoil, it is impossible to allocate the cost increases among specific causes. What is more critical is that for some years at least we can expect the costs to continue rising in real as well as monetary terms. The unattractiveness of coal mining is likely to continue forcing substantial wage increases and the present climate will make it difficult even to restore 1969 levels of output per worker by 1980. At the same time, little evidence is available on the sensitivity of cost trends to cumulative production levels. In principle, increased cumulative output will deplete the cheapest to exploit reserves and lead to higher mining costs. The implicit assumption here is that the exhaustion of cheaper-to-mine resources will have much less impact than the other forces considered. The 1973 dollar cost of Eastern coal probably will rise to 40–50 cents a million BTUs by 1980 largely as a result of the forces affecting labor costs and productivity in mines exploiting reserves comparable to those presently employed.

Oil prospects
Turning to oil, here again the uncertainties are vast. Adelman's work on oil makes clear that existing imported oil prices are inflated by the ability of the producing countries to keep prices well above marginal costs. It is, therefore, possible to rig the analysis to secure any result desired. Sufficient pessimism about further price rises can lead to forecasts of total inability to compete; conversely, if you forecast significant enough weakening of oil prices, you can conclude that oil will conquer the whole market. A middle course is taken here – a 1973 dollar price pattern roughly similar to that prevailing in mid-1972 is assumed. At that time, the price of low-sulfur oil delivered on the US East coast was about 67 cents a million BTUs and high-sulfur oil was selling for about 40 cents. This 27-cent premium for low-sulfur oil exceeded the standard estimate that desulfurization would cost around 17 cents a million BTUs. Presumably the differential arises from the short-term scarcity of desulfurization capacity and will disappear in time. However, for present purposes, it is assumed that low-sulfur oil prices remain at 67 cents and high-sulfur oil prices rise to 50 cents. It appears that the oil could be pipelined to most locations east of the Mississippi for less than 10 cents a million BTUs and barged at prices no greater than 15 cents for the furthest locations on the inland waterway network. Chicago costs might be about 5 cents for

pipelines and 10 cents for barges. However, Chicago prices here are set conserva-
tively at 80 cents for low-sulfur oil (an implicit transportation charge of 13 cents)
and at 63 cents for high-sulfur oil. [Editors' note: Oil prices have substantially increased since mid-1972. This will make coal and nuclear power more competitive
and increase the already excess demands for natural gas. However, the higher oil
prices move both oil shale and tar sands closer to full commercial feasibility.]

Possible patterns of fuel use
From the prior data follow the conclusions that Eastern coal could face considerable difficulties but that the role of other fuels remains somewhat uncertain. As
Table 3 shows, Western coal could possibly be as cheap as Eastern coal delivered
in Chicago and the highest premium for Western coal considered is 35 cents. Some
combination of such a high premium and low scrubber costs is necessary to allow
Eastern coal to remain competitive in existing or new plants in Chicago. Oil, in
contrast, is projected to cost 20 to 30 cents more than Eastern coal – even using
a mid-1972 price-comparison basis. Again, low scrubber costs are critical in
allowing Eastern coal to remain viable in either old or new facilities. However,
the comparative position of Western coal and oil in Chicago and thus the implied
division of the national market between the two fuels is extremely uncertain. In
contrast, under the prices assumed here, nuclear power is clearly cheaper than
conventional fossil-fuel plants not serving markets near Western coal fields.

Ambiguity returns when the prospects of the combined cycle are added. My
estimates for coal and oil prices allowable when using the combined cycle are too
broad to resolve the issue of viability against nuclear power. The figures do suggest that should oil prices in the 1980s not markedly exceed those of 1972, oil
will be in a stronger position than coal. A rough estimate is that coal must sell
for less than 52 cents to compete with gasification of 63 cent high-sulfur oil, and
42 cents to compete against direct use of 80 cent low-sulfur oil.

It should be once again recalled that all these numbers are subject to considerable uncertainty and serious forecasting errors could have been made. Moreover,
two inherent limitations should be noted. The focus on Chicago leaves uncertain
the exact pattern in other parts of the country since no effort was made to determine the variation in transportation costs. Moreover, the implicit assumption of
all these price estimates is that the exhaustion of lower cost deposits is not as significant an influence on prices as other forces. This argument is consistent with
the prior analyses of all fuels but Western coal. The potential limitations to its
supply could force prices well above 25 cents FOB mine and weaken its expansion potential.

[Editors' note: The fuel cost differentials discussed above assume that in some
geographic markets a particular fuel, fuel source, and technology will be dominant.

TABLE 3

Possible relative position of fuels for electric power generation in Chicago
(cents/million BTUs, 1973 dollars)

Case 1: Western coal compared to oil and Eastern coal in existing plants

	Greatest advantage to Western coal	Least advantage to Western coal
1 Delivered price of Western coal (from Table 2)	60	85
2 Delivered price of Eastern coal (from Table 2)	60	50
3 Excess of Western coal delivered price over Eastern coal delivered price (1–2)	0*	35
4 Premium allowed for Western coal over Eastern coal (from Table 1)	85	23
5 Delivered price of oil (from Table 2)	80	80
6 Excess of Western coal delivered price over oil price (1–5)	–20*	5
7 Premium allowed for Western coal over oil (from Table 2)	10	5

Case 2: Oil compared to Eastern coal in existing plant

	Greatest advantage to oil	Least advantage to oil
8 Excess of delivered oil price over Eastern coal delivered price (5–2)	20*	30
9 Premium allowed for oil over Eastern coal (from Table 1)	79	20

Case 3: Oil compared to Eastern and Western coal in new plants

	Greatest advantage to oil	Least advantage to oil
10 Excess of delivered oil prices over Eastern coal delivered prices (item 8 above)	20*	30
11 Premium allowed for oil over Eastern coal (from Table 1)	79	20
12 Excess of delivered oil prices over Western coal delivered prices (item 6 above adapted to this case)	–5*	20
13 Premium allowed for oil over Western coal (from Table 1)	16	8

TABLE 3 continued

Case 4: Eastern coal compared to Western coal in new plant

	Greatest advantage to Western coal	Least advantage to Western coal
14 Excess of delivered prices Western coal over Eastern coal (item 3 above)	0*	35
15 Premium allowed for Western coal over Eastern coal (from Table 1)	79	20

Case 5: Nuclear power

	Most favorable to nuclear	Least favorable to nuclear
16 Eastern coal delivered prices	60	50
17 Allowable price of Eastern coal (from Table 1)	-32	39
18 Western coal delivered prices	85	60
19 Allowable price of Western coal (from Table 1)	31	51
20 Oil delivered price	80	80
21 Allowable price of oil (from Table 1)	39	67

* Excess of predicted price over rival fuel price low enough to insure viability.

'Dominance' is here defined to be least cost when all capital, operating, transportation, and environmental costs are included. Under some circumstances, a particular fuel may be dominated in all markets by one or another of the alternative fuels. In other situations, there may be well-defined boundaries between areas of dominance. At these boundaries, the laid-in costs of two or more fuels and technologies will be equal. The boundaries may in fact be wide grey zones where the choice is swung from one fuel, fuel source, and technology to another by relatively modest cost changes that are well within the forecast errors of relative fuel prices. Those grey zones of indeterminacy may be belts that are several states wide. It is the existence of such grey areas which puts the challenge into investment decision-making. Another way to look at the problem which Professor Gordon is discussing would be to attempt to define the location and width of the boundaries between various fuel and technology pairs and the sensitivity of these boundaries to changes in various cost components. Such an attempt is beyond the scope of Professor Gordon's paper and the limits of reporting for these volumes.]

In any event, the future of coal as an electric utility fuel is severely threatened. Unless nuclear power proves far more costly than expected or the economics of coal use are greatly improved, nuclear power clearly represents a cheaper long-run alternative. It may in turn be displaced by oil but that depends upon the ability of oil consumers to resist rising prices abroad. Clearly, better methods of utilizing coal are needed if the industry is to remain viable but they are not sufficient to overcome completely the threats of rival fuels. Equal emphasis must be placed on developing cheaper, safer, and less environmentally destructive methods of coal mining. Whether the task is worth attempting is another matter. Countless observers insist that success is inevitable. Most of these advocates unfortunately base their arguments on belief that other promising alternatives do not exist.

Whatever really happens ultimately, a long and difficult transition period is likely. The critical point here is that the future of coal in its traditional markets has become nearly impossible to forecast. We have no idea what the economic optimum will prove to be, let alone whether public policies will be well designed to attain such an optimum. It may be argued that this is actually a highly positive policy conclusion. All too much policy discussion assumes that the right answer is either already known or easily found if we only studied the matter a bit more. It may be useful to recognize that things are not this simple and that decision-makers cannot design a solution tomorrow that will last for thirty days let alone for thirty years.

SYNTHETIC FUELS FROM COAL[26]

Turning to synthetic fuels, a wide variety of processes for producing close substitutes for oil and natural gas have been considered. Their status differs widely. At one extreme, work is moving ahead in adopting the long-proven German Lurgi process for gas manufacture in the US. The process to date has only produced a low BTU gas but it is hoped that a methanation step that adds the hydrogen required for a high BTU gas can be developed before the proposed projects are completed. Other more advanced systems are at various stages of development. It appears that such advanced developments cannot be completed until the early 1980s at best.

The cost data on these processes are limited in quantity and quality. It is a standard estimate that coal gas would cost at least $1 when produced using strip mined Western coals. For example, data in a 1972 study by the National Petroleum Council suggest that the cost of coal gas per million BTUs would run from $0.75 to $1.00 plus about 1.5 times the price per million BTUs of coal (since about 1.5 million BTUs of coal would be needed for a million BTUs of gas).

Thus, if non-coal costs are at 75 cents, the total cost of gas is about $0.98 with the 15-cent coal prices now prevailing in the West, $1.13 if these costs rise to 25 cents, and $1.50 if it becomes necessary to use 50-cent underground-mined coal. The respective figures rise to $1.03, $1.38, and $1.75 if non-fuel costs are $1.00. Clearly, these figures exceed not only the present costs of gas, but also the more optimistic estimates of the market-clearing price for gas. Even less needs to be said about coal liquefaction. The NPC indicates the lowest conceivable cost is $5.75 a barrel FOB mine mouth plant and that costs could exceed $8.00.

Quite clearly, the prospects for coal liquefaction depend entirely upon sharp rises in world oil prices. The leading oil-producing countries abroad would have to raise prices to the level of alternative supplies and these would have to be extremely expensive. For example, oil in North America would have to become very costly. The presumption that coal liquefaction will become important is essentially a forecast that OPEC control of foreign oil prices keeps getting stronger and that supplies in Alaska, the Canadian Arctic, and offshore in the US all prove inadequate to meet demands without massive price increases.[27]

The case for coal gas involves these presumptions plus pessimism about conventional gas supplies and the ability of gas users to convert to oil. In short, there is little a study of coal can contribute to analysis of synthesis beyond the observation that it is expensive by the standards applicable up to 1973. It remains for students of oil and gas markets to appraise the prospects. The published literature can provide support for any position. Adelman's work on oil makes clear that (assuming that it is not determined that nuclear power has marked environmental advantages over low-sulfur oil) oil has the lowest real resource cost for all purposes including electric power generation. Should oil not be viable, it will only be because foreign oil producers kept prices well above marginal costs. Visions of future oil price patterns range from a feeling that the price rigging cannot last to conviction that the producing countries are invulnerable. The argument can be appropriately complicated by alternative views of such issues as the nature and effect of natural gas policy and the success of exploration activities in Alaska, the US outer continental shelf, and the Canadian Arctic. Again, the only documentable conclusion is that coal synthesis is not a guaranteed success. The reader may decide for himself whether to share the impression that the barriers are so formidable that the prospects are extremely dubious. Thus, the golden future expected for coal is much less than fully assured.

NOTES

This study draws upon research on coal economics supported by Resources for the Future Inc. and a review of industrial fuel markets supported by the

Richard L. Gordon

National Science Foundation; the assistance of both is gratefully acknowledged. The opinions here are mine. Much of the material in this study summarizes a manuscript on coal markets presently under review at Resources for the
Future; the manuscript provides greater detail. In any case, the underlying data
were obtained from a combination of literature surveys and interviews with
officials in the electric utility and coal industries. Unless an explicit source is
provided, it may be presumed that the data are largely drawn from these interviews.

1 Data on the coal industry can be found in US Bureau of Mines, *Minerals Yearbook* (Washington annual). On the reserve picture and many other issues, the
   National Petroleum Council's full report dated December 1972 on *U.S. Energy
   Outlook* and the supporting task force reports may be consulted. The report
   should not be confused with a similarly titled summary version.

2 See US Bureau of Mines, *Minerals Yearbook*

3 The coke serves several functions in iron-making but the critical one of supporting the ore burden requires a solid fuel.

4 See R.L. Gordon, *The Evolution of Energy Policy in Western Europe* (New
   York 1970), for a review of such policies.

5 See US Federal Power Commission, *The 1970 National Power Survey*, vol. I
   (Washington 1971) for a description of the electric power industry.

6 The BTU is the amount of heat required to increase the temperature of one
   pound of water one degree Fahrenheit. Since fuels, particularly coals, differ
   widely in BTU content per ton, it is conventional to present costs on a heat-
   content basis. Strictly speaking, no fuel user buys entirely on a heat-cost basis,
   but in the case of electric utilities the assumption is a close enough approximation to justify its use. See also note 28.

7 The most recent data on existing abilities to convert among fuels appear in
   Thomas E. Duchesneau, *Interfuel Substitutability in the Electric Utility Sector of the U.S. Economy,* a staff report to the Federal Trade Commission
   (Washington 1972), p. 36. In 1969 40.8 per cent of capacity was able only to
   burn coal, 28.7 per cent coal and one or two other fuels. These figures were
   tabulated from data on plant characteristics compiled from data filed with the
   Federal Power Commission and reported in National Coal Association, *Steam
   Electric Plant Factors.* Examination of the Coal Association reports suggests
   two possible biases may prevail. First, coal capability apparently is defined as
   the installation of coal-handling equipment; plants that have converted to oil
   and removed such handling equipment are no longer credited with coal-use
   capability. Thus, the figures only relate to immediate abilities to use coal. Conversely, the capabilities relate to the entire plant and it is quite likely that in

plants in which several separate boilers have been installed some boilers will not be able to use coal.

8 This figure is a rough adjustment for retrofitting penalties of the costs discussed below of adding coal-use capability to a new plant.

9 See National Petroleum Council, *U.S. Energy Outlook,* p. 232 for the 1972 estimate. The projection comes from F.L. Robson, et al, *Technological and Economic Feasibility of Advanced Power Cycles and Methods of Producing Nonpolluting Fuels for Utility Power Stations,* United Aircraft Research Laboratories, 1970 (available from National Technical Information Service as PB 198 392). This is a detailed presentation of the case for the combined cycle using synthetic low BTU gas.

10 See *1970 National Power Survey,* p. I-8-4

11 See ibid., chap. 10 and 11 for a review of these issues.

12 Nitrogen oxides are largely formed by reaction between heat and oxygen and nitrogen in the atmosphere. Nitrogen in the fuel can increase the formation. Coal creates greater amounts of nitrogen oxides both because it tends to be burned at higher temperatures and because it contains more nitrogen than other fuels. Control difficulties arise because the techniques designed to modify combustion to retard formation thus far have not worked satisfactorily for coal.

13 The optimistic arguments on the feasibility and low cost of sulfur scrubbing appear in Sulfur Oxide Control Technology Assessment Panel, *Final Report on Projected Utilization of Stack Gas Cleaning Systems by Steam Electric Plants,* 1973. A dissent was registered by Robert M. Jimeson who represented the Federal Power Commission on the panel. His views appear in Alexander Gakner and Robert M. Jimeson, *Environmental and Economic Cost Considerations in Electric Power Supply* (paper presented at the annual meetings of the American Institute of Chemical Engineers, 1973).

14 See Commonwealth Edison Company, *Memorandum regarding SO$_2$ Removal Experience and Cost Estimates,* 1973

15 A good laymen's introduction to the issues, presenting the pro-nuclear position, is provided by US Atomic Energy Commission, *The Safety of Nuclear Reactors (Light-water Cooled) and Related Facilities* (Wash-1250) (Washington 1973). The last chapter of this study reviews and cites many of the major critics.

16 Space does not permit an elaborate review of the profusion of pollution rules. The US government imposes two types of minimum standards – one applied to over-all air quality and another for emissions from particular sources. The over-all standards are designed to prevent threats to health and welfare, but

Robert L. Gordon

the standards for specific sources apparently are based on what allegedly is technically attainable. The figure cited above is actually a translation of 1971 standards applicable to all new electric power plants into its equivalent for a high BTU coal. It should be considered roughly representative of the requirements that will ultimately apply at least to Eastern coals; Western coals will face stricter requirements. A lower allowable per cent weight sulfur content is implied when the US standard is applied to the low BTU Western coals, and Western states are adopting much stricter emission standards than the US government imposed.

17 No systematic compilation of the costs of conversion to oil is available but a survey of scattered data in company annual reports and discussions with individual companies suggests a $10–20 a kilowatt cost which probably roughly levelizes to the figures in the text when an old plant is involved.

18 This figure comes from the sources cited in note 19.

19 The data are mainly scattered in different hearings of the US Congress Joint Committee on Atomic Energy, particularly in the annual *AEC Authorization Legislation* volumes. A compilation of earlier material appears in a Joint Committee print called *Nuclear Power Economics – 1962 through 1967*. The Oak Ridge group's 1973 estimates appear in the January 1973 issue of *Power Engineering*. It may be noted that non-fuel operating costs are ignored here, as all sources indicate these costs do not differ among nuclear and different types of conventional fossil plants. Nuclear fuel costs here include special nuclear insurance fees.

20 The AEC's case for the breeder appears in *Updated (1970) Cost-Benefit Analysis of the U.S. Breeder Reactor Program* (Wash-1184) (Washington 1972) and makes the importance of rising uranium prices clear. A view of uranium supply prospects appears in National Petroleum Council, *U.S. Energy Outlook*, chap. 6.

21 The combined cycle data are entirely from Robson, *Nonpolluting Fuels*.

22 The published literature is very vague on costs so that interviews were the main basis of the appraisal.

23 The calculation is based on data in National Petroleum Council, *U.S. Energy Outlook*, pp. 162-8 that indicate a 67 per cent conversion efficiency. 8000 BTUs per pound was used here as the heat content of the coal and 1000 BTUs per cubic foot, as the heat content of the gas. The 26.7 billion tons of coal could be produced at a rate of .9 billion tons or 14 quadrillion BTUs per year for thirty years. This means 9.5 quadrillion BTUs or 9.5 trillion cubic feet of gas per year.

24 See US Council on Environmental Quality, *Coal Surface Mining and Recla-*

mation, report to the Senate Committee on Interior and Insular Affairs (Washington 1973) for a review of these problems.

25 See US Department of the Interior, *Southwest Energy Study,* 1973, for a review of the plans and their environmental impacts.

26 H.C. Hottel and J.B. Howard, *New Energy Technology – Some Facts and Assessments* (Cambridge, Mass. 1971), reviews these synthetic fuel processes and many other new energy technologies, but the cost data reported are obsolete. See National Petroleum Council, *U.S. Energy Outlook,* for more recent cost data.

27 This paragraph should be reinterpreted, in the light of the sharp subsequent rises in oil prices, as arguing that the Middle Eastern prices of January 1974 are unsustainably high. The evidence on oil shale suggests it could provide synthetic crudes at a price well below that of crude oil from coal (and 1974 Middle Eastern oil prices). Moreover, a distinct possibility exists that an all-out effort at expanding US conventional crude oil production would be cheaper than developing oil shale.

28 A discussion of the general concept of the levelized cost approach may be found in any basic engineering economy text. The details of the specific application of the levelized cost approach may be obtained by referring to Professor Gordon's forthcoming RFF volume, or by writing to Professor Gordon himself for a briefer mimeo available from him.

A coal-fired electric generating plant would consume 74 million pounds of coal to generate sufficient electricity for electric toothbrushes in the United States in 1969. This coal when burnt would emit 1.5 million pounds of sulfur by-product; if stripmined, it would leave 7 acres of soil disturbed.

From this simple example, Chapman builds up an analysis of the demand for and supply of electricity in the US. He presents projections of electricity demand in 1980, significantly lower than the predictions of five recent studies. As our introduction suggests, anticipated price rises because of difficulties on the supply side will diminish the quantity of electricity demanded. Energy sources for electricity will, twenty years in the future, be predominately nuclear, then coal, and to a lesser extent oil. The environmental consequences of each of these fuels is examined.

The way out of the crisis – black-outs and brown-outs – obviously not the best means of sharing these higher costs. A price increase would be a mor effective policy to stimulate action – on the side of consumers to minimize energy loss, and on the side of regulators and producers to see that the correct incentives are operative.

76

DUANE CHAPMAN

Electricity in the United States

The nature of the physical processes of production and use of electricity suggests the economic problems we face. In this paper we will examine both these aspects, summarizing the physical process and noting the connection between consumer use, power generation, and environmental problems as we discuss some of the personal and public policy options we have.

Electricity is electric energy. Its production in a fossil fuel plant involves burning coal, oil, or gas to boil water and drive a steam turbine. A nuclear plant transforms matter to create the necessary heat and steam. Hydroelectric stations use a water wheel to drive the turbine. The shaft of these turbines is connected to the armature of an electric generator. The generator changes mechanical energy (of the turbine) into electric energy, which is then carried over transmission lines to consumers who use it to do work. A rigorous definition of 'energy' is, in fact, 'the ability to do work.'

All ordinary matter is composed of atoms: massive positive nuclei surrounded by a cloud of enough negatively charged electrons to make the atoms as a whole electrically neutral. If an electron is moved away from its home atom, an electric force on neighbor electrons due to the resultant *net* positive charge is created. A neighbor electron jumps to fill in the gap, leaving its own home atom positively charged. This process of 'charge displacement' continues and is what we call 'electricity.'

The ultimate source of the energy in our homes is the sun which has always provided the energy of plants and animals via photosynthesis of starches and sugars. Coal is fossilized vegetable matter, consisting of carbon, hydrocarbons, and various other complex compounds. Petroleum, formed by the decomposition of microscopic marine organisms, is a mixture of many different hydrocarbons. Natural gas has an origin identical to petroleum and is mostly methane. It is the burning of these earth fuels that changes their stored chemical potential energy into heat, and produces the steam which passes through a steam turbine (which is like a water-wheel running on steam) and runs the generator.

In a nuclear power plant, however, the fission of atomic nuclei in a controlled chain reaction is the source of heat for steam. These atomic nuclei were not created by our sun but were formed in stars which exploded before the creation of our earth and sun.

USE OF ELECTRICITY

Americans used 80 million kwh for electric toothbrushes in 1969.[1] Consider our illustration in Figure 1: a coal-fired plant would require 74 million pounds of coal to generate the power for the toothbrushes. A typical sulfur content of 2 per cent would indicate the emission of 1.5 million pounds of sulfur as a byproduct of electric toothbrush use. At 5000 tons of coal per acre from strip mining, the nation would need to strip seven acres of coal to power its toothbrushes. But these power toothbrushes are an insignificant user of energy.

Let us take the 199 million people in 1968 and the reported 60.4 million households to define an average family of 3.3 persons. This average family used 22,000 kwh directly and indirectly in 1968, but only 5 kwh for the electric toothbrush. (Only one-fourth of the households had these machines in 1968.) A family uses much more electricity indirectly, outside of the home, than it does directly with electrical appliances. The upper part of Table 1 shows that the family's share of manufactured products required 10,000 kwh. Iron, aluminum, and other metal products have heavy energy requirements. The metal products used in an average day's work and at home has 10 per cent of the family's energy budget. Chemicals – from fertilizer to nylon for suits – require even more electricity. We have less information about commercial consumption of electricity, but the family uses more power for air conditioning in stores and offices than in any single home use. In 1968 the typical all-electric home required 32,000 kwh per year. If the future means we all move towards all-electric homes, our per capita use can easily quintuple in a short time. In fact, the recent past has seen regular and significant increases in electricity use. The pattern has been so regular that most experts have simply extrapolated past growth into the future.

PREDICTING FUTURE GROWTH

An illustration is persuasive. In the five-year period 1962-7 total national electricity sales grew on average 7.3 per cent per year to 1.11 Tkwh (trillion kilowatt hours).

TABLE 1

Purchased electricity use per household, 1968 (a 3.3 person household)

INDUSTRIAL	
Chemicals and fibers	2864
Iron, aluminum, and other metals	2285
Food	596
Paper and cardboard	497
Concrete, glass, etc.	497
Petroleum	397
Other (bombs, lumber, etc.)	2781
Total industrial product use of electricity per family	9917
HOME USE	
Refrigerator	1097
Hot water	978
Heating	719
Air conditioning	676
Lighting	658
Television	562
Cooking	421
Freezer	351
Dryer	224
Other	412
Transmission line losses, etc.	645
Total electricity for home use per family	6743
COMMERCIAL USE (offices, schools, shopping centers, etc.)	
Lighting and other	3278
Air conditioning	1573
Cooking	381
Total electricity for commercial use per family	5232

Total per family in 1968 was 21,892 kwh

Total for country was 1.3 trillion kwh

Suppose in 1968 a prediction of 1972 sales had been made assuming exactly the same growth rate. The 1972 prediction would have been 1.58 Tkwh. And 1972 sales were that precise amount. This kind of successful experience, repeated at the utility, state, and national level, has led industry and government analysts to depend upon compound growth rates as a method of predicting future growth.

Duane Chapman

TABLE 2

Recent predictions of future growth: government, industry, and academic

Source	Electricity generation (T kwh)					
	1970	1975	1980	1985	1990	2000
Office of emergency preparedness	1.54	2.13	2.98	3.97	5.52	
Electrical world	1.54	2.23	3.16	4.39	5.93	
Cornell-NSF workshop	1.54	2.15	2.92	3.96	5.38	10.25

Table 2 shows three sets of projections made in 1972 by government, industry, and university groups.[2] The similarity in forecasts is impressive. Most experts of whatever background anticipate future growth will approximate past growth, nearly doubling every ten years. And these projections in Table 2 coincide closely with projections by the Federal Power Commission and the National Petroleum Council.

I believe the five projections noted here are incorrect, and much too high for the late 1980s and 1990s. One and probably two of the basic factors influencing demand growth have irreversibly altered their courses. In every year from 1946 to 1970 the (deflated) average price of electricity fell, declining at 3.5 per cent per year over the period.[3] There are a number of reasons for this, including the success of the industry in achieving production and distribution efficiency, the economies of scale achieved through larger generating facilities, and the exclusion of the human and environmental cost of power generation from the price of energy. We shall take this point up again later. However, we may be near the end of scale economies, and the bill for environmental protection is now being presented. This, coupled with rising energy costs, means that the era of falling electric rates has passed. Beginning in 1970 rates began rising in most parts of the country and will continue to do so for many years. Necessarily, this will affect the way in which we choose to use electricity in the future; the impact must be a reduction in the rate of growth.

The picture is less clear with respect to population trends. Population grew at 1.3 per cent per year through the 1960s. However, in 1971 fertility rates approached the zero population growth level, and fell below that level in 1972. Consequently, population growth has slowed at a decreasing but perceptible pace.[4]

Most of our research work at Cornell University has been focused upon the statistical estimation of the significance of prices, population growth, and income growth as they influence the demand for electricity.[5] This kind of work is mathe-

TABLE 3

Electricity demand

Factor	Relationship to electricity demand growth	Likely pattern for future
Electricity prices	Demand responds negatively to price increases, and the demand changes faster than price	Increasing electricity prices, perhaps doubling in 30 years
Population	Demand is proportional to population	Population growth seems to be declining
Per capita income	Demand responds positively to income increases, but demand doesn't increase as much as income	Rapid growth in last two years: future = ?
Gas prices	Electricity demand grows if gas prices rise, but only a small impact	Gas prices will probably rise faster than electricity prices

Summary: Continued growth but at declining rates

matical by nature but can be summarized as in Table 3. One important finding not shown in the table is the lengthy period necessary for changes to become visible in electricity demand. Since electricity is used through machines and appliances, we don't really begin to affect demand until our preferences change and different items or designs are chosen. As an example, a 100 per cent rise in electricity rates won't affect the use of a fourteen cubic foot frost-free refrigerator in my home today. But if I move or it wears out, the large price increase may lead me eventually to choose a twelve cubic foot refrigerator using only 40 per cent as much power each year. This time lag characterizes most personal and business consumption of energy.

These findings lead us to disagree with most other observers. Ten trillion kwh sales in 2000 seems unlikely. Obvious qualifications must be kept in mind, however. Widespread substitution of electricity for oil in transportation (cars, transit) and for oil and gas in heating could conceivably more than quadruple per capita use by the end of the century. My guess is that such changes are unlikely, in the long-term future, but the predictions in Table 2 are likely to be quite accurate for 1975.

The question yet to be answered relates to the interaction between consumption and production: Would paying higher rates for environmental protection result in a gradual reduction in the rate of growth? This subject will be taken up

Duane Chapman

below; the next section outlines the major methods of generating electricity and
their environmental consequences.

ELECTRICITY GENERATION
AND ENVIRONMENTAL IMPACT

A year ago I talked with the mayor of a small town and some of her friends about
power problems. Their area is a prime candidate for pumped storage facilities for
peak electricity needed for air conditioning. She believed the power company
hadn't given sufficient thought to solar power as an alternative energy source. A
few months later I met with a group from another small town which is a likely
candidate for numerous nuclear power plants. They had heard of windmill power,
and thought windmills on floating platforms could be alternatives to nuclear
plants.

Both groups face difficult dilemmas, and responded with a desire to seek out
positive alternatives. My own opinion is that these and other 'clean energy' forms
are unlikely to produce significant amounts of power in the foreseeable future.
Geothermal heat, tides, winds, and sunlight are indeed clean, but poorly designed
for the production requirements of our present level of consumption. All major
electricity and energy sources are derived from the sun, either through photosynthesis (the fossil fuels), evaporation (the source of precipitation and hydropower), or synthesis of heavy nuclei before the earth's creation (uranium and
nuclear power). We rely upon eons of natural processes to convert solar and stel-
lar energy into forms we can use, but it is doubtful that direct conversion to electricity will be practical on a large scale.

In Figure 1 coal is seen to be the main source of power at present, generating
almost one-half of the total.[6] It is the major source of fuel for power generation
in and near states with significant coal production (see Figure 2).[7] If electricity
consumption grows at the rates anticipated by the studies in Table 2, coal will be
the major source of new power in the near future. The basic environmental consequences of coal use can be expressed in a manner relating these consequences
to the family energy budget discussed above. A 1000 megawatt (mw) plant is
representative of new plants being built today and produces annually about 6.6
billion kwh. Generation for the average household in 1971 was 25,000 kwh (in
1968 22,000 kwh). So this 1000 mw plant could supply about 260,000 families
in 1971.

About two-thirds of the coal used in the US is for power generation, and about
one-half of this coal is strip mined. Essentially, then, the problems of coal are the
problems of electricity consumption. Other chapters in this volume on coal and
on environment develop these problems in detail. In the context of electricity

82

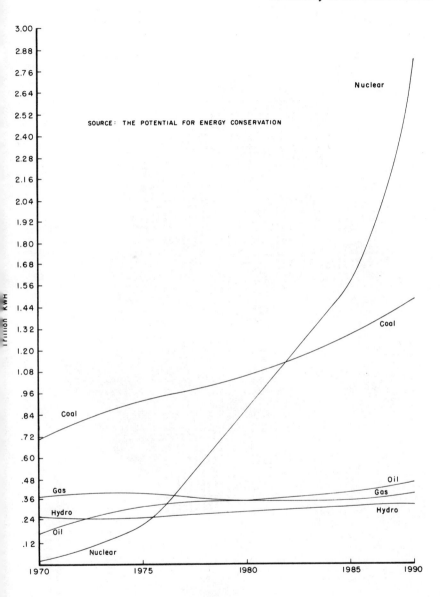

Figure 1   Energy sources for generation

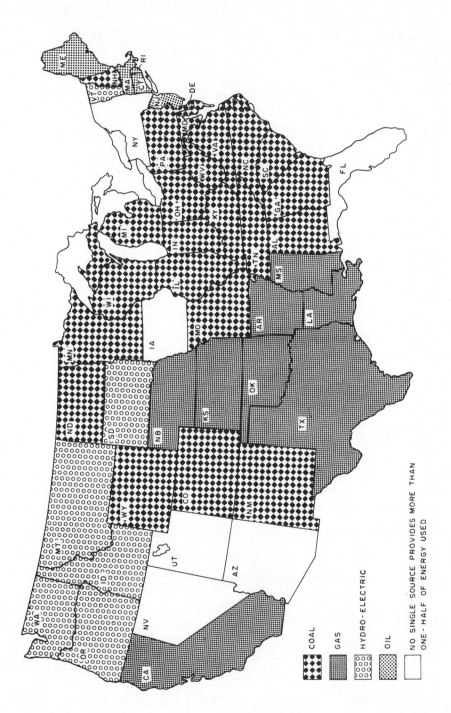

COAL
GAS
HYDRO-ELECTRIC
OIL
NO SINGLE SOURCE PROVIDES MORE THAN ONE-HALF OF ENERGY USED

Figure 2. Major energy sources (supplying more than half the energy used) by state.

generation, we shall note only the most summary kind of statistics dealing with environmental impact.

Concerning underground mining of coal, the most salient environmental problem is the physical danger to the miners. About 200 men were killed each year in the recent past. Last year the figure fell to about 160; perhaps the new health and safety regulations helped. But counter-balancing this is the Buffalo Creek mine dam disaster which killed 120 residents along Buffalo Creek in West Virginia. The health picture is equally grim. About 300,000 men now have black lung disease and the figure is certain to rise. Payments from the federal treasury to black lung victims will approach $1 billion per year. Eventually, if dust control programs become effective, the number of afflicted men will decline.

Strip mining is safer, and far fewer men are needed to do the work. As we all know by now, the major negative consequence of this kind of mining is its impact on land and water. We now have two million acres of unreclaimed strip mined land, and another two million acres with various degrees of reclamation.

The environmental consequences of burning coal for power generation are of an equal magnitude. About eight million tons of sulfur a year are emitted into the air by power plants (about half of the US total), and three to four million tons per year of soot (about one-eighth of the US total). According to a widely cited Public Health Service study by Barrett and Waddell,[8] these sources cause $5\frac{1}{2}$ billion a year damage to health and materials. While oil-fired plants contribute to sulfur pollution, most of this air pollution damage comes from burning coal.

With the help of a recent Council on Environmental Quality (CEQ) study[9] we can express these major environmental impacts in an approximate manner as they relate to specific power plants and individual families. The 1000 mw plant in Table 4 is presumed to use half of its coal from underground mines and half from strip mines. Noting the 260,000 families per plant figure above, we can express the impacts on a per family basis. To convert any figure in Table 4 to an annual basis, divide by 30. Three or four men will die each year in accidents mining the coal and getting it to the power plant. Thirty-one thousand acres of land are needed for strip mining and transmission lines. The air pollution damages caused by the power use of a representative family may be $300 per year and $10,000 over the life of the plant.

However, we should qualify these rough estimates by noting influences working to change the magnitude of these impacts in both directions. First, the kind of growth predicted in Table 2 means per family use would increase six or seven times by the end of the century. Instead of providing power for a quarter of a million families, the 1000 mw plant would serve the needs of 40,000 families. Each 'family share' in Table 4 would be multiplied by six or seven for this kind of growth.

Duane Chapman

TABLE 4

Major environmental impact of a
1000 megawatt coal plant over its 30-year life

	Total	Family share
Coal mining and hauling		
Deaths from accidents	100	.0004
Black lung: man days lost	120,000	.5
Accidents: man days lost	275,000	1.1
Acres strip mined	14,000	.05
Acres for transmission line right of way	17,200	.07
Heat discharge, billion BTUs	915,000	3.5
Sulfur emission, tons	1.9 million	7.3
Damage, dollars	$1.1 billion	$4300
Soot emission, tons	6.1 million	23.5
Damage, dollars	$1.5 billion	$5800

Some of these impacts can be significantly lessened if we are willing to pay for environmental improvement. As an illustration, the generating costs of a coal-fired 1000 mw plant can be taken as about .8 of a cent per kwh, and the average total cost of generation and distribution to all customers in 1972 was 1.8 cents per kwh. The same CEQ study estimates that 'complete reclamation' of strip mined land would add 4 per cent to generating costs, and nearly complete removal of sulfur and soot would add 25 per cent to generating costs. The heat discharge into waterways could be discharged into the air via air cooled towers at 4 per cent of generating costs.

According to Figure 1, nuclear power is a major source of energy for new generating plants. It is not well understood, but one reason the electric utility industry is turning to nuclear power is to meet present and future environmental restrictions on other power sources. Nuclear power has essentially no air pollution, relatively little land effect, and has been significantly safer in terms of deaths, disease, and injuries than coal power.

In two significant aspects nuclear power does not fare as well as coal power. One is heat discharge into water. A coal plant converts heat into electricity somewhat more efficiently, and discharges some of its heat into the air by its smokestack. Compared to Table 4, the nuclear plant discharges 60 per cent more heat directly into the water. Let us imagine a stretch of Pacific Ocean beach. Consider a slice of ocean 2500 feet wide and twenty feet deep at an average temperature of 55°F. According to the standard prediction in Figure 2, the 2.8 trillion kwh in 1990 from nuclear power translates into 430 1000 mw nuclear plants. The waste heat of 22 quadrillion BTUs (British thermal units) would boil a section of water 8300 miles long.

The second environmental problem of nuclear power has no handle. It is the question of catastropic accident. Hammond, Metz, and Maugh provide a comprehensive summary:[10] 'The concerns include reactor operating hazards, particularly the chances of a serious accident, the difficulties of safeguarding fissionable materials used as reactor fuels, and the still unsolved problem of long-term storage for radioactive wastes. Technological failure, earthquakes and other unforeseen natural disasters, and human actions ranging from carelessness to deliberate sabotage are of unusual moment with nuclear power systems. Indeed, the consequences to human health and to the environment of any large release of radioactive substances make nuclear fission potentially the most hazardous of all sources of energy.' This is the paradox: historically, nuclear power has proven to be safer for humans and for the environment than coal and oil power; potentially, it might be the most destructive form yet developed. [Editor's Note: The papers by Kreese and by Carnesale and Elleman discuss the problem of catastrophe.]

In Figure 1 oil use for power is shown increasing two and one-half times. In both extraction and combustion, oil is cleaner than coal. Compared to Table 4, an oil facility causes one-tenth of the deaths, one-fifth of the illness to workers, disturbs somewhat less land (and disturbs it less destructively), causes only 1 per cent as much soot emission, and less than half of the sulfur emissions. However, the heat discharge and transmission line acreages are essentially identical for coal and oil plants. Oil contamination from wells and ships is a distinct problem.

Seemingly, we should turn to oil rather than coal for power generation, but we cannot. The United States can no longer meet US consumption with domestic production. Oil in the future will be much more expensive. Import prices are rising, and production costs at offshore sites are costlier than at the conventional land sites used in the past. Any major new sources such as Alaskan oil, oil from Western shales, and coal liquefaction will also be costly.

Natural gas gets better marks than petroleum for human and environmental health and would clearly be the preferred fuel source. But there is a major problem: while it may be clean, its potential supply is limited. Hence natural gas will not likely grow in use in power generation.

Hydropower faces identical constraints for any future growth. There is essentially no unused capacity at existing power reservoirs. The new hydropower sites tend to be for pumped storage, and these sites are very controversial. Basically, they require excavating the top of a mountain, and then coupling the mountain top reservoir with a river reservoir. Water runs down the mountain in a pipe on a hot summer day to run air conditioners and for other peak uses, but the water must be pumped up the mountain at other times. So a pumped storage facility is necessarily a net consumer of energy. Given the generally polluted air in large cities in the summer, air conditioning is an environmental improvement for the city dweller. But the air conditioner causes serious despoilation in the country-side, and requires a form of power generation which is a net user of power.

In this section we have noted some of the aspects of present and future patterns of power generation, and the environmental consequences of these processes. The increased costs for environmental protection would raise the cost of electricity and the price we pay, leading us to reduce our growth in electricity use. Also, our indirect use of electricity would be affected. As Table 1 revealed, the greatest household shares of electricity are for uses in business and industry. Cost increases in electricity will lead business to lower its growth in consumption by turning to other processes. If plastics, metals, and the like become more expensive because of higher power costs, we might alter our consumption of these products and thereby further the reduction in the growth of demand for energy. This suggests some important policies which are taken up in the last section.

QUESTIONS OF POLICY

We do not usually think of ourselves as policy-makers, but each of us has a personal and family energy policy just as the nation has its policies. In this concluding section we shall note some of the policies available to the family, the community, and the state and federal governments.

At the household level the most significant decision is whether to use gas or electricity as the basic home energy source. Generally, gas systems cost less to operate, are cleaner (as noted above), and need less total energy. Table 5 shows one estimate of savings in energy from using gas appliances.[11] Unfortunately, there is a major barrier to widespread expansion of gas use: the limits of domestic natural gas supply may be reached in ten to thirty years.

The next most significant household choice is insulation. Until recently, little attention has been given to this subject. But now architectural engineering studies show a typical electrically heated house in New York (one built to pre-1971 FHA standards) is wasting one-half of its heating energy because of unnecessary heat loss. Putting significant insulation into this typical house and adding storm windows saves this unnecessary loss, and should save $100 to $200 per year in heating bills. For gas heat the energy saving is comparable, but the financial saving is less because gas is less expensive.

How did we get into a situation where so much energy is thrown away in heating? Basically, I think there are two reasons. First, the nature of home building induces a 'pay later' psychology. The builder might prefer to save on insulation construction cost and have the tenants pay higher utility bills. The second reason

TABLE 5

Energy savings from gas rather than
electric appliances, total system

Appliance	Percent savings with gas
Heating	55
Water heater	50
Clothes dryer	58
Range	29
Air conditioning	44

NOTE: Total system defines total energy as it
passes through extraction, processing, transportation, conversion (for electricity), and home
use.

is that most of us never thought much about it a few years ago. It has been the
advent of environmental and energy concerns that have highlighted this problem.

The thermostat setting is another small but important household factor. Lowering its regular winter setting from 75° to 70° may save 15 to 20 per cent of
heating requirements. Turning down the thermostat at night saves energy but not
as dramatically, as the home and its contents must be reheated each morning.

Table 1 reveals measures to reduce the indirect use of electrical energy. The
five largest categories of family use are outside the home. Walking and bicycling
saves electrical energy used in manufacturing cars, gasoline, and paving materials.
Natural fibers such as cotton and wool require less electricity than nylon and
rayon. Similarly, wood for construction requires less energy than aluminum or
steel. But there is a problem with this kind of indirect energy conservation because it usually would cost more to practise. When we discuss gas v electricity,
insulation, and thermostat settings, we are considering choices which save the individual money. When we talk about changes in our use of products, we may be
considering either more expensive or more difficult ways of life. In focusing
upon the use of commercial and industrial electricity we need to discuss pricing
policies (which will be taken up later in this section).

The second level of decision-making is at the local level of the community and
utility service area. A common controversy is whether new capacity should be
nuclear, coal, or some other energy source. In the preceding section we presented
a generalized discussion of the environmental effects of nuclear v coal power.
Many citizens' groups oppose nuclear plants without being fully aware of the environmental consequences of coal plants.

Duane Chapman

Concerning the utility service area, individual utilities can contribute to the success of energy-saving efforts by individuals. In Michigan, the Public Service Commission and the utilities are working on a plan to insulate old homes and finance the $100 to $200 investment through utility billing. It is expected that this program will save both money and energy.

Finally, communities may make some contribution to energy conservation by designing roads, sidewalks, and transportation plans to encourage walking, bicycling, and transit use.

Federal policy should be seen as establishing regulations and incentives for the proper functioning of the electric utility industry. There are about 500 privately-owned and 3100 publicly-owned electric utilities in the United States. While there is some industrial generation (such as by aluminum plants), it produces about 6 to 7 per cent of total generation. Imports of power from Canada and Mexico are insignificant, less than one-tenth of one per cent of the total. Thus, the electric utilities in the US produce 93 to 94 per cent of our total consumption. While the number of public companies exceeds that of private companies, private companies account for more than three-quarters of the industry's generation. Federal agencies produce one-eighth of the industry total, municipal companies about one-twentieth, and consumer cooperatives about the same. Thus we need to consider this structure in calculating the effectiveness of federal and state policies.

From my point of view the four major policy problems federal and state agencies must deal with are growth in consumption, environmental protection, rate structures, and adequate production. These questions are of current significance, and any comments here may soon be overtaken by events.

Throughout our discussion we emphasized the interactions between individual and family consumption, aggregate demand, generation, and environmental consequences. In a broad way we can show how environmental policy interacts with costs, demand growth, and supply requirements. Environmental protection is expensive, and satisfactory levels of air pollution control, strip mine reclamation, mine safety, and nuclear power plant design may easily double our costs. Let us suppose federal and state agencies encourage and require these higher levels of environmental protection. Further, let us suppose these same agencies allow the privately-owned companies to pass these costs along to us as legitimate expenses. Can we perceive the consequences of such a policy?

Figure 3 shows a series of projections of future total US generation. The top line is an 'official' projection, a composite of the industry, government, and university projections in Table 2. The second line is a total of 141 separate projections of states' and consumer classes. The basic difference between these lines is that the second is based upon a quantitative specification of our response to price increases (eg, see Table 3), and prices are assumed to increase 19 per cent from

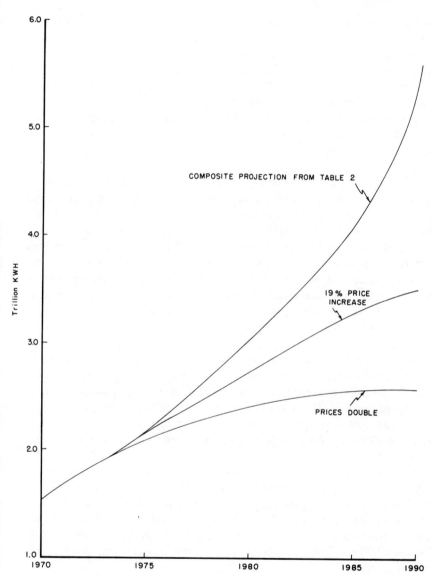

Figure 3   The effect of price increases on demand growth (Tkwh)

1968 to 1990 because of higher environmental protection and fuel costs.[12] In other words, we respond to the higher electricity rates induced by environmental protection, and the response takes the form of altering our habits of accelerated consumption. The second line follows the 'official' projection closely for the next few years. The significance of this is that we can't depend on price increases to ease supply problems in the near future. But - and this is an important conclusion - adequate environmental protection helps insure future supplies by inducing us to change our habits because of higher prices. If these prices double over the rest of the century (the third line), the conclusions reached above are reinforced.

Rate structures have been widely discussed as a tool for reducing demand growth. The discussion usually has three forms: the declining rate schedule, peak rate differentials, and differentials between types of consumers. While a large business may keep careful track of its electric bill and rate schedule, most consumers do not know how their bill is calculated. Typically, there is a very high charge for the first few kilowatt hours, perhaps 15 cents/kwh for the first 10 kwh. But this means only one light bulb a few days a week. There will generally be other 'steps' with declining rates until the step with the average customer is reached, that is, the second 500 kwh might cost 2 cents/kwh. If electric heating is used in the home, electricity use for many months will be over 1000 kwh per month, and these kwh will typically cost much less than 2 cents/kwh.

Would charging the same rate for all residential customers in a utility area affect use? Perhaps not. As an illustration, if a utility charged a 2 cent rate for all kilowatt hours it would lower bills for below-average users and raise bills for above-average users. This might lead the below-average users to buy more appliances, and some potentially above-average users to decide against electric heating or air conditioning. The net effect cannot be determined, but it may be insignificant.

Peak rate differentials are based upon the nature of the generating process. In a peak use period (eg, air conditioning peaks in the late afternoon on a summer day), older and smaller generating units are brought into use. These units are generally more expensive to operate than larger or newer units. Thus, one example of a peak rate differential is to charge higher rates in the peak use period (eg, between 2.00 and 7.00 PM in the summer). This might reduce the need for peak period generation.

To some extent many areas already have peak rate differentials, but they pass as trough differentials. Many utilities offer lower rates for night use, sometimes as low as 50 per cent of day rates. This leads consumers who choose this option to operate their water heaters and dehumidifiers at night, saving money for themselves and reducing peak period stress for other consumers and the utility. The

TABLE 6

US demand in 1990 with rate equalization, T kwh (overall costs grow 19 per cent)

Rates	Demand			Total generation
	Residential	Commercial	Industrial	
Not equalized	.92	.91	1.25	3.53
Equalized	1.25	1.16	.54	3.38

success of these off-peak rates suggests a peak period rate premium might be equally successful.

Finally, the subject of class differences is illustrated by noting that in 1971 the average residential price was 2.2 cents/kwh, the commercial price was 2.1 cents/ kwh, and the average kilowatt hour to industry cost 1.0 cents. (Of course there are substantial regional variations; electricity costs only one-quarter to one-third as much in Washington State as it does in New York.) The rationale for the rate differential between residential-commercial customers and industrial customers has been based partly upon the economies of scale in generation. A typical industrial customer might use two million kwh per year, far more than the seven thousand kwh the individual residential customer now uses. However, if we can no longer anticipate significant scale economies the rationale for the difference is lessened. Is it possible that charging the same price to residential and business users would affect demand growth and environmental impact?

The demand projections in Table 6 are similar in nature to those in Figure 3. The second line shows demand with rate equalization. Residential and commercial demand increases, and industrial demand falls. Presumably this means that rate equalization would induce us to use more air conditioning and electric heating in our homes and offices, but lead industrial users to employ manufacturing processes which require less electricity. But the environmental impact might be nil because total generation is essentially unchanged.

Thus far we have noted that proper decisions by individuals, communities, utilities, and state and federal agencies may potentially work towards future harmonious reconciliation of reduced demand growth, environmental protection, and adequate supply. I see no similar comfort for resolution of immediate problems. Power shortages in many areas will persist for the next few years. First, on the demand side, next year's production and construction plans for homes, cars, freeways, electric heating, and so on are already established. No matter what kind of projection we rely upon, electricity demand will continue to grow rapidly in the next few years. I see no method for immediate significant reductions in demand growth other than rationing. Current policies of gas rationing and voltage reductions are likely to continue, and may even increase. The extent to which rationing will be unnecessary will depend partially upon the degree to which we loosen our commitment to environmental and health protection. Coal-fired plants can be built in increasing numbers, but the impacts outlined in Table 4 may not change much.

Utilities may turn to oil because of its lower sulfur content, but utility use of oil cannot be further accelerated while we simultaneously accelerate our use of automobile gasoline and home heating fuel. Gas cannot be increased for power generation because of its short supply and desirability of use in homes. Adoption of nuclear power generation can be accelerated in the near term, but it would require ever more communities to lower their concern about heat discharges and radioactivity release.

My guess is that areas with supply problems will make efforts in more than one of these areas. It is probable that most areas of the country will have adequate supplies, but some areas will experience rationing and shortages. The environmental picture will be mixed with pluses in improved mine safety and reduced soot emissions, and large minuses in increased sulfur emissions, heat discharge, strip mine damage, and offshore oil spillage. In the 1970s we have to contend with the consequences of decisions made over the past thirty years. Whether the picture deteriorates or improves in the 1980s depends upon the decisions all of us – at all levels – make today.

NOTES

The description of the physical nature of electricity was written by Steven Ostro. Jeanne Ostro carried out the computer analysis of demand projections and prepared and edited the manuscript. Joseph Baldwin prepared the original drafts of the figures. The research on demand analysis discussed here was supported by the National Science Foundation RANN Program through the Environmental Program at the Oak Ridge National Laboratory and by the Cornell University Agricultural Experiment Station; Timothy Mount, Timothy Tyrrell, and Martha Czerwinski have been active in this basic research. None of these individuals or organizations assumes any responsibility for the accuracy or opinions in this chapter; this responsibility is mine.

1 The discussion of electricity use here and in Table 1 is based upon information available in *Patterns of Energy Consumption in the United States,* prepared by the Stanford Research Institute for the Office of Science and Technology, Jan. 1972; the Edison Electric Institute (EEI), *Statistical Year Book of the Electric*

Utility Industry; the *Statistical Abstract of the United States*; and 'Coal Surface Mining and Reclamation,' prepared by the Council on Environmental Quality for the Senate Committee on Interior and Insular Affairs, March 1973.

2 The three forecasts in Table 2 are taken from *The Potential for Energy Conservation* by the Office of Emergency Preparedness, Oct. 1972; the '23rd Annual Electrical Industry Forecast' by Leonard Olmstead in the 15 September 1972 issue of *Electrical World*; and the 'Summary Report of the Cornell Workshop on Energy and the Environment Sponsored by the National Science Foundation,' prepared for the Senate Committee on Interior and Insular Affairs, May 1972. The other two cited forecasts are the Federal Power Commission's *The 1970 National Power Survey* and *U.S. Energy Outlook: A Summary Report of the National Petroleum Council*, Dec. 1972.

3 Information on electricity revenues and sales is reported in the EEI *Yearbook*. The average price is calculated by dividing the total revenues in dollars by the total sales in kilowatt hours. A price is deflated by a price index which measures the overall growth in prices; in this case, the Gross National Product deflator as reported in the *Survey of Current Business*.

4 The *New York Times* regularly reports the latest status of Census Bureau measures of fertility rates and growth rates.

5 The reader interested in statistics and econometrics may wish to read 'Electricity Demand in the United States: An Econometric Analysis' by Timothy Mount, Duane Chapman, and Timothy Tyrrell, Oak Ridge National Laboratory, Oak Ridge, Tennessee, June 1973. A summary appears in *Energy: Demand, Conservation, and Institutional Problems*, ed. Michael Macrakis (1973). A more detailed examination of electricity demand growth appears as 'Electricity Demand Growth and the Energy Crisis' in the 17 Nov. 1972 issue of *Science*, and 'Electricity Demand Growth' in the Oct. 1973 issue of *Environment*. Both of these articles are based upon 'Electricity Demand Growth,' a statement prepared for the Subcommittee on Science, Research, and Development of the House Committee on Science and Astronautics for their hearings on *Energy Research and Development*, May 1972. These studies are the basis for much of the discussion of future growth and for Table 3.

6 Figure 1 is based upon the Office of Emergency Preparedness study included in Table 1.

7 The map for Figure 2 is based upon information in the 1971 EEI *Yearbook*.

8 Larry Barrett and Thomas Waddell, 'The Cost of Air Pollution Damages: A Status Report,' Public Health Service, July 1970. Their damage estimates for 1968 were adjusted for 1972 value by the price index discussed in note 3.

9 Most of Table 4 is based upon *Energy and the Environment: Electric Power*, prepared by the Council on Environmental Quality, Aug. 1973. The source of

damage estimates in Table 4 is explained in the preceding note. Other sources used in the discussion of environmental impact are 'Coal Surface Mining,' cited above; 'Factors Affecting the Use of Coal,' prepared for the Senate Committee on Interior and Insular Affairs, 1973; *The Economics of Clean Air,* Annual Report of the Administrator of the Environmental Protection Agency, March 1972; *Environmental Quality,* Annual Report of the Council on Environmental Quality, Aug. 1972; James Ridgeway, *The Last Play* (1973); and the National Coal Association, *Bituminous Coal Facts*

10 Allen Hammond, William Metz, and Thomas Maugh III, *Energy and the Future* (1973)

11 Table 5 is prepared from *Energy and the Environment* cited above. Other sources used in discussing policy issues include 'Individual Action for Energy Conservation,' prepared for the Subcommittee on Energy of the House Committee on Science and Astronautics, June 1973; Eric Hirst and John Moyers, 'Efficiency of Energy Use in the United States' in the 30 March 1973 issue of *Science*; the Federal Power Commission's *Statistics of Publicly Owned Electric Utilities in the United States*; and the EEI *Yearbook.*

12 The demand projections in Figure 3 and in Table 6 are taken from unpublished work prepared in association with the 1973 National Power Survey. The methodology is similar to that employed in the demand growth studies cited in note 5.

STEPHEN W. MILLSAPS, ROBERT M. SPANN,
AND EDWARD W. ERICKSON

The US petroleum industry enjoys special tax advantages relative to most other industries. These special tax provisions are usually called 'the depletion allowance,' but they include other features as well. These tax provisions have long been a base of contention in discussions of public policy as it affects the petroleum industry. Tax reform groups have attacked the depletion allowance as a special subsidy. The petroleum industry has defended it as necessary to adjust for the special circumstances of the industry and as vital to the national security.

Economists have debated the incidence of the corporate income tax (whether it falls on suppliers of inputs or on the buyers of output) and whether or not the depletion allowance and its related tax advantages are neutralizing or non-neutralizing (make the social allocation of resources more or less efficient). It does not appear that these questions will be solved directly in the near future. But three facts do seem clear. First, the depletion allowance does not result in inflated long-run after-tax earnings for the petroleum industry. Second, the depletion allowance and its related special tax provisions do result in the domestic industry holding a greater stock of reserves at any given price than would otherwise be the case. And third, a percentage point change in the economic incentives the industry faces is a percentage point change in incentives – regardless of whether it comes from tax policy or price effects.

Even if the economics of the depletion allowance were clear and all economists agreed that it was a neutralizing adjustment, it would still be a lively topic of political debate. As such, it would confuse the debate about a national energy policy. An important element of such a policy is allowing energy

97

markets to clear, but allowing energy markets to clear is viewed by many as an unwarranted concession to the petroleum industry. In the current situation of price expectations which are being dramatically revised upwards, Professors Millsaps, Spann, and Erickson suggest that the industry is a unique position to clear some of the air with respect to the energy policy debate and trade the depletion allowance for deregulation of the wellhead price of natural gas and decontrol of the field markets for crude oil.

It is unlikely that such a trade would be consummated. In terms of the Byzantine development of energy policy, it would be too simple.

This chapter should be compared to the Hyndman & Bucovetsky chapter on the Canadian tax system. It should also be compared to the Erickson & Spann chapter on the US petroleum industry and the Starratt & Spann chapter on natural gas regulation. Finally, it should be compared to the MacAvoy and McDonald chapters on other elements of the energy policy mix.

S.W. MILLSAPS, R.M. SPANN, AND E.W. ERICKSON

Tax incentives in the US petroleum industry

Taxes are a powerful instrument of public policy. They transfer resources from the private sector to the public sector. These resources, in turn, are used to carry out the functions of government and to support other instruments of public policy. The United States Supreme Court once wrote, 'The power to tax ... is not only the power to destroy, but also the power to keep alive.' Perhaps the respect and fear of such centralized power explains why there is always intense emotional debate over how, and from whom, those taxes will be collected. Debates in the taxation area usually stem from (1) differences in the evaluation of effectiveness (costs vs benefits) of governmental policy; (2) differences in assessment of the incidence of taxes; (3) differences in opinion over the efficiency of public vs private enterprise. It seems tax debate is just as inevitable as the tax itself.

The petroleum industry is no exception. Percentage depletion is one of the most hotly debated sections of the Federal Tax Code (henceforth, percentage depletion is used as a shorthand expression for the whole package of special tax provisions affecting the petroleum industry). A large part of the debate has centered around the effects of percentage depletion on the distribution of income (is the petroleum industry's tax burden 'too low' or 'too high'?) and the allocation of resources within the economy (including risk compensation and tax neutrality).

These are not the only issues involved in the percentage depletion debate, however. Any discussion of percentage depletion must also consider the fact that the special tax provisions enjoyed by the petroleum industry are the result of purposeful decisions by policy-makers. These policy decisions were made in the pursuit of certain goals, stated or unstated. It is important, therefore, to determine whether or not percentage depletion does in fact achieve those goals and to determine whether or not percentage depletion is the least-cost method of achieving those goals.

In addition, there are four important and interrelated considerations in any discussion of the consequences of altering the special tax provisions currently affecting the petroleum industry. They are the size of US oil reserves, the tax policies under consideration, the price of domestic petroleum output, and the degree of US dependence on foreign oil. If a change is made in any one of these critical variables, there may have to be compensating changes in one or more of the other variables. For example, consider a case where percentage depletion and its attendant provisions were eliminated, but the United States desired to maintain a constant domestic real price of crude oil. If the tax change is made, the United States must then be prepared to rely upon an increasing fraction of domestic oil usage being supplied from foreign sources. Also, domestic oil exploration and production would become less profitable and resources would flow to alternative uses; in the long run domestic oil reserves would fall under this policy. With a fully employed domestic petroleum industry, there are no free lunches. The domestic industry is now practically fully employed.

Policy-makers and citizens must often feel a profound sense of exasperation with economists and their analyses. Not only is there a perplexing lack of unanimity in economists' policy prescriptions, but by the time the analytical dust has cleared, policy decisions have often rolled through the issues to which the analysis may once have been relevant. Taxes, however, always remain.

In this paper, we try to avoid controversy. Such a claim is always suspect, but we have tried to present a standard analysis that is rooted in the simplest common denominators of economics – supply and demand theory and marginal analysis. In what follows, we examine the analytical and theoretical dust in the petroleum taxation field in an attempt to clarify what is known and essentially agreed upon and make some conclusions which we believe represent a consensus of professional economists. The major conclusions are:

1 That the dominant argument for percentage depletion must be national security;

2 That tax expenditures are not likely to be the most efficient means for achieving any given security goal.

SPECIAL TAX BENEFITS
FOR THE EXTRACTIVE INDUSTRIES

The Internal Revenue Code contains three basic special tax benefits for producers of petroleum, natural gas, and hard minerals. There are:

1 The percentage depletion deduction – section 613 of the code.

2 Special provisions which permit the *current* write-off of intangible drilling and development costs for producing oil and gas wells – section 263(c).

3 Special provisions which permit hard mineral exploration and development costs to be written off currently, subject to certain limitations – sections 615 through 617.

In addition, the Treasury Regulations on Income Tax permit oil and gas producers who have elected to capitalize intangible drilling and development costs (instead of a current write-off as in section 263(c) of the Internal Revenue Code) the additional option of either expensing or capitalizing their dry-hole costs – section 1.612-4(b) (4). Sections 901 through 906 of the code also provide foreign tax credit benefits.

Percentage depletion allows a standard tax deduction of 22 per cent of gross income (price times quantity sold) from oil and gas production and results in a reduced effective tax rate for the industry. The percentage depletion, however, may not exceed 50 per cent of net income. This provision limits the effect of the benefit. This is an extraordinary tax benefit because it permits the tax-free recovery of dollar amounts which are far greater than the taxpayer's original investment in the depletable property. This is why the depletion deduction is a subsidy and not just a simple mechanism for depreciating the taxpayer's capital investment. In addition, that portion of the percentage depletion deduction which represents ordinary tax-free recovery of capital investments is usually recovered more rapidly than would be the case if computations were made analogously to the computation of depreciation in non-extractive industries. Thus, percentage depletion confers a double benefit, both deductions in excess of initial costs, and deductions of initial costs that are usually accelerated relative to non-extractive industries.

Costs of labor, materials, and other goods incidental to drilling are considered 'intangible costs of drilling' and can be expensed as soon as a well becomes productive. This is a benefit because it permits the immediate tax-free recovery of capital investments. By most criteria, exploration and development costs would be considered an investment in capital and therefore subject to a depreciation allowance over the useful life of the capital asset.

Expenditures for tangible equipment such as pumps, tanks, and pipes are classified as 'tangible costs of drilling.' These are treated exactly as depreciable assets in other industries. Geological surveys, lease bonuses and rentals are also considered as expenses to be deducted over the useful life of the asset. These costs cannot be expensed if the 22 per cent percentage depletion allowance is used; they can be expensed if percentage depletion is not used.

Consider the hypothetical example of a firm operating two productive properties as outlined in Table 1.[1] The two properties have the same gross income after

101

S.W. Millsaps, R.M. Spann, and E.W. Erickson

TABLE 1

Computation of allowable percentage depletion deduction
and federal income tax liability for a hypothetical firm

	Properties	
	A	B
1 Allowable percentage depletion deduction		
Gross income after royalty	$500,000	$500,000
Less: cost attributable to property[a]	200,000	350,000
Net property income before depletion	300,000	150,000
(22% of gross)	(110,000)	(110,000)
(50% of net)	(150,000)	(75,000)
Less: allowable depletion	110,000	75,000
Net property income after depletion	$190,000	$ 75,000

	Consolidated properties
2. Federal income tax liability	
Gross income after royalty	$1,000,000
Less: costs attributable to individual properties	550,000
Net property income before depletion	450,000
Less: allowable depletion deduction	185,000
Net property income after depletion	265,000
Less: all other costs of doing business[b]	115,000
Net taxable income	150,000
Less: federal income tax[c]	72,000
Net income after tax per tax return	$ 78,000

a Includes production expenses, *ad valorem* taxes, depreciation of tangible well investment, costs of dry holes drilled on property, and intangible drilling expenses. Lease acquisition and capitalized exploration costs not included.
b Includes costs of dry holes not attributable to producing properties, lease rentals, and overhead and miscellaneous expenses attributable to non-producing properties.
c Forty-eight per cent uniform tax rate.

royalties. However, property B is allowed a depletion deduction of only $75,000 due to the 50 per cent of net limitation, while property A is allowed $110,000, the full 22 per cent of gross income. Notice that the costs attributable to the properties include dry-hole costs and the intangible expenses of drilling productive wells on them. Thus, it is possible for finding and development outlay expensing to be competitive with, rather than supplementary to, the percentage depletion deduction.

102

The firm's income tax liability is based on the consolidated net income derived from the two properties after an additional deduction for business costs not attributable to either property; the distinction between properties is important only for computing the total allowable depletion for the firm. In the computation of the income-tax liability of the firm the costs of unsuccessful exploration not attributable to producing properties are not competitive with percentage depletion. While no firm would deliberately incur exploration expenses that it knew would be unsuccessful, the deductibility of unsuccessful expenses might induce a firm anticipating income tax liability on current producing properties to increase its exploratory drilling.

In the example, the total depletion deduction is $185,000, which is 18.5 per cent of gross income as compared with the maximum allowable rate of 22 per cent, that is, the effective depletion rate is 18.5 per cent. Suppose the firm had taken $35,000 in deductions based on capital lease acquisition costs and capitalized exploration costs attributable to producing properties (which cannot be deducted from gross income if percentage depletion is taken). In this case the depletion deduction would exceed the alternative cost-based depletion by $150,000 ($185,000 minus $35,000). This is to say that the total deductions from gross income for tax purposes would exceed by $150,000 the total costs actually incurred by the firm and attributable to the income period. It is this excess which measures the advantage of percentage depletion to the firm. The firm's financial net income after taxes, as reported to management and stockholders on the basis of conventional accounting practices, would be $228,000 rather than the $78,000 reported on the tax return. In summary, the effect of percentage depletion can be viewed as a reduction of the effective tax rate on income from oil and gas production (the effective rate in this example is 24 per cent rather than the nominal 48 per cent).

To summarize, the initial value of an asset in most industries is its supply price, and depreciation is claimed on this initial cost. However, in oil extraction, exploration and development costs – that is, the investment in the capital asset – may have little relation to the initial value of the resulting capital asset; this is entirely due to the depletion-related special tax arrangements which provide the petroleum industry (and other extractive industries as well) with extraordinary benefits relative to non-extractive industries. In the next section we analyse the major stated goals presented as justification for conferring these benefits.

THE GOALS OF SPECIAL TAX PROVISIONS

The special tax provisions currently enjoyed by the extractive industries are the result of purposeful public policy decisions by responsible government officials.

S.W. Millsaps, R.M. Spann, and E.W. Erickson

These policy decisions must be made in the pursuit of certain goals, stated or unstated. We limit our analysis to stated goals of the special tax provisions applicable to the petroleum industry. They include (1) the risk argument; (2) the strong mineral industry argument; (3) the tax neutrality argument; and (4) the national security argument.

The 'risk' argument

This argument contends that mineral producers operate under exceptionally high risk, and therefore deserve compensatory tax relief, that is, that mineral production is riskier than most other types of income-producing ventures. In this context, we are discussing *relative* risk taking. Obviously some ventures are riskier than others and the market works to compensate those who succeed at the more risky undertakings. Policemen might argue that walking-the-beat is riskier than school teaching, and they might be right; school teachers might argue that their job is riskier than operating a filling station. The point is obvious: if we do choose to subsidize riskier ventures we must decide, Risky relative to what? 'Exceptional' is no help. We must ask, Exceptional relative to what? and the essential circularity of the argument is reintroduced. A simplifying assertion is that mineral industry ventures are riskier than ventures in non-mineral producing industries (which are themselves not risk free).

Riskiness is difficult to define. In part this is because a large element of the appraisal of risk, as of beauty, is in the eye of the beholder, and also because the analytics of the concept are slippery, even for people consciously trying to consistently discuss the same thing. A measure of risk is the relative frequency with which an outcome other than the expected outcome occurs. The ratio of successful to unsuccessful wildcat oil wells is about 1:9. Because no one would commit the resources necessary to drill a wildcat well unless he 'expected' it to be successful, this 1:9 ratio is frequently used to argue that petroleum exploration is exceptionally risky. However, the ratio itself is remarkably stable. There is variation in the ratio and it is a conditional measure that is itself economically determined [see Fisher (1964), Erickson and Spann (1971)], but that is a detail that does not alter the argument here. Thus, in our simple example, if a firm were to drill ninety-nine wells, it could expect about eleven successes, although it would not know in advance which of the wells would be the successful ones. From the vantage point of an overall exploration campaign, then, the search for petroleum does not appear as risky as it does when only a single well is considered. An analogy to roulette is apt. No one can predict a single turn of the wheel. But for a large number of spins, the proportion of outcomes which are, say, red and odd can be confidently bounded. This safety in numbers does not preclude the possibility of losing large sums on a single venture. This characteristic, however, does not automatically make petroleum exploration more or less risky than other industrial activities. Other industries also display investment outcomes which involve large losses on a single venture. Examples are corfam, the Edsel, and the Fermi nuclear power plant.

Even if mineral production is riskier, the market mechanism and a uniform corporate income tax could be relied upon to spread risks successfully among different groups, thereby reducing risks to any single person. One might argue that there would be more resources in the oil and gas industry if there were a scheme of risk compensation particular to that industry. Even if this is true, we must ask 'to what purpose?' If the answer is, 'we need the extra resources for national security reasons,' then it must be determined that special tax expenditures are the least-cost means to achieve this end.

In summary, the risk argument rests upon two central pillars. The first is that oil and gas exploration is riskier than alternative business activities. Given the continued success of many large petroleum-producing enterprises, this assertion is difficult to prove. The second pillar is a lack of faith in the ability of market processes to adapt to risks. We know the market will adapt to equalize the monetary value of differential riskiness; there are virtually no risk-free enterprises. If there is differential riskiness in petroleum exploration and production, then it is necessary to show that any increased reserves and output under a subsidy are worth the tax expenditure currently being made to achieve them.

The strong mineral industry argument

We want a strong oil and gas industry. We also want a strong steel industry, a strong technical-instruments industry, and a strong chemical industry. We want all our industries to be strong, but cannot afford to subsidize them all. Subsidies reduce the market price to the consumer. At the same time, the American consumer is the American taxpayer; he also pays for the subsidy.

One may argue that we need a strong oil and gas industry in case of a national emergency. This is a national security argument, not a strong mineral-industries argument. In the extreme, the strong industries argument is vulnerable. If many industries contribute to the national defense potential, then a partial measure of national security capacity is GNP itself. Because a series of *ad hoc* industry specific subsidies results in an inefficient allocation of resources, the total GNP is smaller in the presence of such subsidies than it would be without them. Thus, in this very general context, the overall defense capacity is adversely affected by piecemeal subsidies designed to strengthen particular industries.

S.W. Millsaps, R.M. Spann, and E.W. Erickson

The tax neutrality argument: the McDonald debate
There has been an extended debate among several well-known economists as to whether the present tax treatment of the petroleum industry is 'neutral.'[2] The neutrality at issue in the debate is whether the corporate income tax affects the allocation of resources in the economy as a whole, including non-extractive industries. The relevant comparison involves, at the least, a uniform corporate income tax and the present system of special provisions affecting the petroleum industry. More precisely, a three-way comparison is necessary. We must compare resource allocation in the following situations:
1 No corporate income tax;
2 A uniform corporate income tax with no special provisions for the petroleum industry (and other extractive industries); and
3 The present system of a corporate income tax with special provisions for the petroleum industry (and other extractive industries).
The present system is neutral if the allocations are the same as they would be in the case of no corporate income tax. In this situation, the special provisions affecting the taxation of income earned in petroleum production promote neutrality. If the allocation of resources under the present system is different from that under no corporate income tax, then the present system is non-neutral. If the special provisions affecting petroleum cause the allocation of resources among industries under the present system to be farther away from the no-tax special provisions, then the special provisions are themselves non-neutral.

Efficiency is crucial in this discussion, for it affects national income and therefore our standard of living. However, it must be understood that whether the conclusion is neutrality or non-neutrality, it has no current public policy significance. The reason for this seeming anomaly goes back to the earlier discussion of the economic analysis of public policy decisions. The efficacy of the special tax provisions does not depend upon neutrality or non-neutrality. Rather, it depends upon the policy goals and the alternative means of achieving these goals. Nowhere in this paper is it said that the principal goal of the current special tax provisions is of minor importance. Even if the special tax provisions are non-neutral, if they are the least-cost way to achieve a well-defined national security goal, then the security gains may be worth the efficiency costs. To the extent that the current structure of tax rates and regulations reveals the intentions of policy makers, it would have to be concluded that tax neutrality is very low on the priority list of policy. Nowhere is it said that tax neutrality is the policy goal of the special tax provisions. However, this debate has provided some useful quantitative information in this area. Therefore we will discuss it in more detail in a later section.

The national security argument

The national security argument is that extra productive capacity (called reserves) is needed for use in the event of war or other national emergency, and that the special tax provisions are needed to encourage the creation of such reserves. Proved reserves (a concept embracing the potential to bring oil into production at present and expected near-future prices) are the main elements of crude-oil production capacity. Current output rates (at a given incremental cost per barrel) are positively related to proved reserves. If proved reserves are allowed to dwindle, a specified output rate could only be sustained at increasing costs per barrel.

There is a difference between wartime and peacetime needs. In peacetime, national security policy would be focused on developing and maintaining a pool of 'extra' proved reserves primarily to avoid being vulnerable to foreign supply restrictions. Therefore, policy should be geared to expanding reserves, but not production. Stimulating both could be self-defeating; more resources would be devoted to expanding reserves than would be necessary if production had not been stimulated. In wartime, policy must be focused on the continued flow of output during the conflict. Oil is an important input in conventional war and less necessary for a nuclear confrontation. If reserves start to dwindle during the conflict, leading to increasing costs, at some point it would become cheaper to divert resources to acquiring new reserves rather than try to maintain the needed output rate from the reduced reserve capacity. Thus, during wartime, policy would have to be geared to stimulating both production and proved reserves sufficiently to meet war requirements. There are two key variables, current output and proved reserves, which must be considered in formulating a national security policy for the oil industry. The acceptability of any tax-oriented policy would depend on its impact on reserves alone in peacetime, and its impact on reserves and production in wartime.

Given current discussion regarding the 'energy crisis,' the increased militance of oil-producing nations [specifically the cartels known as the Organization of Oil-Exporting Countries (OPEC) and the subset of OPEC known as the Organization of Arab Oil Exporting Countries (OAPEC) which have boosted prices and made them stick], and Israeli-Arab tension in the Middle East, it is concluded that if there is a policy goal of the special tax provisions to the petroleum industry (other than the unstated goal of income redistribution), then the dominant goal must be to encourage extra productive capacity (called proved reserves) which the US might need during a national emergency. In light of this conclusion, we proceed with an analysis of the resource-allocation effects of the special tax provisions.

S.W. Millsaps, R.M. Spann, and E.W. Erickson

THE SIMPLE ECONOMICS
OF THE PETROLEUM INDUSTRY

An economist's primary concern is with the efficient allocation of the scarce resources of the economy. Efficiency is defined in a very special way. There is an efficient allocation of resources when it is impossible to change prices or outputs to make some consumers better off without simultaneously making others worse off. In a generally competitive economy with no glaring externalities or unexploited economies of scale, the action of market forces results in an efficient allocation of resources. With the exceptions of distortions caused by government (state and federal) policies, the US petroleum industry has been and is now a competitive industry. Furthermore, the US economy is, in general, sufficiently competitive to make the implications drawn from the competitive model useful guides for policy analysis.

In Figure 1, let DD represent the industry demand curve for oil,[3] and SS represent the industry supply of oil.[4]

In the absence of an energy crisis, the equilibrium price and quantity of oil is at Q_1 and P_1. The effects of the energy crisis and price controls are discussed below. For graphical simplicity, we assume no import sector. This does not affect the logic of the analysis. It is helpful for policy analysis to think of DD as the marginal social benefit curve (MSB) – the value society places on the benefits derived from one more unit of oil, and to think of SS as the marginal social cost curve (MSC) – to include *all* costs to *society* of producing additional units of oil. Thus the efficient allocation of resources in the oil industry, depicted in Figure 1, is *defined* to be the resources required to produce that output at which MSB equals MSC, that is, the resources required to produce output Q_1. At any output greater than Q_1, there are 'too many' resources in the industry by efficiency standards; at any output less than Q_1, there are 'too few' resources in the industry.

The depletion allowance is essentially a negative *ad valorem* tax [Davidson (1970)]. It shifts the supply curve of oil to S^1S^1, lowering the price of crude oil to P_2[5] and increasing the output of crude oil to Q_2. This leads to an inefficient allocation of resources ('too many') in the oil industry. The cost of this output increase, in terms of real resources, is the area Q_1ACQ_2 under the SS curve. Consumers value the increased oil output (Q_2-Q_1) by an amount equal to the area Q_1ABQ_2.

The difference between the social costs and benefits of the subsidy, in terms of inefficient resource allocation, is the triangular area ABC (area Q_1ACQ_2 minus Q_1ABQ_2). This is not to say that the special tax provisions are socially undesirable, just that they are inefficient from an economic point of view.

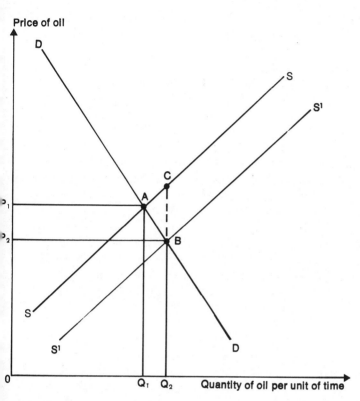

Figure 1

To evaluate a given public policy decision, one must know what the decision is trying to accomplish. The dominant argument for the special tax provisions to the petroleum industry is national security. Two major issues arise with regard to the depletion allowance. First, we do not know whether national security actually requires greater reserves than the market would generate without the tax provisions; and if so, what absolute and relative incremental reserves are required. The submissions to and analysis by the Cabinet Task Force on Oil Import Control suggest that the contribution of domestic conventional reserves to the national security, narrowly or broadly defined, is not nearly so precise or inexorable as simplistic statements often assert [see *The Oil Import Question* (1970)]. This is a particularly important point when the costs of creating and holding conventional reserves are compared to some substitute means to achieve the same national security objective – for example, strategic stockpiles.

The national security problem requires an answer to the following questions:
1 Does national security require the resources to produce an output such as Q_1, the amount the market would generate without the tax provisions?
2 Or does the national security require the greater resources necessary to produce an apparently inefficient output such as Q_2, the amount generated by the oil and gas industry operating with special tax provisions?[6]
3 Finally, if there is a need for greater domestic reserves, is the necessary increment less than, equal to, or greater than Q_2-Q_1?

The second major issue involves the relation between the size of the special tax provisions and the amount of the shift in the supply curve of petroleum. We have little explicit empirical evidence about the extent to which the present special tax provisions actually do create additional reserves. The change in the volume of reserves per percentage-point change in the depletion rate is not now known. Such knowledge is crucial for a determination of how much additional defense capacity[7] (measured by increased reserves) is achieved per dollar of expenditure of taxes foregone and resources misallocated; that is, the cost-effectiveness of the percentage depletion tax program in achieving the national security goal.

In the presence of an energy crisis, the situation is a little more complicated. As a result of the regulation-induced shortage of natural gas, poor planning with regard to the relaxation of oil import quotas, environmental and other restrictions on the production and consumption of coal, the effect of emission controls on automobile gasoline mileage, growth in the economy, and the Arab oil embargo, the demand for domestic oil production has increased to D^1D^1 in Figure 2.

At the same time, there are price controls on US crude oil. There has been some relaxation of these controls with respect to 'new' oil production, but the average price of US oil is nevertheless held below that of alternative imported oil. Thus, there is an effective quasi-ceiling price on US oil production. The result is excess demand for US oil at the going market price of P_2 equal to the difference between the quantity demanded at P_2 and that supplied at P_2. This difference is Q_3 minus Q_2. The excess demand for US oil production represents a shortage at the going market price.

Some policy-makers have suggested additional tax incentives for the industry as a means of eliminating the shortage. Additional tax incentives, if they were sufficient to eliminate the shortage, would induce a shift in the domestic supply curve to S^2S^2. The effect of such a tax-subsidy-induced supply shift in terms of inefficient resource allocation would be to increase the social cost of the depletion allowance (and related tax provisions) from an amount measured by the area of the triangle ABC to an amount measured by the area of the triangle DEF.

An alternative policy which would be consistent with conservation of scarce energy resources (the tax subsidy induces increased consumption), elimination

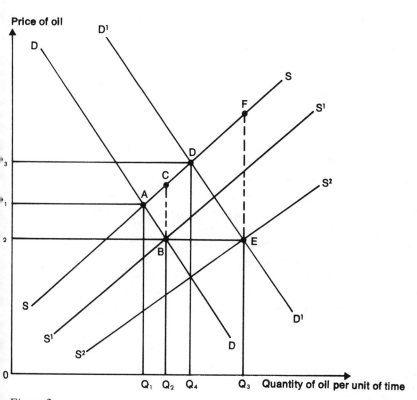

Figure 2

of the shortage, and efficient resource allocation would be to eliminate simultaneously the depletion allowance and the ceiling price. Such a move would curb tax-subsidy-induced consumption and expand domestic supply. In Figure 2, domestic markets would clear at a price of P_3 and an increased volume of oil production of Q_4.

The depletion allowance is a political as well as an economic issue. It could well be that the only way to achieve the benefits of market-clearing prices in domestic field markets for oil and gas is for the petroleum industry and its spokesmen to compromise on the depletion allowance. In effect, the industry might be able to trade the depletion allowance for deregulation of the well-head price of natural gas and decontrol of the field-market price of crude oil.

In this connection, the industry is currently in a unique position. Existing contracts have been written in such a way that they include within them both a given historical set of price expectations and the capitalized value of the depletion allow-

111

ance. With no change in prices, elimination of the depletion allowance would create capital losses for the domestic industry. At the moment, however, historical price expectations are increasingly obsolete and a substantial upward revision of anticipated prices is occurring. Thus, the industry is in an economic position to trade away the depletion allowance without incurring capital losses or adjustment costs. The social benefits of such a trade would be substantial. These benefits would include:

1 Elimination of the regulation-induced shortage of natural gas;
2 Permitting the domestic supply of oil to respond to across-the-board increases in domestic oil prices;
3 Use of the price mechanism to ration oil usage and restrict consumption to that amount at which marginal social costs and benefits were equal;
4 Removal of the depletion allowance as a confounding and acrimonious element in the debate about national energy policy;
5 Defusing the issue of windfall gains as an objection to allowing market prices to become equilibrium prices; and
6 Improvement in the efficiency of resource allocation.

At a time when the United States is teetering on the brink of prolonging the energy crisis through expansion of inept government controls of fuel markets, such a trade appears especially advantageous.

The remaining sections of this paper review the existing empirical literature which examines the relationship between tax expenditures and incremental reserves.

TAX NEUTRALITY AND RESOURCE ALLOCATION

As mentioned above, there has been debate among economists as to whether the present tax treatment of the petroleum industry is 'neutral' with respect to resource allocation, that is, do the taxes imposed cause resources to be allocated differently than if those taxes had not been imposed?[8] The debate has proceeded at two levels – efficiency and equity; are more resources devoted to oil extraction than would have been under a system of neutral taxation (the efficiency question)? And is the national income distributed differently from what it would have been under neutral taxation (the equity question)? We are most interested in the efficiency question in this analysis.

The debate began when Harberger (1955) and Steiner (1959) concluded that the distinctive tax treatments accorded to petroleum producers were non-neutral with respect to resource allocation because these special provisions made it profitable to invest more resources in petroleum than in less favored industries. In the basic model, the effect of a corporate income tax is illustrated in Figure 1 as a shift in petroleum supply from SS to S^1S^1. If all industries were alike, the depletion-induced shift would differentially favor the petroleum industry and result in more resources being allocated to the petroleum industry than are strictly justified by the equality of marginal social benefits and marginal social costs.

The assumption that all industries are alike was challenged by McDonald (1961). He argued that if we assume perfect forward shifting from producers to consumers (and certain other assumptions he thought realistic), the standard corporate income tax alone discriminated against the more capital intensive (a larger amount of plant and equipment relative to labor and materials) and/or the riskier industries. He argued that the petroleum industry fell in this group and therefore would be subject to tax discrimination without some special compensating tax advantages.

Susan Agria (1969), using an approach similar to that developed by Harberger and later by Steiner, compared the total amount of resources invested in petroleum development (operating with special tax incentives) with that devoted to other forms of investment (non-mineral and subject to normal depreciation and tax rates). She found the ratio of petroleum investment to ordinary investment, adjusted for economic rents in the form of lease costs and severance taxes, to be in the range of 1.2 to 1.3; that is, 20-30 per cent more capital was invested in petroleum production than would be in other assets operating without the special tax benefits. She also found that the incentive to develop existing wells was greater than the incentive to explore primarily because intangible drilling expensing favors drilling productive wells (remember dry holes can be written off immediately) and the depletion allowance deduction varies directly the value of output.

The neutrality or non-neutrality of the special provisions affecting the taxation of income earned in the petroleum industry ultimately depends upon the relative riskiness and capital intensity of the industry, the size of the provisions, and whether or not the corporate income tax is shifted forward to consumers. In a recent article, McDonald (1970) has provided the capstone for the debate. He concludes '... the combined effect of percentage depletion and expensing privileges is probably unneutral, thereby inducing an uneconomical allocation of resources to oil and gas production. Under assumptions less favorable to the industry but more consistent with majority professional opinion, we conclude that the distinctive tax provisions are markedly unneutral. Consequently, there are important misallocative effects.' [Editors' note: This conclusion rests in part on an assumption that the corporate income tax is not shifted forward. The state of economic knowledge on this subject is very murky. The best assumption may be that part of the tax is shifted forward, part of it is shifted backward to non-capital factors of production, and part of it is borne by corporate stockholders.]

It is also agreed that in order to restore neutrality, all relatively capital intensive industries would have to be taxed at effective rates below the uniform rate, and firms in relatively non-capital intensive industries would have to be taxed at rates higher than the uniform rate. As outlined earlier, the policy implications of the findings to date are nil. Nowhere is it said that tax neutrality is the policy goal of the special tax provisions.

Steiner (1959) left the door open when he argued that deliberate tax non-neutrality may be in the best interests of public policy. He wrote: 'The central issue of public policy does not concern whether such provisions affect the allocation of resources among industries but rather whether the social benefits of such effects are worth the costs involved.'

The general problem is one of evaluating the costs and benefits of economic incentives such as tax subsidies, direct subsidies, or import controls to alter free market solutions in order to achieve some policy goal. For example, the Cabinet Task Force on Oil Import Control favored relying upon existing domestic capacity and reserve storage stockpiles to 'increase the ability of consuming countries to respond to a supply interruption.'[9] They also concluded that 'the present (1970) import control program was not adequately responsive to present and future security considerations.' The same basic analytical problem applies to tax subsidies. This leads us to the major empirical attempts to measure the quantitative 'cost-effectiveness' of present tax policy towards the oil industry.

THE CONSAD REPORT
AND THE NCSU/VPI MODELS

The CONSAD report
One major attempt to estimate the effect of the special tax provisions for income earned in oil and gas production on the reserve-holding behavior of the domestic petroleum industry was a study done by CONSAD Research Corporation under commission from the US Treasury (CONSAD 1969). The CONSAD report developed two models – a user cost of capital (reserves) model and an industry simulation model. In order to estimate the effects of changes in tax policy on oil reserves, CONSAD first calculated the effect of tax changes on economic incentives while assuming production was held constant.[10] This assumption seriously biased the CONSAD results in the direction of underestimating responsiveness. For a complete discussion of the modeling problems involved, see CONSAD (1969), Mid-Continent Oil and Gas Association (1969), Spann, Erickson, and Millsaps (1973), Erickson and Millsaps (1971), Cox and Wright (1973), and Millsaps (1973).

The CONSAD report developed numerical estimates of the changes in liquid hydrocarbon and natural gas reserves which would occur if the percentage depletion allowance were reduced (or eliminated) and if the option to expense intangible drilling costs were removed. These estimates were developed on the assump-

114

tion that the resultant tax increase was absorbed entirely by the petroleum producers (that is, *not* passed forward to consumers or backward to land owners).[11]

The specific conclusions of the CONSAD study were:

1 'The elimination of percentage depletion as an option would reduce existing reserve levels by 3 percent and result in an additional $1.2 billion in tax revenue at current production levels.

2 'Elimination of the option to expense intangible drilling costs would reduce existing reserve levels by from 1.9 percent to 4.0 percent depending on the alternative tax policy.

3 'Percentage depletion is a relatively inefficient method of encouraging exploration and the resultant discovery of new domestic reserves of liquid petroleum. This is in part due to the low sensitivity of desired reserve levels to the price subsidy represented by percentage depletion, and in part to the inefficiency of the allowance for this purpose since over 40 percent of it is paid for foreign production and non-operating interests in domestic production.'

CONSAD also provided estimates of the size of the recent tax benefits to the extractive industries and of the size of the stimulus to creation of new reserves of petroleum. Tax expenditures due to the excess of percentage depletion over cost depletion, plus expensing of exploration and development costs, were estimated to have run at an annual rate of $1.7 billion, $1.4 billion of which were estimated to have gone to the oil and gas industry. CONSAD estimated that the tax policies then in effect resulted in additions to petroleum reserves worth approximately $150 million per year. If these figures are even approximately correct, spending $1.4 billion to achieve $150 million in additional reserves is extremely inefficient. This judgment, of course, depends upon the accuracy of the CONSAD estimates and the presumption that there is a lower cost means for achieving at least as many additional reserves that are in fact a national security reserve.[12] As noted above, however, the assumptions in the CONSAD report biased their estimate of the tax subsidy induced incremental reserve holdings downward.[13] Nevertheless, the relative magnitudes of the costs and benefits estimated by CONSAD are consistent with an inefficient allocation of resources.

The NCSU/VPI models
In conjunction with the energy economics research underway at North Carolina State University and Virginia Polytechnic Institute and State University, two models of the effects of tax incentives on the domestic petroleum industry have been developed [Spann, Erickson, and Millsaps (1973) and Millsaps (1973)]. The results of these models are generally consistent with each other. The first model is a mathematical model which uses existing econometric estimates of the supply responsiveness of the US petroleum industry to calculate the effects of changes

in tax policy. The second model is a direct econometric estimation using an alternative econometric model of these same effects.

When the mathematical model is used to estimate the long-run effects of changes in the special tax provisions on domestic crude oil reserves, production, and prices and to illustrate the numerous trade-offs involved with various tax policy changes, the primary conclusions are:

1 Elimination of the package of special tax provisions accorded the petroleum industry would, over the long run, increase crude oil prices by approximately 24 per cent, reduce domestic crude oil output and discoveries by approximately 10.5 per cent, and reduce crude oil reserves held by about 24.4 per cent.

2 Elimination of percentage depletion while retaining the expensing of intangibles would increase crude oil prices by about 9 per cent, reduce crude oil output by approximately 4.3 per cent, and reduce reserve holdings by about 11.2 per cent.

3 Using 1971 as a base, the import ratio[14] would have had to increase to about 37 per cent in order to hold crude oil prices constant if the special tax provisions accorded the petroleum industry were not in force then. For the case in which only percentage depletion were eliminated, the import ratio would have had to have been 28.7 per cent in order to hold wellhead crude oil prices constant.

4 The special tax provisions accorded the petroleum industry have significant costs. The tax revenue foregone due to these provisions is approximately $2.5 billion. The social cost of the tax provisions in terms of the misallocation of resources attributable to those provisions is approximately $300 million:[15]

The estimates presented here are considerably higher than the CONSAD estimates and indicate a more pronounced effect of percentage depletion and expensing of intangibles on the long-run level of domestic oil reserves.

The direct econometric estimation model confirms these results. It has been suggested by industry spokesmen that tax incentives are a more powerful inducement than prices to encourage the domestic petroleum industry to discover and develop new petroleum reserves.[16] The direct econometric estimation model was developed to test this hypothesis.

The results of the direct econometric estimation model with respect to the price and tax effects on the industry's behavior and economic performance are as follows:

1 An increase in prices or a decrease in effective taxes each improve the incentives to discover and develop petroleum;

2 Both price-induced and tax-induced increases in economic incentives have a significant effect upon the behavior of the industry with regard to discovery and development of new petroleum reserves;

3 Equal percentage changes in the economic incentives the industry faces, whether price induced or tax induced, have equal effects upon reserves.

The mathematical and econometric models are both consistent with the position that discussion of tax policy changes should not be approached cavalierly. Significant tax policy changes would have significant effects upon the US energy balance. However, price policy is an effective substitute for tax policy. Were deregulation of the wellhead price of natural gas and decontrol of the field market price of crude oil to be substituted for the depletion allowance and its related provisions, market clearing equilibrium prices would be higher than current estimates indicate. But existing empirical evidence suggests that both the efficiency of resource allocation and the overall US energy balance would be improved by such a combination of policy changes.

CONCLUSIONS

The relevant public policy goal of the special tax provisions which affect the domestic petroleum industry is national security. The Arab oil embargo is an example of a security risk. The depletion allowance has resulted in larger levels of domestic petroleum reserves than would otherwise have been the case. But price incentives would be just as effective as tax incentives to encourage discovery and development – and more efficient. However, if these reserves are fully committed to support domestic production, there is no national security reserve. Moreover, there are social costs associated with the depletion allowance because it induces incremental consumption of our scarce petroleum reserves beyond the point where marginal social costs begin to exceed marginal social benefits. A more reliable and administratively flexible way to provide national security reserves would be through the use of the strategic petroleum stockpiles. This approach was part of the recommendations of the Cabinet Task Force on Oil Import Control. At this time, a politically feasible and economically desirable set of policy changes would be to eliminate percentage depletion, deregulate the wellhead price of natural gas, and decontrol the field markets for crude oil.

NOTES

1 This example follows McDonald (1963), pp. 19-22.
2 The main contributors to this literature are the following: Davidson (1963); McDonald (1961), (1962), (1964), (1967), (1970); Steiner (1963), (1964); Harbarger (1955); Agria (1969).
3 The demand curve slopes down and to the right in the oil industry [see Balestra and Nerlove (1966), Burrows and Domenich (1970), McDonald (1970)].
4 The supply curve slopes up and to the right in the oil industry [see Erickson and Spann (1971), Erickson (1968), Eldridge (1962)].

5 Note that the depletion subsidy lowers the price of oil to consumers – from P_1 to P_2. This result, however, is not a free lunch for consumers. It is consumers, after all, who intially provide the subsidy. If the federal budget is independent of the size of the depletion allowance, then other taxes must be sufficiently high to offset the tax revenue lost due to the special tax provisions enjoyed by the oil industry. These offsetting taxes cause the prices for other industries and the personal income tax to be higher than they would otherwise be. The amounts involved are large. For example, one special provision, expensing intangibles, costs the treasury about $400 million a year in foregone tax revenue from the petroleum industry.

6 This is a different question from that whether any additional war-making potential created by specific capacities such as Q_1Q_2 causes our foreign policy-makers to be less cautious than they would otherwise be. If this is the case, we may produce more war than the global optimum allocation of resources requires. There is evidence, however, that suggests that the causality runs from war-making propensities to the existence of the capacities such as Q_1Q_2, rather than the other way around. Almost none of the petroleum used in Southeast Asia was produced from US reserves.

7 We ignore the problem of whether state agencies which control production would allow the incremental reserves to be realized as increased production. The assumption here is that in a real national security emergency the decisions of federal policy-makers would be paramount.

8 See Cox and Wright (1973) for an in-depth summary of this issue.

9 *The Oil Import Question,* pp. 53-6

10 The Mid-Continent Oil and Gas Association immediately criticized this technique in a paper (Mid-Continent 1969) submitted to the US House Ways and Means Committee. Mid-Continent asserted that (a) 'the required level of reserves is technologically determined by the level of production' and (b) 'the effect of an increase in income taxes on oil companies would be a decline in production not a change in the ratio of reserves to production, which by (a) is technologically determined.' From these assertions, Mid-Continent concluded that the way CONSAD formulated the problem was foreordained to show little responsiveness of reserves to taxes when production was fixed, because fixed production means fixed reserves. Although the reserves production ratio is not strictly a technical relation, this assumption affected CONSAD's results.

11 This assumption represents the 'worst case' impacts. If the net increase in tax payments can be passed on to consumers, or be compensated for by a reduction in costs, then the effect on reserve stocks will be smaller than that estimated in this study. In actuality, the result of the increase in taxes would probably be a combination of passing forward to consumers [see Jameson

(1968)] and passing backwards to landowners [see Davidson (1970)], reducing costs [see *JPT* (1958) and *Oil and Gas Journal* (1965)], and shutting down excess wells in overdeveloped fields [see *Oil and Gas Journal* (1962)].

12 For discussions of stockpiling, see *The Oil Import Question* and Mead and Sorenson (1971).

13 There is a growing body of econometric literature which indicates that petroleum discoveries are relatively sensitive to price changes. [For example, see Erickson and Spann (1971), Erickson (1968), and Spann (1973).] If petroleum discoveries are relatively sensitive to price, then it is not intuitively appealing that reserve holdings should be insensitive to changes in economic incentives.

In addition, there are a number of problems in the formulation and estimation of the CONSAD model. First, the desired stock of reserves cannot be directly observed. CONSAD used alternative series of *ad hoc* proxies for this variable.

Second, the CONSAD formulation of user cost and some of the data elements in the measure they used can be improved. In a working paper, Wright and Cox have shown that CONSAD failed to incorporate directly a term for percentage depletion in its user cost formula causing bias.

Third, inclusion of output directly in the estimating equation poses conceptual and statistical problems. The reserves/production ratio is an economic variable, but it is bounded by technological limits. Estimating the responsiveness of reserves to tax policy while holding production constant biases the effect of changes in economic incentives toward zero. In addition, in the presence of a supply relation between price and output, simultaneous inclusion of both price and output as principal explanatory variables for desired reserves causes the X^1X matrix to approach singularity.

Three major points must be made with respect to the problems just discussed. First, they are not trivial. Correct respecification, variable redefinition, and reestimation of a user cost model can be expected significantly to change the results. Second, such an effort is possible. And third, the initial CONSAD work should not be regarded lightly. A considerable amount of opprobrium has been directed toward the CONSAD work. This is understandable in an adversary context. But the CONSAD effort can be viewed in another light. It was a major exploratory effort in an undefined province. Economic research, as does petroleum exploration, produces dry holes. But just as in petroleum exploration, these dry holes may give significant direction to subsequent efforts.

14 The import ratio is defined as the ratio of crude imports to domestic consumption of crude oil.

15 This is an estimate of the inefficient resource triangle *ABC* in Figure 1. These

estimates are based on historical average prices of crude oil; oil prices are now substantially higher. As a result of Cost of Living Council controls there are now two prices for oil. The prices of 'old' oil are approximately $5/barrel. The prices on 'new' oil are approximately $7–$10/barrel. This rise in oil prices would increase the social costs of the resource misallocative effects of the tax provisions.

16 See, for example, the statement by Richard J. Gonzalez in the panel discussion on general tax reform before the Committee on Ways and Means, House of Representatives, Ninety-third Congress (Washington 1973), pp. 1328-64.

REFERENCES

1 Agria, S.R., 'Special Tax Treatment of Mineral Industries,' in A.C. Harberger and M.J. Bailey, eds., *The Taxation of the Income From Capital* (Washington 1969)

2 Balestra, P. and M. Nerlove, 'Pooling Cross-sectional and Time Series Data in the Estimation of a Dynamic Model: The Demand for Natural Gas,' *Econometrica*, XXXIV, 3, July 1966

3 Burrows, J.C. and T.S. Domenich, *An Analysis of the United States Oil Import Quota* (Lexington 1970)

4 Cabinet Task Force on Oil Import Controls, *The Oil Import Question* (Washington 1970)

5 CONSAD Research Corporation, *The Economic Factors Affecting the Level of Domestic Petroleum Reserves*, Part 4 of US Congress Committee on Ways and Means and Senate Committee on Finance, *Tax Reform Studies and Proposals*, US Treasury Department (Washington 1969)

6 Cox, J.C. and A.W. Wright, 'The Economics of the Oil Industry's Tax Burden,' in *The Petroleum Industry's Tax Burden* (Washington 1973)

7 Cragg, J.C., A.C. Harberger, and P. Mieszkowski, 'Empirical Evidence on the Incidence of the Corporation Income Tax,' *Journal of Political Economy*, LXXV, 6, Dec. 1962

8 Davidson, P., 'The Depletion Allowance Revisited,' *Natural Resources Journal*, Albert E. Utton, ed. (Albuquerque, January 1970)

9 Davidson, P., 'Public Policy Problems of the Domestic Crude Oil Industry,' *American Economic Review*, LIII, 1, March 1963

10 Eldridge, D., 'Rate of Return, Resource Allocation and Percentage Depletion,' *National Tax Journal*, XV, 2, June 1962

11 Erickson, E.W., 'Economic Incentives, Industrial Structure and the Supply of Crude Oil in the U.S., 1946-58/59' (unpublished PhD dissertation, Vanderbilt University, 1968)

12 Erickson, E.W. and S.W. Millsaps, 'Taxes, Goals and Economic Efficiency: Petroleum and Defense,' *The Economics of Federal Subsidy Programs,* Part 3, Tax Subsidies, Joint Economic Committee (Washington 1972), pp. 286-304

13 Erickson, E.W. and R.M. Spann, 'Supply Response in a Regulated Industry: The Case of Natural Gas,' *Bell Journal of Economics and Management Science,* II, 1, spring 1971

14 Fisher, F.M., *Supply and Costs in the U.S. Petroleum Industry, Two Econometric Studies* (Baltimore 1964)

15 Harberger, A.C., 'The Taxation of Mineral Industries,' in US Congress, Joint Committee on the Economic Report, *Federal Tax Policy for Growth and Stability* (Washington 1955)

16 Jameson, M., Executive Vice President of the Independent Petroleum Association of America, news service interview, 11 Sept. 1968

17 *Journal of Petroleum Technology* (JPT), X, 1958

18 McDonald, S S., *Federal Tax Treatment of Income from Oil and Gas* (Washington 1963)

19 McDonald, S.L., 'Distinctive Tax Treatment of Income from Oil and Gas Production,' *Natural Resources Journal,* Albert E. Utton, ed. (Albuquerque, January 1970)

20 McDonald, S.L., 'The Non-neutrality of Corporate Income Taxation: A Reply to Steiner,' *National Tax Journal,* XVII, 1, March 1964

21 McDonald, S.L., 'Percentage Depletion and Tax Neutrality: A Reply to Messrs. Musgrave and Eldridge,' *National Tax Journal,* XV, 3, Sept. 1962

22 McDonald, S.L., 'Percentage Depletion and the Allocation of Resources: The Case of Oil and Gas,' *National Tax Journal,* XIV, 4, Dec. 1961

23 McDonald, S.L., 'Percentage Depletion, Expensing of Intangibles, and Petroleum Conservation,' in Mason Guffrey, ed., *Executive Resources and Taxation* (Madison 1967)

24 Mead, W.J. and P.E. Sorenson, 'A National Defense Petroleum Reserve Alternative to Oil Import Quotas,' *Land Economics,* XLVII, 3, Aug. 1971

25 Mid-Continent Oil and Gas Association, *Analysis and Comment Relating to the CONSAD Report on the Influence of U.S. Petroleum Taxation on the Level of Reserves.* Part 9 of US Congress Committee on Ways and Means and Senate Committee on Finance, Tax Reform, 1969 (Washington 1969)

26 Millsaps, Stephen W., 'Tax Incentives in the United States Petroleum Industry' (unpublished PhD dissertation, North Carolina State University, 1973)

27 *Oil and Gas Journal,* 21 June 1965

28 *Oil and Gas Journal,* 22 Aug., 26 Sept., and 5 Dec. 1962

29 Spann, R.M. and E.W. Erickson, 'Deregulation of the Wellhead Price of Natural Gas, Oil Import Controls and National Energy Policy,' presented at the Southern Economic Association Meetings 1972

30 Spann, Robert M., Edward W. Erickson, and Stephen W. Millsaps, 'Percentage Depletion and the Price and output of Domestic Crude Oil.' Reprinted in *General Tax Reform, Panel Discussion before the Committee on Ways and Means,* US House of Representatives, 93 Congress, 1 session, Part 9 of 11 (26 Feb. 1973)

31 Spann, R.M., 'The Supply of Natural Resources: The Case of Oil and Natural Gas' (unpublished PhD dissertation, North Carolina State University, 1973)

32 Steiner, P.O., 'The Non-neutrality of Corporate Income Taxation – with and without Depletion,' *National Tax Journal,* XVI, 3, Sept. 1963

33 Steiner, P.O., 'Rejoinder to McDonald,' *National Tax Journal,* XVII, 1, March 1964

34 Steiner, P.O., 'Percentage Depletion and Resource Allocation,' in US Congress, House Committee on Ways and Means, *Tax Revision Compendium* (Washington 1959), pp. 949-66

PART TWO

Canada

Canadian oil policy, called the National Oil Policy (NOP), has attempted to maintain Canadian markets west of the Ottawa Valley for domestic Canadian producers. Imported oil supplied demand east of the Ottawa Valley (Quebec and the Atlantic provinces).

Until 1971, these eastern users paid 25 to 35¢ per barrel less than customers consuming domestic crude. Debanné argues that the National Oil Policy did nothing but formalize existing multinational company policy; the policy was one which maximized the profits of the oil companies. Quebec and the Maritimes acquiesced because they received cheaper oil than Ontario. Ontario abided by the federal policy in return for the establishment and expansion of a large refining and petrochemical industry. The west agreed because of the guaranteed markets. Debanné argues that the Canadian pattern of imports and exports would have been unchanged had there been no government-enforced National Oil Policy.

The sharp dislocations of the world oil market have crushed the NOP. The Canadian federal government has announced an extension of the west-east pipeline through Quebec, has maintained a domestic price freeze on crude (at $4.10 per barrel), and has levied an export tax on oil shipments to the US. Debanné argues, and we concur, that these policies are clearly discriminating and wasteful.

Debanné suggests that Canada has other policy options available including shutting back production as an emergency stockpile for North America.

As corresponding papers, read Spann and Erickson on US oil, Waverman on Canadian-American energy relations, McDonald on prorationing, Quirin on alternative technologies, and MacAvoy on policy disharmonies (all in this volume), and the papers by Adelman, Mabro, Crandall, and Steele in the first volume.

124

J. G. DEBANNÉ

Oil and Canadian policy

Canadian oil policy during the past decade cannot be properly understood unless
it is studied within the context of United States oil policy and the dominant role
of multinational oil corporations. This dominance is declining rapidly for three
reasons:
1 the changing position of the US from an almost self-sufficient importer of oil
in a buyer's market to an increasingly oil-deficient nation in a seller's market,
2 the emerging role of OPEC in oil pricing and oil-supply policy and the corresponding decline of the multinationals' power in these fields,
3 the growing mood in Canada for more control over the Canadian economy and
over Canadian natural resources in particular.

Whether or not this decline in influence of the United States and the multinationals on Canadian oil policy will continue remains to be seen; nevertheless
it is necessary to focus on US oil policy over the past decades in order to understand Canadian oil policy until the early seventies.

THE US OIL IMPORTS QUOTA POLICY
AND THE OVERLAND EXEMPTION

From US oil surplus to oil deficit
The writing was on the wall as of 1948 when the largest producer of oil in the
world (the US) ceased to be a net exporter of oil. These imports by the multinationals grew and alarmed the independent oil producers in the US. As a result,
a voluntary oil imports limitation program was initiated by the Eisenhower administration in 1957. Its failure to curb imports led to the establishment in 1959

125

of a mandatory oil imports limitation program which imposed a ceiling of 12.2 per cent of domestic US oil production on imports of foreign crude.[1] However, the new policy featured an exception, the 'overland exemption,' in favor of Canadian and Mexican oil imports. These were not officially covered by the quota but were allowed to displace part of the overseas imports to the US. The overland exemption found supporters among those in the US government who were concerned about the security of oil supply. A typical argument in favor of this policy was that Canadian oil imports ought to be given a privileged position because this source of supply 'is as secure a source as any domestic production.' Naturally the Canadian government and the western oil-producing provinces actively supported the US quota system and its overland exemption clause because it secured an export market for Canadian oil at favorable prices. Moreover, both governments seemed anxious to maintain the appearance and – in the case of Canada – the substance of a privileged position for Canadian oil in the US market.

The rising cost of finding and developing new domestic oil reserves in the US was making it increasingly difficult for the domestic oil-producing industry, particularly the independents[2] who did not have large inventories of cheap oil reserves in the ground. While the Mandatory Oil Imports program appeared to promise a good measure of protection and relief from the competition of cheaper overseas oil imports, the 'overland exemption' was increasingly looked upon with concern by the independents. This led the US government to seek and obtain, in 1968, a commitment from the Canadian government to 'limit voluntarily' Canadian oil exports to the US east of the Rockies to 280,000 barrels a day and to limit annual growth of these exports to 26,000 barrels a day.[3]

The price differential between overseas crude imports and US domestic oil was estimated by the Office of Oil and Gas (US Department of the Interior) at 95 cents per barrel[4] in 1969 and prevailed throughout the sixties, up to the Teheran and Tripoli agreements with OPEC in 1970 and 1971. Support of the multinationals for the mandatory import quota was secured by allocating the bulk of this quota and the corresponding profits of 95 cents per imported barrel to the traditional importers of oil, mainly the same multinationals.

Although the 'overland exemption' reduced overseas oil imports and the associated profit per imported barrel, it was actively supported by the multinationals who wielded at the time considerable influence on US and Canadian oil policy.

The production-imports-exports triangle
To understand the attitude of the multinationals at the time one must look at North America as an integrated oil supply distribution system. The multinationals were the major importers of oil in the United States as well as in Canada. The allocation pattern of imported oil and domestically produced (i.e. Canadian) oil is

TABLE 1

Crude oil and equivalent supply to Canadian refineries, 1950-71 (thousands of barrels daily)

Date	British Columbia		Prairies		Ontario		Quebec and Atlantic provinces		Canada	
	Imports	Total supply	Imports	Total supply	Imports	Total supply	Imports	Total supply	Imports	Total supply
1971		127		224	5	379	664	669	669	1399
1970		120		220	6	372	564	564	570	1280
1969		107		216	1	342	520	520	521	1185
1968		112		205	1	330	485	485	486	1132
1967		102		200	1	312	446	446	447	1060
1966		94		195	1	313	433	433	434	1035
1965		81		189	2	301	393	393	395	964
1964		82		180	1	283	392	392	393	937
1963		73		173	3	271	400	400	403	917
1962		80		168	1	235	370	370	371	853
1961		67		143	7	227	358	358	365	796
1960		66		145	10	207	337	337	347	755
1959		64		153	7	205	312	312	319	734
1958		58		154	4	160	277	277	281	649
1957		61		153	22	163	284	284	306	661
1956		60		163	25	159	266	267	291	649
1955		53		151	28	139	210	210	238	553
1954	5	42		126	24	119	181	181	210	468
1953	16	23		145	30	95	177	177	223	440
1952	20	21		109	37	93	168	168	225	391
1951	22	22		93	44	82	162	162	228	359
1950	21	21	1	80	69	70	133	133	224	304

SOURCE: Canadian Petroleum Association, *1971 Statistical Yearbook*; Department of Energy, Mines and Resources, 'Petroleum and Natural Gas Industry in Canada, 1963-1968,' *Mineral Information Bulletin*, MR 104

presented in Table 1. This table shows that as early as 1958, when the Borden Commission on Energy was holding its hearings on Canadian oil policy, Canada west of the Ottawa River was almost entirely supplied from Canadian sources. Likewise, Table 1 shows that Quebec and the Atlantic provinces (Canada east of the Ottawa River) have always been exclusively supplied with oil imports. This allocation pattern, which was to be officially endorsed in 1960 as Canada's national oil policy,[5] was in fact the pattern already adopted by the multinationals for Canada.

By 1960 the multinationals controlled a dominant share of the oil production in Western Canada and controlled also the Interprovincial Pipeline which supplied the Ontario market. [Editors' note: Foreign ownership of Canada's petroleum industry, including production, refining, and marketing has remained relatively unchanged throughout the sixties in terms of assets, ranging from 77.3 per cent in 1960 to 76.8 per cent in 1970.] Although it was obvious at the time that western Canadian oil fields had the potential to supply eastern Canada, the multinationals preferred to seek instead a market for this crude in the US mid-continent under the umbrella of the 'overland exemption.' There are many factors which, if appropriately weighed, give a clue to the motivation behind the determination of the multinationals to displace profitable overseas oil imports quotas (to the US) by more expensive western Canadian oil.

One important consideration was that the multinationals had major producing interests in the US and Canada and quasi-exclusive control of production from the Middle East as well as from Venezuela and the Caribbean.[6] All other things considered equal, economies of transport would be realized by routing Alberta oil to the nearby mid-continent and Pacific Northwest markets instead of transporting this oil by pipeline further east to Montreal. In short, transportation economics favored entry of Alberta oil into the US mid-continent[7] rather than into the more distant eastern Canada market. Furthermore, the north eastern tip of the North American continent, i.e. Quebec, the Maritimes, and New England, is the most expensive destination for North American-produced oil delivered by pipeline; hence it is the region to be supplied by tanker with overseas imported oil.

Another reason was that US and Canadian oil production is 'prorated' among all producers, while production from Venezuela or the Middle East is 'owned,' by the multinationals. This allows, for example, the Jersey- or Shell-controlled refineries in Montreal to be exclusively supplied from Jersey- or Shell-controlled oil pools respectively and to have much of this oil transported in company-owned tankers. In other words, more Jersey or Shell oil is sold for every barrel of oil imported by Imperial and Shell refineries in Montreal than if this oil originated from 'prorated' production in Alberta. This is because Shell and Imperial production in Alberta is 'diluted' by the proration formula which allocates 'production allowables' to all Alberta producers. [Editors' note: For a discussion of prorationing see the McDonald paper in this volume.]

The advantages of 'owned' production over prorated production provide one good reason why overseas oil rather than Alberta oil served the Montreal market and Canada east of the Ottawa River. They do not explain why Alberta oil was allowed to displace overseas oil imports quotas to the US. Part of the expanation was that Alberta oil was to be provided with an expanding market, and the multinationals could not prevent its entry to both the eastern Canada market and the US (mid-continent) market. After all, the multinationals had large investments in western Canadian oil reserves; accordingly, an expanding market for western Canadian oil was necessary to ensure an adequate return on their Canadian investments.

Another important consideration was that the multinationals had important oil reserves in Venezuela, where their concessions were to run out much sooner than in the Middle East. Moreover the government 'take' was substantially larger in Venezuela than in the Middle East (97.2 cents a barrel in Venezuela as compared to 75.7 cents a barrel in the Middle East in 1962).

There were good reasons to suspect at the time that Venezuelan demands for a still larger government 'take' would continue to be pressed and would outpace demands of Middle East governments. This proved to be true as the respective government revenues per barrel remained consistently higher in Venezuela than in the Middle East up to 1971 (146.2 cents a barrel versus 124.5 cents a barrel in 1971).[8] Accordingly, the multinationals were anxious to produce their Venezuelan oil as soon as possible while conditions were favorable. Since this oil was higher priced than Middle East oil, both at the source and at North American ports of entry, the multinationals preferred to route as much Venezuelan oil to eastern Canada where they were able to maintain higher retail prices than in comparable regions of the US, such as New England.[9, 10] As a result, the growth of Canadian oil exports to the US under the umbrella of the 'overland exemption' was more than compensated by overseas oil imports east of the Ottawa River (Borden Line) since adoption of the National Oil Policy in 1960. From 1961 to 1971, total imports of crude and refined products to eastern Canada increased from 446.3 thousand barrels a day to 825 thousand barrels a day. During that period, oil and refined products exports increased from 189.7 thousand barrels a day to 787.8 thousand barrels a day. This increase in exports grew also in importance from 10 per cent of all US oil imports in 1961 to some 40 per cent in 1968.

J.G. Debanné

Inasmuch as compliance with both Canada's national oil policy and 'overland exemption' in the US oil policy were to be 'voluntary,' it was essential that the policy appeal to most if not all the participants. The price of Venezuela crude FOB Montreal resulted in a calculated differential with Alberta oil FOB Montreal which was until very recently moderately in favor of imported oil (25 to 35 cents). Moreover, the additional cost to move Venezuelan oil to the southern Ontario market already supplied from western Canada did not leave much of a differential. This eased the pressure for shipments across the Borden Line of Venezuelan crude bought at the official posted price.

The western provinces and the independent oil producers in western Canada would have liked to serve the Quebec crude oil market; however, they had to face a calculated price differential of about 25 to 35 cents a barrel in favor of Venezuelan crude. This differential discouraged the west from lowering the posted price of oil in Alberta which stayed between $2.62 and $2.67 a barrel for Redwater crude throughout the sixties until 1969. Oil imports east of the Borden Line resulted in a modest price advantage at the retail level in the Montreal region and other refining centers over retail prices in the Ontario market. Surely Quebec and the Maritimes would have preferred still lower retail prices, comparable to those prevailing in New England, which would have been possible if the bulk of crude oil imports were lower priced Middle East oil or 'discounted' Venezuelan oil. Except for the occasional spot purchase by independents of lower priced crudes and products, the bulk of crude oil was purchased by the multinationals from Venezuela at the official posted prices rather than at discount prices which were about 50 cents per barrel lower.[11] This was to be expected since the multinational refiners in Eastern Canada bought crude from their respective affiliates in Venezuela, Colombia, and the Caribbean.

Provincial governments accepted this state of affairs because they took it for granted until very recently that overseas crude oil purchases were entirely out of their hands. Recent evidence that this might not be the case in the future appears in the Quebec government's report on Energy Policy and the creation in 1970 of SOQUIP (Société Québécoise d'Initiatives Pétrolières) which has recently been vested with the responsibility of negotiating oil-supply contracts with overseas producers.

Alberta oil, priced with the delivered price of Alberta crude in Ontario, was slightly higher than the calculated price of overseas oil if transported from Montreal to Sarnia, Ontario by pipeline. The fact nevertheless remains that cheaper spot purchases of overseas oil products were possible FOB southern Ontario during the navigable season of the St Lawrence Seaway. The independent refiners and marketers were quite aware of these possibilities and violated the Borden Line and the national oil policy by importing from time to time a shipment of petroleum or products at bargain prices. Finally the issue reached the law courts between the National Energy Board and Cal Oil, an independent refiner. The Ontario government was then faced with a dilemma of its own: either to encourage such violations of the national oil policy in order to maintain a downward pressure on retail prices, or else side with the NEB and the predominantly multinational refiners in Ontario. The Ontario government had mixed feelings about this issue, and a convincing indication of its 'reluctant compliance' with the national oil policy is that it did not actively intervene when the NEB sought, and finally obtained in 1971, legal powers to prevent the flow of gasoline and other products from Quebec to Ontario.

Another factor which helped placate Ontario is that the NEB sought to discourage the expansion of refining capacity east of the Borden Line and succeeded in its efforts, principally with the multinationals. It is significant to note in this respect that, as of 1969, projected new refining capacity totalling 465,000 barrels a day in Quebec and the Atlantic provinces was largely planned by independent refiners eyeing the possibilities of exports to the US and Ontario as well as of expansion of the local market in Quebec and the Atlantic provinces.[12] In short, Ontario accepted the national oil policy and the higher retail prices entailed by this policy in return for the concentration and expansion of a large refining and petrochemical industry in the province.

CONGRUENCE OF MULTINATIONAL AND NATIONAL INTERESTS

US national interests

The Mandatory Oil Imports system was initiated in order to encourage the development of a healthy domestic oil-producing industry primarily for national security reasons. For these same reasons the US government genuinely wished to nurture and develop close ties and co-operation with its northern neighbor in the spirit of the Hyde Park Agreement of 1941, which Dean Acheson sought to expand after the war.[13] The Leduc oilfield discovery in 1949 which triggered the second oil boom in western Canada was very important by North American standards and did not pass unnoticed by the US government and its oil industry, particularly since the US had become a net importer of oil two years before in 1948.[14]

While far more important discoveries of oil reserves were to be made in other parts of the world, largely with US capital, a number of events up to 1959, when the 'overland exemption' became US policy, enhanced the value of Canadian oil reserves as 'secure' reserves for the US industry as well as for the US government in case of necessity, particularly in case of another war. The Iranian oil nationalization by Mossadegh in 1951, the disruption of the Suez Canal in 1956, the Biafran war, the Iraqui, Libyan, and Venezuelan revolutions, and other events confirmed the conviction that Canada deserved special treatment by the United States as an oil-exporting country.

Within a wider perspective of western hemisphere security, it was naturally in the interest of the US that Venezuela enjoy a healthy economy. Accordingly, Venezuelan oil exports to Canada at relatively good prices benefited the Venezuelan economy and was no doubt favorably viewed by the US government.

Venezuela's national interests[15]

Venezuela was becoming increasingly edgy about the exploitation of its petroleum resources by the multinationals. It was the first host oil-producing country overseas to impose (in 1948) an income tax on the profits of the multinationals. This brought the total share of the state to 50 per cent and thus became the first *de facto* '50-50 split' arrangement between any host country and the multinationals. By the time the Borden commission hearings were being held in Canada (1958-9) new tax reforms in Venezuela brought the total state share to between 55 and 60 per cent of oil profits. Furthermore, Venezuela was actively seeking higher prices for its crude and was earnestly seeking an accommodation with Middle East oil-producing countries, whose crudes had reached the eastern seaboard of the US by 1958. It was then evident to the multinationals that the end of their concessions in Venezuela were ominously close and that these concessions would not be renewed. Accordingly, one of their major concerns at the time was to devise exploitation plans in order to derive maximum profits from their Venezuelan concessions before these expired. They therefore sought to safeguard outlets for Venezuelan oil exports such as eastern Canada and to obtain the highest possible price for these exports, an objective which also coincided with the interests of the Venezuelan government.

Canada's national interests

The report of the Royal Commission on Energy (Borden report) judged these oil imports to the Maritimes and Quebec to be in Canada's national interest because of 'international relations' and 'external trade' considerations.

To what extent Canada was expected by the US to help keep Venezuela solvent may not be ascertained without a study of the secret correspondence between the US Department of State and the Canadian Department of External Affairs on this issue. It seems, however, that Venezuela, which enjoyed the highest per capita income in South America and exported the major portion of its oil to other countries than Canada, would have remained comfortably solvent without its oil exports to Canada. In 1970, for example, out of a daily Venezuelan production of 3.74 million barrels a day of which 3.4 million a day were exported from Venezuela, Canada imported half a million barrels a day or less than 15 per cent. Venezuela would certainly not have been bankrupt by the loss of the eastern Canadian market.

Likewise, the 'external trade' argument appears to be given undue importance. For example, the countries which accounted for more than 99 per cent of oil exports to eastern Canada in 1968 (Venezuela, Kuwait, and Saudi Arabia) absorbed a minute portion of Canadian exports; certainly there was no reason to fear 'disastrous consequences on Canada's external trade, that restrictions on Canadian oil imports might provoke' (Borden report, French version, p. 143).

As expected, the independent oil producers of western Canada who did not have at their disposal the variety of options open to the multinationals were eyeing the Montreal market for western oil and invoking the traditional Canadian policy in favor of east-west trade, a favorite and popular theme (the 'National Policy') since the construction of the Canadian Pacific Railway during the last century. National policy was adhered to in 1957 for natural gas when the Canadian government forced the construction of the Trans-Canada Pipeline from Alberta to eastern Canada on Canadian soil, notwithstanding the economic advantages of north-south gas flows and the unwillingness of industry to finance the Trans-Canada Pipeline. Two years later, the Borden commission rejected the east-west trade argument for supplying Montreal with Alberta oil, stating candidly that the multinationals would not support such a policy and would be unwilling to finance an oil pipeline from Sarnia to Montreal. The official reason put forward by the multinationals in their briefs to the Borden commission was that it would be more economical to import overseas oil to the Montreal market than to supply this market with western Canadian oil. The Borden commission opted therefore for the scheme already adopted for Canada by the multinationals. This was essentially an endorsement of the status quo with due recognition to export possibilities to the US. It would therefore be more appropriate to talk about Canada's 'multinational oil policy' rather than of a 'national oil policy.' The multinationals tailored this policy for Canada with due regard to Canadian interests and to their own interests, as indeed they have done in the US and in Venezuela.

Post-mortem

Canada's national oil policy ran its course as the good old days of cheap oil imports ended in the early seventies. It was officially declared dead by Prime Minister Trudeau in his Parliament speech of 6 December 1973.[16]

J.G. Debanné

The multinationals, who are the real authors of Canada's national oil policy since 1959, need not apologize as far as Canada is concerned, because their plan was economically advantageous to this country. Furthermore, it is probably in good part due to the representations of the multinationals that the 'overland exemption' for Canadian oil was included in the US oil imports policy. Western Canadian oil was guaranteed its natural market for expansion, the US midwest, and was safeguarded against competition from cheaper oil where such competition could have hurt, namely, in the Ontario market. Quebec and the Maritimes enjoyed marginally lower prices than would have otherwise been possible if supplied by western Canadian oil and the Canadian government was happy at the beneficial effect on the Canadian balance of payments of importing 'cheap oil' east of the Borden Line and exporting 'expensive oil' to the US. In effect, this advantage allowed eastern Canada to benefit from its geography – its accessibility by sea – and allowed western Canadian oilfields to take advantage of their relative proximity to the US mid-continent and Pacific Northwest oil markets.

Actually the development of oil imports and exports would essentially have taken place anyway even if the national oil policy was never officially adopted. The multinationals who control the Canadian petroleum industry would have stuck to this plan which was theirs in the first place. However, the official adoption of the policy and the vigilance of the National Energy Board made it more profitable to the multinationals throughout the years as importation by the independents of cheaper gasolines into Ontario was successfully discouraged, thereby eliminating downward pressures on retail prices of petroleum products.

In all fairness it must be recognized that the plan of the multinationals was economically advantageous for Canada as long as a price differential existed between western crude and cheaper overseas crude and for as long as the US Imports Quota system was in force. It would have been more advantageous however to the Canadian consumer if the oil supply-imports-exports scheme for Canada were not enshrined in a national oil policy, as this allowed the multinationals with the help of the NEB to suppress competition by the independents in the vulnerable Ontario market. Throughout the sixties and up to March 1973, when oil export permits became mandatory in Canada, the national oil policy helped continental security of oil supply inasmuch as Canada stood ready to supplement United States oil production in the midwest market area, subject of course to limits to Canadian crude imports that Washington considered tolerable with due respect to the concern of independent oil producers in the US. Throughout the sixties, therefore, implementation of Canada's national oil policy featured persistent overtures to Washington for more US imports of Canadian oil and for a larger share of the oil market in the mid-continent. Guarantees for an expanding share of the US oil market were furthermore sought by Canada in the form of a continental energy policy.

Throughout that period, Washington allowed Canadian oil imports to grow because this stimulated the development of new petroleum reserves in western Canada, hence contributing to the continental security of energy supply (see Table 2). However, the US preferred at the time to leave its options open and was not ready to commit itself to long-term Canadian oil imports, i.e. to a continental oil policy. Nevertheless, throughout this period the 'special relationship' between Canada and the United States regarding oil was officially recognized by the 'overland exemption.' Canada's oil exports to the US were 'voluntarily restricted' by industry. Violations of the import limits set by Washington drew pleas for restraint by US government officials but never a formal curb on Canadian oil imports by Washington.

The end of an era
Since 1970 a steady but rapid change in relationships between Washington and Ottawa has taken place, triggered by the Teheran agreements with OPEC regarding the pricing of overseas crude, the vanishing of surplus oil-producing capacity in the US, the increasing costs of finding and developing new oil and gas reserves south of the 49th parallel, the delays in developing and moving Alaskan oil, and the mounting opposition to nuclear and coal-powered generation plants and petroleum refineries.

Since 1970 Washington has been increasingly eager to expand imports of oil and gas from Canada and to explore the possibilities of a continental energy policy. Ottawa had by that time changed attitudes and was no longer eager to expand its share of the mid-continent oil market. The very notion of a continental energy or resources policy became taboo in Canadian politics. Yet, the tradition of a 'special relationship' regarding Canadian oil seemed to remain intact inasmuch as the restrictions to oil exports that Canada now wanted to impose were to be implemented on a 'voluntary' basis by industry rather than through the requirement of an export permit as was the case for natural gas and electric power.

It has somehow proven impossible to maintain the outward appearance of the 'special relationship,' and the Canadian government found it necessary to impose export controls on oil for the first time as of March 1973. One can safely surmise that the increasingly oil-hungry refiners of the midwest would not commit themselves to oil-import restraints and apparently left the NEB in the dark as to the volumes of Canadian oil they would 'nominate' (i.e. order) for March 1973.[17] Since concern about meeting Canadian oil requirements in Ontario was becoming

135

TABLE 2

Historical record of remaining proved oil reserves in Canada (thousands of barrels)

Year	Remaining at beginning of year	Gross additions			Total additions	Net production	Remaining at end of year	Net change in reserves during year
		Revisions	Extensions	Discoveries				
1951	1,202,607	83,100		138,211	221,311	47,318	1,376,600	173,993
1952	1,376,600	60,948		302,461	363,409	60,500	1,679,509	302,909
1953	1,679,509	151,932		94,891	246,823	80,910	1,845,422	165,913
1954	1,845,422	359,589		98,219	457,808	95,616	2,207,614	362,192
1955	2,207,614	365,861		63,566	429,427	127,507	2,509,534	301,920
1956	2,509,534	460,966		48,191	509,157	169,321	2,849,370	339,836
1957	2,849,370	167,014		39,823	206,837	181,753	2,874,454	25,084
1958	2,874,454	448,184		9,311	457,495	166,045	3,165,904	291,450
1959	3,165,904	421,107		93,852	514,959	183,739	3,497,124	331,220
1960	3,497,124	350,478		22,044	372,522	191,104	3,678,542	181,418
1961	3,678,542	694,656		21,399	716,055	221,028	4,173,569	495,027
1962	4,173,569	531,361		20,655	552,016	244,883	4,480,702	307,133
1963	4,480,702	450,436	178,596	28,245	657,277	256,487	4,881,492	400,790
1964	4,881,492	1,238,344	220,912	107,697	1,566,953	270,799	6,177,646	1,296,154
1965	6,177,646	349,738	279,270	196,175	825,183	291,592	6,711,237	533,591
1966	6,711,237	657,812	357,200	381,555	1,396,567	316,053	7,791,751	1,080,514
1967	7,791,751	459,788	70,730	190,811	721,329	344,156	8,168,924	377,173
1968	8,168,924	371,847	87,053	125,257	584,157	371,468	8,381,613	212,689
1969	8,381,613	477,630	74,113	79,852	631,595	393,403	8,619,805	283,192
1970	8,619,805	276,068	68,654	32,476	377,198	438,023	8,558,980	−60,825
1971	8,558,980	178,431	57,998	17,804	254,233	480,126	8,333,087	−225,893

SOURCE: Canadian Petroleum Association, *1971 Statistical Yearbook*

serious because of insufficient oil pipeline capacity from western Canada, the Canadian government announced in February 1973 that henceforth export permits would be required to ship oil to the US. This decision marked the end of an era. In effect, Canada told the US to seek oil elsewhere because Canadian oil reserves and oil-producing capacity were too small to materially help fill the widening gap between US demand and US oil-producing capacity (see Table 2 for remaining Canadian oil reserves and annual producing rates). This argument is backed up by evidence of declining proven oil reserves in western Canada which are down to a 13-year life at current rates of production as compared to a 30-year life in 1950.

This argument made the change of status more palatable to the United States and it appears that Washington took it philosophically. Accordingly, when the new US oil policy was announced, lifting all restrictions on oil imports, no special provision was made for Canadian oil. This event did not pass unnoticed in Canada where the *Financial Post* announced it in a prominent headline: 'Nixon serves Canada with Divorce Papers!' Canadian oil was relegated to the status of any other foreign oil because for policy-makers it seemed to have lost one particular quality which rendered it more valuable than any other foreign oil, namely, the security of its supply.

CANADA'S NEW OIL POLICY

The fast-changing energy scene
The energy scene has been changing very quickly in Canada and the United States since the summer of 1973. The gasoline shortage which developed in the US during the summer of 1973 spurred demand for Canadian gasoline exports from refineries in eastern Canada. Public concern about a resulting gasoline shortage in Canada caused the federal government to extend export controls on all petroleum products, thereby closing all remaining loopholes in the newly erected barrier to the free flow of liquid hydrocarbons between the US and Canada. Since the summer of 1973, the Canadian government has released a succession of reports, policy statements, and trial balloons dealing with energy policy. The first instalment featured a report in two volumes, entitled *An Energy Policy for Canada, Phase I*, which presented facts, figures, and certain options. The last instalment to date is the Prime Minister's energy policy speech to Parliament of 6 December 1973.

In the intervening period a 'voluntary' freeze on the price of Canadian oil was imposed on 4 September 1973 until 31 January 1974 and an export tax introduced for the first time on Canadian oil exports. This tax was designed to close the price gap between the frozen price of Alberta oil and the going price of oil in the Chicago market, thereby avoiding a subsidy to US importers of Canadian oil at the expense of Canadian producers and royalty holders. The petroleum industry and the Alberta government strongly objected to the tax which was depriving them of revenues to which they felt entitled. The federal government sought to compromise by sharing the proceeds of the export tax on a 50-50 basis with the producing provinces and later on offered to earmark the federal share of the oil export tax, for future development of oil reserves in Canada.

The Middle East war in October 1973, the resulting OAPEC (Organization of Arab Petroleum Exporting Countries) reduction of oil production, and the oil embargo against the US triggered a sharp rise in overseas oil prices and widened the gap between the frozen price of Canadian oil and the price of overseas oil delivered in Montreal and Chicago. The Canadian government decided to close this gap by increasing the export tax to $1.90 a barrel instead of letting the price of Canadian oil rise. The vehement protests of the Alberta government and of industry caused the federal government to back down and agree to a gradual rise of the price of Alberta oil after 31 January 1974. This measure would also have helped reduce the widening gap between the price of oil in eastern Canada and the frozen price of Alberta oil in Ontario and the western provinces. However, the New Democratic Party (NDP), which holds the balance of power in Parliament and who claimed credit for the oil price freeze because of its strong leverage position over the government, threatened to withdraw its support and bring down the government over what it perceived as a sellout to the oil companies and an about-face by the Minister of Energy, Mines and Resources.[18]

The Trudeau speech
It was at this point that Prime Minister Trudeau took personal charge of the energy problem and presented Parliament and the country with an eleven-point oil policy proposal on 6 December 1973.[19] While some aspects of the proposal may have been intended as a compromise to secure NDP support, such as the extension of the price freeze from January 31 to the end of the heating season, other aspects denoted a realistic assessment of energy priorities, such as the need to develop oil reserves in the frontier regions of Canada rather than in oil-depleted regions and the need to develop the tar sands.

Inasmuch as Mr Trudeau's oil-policy speech was at variance with previous statements of his government on the subject it is here taken for granted that the Prime Minister's views superseded earlier pronouncements by his ministers and represented the current – although not definitive – posture of the Canadian government on national oil policy. Mr Trudeau's policy statement called for:
1 establishment of an Energy Supplies Allocation Board to ensure equitable allocation of petroleum products in times of shortage, such as at present;[20]

2 abolition of the 'Ottawa Valley Line' or 'Borden Line' so that 'the Western provinces will have a guaranteed outlet for increased production; and the eastern provinces will be guaranteed security of supply';

3 'establishment of a pricing mechanism which will provide sufficient incentives for the development of our oil resources, both frontier oil resources such as Arctic reserves and non-conventional resources such as the tar sands';

4 a declaration of intention not 'to cut off exports' (to the US) and not 'to reduce imports from reliable suppliers';

5 'enactment of measures to ensure that any escalation in returns and revenues as a result of higher prices will be used in a manner conducive to security and self-sufficiency';

6 establishment of a 'publicly owned Canadian petroleum company principally to expedite exploration and development';

7 'early completion of a pipeline of adequate capacity to serve Montreal and as required more eastern points';

8 intensification of research on oil sands technology to permit their full and rapid development;

9 the price of domestic heating oil will be maintained during the present heating season and the government will 'undertake discussions with the government of Alberta and with the oil companies to secure their agreement to maintain the price of domestically produced oil at the current level at least until the end of this winter.' (This last point was in part intended to placate the NDP and save the government; however, Mr Trudeau did acknowledge that 'prices must go up in the long run, if we are to have adequate supplies.')

10 the federal government will continue to levy a tax after 1 February 1973 on exported oil, equal to the difference between the domestic price and the export price as determined by the National Energy Board;

11 the 'federal government's offer to share the proceeds of the tax to January 31 with the producing provinces on a 50/50 basis' is extended after that date and the scheme is to be discussed with the provincial premiers in February.

Indeed the entire proposal was to be discussed at the forthcoming premiers' conference, which suggested an open attitude and a willingness to compromise on the part of the prime minister on the oil policy issue. In the hope that it is not too late to influence Canadian energy policy the following remarks are intended as constructive guidelines towards an improved version of the prime minister's proposal, in the best interest of all concerned.

GUIDELINES FOR A CANADIAN OIL POLICY

Oil exploration and development technology and know-how have enormously increased the effectiveness of the search for conventional petroleum reserves

139

during the past two decades. The bulk of the substantial oil pools and reservoirs accessible to the exploration teams of the multinational oil companies has been discovered on land throughout the world and on the shallower portions of continental shelves opened up for exploration. The stark fact is that no significant oil discovery has been recorded on land for several years, either in Canada or the US south of the 49th parallel, or in the Middle East, or anywhere else in the 'free world.'[21] [Editors' note: This is Professor Debanné's opinion. We do not share it. The complex interplay of government policies and uncertainties has likely retarded exploration. Steele's paper on Latin America shows large discoveries and discovery potential. The papers on China and Russia indicate substantial reserves probably available to the 'free world.'] It has been recognized for some time that mainly in new, heretofore unexplored territory, such as further north in the Canadian Arctic or further out in the oceans, are there still interesting prospects for important oil and gas discoveries. The northern slope 'play' in Alaska and the North Sea play in Western Europe substantiate this prediction, but also establish the fact that these less accessible reserves are considerably more expensive to find, produce, and transport.

The oil-producing regions and states such as Alberta, Iran, or even fabulously rich Saudi Arabia can see the writing on the wall and in the case of Alberta and Iran are increasingly convinced that their reserves, respectively sufficient for ten and twenty years of production at current producing rates, have peaked out. They are also aware that demand for petroleum products has barely started to take off as affluence spreads throughout the world. Likewise they feel that oil and its products are irreplaceable in many fields of application, such as automobile and aviation fuel or as a home-heating fuel in many parts of the world.[22] Their state of mind is somewhat comparable to that of the Burgundy wine grower who knows from experience that truly great vintage years are extremely rare and that he might never in his lifetime replenish his dwindling stock of great vintage (1969) red burgundy. Soaring demand for this vintage has driven the price up to say twenty-five dollars a bottle and it would be unthinkable to compel this wine grower to sell his remaining stock of 1969 burgundy at say, five dollars a bottle on the ground that it cost him only two dollars a bottle to produce.

Likewise, there has never been and probably never will be a relationship between the cost to find, develop, and produce conventional oil and the price of that oil. What determines the price of oil is its opportunity cost (replacement cost) as perceived by the price leader, which used to be the Jersey group until the price leadership was wrested away by Lybia and more recently by Saudi Arabia. All other producers perceive it in their best interest to behave as price takers, i.e. to achieve price equilibrium with the price leader. They therefore feel it is their basic right to secure as high a price as possible for their depletable oil resources by following the price leader. In the final analysis, the acid test of a just and reasonable price is the cost of an alternate source of supply in adequate quantities.[23]

North American society has now come to realize that the value assigned to petroleum products is much higher in most technologically advanced countries than in Canada and the United States. Italians, for example, have for years been paying over $1.00 a gallon for gasoline and are now paying over $1.30 a gallon. The net effect of such high prices for gasoline has been beneficial because the motorized passenger transportation fleets are considerably more efficient in Italy and other technologically advanced countries than in Canada or the US in terms of BTUs per passenger mile. [Editors' note: The efficiency of European cars is a product of four things – higher prices for gasoline, small roads, low income, and taxes on horsepower. No study we are aware of has proven that the high price of gasoline is the major cause of efficiency.]

Insulating all or part of Canada from the long-overdue readjustment of energy prices with respect to the prices of other services and commodities may be unavoidable over the very short term, but this will help maintain energy waste. Insulating part of Canada against the rise in oil prices will have the additional disadvantage of creating inequities within Canada. This would place all or part of eastern Canada and its industries at a disadvantage with respect to energy-subsidized industries in other parts of Canada and would inevitably result in charges of unfair treatment against the federal government. Indeed, the successive variations of and contradictions to the original 'two-price' oil policy issued by the federal government on 4 September 1973 are evidence of the pressures and strains to which that government has been subjected to by provinces, political parties, and industry on the oil-pricing issue. Furthermore, it is significant to note that the Prime Minister's oil-policy speech of December 6 was quite noncommittal and vague about the oil-pricing structure in Canada, other than that domestic crude prices would remain frozen until the end of this heating season at least, but that oil prices are expected to rise in the long run to foster the development of new conventional oil reserves and tar sand oil.

In the light of the foregoing it is very hard to justify the position that the oil-producing provinces and the oil companies have no right to sell their oil in Canada at the going price, particularly since the federal government makes sure, by imposing an oil-export tax, that the American market pays the going price for Canadian oil. This policy is discriminatory against oil producers just as it would be against landowners if they were prohibited to sell land at the going price. As such, it undermines Canadian unity by forcing Alberta, and particularly its oil-producing industry, to sell Alberta oil at unjustly low prices with respect to the opportunity cost of oil. Surely, if Alberta were an independent state it would choose to sell all its oil production at the going price. Alberta's membership in Confederation is no reason why it ought to be subjected to discriminatory practices, forcing it to sell its oil, a depletable resource, at far below market value.

One province which would be happy about such a price structure is Ontario, even if the oil price in that province were propped up to parity with overseas oil delivered in Montreal, as was suggested at some point by federal officials in order to placate Quebec. Actually, Ontario can claim a right to preferential treatment, because it is the largest tax-generating province and can point to the gross inequity created by the 'depletion allowance.' This preferential tax treatment is mainly designed for the benefit of the oil- and gas-producing industry in the western provinces and costs the federal treasury several hundred million dollars in lost tax revenues every year. The depletion allowance is blatantly discriminatory and ought to be repealed because it has failed to accomplish its objective, namely, to encourage exploration and development of new oil and gas reserves. The depletion allowance has mainly served to finance the huge cash bonuses paid for exploration permits and mineral rights rather than to finance oil and gas exploration and development operations. The depletion allowance also generates additional dividends to the shareholders, which was not its intention.

Professor Bruce W. Wilkinson estimates that there is a 7.73 per cent net loss to the Canadian economy on any increase to the price of Canadian oil because some 86 per cent of the additional dividends and retained earnings generated by the price increase go to the parent corporations outside Canada.[24] [Editors' note: Professor Wilkinson's estimates, like all others of this type, are approximations based on certain assumptions, such as the appropriate tax rate etc. See a similar estimate for national gas in the Hamilton paper.] Repeal of the depletion allowance would certainly correct this situation because the oil companies would then be paying their full share of taxes. Furthermore, there is no reason why the federal government could not consider requiring that oil companies prove up new oil and gas reserves equal to the quantities produced as of the date when the oil price freeze is lifted.[25] Those oil companies which may have remaining net earnings after proving up reserves equal to the quantities they have depleted may export these earnings if they wish. Such a scheme would make sure that profits from the sale of oil are used to find new oil and would be far preferable to the depletion allowance.

An equilibrium price structure and security of North American oil supply
It has been established by Waverman[26] in the case of natural gas and by Debanné[27] in the case of oil that the minimum cost allocation of these respective commodities in North America, taking into account transportation costs from sources of

supplies to market centers and lifting governmental constraints to flows, lies along north-south lines. Any distortion of this optimal allocation structure results in inefficiencies and higher costs that somebody must pay for: either the consumer in terms of higher prices or the producer in terms of price discounts.

The equilibrium price structure in Canada is that which uses as a reference market that region situated at the neutral point, or midpoint in terms of transportation cost, between the center of oil imports on the eastern seabord and the center of oil production in western Canada. This point is located in the Chicago area for the northern-tier states of the US and for Canada. Moving this reference point further east to Toronto would penalize Alberta which would have to reduce its field price of oil by the cost of transportation from the Chicago region to Toronto. Alberta oil would suffer a further discount if it were priced with reference to Montreal to be in equilibrium with overseas oil prices.

It would be far simpler and preferable to let oil prices reach equilibrium in the market place instead of distorting the price structure and compensating for the distortions by subsidies and tax levies. Therefore, from a purely economic viewpoint and assuming undistorted equilibrium prices, it is advantageous to supply eastern Canada with overseas oil. When the federal government launched its two-price oil policy aimed at decoupling Canada from the United States and the rest of the world, a 'one Canada' oil policy was simultaneously launched, aimed at placing the Montreal oil market within the orbit of the Alberta oil supply system. Linking Montreal to Alberta oil by pipeline is the most expensive and wasteful way to supply Montreal with oil, and this fact generated serious concern among those likely to pay for the additional costs, namely Alberta, Quebec, and the petroleum industry.

The freeze on domestic oil prices announced in September 1973, however, made the Sarnia-Montreal pipeline appear economically attractive to Quebec as overseas oil prices continued to rise. Moreover, the OAPEC oil embargo brought to bear in October 1973 occurred at a very opportune time for the proponents of the controversial policy to supply the Montreal market and perhaps other markets further east with Alberta oil.

It is here contended that the security-of-oil-supply problem in eastern Canada demands a global solution and a much wider perspective than that underlying the policy to decouple the Canadian oil market from the world oil economy. Security of supply may well be achieved through interdependence rather than through independence of the Canadian oil economy. It is high time that comprehensive studies be made of the major options for security through interdependence. One of these options would feature, for example, a Montreal to Sarnia oil pipeline link which would supply part of the growing Ontario oil market. A strategic oil reserve would be accumulated in the immense underground salt reservoirs underlying the Magdalen islands. This reservoir can hold several years' supply of oil for eastern Canada, including Ontario and part of New England as well.

The higher oil prices that Alberta oil would command in its natural market (the Chicago market) would then justify a reduction of oil-producing rates from the high-productivity oilfields of western Canada. These oilfields would then serve as a strategic oil reserve to meet peak demand in the markets linked to Alberta by pipeline. Alberta's oil reserves are quite modest by Middle East standards; but the productivities, that is, the capacity to produce from certain oilfields of western Canada, are comparable to those in the Middle East. Leduc reef reservoirs such as the Bonnie Glenn or Wizard Lake fields in Alberta are presently prorated at a small fraction of their potential producing capacity. Throttling back such oilfields to the current allowable producing rates is a misuse of capability, somewhat comparable to the misuse of a Ferrari engine to power a city bus. It would be preferable to hold back still further or even shut down such oilfields under normal demand conditions and open them up at high rates of production during peak demand periods. In effect this option would capitalize on the reserve production capacity of western Canada's high-productivity formations and provide not only the commodity (barrels of oil) but also the service, in terms of added security of supply to meet peak demand and emergency shortages. This service is a function of the value assigned to security of oil supply and of the savings realized in synthetic oil-producing capacities such as tar sand oil plants and coal liquefaction (methanol) plants. Idle capacity in such plants would be several orders of magnitude more expensive than in high-productivity oilfields such as the Leduc reef reservoirs of western Canada.

This option is one of many that ought to be assessed before deciding on Canada's oil policy in the coming decades. Many important multinational considerations seem to have been overlooked in the policy studies performed to date. One such consideration is that it is in the interest of Canada and the US to see the world price of oil increase, first because both countries are marginally dependent on foreign oil imports, unlike their industrial competitors such as Western Europe and Japan; secondly, because an increase in the price of oil enhances the economic attractiveness of alternate sources of North American oil supply such as arctic oil and synthetic crudes. Likewise, not enough thought has been given to the proposition that another oil embargo by OAPEC is very unlikely in the future. There are good reasons to believe that the present Geneva negotiations for a Middle East peace should provide a few years of relative peace and avert another oil embargo during the critical five or six years needed by the United States to become energy-sufficient in time of crisis. An oil embargo in five or six years or any time thereafter would have little effect on the US and would therefore cease to have any leverage value to OAPEC on US foreign policy in the Middle East.

It also seems that the avenues for mutually beneficial co-operation between Canada and the United States in the energy field are highly promising and should be seriously explored. Tar sand oil and refined petroleum products for the US market offer very attractive prospects for Canada within the context of a North American economic community or common market. Likewise, the possibilities of Canada-OPEC co-operation are very promising if eastern Canada becomes the major importer and refiner of oil for the eastern seabord, including New England.

Finally, not enough thought seems to have been given to the pros and cons of a single Canadian national oil company as opposed to provincial oil companies or agencies such as SOQUIP in Quebec or Alberta's Oil Marketing Board. These can more effectively operate within a regional competitive system to serve the best interest of their respective provinces. A national oil company engaged in oil supply and distribution would inevitably draw upon itself suspicions of favoritism and unfair treatment from the various regions of Canada, the interests of which are so diverse.

In the field of oil and gas exploration, the industry's great asset is its talent and experience. Devising appropriate incentives to direct this talent to develop the needed domestic oil and gas reserves would be far preferable to alienating this talent through arbitrary and unfair prize freezes. Conversely, it should be pointed out that while government-controlled corporations have proven quite effective in some instances in the oil refining and products retailing operations such as in Italy, they have conspiciously failed to date to find significant oil and gas reserves except in the USSR.

In the light of the foregoing, it is concluded that the Prime Minister's energy policy proposal of 6 December 1973 should be viewed as a basis for discussion rather than as a blueprint for Canadian oil policy in the coming decades. Important policy options are yet to be assessed and it is hoped that the participatory democratic process which Mr Trudeau has endeavored to promote will have an opportunity to help shape Canada's new oil policy.

NOTES

1 Bernard Cloutier et David Vincent, *Evolution de la Structure Mondiale de l'Industrie Pétrolière,* Société Québécoise d'Initiatives Pétrolières, Editor, Ste Foy, Québec, Dec. 1973, p. 34
2 Paul D. Torrey, *Problems Created by Petroleum Imports,* Congressional Hearings, Eighty-Seventh Congress, pursuant to H.Res. 46, Washington DC, 27-29 Nov. 1961, pp. 842-8

3 J.W. Fraser and W.G. Lugg, 'Petroleum and Natural Gas Industry in Canada 1963-1968,' *Mineral Information Bulletin* MR104, Department of Energy, Mines and Resources, Ottawa, 1970, p. 114

4 Office of Oil and Gas, *Cost of the Oil Import Program to the American Economy*, Report of the Department of the Interior, Washington DC, 14 Jan. 1969, p. 1

5 Henry Borden, et al., *Second Report of the Royal Commission of Enquiry on Energy*, chapter 6, Conclusions and Recommendations, Ottawa, 1960

6 Department of Energy, Mines and Resources, *An Energy Policy for Canada*, Phase 1, Volume II, pp. 218-24

7 J.G. Debanné, 'A Model for Continental Oil Supply and Distribution,' *Journal of Petroleum Technology*, September 1971, pp. 1089-1100

8 *Petroleum Press Service*, Sept. 1972, p. 321

9 Unlike the US where the multinationals have been harassed for years for alleged price-fixing practices, little if anything was ever done in Canada before 1973 to control retail prices of petroleum products.

10 Bernard Cloutier et David Vincent, *Evolution*, pp. 181-2

11 Spot purchases of Venezuelan crude from independent producers are reported at discounts of $0.75 /Bbl (*Platt's Oilgram*, 30 Jan. 1958) and at $0.50 to $0.59 /Bbl (*Platt's Oilgram*, Nov. 1971).

12 *Petroleum Press Service*, Sept. 1972, p. 321

13 Henry Borden et al., *Second Report*

14 The first oil boom took place during World War II in the Turner Valley field and was stimulated by government financial assistance for security-of-supply reasons.

15 Bernard Cloutier et David Vincent, *Evolution*, pp. 181-2

16 P.E. Trudeau, *Hansard*, Ottawa, 6 Dec. 1973, pp. 8478-84

17 Bernard Cloutier et David Vincent, *Evolution*, p. 68; 'U.S. oil companies unable to fill orders from garages,' *Ottawa Journal* (*Associated Press*), 31 March 1973, p. 20

18 T.C. Douglas, *Hansard*, 5 Dec. 1973, p. 8452

19 P.E. Trudeau, *Hansard*

20 Department of Energy, Mines and Resources, 'Bill C-236,' First Session, Twenty-Ninth Parliament, House of Commons, Canada, 3 Dec. 1973

21 J.G. Debanné, 'Canadian Energy Resources for Home Consumption or Export,' *Proceedings of the Energy 2001 Seminar*, Sarnia Professional Council, Sarnia, February 1973

22 Mohammed S. Al-Mahdi, 'View Concerning some Future Prospects of the Oil-Exporting Countries,' *International Symposium on Petroleum Economy*, Laval University, Quebec City, March 1973, p. 6

23 J.G. Debanné, 'A Systems Approach for Oil and Gas Policy and Planning in North America,' *Proceedings of the 8th World Petroleum Congress,* Moscow, June 1971, London, Elsevier Publishing Co.

24 As reported by Mr T.C. Douglas, *Hansard,* 6 Dec. 1973, p. 8454

25 In effect, instead of a 'depletion allowance,' we would have a 'reserve maintenance commitment' or a 'depletion obligation'

26 Leonard Waverman, *Natural Gas and National Policy: A Linear Programming Model of North American Natural Gas Flows,* Toronto, 1973

27 J.G. Debanné, 'A Model for Continental Oil Supply'

28 J.G. Debanné, 'La Conjoncture Internationale et l'Approvisionnement en Pétrole L'Outremer,' Report to the Quebec Government, December 1973

Natural gas spearheaded the energy controversy which threatens Canada's national fabric. In the fall of 1972, Alberta – the province producing nearly 90 per cent of natural gas consumed within Canada – demanded that all contracts be rewritten to increase the price of natural gas by 10¢ per mcf (approximately a 40 per cent increase). The low price of gas was probably due to three factors. Trans Canada Pipeline Company is the sole purchaser of gas for resale in Canada east of Alberta, and that pipeline probably used monopsonistic pressure to keep prices low. Second, wellhead regulation of natural gas in the US kept comparable gas prices low. Finally, most gas sales are on twenty-year contracts, with limited escalation clauses. The rapidly rising prices of gas's major competitor – oil – made 1973 gas at 1960 prices a real bargain.

Hamilton details the many currents and cross-currents which have shaped Canadian natural gas policy since the early 1950s. He finds that government policy has largely been ineffective in capturing for Canadians the profits accruing from natural gas production.

As companion pieces read Starratt & Spann on American natural gas, Debanné on oil, Waverman on Canadian policy, and Helliwell on the economics of Arctic gas pipelines.

RICHARD E. HAMILTON

Natural gas and Canadian policy

Canada has the good fortune to possess substantial reserves of natural gas and to enjoy a seller's market. It is also faced with the prospect of having to construct large transportation systems to bring the most recently discovered reserves to market from their isolated locations in the far north, projects so large they could have a significant impact on the economy. The following survey will provide some background and discuss some implications of these features of the Canadian industry. The most important conclusion will be that increased United States demands will necessitate fundamental changes in government policy if Canadians are to capture the rent resulting from the expected higher prices.

PRODUCTION AND RESERVES

Some historical statistics for the Canadian gas industry are shown in Table 1. In 1972 domestic sales of domestic natural gas were 1146 billion cubic feet (Bcf), exports were 1009 Bcf, and imports were 16 Bcf. Proved reserves at the end of 1971 were 55.5 trillion cubic feet (Tcf). These reserves, together with expected additions in western Canada, are probably enough to meet Canadian requirements, plus existing export commitments of 17.2 Tcf, until the late 1980s. Since this point is relevant for the question of whether Canada can afford to postpone the construction of a Mackenzie Valley gas pipeline, it is worth while to quote at length from some evidence given by the vice-chairman of the National Energy Board (NEB).

'If one assumes that this historical rate (of additions to "established reserves" of 3.8 Tcf per year from the western Canada sedimentary basin) will continue

149

TABLE 1

Selected statistics for the Canadian gas industry 1955-72
(billion cubic feet)

Year	Remaining proved reserves at beginning of year[1]	Revisions and extensions[1]	Discoveries[1]	Net change in underground storage[1]	Net production[1]	Net change in reserves during year[1]	Domestic sales[2]	Exports[2]	Imports[2]
1955	12,629	1641	514	4	146	2013	137		
1956	14,642	2157	650	4	193	2619	164		
1957	17,261	515	699	3	244	974	185	16	
1958	18,234	2156	431	2	335	2254	212	87	
1959	20,488	2663	696	34	438	2935	284	85	
1960	23,423	3786	255	5	475	3571	326	91	
1961	26,994	2690	546	-3	694	2542	371	169	5
1962	29,536	2125	393	-4	836	1681	412	343	5
1963	31,217	1494	1159	26	904	1775	452	360	7
1964	32,992	6823	487	28	1009	6327	505	392	10
1965	39,320	1507	623	-8	1088	1035	573	405	18
1966	40,355	3691	512	18	1125	3096	636	432	45
1967	43,450	2840	603	4	1216	2232	695	513	70
1968	45,682	3097	283	-1	1395	1984	766	604	82
1969	47,666	4734	1104	2	1557	4285	845	680	35
1970	51,951	3010	194	20	1799	1425	917	779	11
1971	53,376	3264	776		1953	2086	1001	911	14
1972	55,462						1146[3]	1009[3]	16[3]

SOURCES:

1 American Gas Association, American Petroleum Institute, Canadian Petroleum Association, *Reserves of Crude Oil, Natural Gas Liquids, and Natural Gas in the United States and Canada and United States Productive Capacity as of December 31, 1971* (Volume 26, May 1972), p. 229.

2 *Statistics Canada, The Crude Petroleum and Natural Gas Industry*, annual volumes 1955 to 1972; export figures for 1957 to 1960 are from *Trade of Canada, Exports*.

3 Statistics Canada, *Canadian Statistical Review*, March 1973.

for the next three years and the rate of additions will decline thereafter by gradual steps to a level of perhaps 500 Bcf by the late 1980s and if one assumes that the domestic demand increases about 6 per cent per year (faster than the NEB expects) from a level of about 1.4 Tcf per year estimated for 1972 to 3.3 trillion in 1991, and if one further estimates or postulates that no additional exports will be authorized beyond the present level – this for purposes of discussion – no difficulties are anticipated in meeting the total annual and peak day requirements for gas in the period up to the latter years of the next decade, the eighties.'[1]

While nearly all of Canada's present gas production takes place in the western Canada sedimentary basin, it is probable that large additional quantities could be brought to market by the mid 1980s from the Mackenzie Delta, the Arctic Islands, and eastern offshore areas. Unofficial estimates of proven reserves at the end of 1972 suggest 15 Tcf for the Mackenzie Delta and 13 Tcf for the Arctic Islands.[2] Delta gas discoveries may already have reached the minimum needed to support a pipeline, and the threshold volume of 25 to 30 Tcf for the Arctic Islands may be reached before the end of 1974.

In addition to conventional supplies there are prospects of gas from processing of tar sands, heavy oils, and coal.

Although Canada's natural gas resources are ample to meet its own foreseeable requirements they are not enough to make more than a marginal contribution toward satisfying United States needs. In 1970 Canadian exports of .8 Tcf amounted to only $3\frac{1}{2}$ per cent of United States consumption.[3]

THE CANADIAN GAS INDUSTRY

Two pipeline companies buy gas from producers in western Canada and transport it for sale to domestic distribution companies. They are Westcoast Transmission Company Limited, which serves British Columbia, and TransCanada PipeLines Limited, which serves Saskatchewan, Manitoba, Ontario, and Quebec. These two companies serve not only domestic markets but, along with Alberta and Southern Gas Company Limited and Canadian-Montana Pipeline Company, hold nearly all existing licenses to export gas to the United States. Other companies, including Consolidated Natural Gas Limited, Saskatchewan Power Corporation, Pan-Alberta Gas Limited, and Alberta distribution companies and industries, have purchased gas from producers in western Canada, while several United States companies have made contracts with producers in the Arctic.

The pipeline companies make purchase contracts for periods of twenty years or more, with deliveries beginning two to four years after signing.[4] The contracts usually contain 'take-or-pay' clauses, which require buyers to pay for specified minimum annual quantities whether or not they take delivery of such quantities.

151

They also specify the maximum daily amounts which sellers are obligated to supply at buyers' requests. The contracts stipulate an initial price plus various provisions for price increases in subsequent years. These provisions, which vary from one contract to another, include fixed price escalations at regular intervals, periodic renegotiation of prices, and several types of favored-nation clauses. One type of favored-nation clause, for example, requires the buyer to increase his payments to a particular seller if his price to this seller is less than the average price of all gas purchased by him in the preceding year in the general region.

In the past few years some contracts have provided for lump-sum prepayments to the seller at the time the contracts are executed. These are interest-free loans intended to encourage the establishment of new reserves. They are usually paid back during the early years of gas delivery. Interest-free loans have also been used by American gas-distribution companies as a means to invest large sums of money in exploration ventures in the Arctic and offshore. Commitments for as much as $200 million were made by this means in Canada during 1972.[5]

No full-scale study has ever been made of the nature and extent of competition in field markets for gas in Canada, but what evidence there is suggests that competition has been stronger among producers than buyers. In 1971 the largest single producer accounted for 9 per cent of total Canadian production; the top five producers accounted for 39 per cent, the top ten for 61 per cent, and the top twenty for 77 per cent.[6] Before 1957 TransCanada was the sole major buyer of gas for removal from Alberta and between 1957 and 1968 TransCanada and Alberta and Southern were the only major buyers. Consolidated Natural Gas Limited generated stiff competition for the next two years, but then it withdrew after its export applications were rejected by the NEB in 1970 and 1971. In 1972 Pan-Alberta Gas Limited began making purchases. There is in addition some competition from local buyers. Westcoast has always been the sole buyer in its main supply area, which is in an isolated part of north-eastern British Columbia. As will be explained below, the Alberta government has been attempting to change the imbalance in that province.

The pattern of competition may be different in Arctic gas fields. On the one hand, production is likely to be more concentrated on a few producers than in Alberta. On the other, competition may be greater among buyers than in Alberta since the pipeline companies would act as 'contract carriers' for any buyers who wish to transport gas.

A prominent feature of the Canadian gas industry is the large amount of foreign (chiefly American) ownership. In 1970, 76 per cent of profits of companies in the mineral-fuels, petroleum, and coal-products industries accrued to foreign shareholders.[7] While TransCanada is overwhelmingly Canadian-owned, Westcoast may be less than 50 per cent Canadian, and Alberta and Southern and Canadian-Montana are American-owned and controlled.

The predominance of foreign ownership creates a danger that much of the rent from Canadian gas production could accrue to foreign shareholders as supernormal profits. Rent refers to the value of a natural resource minus the costs of finding and producing including a normal rate of return which takes risk into account. Since the amount of rent varies from zero on marginal projects to very large levels on the most productive and best located projects above the margin, it is difficult to devise methods of ensuring that mineral right owners collect this rent without discouraging investment in marginal projects.[8] A uniform royalty of, say, 10 per cent of the value of production would fail to capture all the rent on the best projects above the margin but would cut into legitimate producer profits on marginal ventures. In Canada, governments own most of the mineral rights. If they are more concerned with encouraging exploration than with capturing rent they may impose overly generous incentives. This policy would result in much of the rent going to the producing companies. For Canadian-owned companies, this creates a problem of the distribution of the rent among groups in the country. For foreign-owned companies, the portion of the rent captured by foreign shareholders would be lost by Canada.

ALBERTA POLICIES

Since Alberta accounts for more than 80 per cent of Canadian gas production, I shall confine my discussion of provincial policies to this province.

The British North America Act gives to the provinces powers to make laws with respect to natural resources located within their boundaries. These powers, together with its possession of subsurface rights to 81 per cent of the land area, have permitted the Alberta government to become deeply involved in the province's gas industry. Indeed, it might be argued that this involvement has gone too far and extends into an area of jurisdiction belonging to the federal government, by virtue of its power to regulate trade and commerce.

Alberta derives revenues from gas producers chiefly in the form of fees, lease bonus payments, and royalties. The regulations governing these revenues are very complicated and vary among various types of government land grants.[9] The following discussion pertains to only one type, called 'Petroleum and Natural Gas Reservations.' On payment of a cash bonus at an auction, a reservation fee of $250, and a performance fee of $2500 for each 20,000 acres or less, an applicant can obtain drilling rights for up to 100,000 acres of land. Reservation holders are given three to five years in which to drill a well, depending upon accessibility, but for the last two years they must pay a fee of ten cents an acre every six months. Further extensions of up to eighteen months can be granted for the purpose of carrying out further exploration. If natural gas is discovered, the reservation holder is allowed to convert up to 50 per cent of his reservation into a ten-year lease for which he must pay a rental of 50 cents per acre per year. A unique feature of Alberta's lease system is that the area converted into lease must consist of blocks either placed in a checker board pattern such that they may touch each other only at corners, or separated from each other by a distance of not less than one mile. The area returned to the government is then auctioned off to the highest bidder. The reservation holder is normally able to retain well over 50 per cent of any pool he discovers in the 50 per cent of the reservation acreage he selects, despite the block-spacing regulations. The revenue, however, received by the government through auctions of the remaining acreage has occasionally been very large.

The government collects a royalty of $16\frac{2}{3}$ per cent of the price of processed natural gas. Since sulphur and other materials are removed from natural gas during processing, the $16\frac{2}{3}$ per cent on processed gas represents a significantly smaller percentage of the value of raw gas in the field. There are indications that the royalty rate will be increased from $16\frac{2}{3}$ per cent of the price of processed gas to 22 per cent of the field price.

Alberta's Energy Resources Conservation Board (ERCB) performs several functions relating to natural gas.[10] First, it attempts to limit the amount of gas flared to the quantities 'which experience indicates would not be economical to conserve having regard for the nature of the production and conservation system.'[11] Whether because of the board's actions or because of the rise in gas prices, the proportion of oil field gas flared fell from 43 per cent in 1961 to 16 per cent in 1971.[12]

Second, the board operates an exportable surplus policy.[13] It will approve for removal from the province only such quantities of gas which it is satisfied are surplus to both the contractable and future requirements of the province. Contractable requirements include existing export commitments plus Alberta requirements defined as the greater of thirty times the requirements for delivery in the first year of the period under consideration or the remaining reserves in those fields committed to and supplying Alberta's requirements. Contractable requirements must be covered by established reserves less reserves from which initial production is deferred beyond three years and which are not under firm contract to a company removing gas from a province. Future requirements include contractable requirements plus estimated growth in Alberta consumption over thirty years, with a cushion for peak day consumption in the thirtieth year. These requirements must be covered out of anticipated additions to established reserves. Not only must there be a surplus for export but the applicant must have under contract approximately 80 per cent of the total volume of gas for which he is seeking an export permit.

In August 1972, following a public hearing, the board published a report in which the principal finding was that the average field price for gas in Alberta of 16 cents was at least 10 cents less than the 'field value' of the gas.[14] The report attributed the depressed price level to insufficient competition among buyers, the NEB's failure to grant export licenses for all the export quantities requested in 1970 and 1971, and the effects of regulatory lag in preventing gas prices to ultimate consumers from rising in response to the large increases which had occurred in the prices of competing fuels. Among its recommendations was a proposal that all purchase contracts covering gas for removal from the province be required to include a base price consistent with the field value of the gas at the time of negotiation of the contract plus regular price escalation amounting to some 3 or 4 per cent of the base price per year.

The Alberta government responded vigorously. In the fall of 1972 the premier, Peter Lougheed, announced the government's intention of forcing buyers of gas for removal from the province to comply with the board's recommendations.[15] In addition, the government demanded that contracts be revised to include provision for price redetermination every two years rather than every five years as recommended by the board.[16] At about the same time Pan-Alberta Gas Limited was making contracts to buy gas at 38 cents per million cubic feet (Mcf) with increases to 42 cents over a five-year period.[17] The company felt confident that such prices were not excessive since it expected that Mackenzie Delta gas would pass through Alberta by 1980 at a price of 75 cents. By spring 1973 the company had accumulated enough gas to apply to the ERCB for a removal permit (the gas is intended for United States markets). In the meantime Alberta authorities have withheld approval from TransCanada to remove large quantities of gas contracted in the past two years because the company has refused to revise its contracts sufficiently to meet the government's new price terms.

The government's intervention has altered the bargaining relationship between buyers and sellers, giving to the latter the advantage that was previously enjoyed by the former. This action comes at a propitious time for producers since prospective price increases resulting from increased United States demands are expected to be enormous. A report prepared by the Stanford Research Institute estimated that the field value of Alberta gas would be 29 cents higher than 1970 prices by 1975, 48 cents by 1980, 71 cents by 1985, and 82 cents by 1990.[18]

Large profits for producing companies do not imply large benefits to Canada. Because of the prevalence of foreign ownership, the gains to Canada from gas price increases in Alberta will likely be small even if the royalty rate is increased to 22 per cent of the field price. To demonstrate this finding it is convenient to divide production into two parts: the part which would occur in the absence of the price change, and the part attributable to higher prices. For part I, Canadian shareholders and governments would receive $56 for every $100 of additional revenue caused by an increase in price from 16 cents per Mcf in 1972 to 40 cents, and foreign shareholders would be entitled to receive $44.[19] It seems legitimate to suggest that prior to 1971 producers did not anticipate prices anywhere close to 40 cents. Therefore, much of the gain to foreign shareholders would probably be windfall profits which could justifiably be taxed away. It would be desirable if a way could be found to tax part I production separately from part II.

The $56 figure measures the gross gain to Canada for part I production. To find the net gain it is necessary to subtract the increased costs imposed on Canadian consumers of Alberta gas. We assume that 53 per cent of part I gas would be sold to domestic customers. This was the actual percentage for 1971.[20] Thus for every $100 increase in gas revenue, Canadian consumers would have to pay $53, which is only $3 less than the gain to Canadian governments and shareholders. For each $100 of revenue obtained from part II production, the net gain to Canada would be $34 and the gain to foreign shareholders would be $13.[21]

To calculate the combined benefits of production from parts I and II, it is necessary to determine the increase in production attributable to higher prices. *The Report on Field Pricing of Gas in Alberta* estimated that a 10 cent increase in field prices would cause a 10 per cent increase in exploration expenditures leading to a 10 per cent increase in annual reserves during the mid 1970s of 300 Bcf, and an increase in the rate of production in 1975 of 20 Bcf.[22] Since 20 Bcf is less than 1 per cent of 1975 production, it seems plausible to assume that the rate of production would increase by more than 1 per cent in later years, perhaps by as much as 10 per cent. Increased recovery of gas in place through longer operation of wells would add 5 Tcf to reserves. Another 5 Tcf would be gained by the inclusion of marginal reserves which have production capabilities that are too small to justify expenditures on wells and pipelines at 1971 prices. These two changes would increase 1975 production by 150 Bcf. A final gain consists of an increment to oil-field gas reserves of 5 Tcf leading to a 10 to 15 Bcf increase in 1975 production. The total increase for 1975 was estimated to be 200 Bcf, approximately 9 per cent. The increase in later years would presumably be greater, perhaps as much as 20 per cent. Even a 20 per cent increase in production is less than one in proportion to the increase in prices.

The Alberta report's assumed field-price increase of 10 cents with the royalty rate unchanged implies a 9.1 cent increase in prices net of royalty. Our 24 cent increase with a higher royalty rate corresponds to a 16.6 cent increase in prices net of royalty. If a 9.1 cent increase in net prices adds only 10 per cent to production in 1975 and 20 per cent in later years, a 16.6 cent increase is unlikely to add more than 15 per cent in 1975 and 30 per cent in later years. An average increase in net prices of 16.6 cents would probably not be achieved until after 1975. Part II production is therefore assumed to be 30 per cent of part I production. This is obviously a rough estimate.

The overall net gain to Canada from combined part I and part II production will vary between $3 and $34 for every $100 increase in revenue, depending on the size of part II production, and the gain to foreign shareholders will vary between $44 and $13. For part II production equal to 30 per cent of part I the net gain to Canada would be $13 and the gain to foreign shareholders would be $34.[23] The net gain to Alberta would be $21 plus regional multiplier effects on income and employment as a result of larger expenditures by the Alberta gas industry.[24] The rest of Canada would suffer a direct loss of $8 plus the indirect effect of resources diverted to Alberta.

FEDERAL TAX AND LAND POLICIES

Federal tax and land policies will be discussed here only briefly since they are dealt with at length in the article by Hyndman and Bucovetsky.

Corporation tax provisions permit producing companies to deduct costs of exploration and development from income from any source. Companies may also deduct one-third of their taxable income as depletion allowances. These provisions strongly favor the petroleum industry relative to other sectors of the economy. In 1970 the ratio of corporate income taxes to profits estimated on the National Accounts basis for corporations in the mineral fuels industry with assets of $1,000,000 or over was only 14 per cent.[25] The average for all manufacturing was 46 per cent and for non-financial industries 38 per cent. The Tax Reform Act of 1971 reduced this bias only partially by ruling that starting in 1977 depletion deductions would have to be limited to amounts 'earned' on the basis of $1 for every $3 of eligible expenditures on exploration and development.

The federal government's present leasing and royalty regulations are much more generous than Alberta's.[26] Permit terms are longer, ranging from nine years to twelve years depending on location, and the fees and rentals are less. Leases are for twenty-one years, and permittees are allowed to convert their entire permit areas into leases, though the 50 per cent of the acreage that is not selected in a block spacing pattern like Alberta's is subject to a higher royalty. The royalty rate on primary leases is 5 per cent of the well-head or plant-gate price for the first three years of commercial exploitation (up to five years north of latitude 70° if production is not continuous) and 10 per cent thereafter. There are indications that in planned revisions of federal land regulations royalty rates may be as high as $46\frac{2}{3}$ per cent on the secondary 50 per cent of the acreage selected by the leaseholder, depending on the rate of production.

A TRANS-CANADA PIPELINE

Two fundamental events in the history of the Canadian gas industry were the decisions to build a west-east pipeline from Alberta to Quebec and to locate the line entirely within Canada.[27] From a continental point of view a more efficient decision would probably have involved a north-south pattern of gas flows with western Canadian gas being exported to United States markets and eastern Canadian consumers being served by American gas. This conclusion is reinforced by the consideration that it was necessary for the federal government to make a loan to TransCanada and to build the northern Ontario portion of the line itself through a crown corporation. Indeed, while TransCanada paid back the loan promptly and purchased the northern Ontario line from the government, the company has never been particularly profitable, and one can argue that an important function to the NEB has been to ensure its commercial viability.[28] With the aid of a linear programming model of North American gas flows, Leonard Waverman has estimated that the decisions to build the TransCanada pipeline and to restrict imports of American gas to the negligible quantities cost eastern Canadian consumers $18,400,000 in 1966.[29]

It is difficult to determine whether the benefits of allegedly greater national unity and greater security of supply exceed the costs. Under free trade eastern Canada might have been exposed to the same shortages which US consumers have experienced in the past few years. Furthermore, the trade policy options available to the Canadian government would have been diminished, since export controls (for example, an export tax) might well have led to United States controls on exports to eastern Canada.

THE NATIONAL ENERGY BOARD'S EXPORTABLE SURPLUS POLICY

The National Energy Board was established in 1959 on the recommendation of the Royal Commission on Energy (the Borden Commission). In accordance with Section 83 of the National Energy Board Act the NEB devised an exportable surplus policy very similar to that in Alberta.

Before recommending the issuance of a new export license, the board must satisfy itself that a surplus exists after fulfilling the condition that 'available' reserves (including 'contractable' reserves plus remaining volumes under existing export licenses) meet Canadian requirements of thirty times the estimated first year demand for Alberta and twenty-five times the estimated fourth year requirement for the rest of Canada, plus existing export commitments. 'Contractable' reserves are defined as established reserves minus 50 per cent of reserves categorized as beyond economic reach, and minus a portion of deferred reserves from which production is not expected to occur within a few years. The board also attempts to determine whether the expected future growth of reserves will exceed the expected growth of domestic requirements, but in its August 1970 decision it recommended that the government grant export licenses even though future reserves appeared to fall short of requirements.[30]

The NEB applies three guidelines to ensure that export prices are 'just and reasonable in relation to the public interest.' The first is that the export price should cover all relevant costs including a fair return on the whole capital investment. The second is that the export price should be 'fair in relation to the prices charged to Canadian distributors in the area adjacent to the point of export, with due allowance being made for variations in the terms and conditions of sale.' The third is that the price charged to foreign buyers should not be appreciably less than the prices of alternative sources of fuel to those consumers.

The August 1970 and November 1971 decisions are the only occasions on which the NEB has turned down applications on grounds of lack of surplus. In 1971 all applications, involving 2.6 Tcf of gas, were rejected. In 1970 the application by Consolidated Natural Gas was refused, and the quantities requested by other applicants were reduced by shortening the terms of the licenses. The overall reduction was from 9 Tcf to 6.3 Tcf. Where previously licenses had been granted for twenty-five-year terms the NEB expressed a preference for fifteen year licenses, but on this occasion it recommended terms of twenty years and nineteen years for TransCanada and Westcoast respectively to facilitate pipeline financing.

The principal rationale for the rule that there be sufficient reserves to meet twenty-five times the fourth year domestic requirement seems to be related to contracting practices by pipeline companies, which in turn are related to financing requirements. On the assumption that Canadian pipeline companies normally make contracts for twenty-five years with deliveries beginning four years after signing, the NEB's formula would help assure Canadian pipeline companies of enough gas for domestic sales before exports are permitted. A plausible economic argument for this formula is that regulatory delays by the NEB and by provincial regulatory agencies could on occasion impose financial hardship on companies serving Canadian markets and thus limit their ability to acquire all the gas they need during periods when there is strong competition from American buyers, with the result that temporary shortages could occur in Canada (i.e.,

159

short-run situations in which ultimate Canadian consumers cannot get all the gas they would like to buy at going prices). If this rationale is accepted, and if buying practices continue to change toward shorter contract terms and earlier deliveries, it might be legitimate for the NEB to relax its rule accordingly.

It would be even more desirable to examine the imperfections that could lead to shortages to see if a better policy can be devised. For the exportable surplus policy imposes substantial costs: regulatory expenses, interest costs for locked-in gas, and costs resulting from uncertainties created by the possibility of exports being prohibited. Nevertheless, it is significant that gas shortages have not been experienced in Canada up to now.[31] Another justification for the exportable surplus policy is to conserve Canadian gas resources for long-term future use. If so, the 25 times 4 formula is only a rough rule of thumb for achieving the optimal degree of conservation. A better approach would involve consideration of the reasons why unrestricted exports are alleged to result in excessively rapid depletion.

The NEB has encountered little difficulty in ensuring that the first two price guidelines are met. The first guideline is most explicitly satisfied by existing Alberta and Southern and Canadian-Montana export contracts which set export prices equal to costs of service, with the result that regardless of how costs move during the terms of export licenses the prices are adjusted by the same amounts so that at no time is it possible for a price to be less than the corresponding cost.

In the 1950s, before the NEB was established, Westcoast was granted a license to make export sales at a price of twenty-two cents per Mcf at the same time as it charged domestic buyers thirty-one cents.[32] This episode is the origin of the second price guideline. Since 1970 the NEB has required TransCanada and Westcoast to incorporate clauses into their export contracts which provide that border prices be at least 105 per cent of rates in the adjacent domestic zones. The board has not been able to apply the second guideline in this direct way for companies which serve only export markets because there is no Canadian market for these companies to serve as a base for comparison, but it has sought to establish that border prices for these companies are reasonable in relation to neighboring domestic prices before granting export licenses.

The most serious difficulties involve the third guideline. The board must estimate the appropriate prices for natural gas and alternative fuels, not only for the first year of licensed export sales but for each subsequent year as well, for up to twenty years into the future, and then it must insist that companies export at these prices. In order to make these estimates it is partly dependent for information on the companies, at least two of whom have an incentive to set border prices at less than maximum levels, as suggested by their use of cost-of-service prices.

Alberta and Southern and Canadian-Montana are both owned by American distribution companies (Pacific Gas and Electric Company and Montana Power Company, respectively). For these companies border prices are intrafirm transfer prices which could be fixed at levels quite different from prices negotiated by unaffiliated companies. There are several reasons why these companies have an incentive to set low border prices. First, if border prices exceed costs producers will insist on higher field prices. Indeed, renegotiation of field prices in this situation was recommended by the *Report on Field Pricing of Gas in Alberta.*[33] Second, if these companies can get licenses from the NEB at low prices they should have less difficulty getting import approval from the Federal Power Commission. Third, there is a withholding tax of 10 per cent on dividends sent abroad to foreign shareholders.

After the August 1970 export decision the government instructed the NEB to undertake regular reviews of fuel prices in export markets served by Canadian gas and to notify the cabinet of any increases in prices of competing sources of energy.[34] In March 1973 the chairman of the NEB admitted to the House of Commons' Standing Committee on National Resources and Public Works that competitive fuel prices had risen significantly relative to Canadian gas prices in US markets.[35] When asked why the board had not reported this finding to the cabinet, the chairman replied that the board considered that its primary duty was to achieve concrete results and that it had been attempting to do this by working directly with the export companies. At the NEB's request, these companies had in several instances amended the price terms in their contracts. He also expressed concern to avoid a confrontation with the Federal Power Commission. One confrontation had already occurred in 1967 after the FPC refused to grant import authorization for gas to be exported by Westcoast on grounds that the price terms were unacceptable. In this case a compromise solution was eventually reached.

To the extent that Alberta's efforts to increase field prices are successful the NEB will be in a better position to ensure that the third price guideline is satisfied on future export licenses. However, there still remains a serious difficulty. Even if the third price guideline is met the benefits of the higher prices will not necessarily accrue to Canada. This problem is due to the prevalence of foreign ownership in both the producing firms and the pipeline companies. We must conclude that the NEB's price policies are by themselves insufficient to maximize the benefits to Canada from export sales of natural gas.

THE MACKENZIE VALLEY PIPELINE

When these words were written (June 1973) it was expected that Canadian Arctic Gas Study Limited would soon make an application to the National Energy

161

Board to build a 48-inch pipeline along the Mackenzie Valley with an extension to Alaska to connect with a line from Prudhoe Bay. Initial deliveries through the 2400-mile line could begin as early as 1978, with rates of more than 4 Bcf per day being achieved by 1980. Although more than 50 per cent of the gas flowing through the pipeline would be of Canadian origin, nearly all would be marketed in the United States, at least in the early years.

The project, which is estimated to cost more than $5 billion, has aroused considerable controversy. It could cause disruption to plant and animal life and could have an adverse impact on the 10,000 Indians, 14,000 Eskimos, and several thousand Métis living in the north, some of whom may have legitimate treaty claims to some of the territories affected by the project. In addition, there is concern that the project could have adverse short-term effects on the Canadian economy. More importantly, the major question is whether Canada, as a whole, benefits from constructing the pipeline at this time. Before approval is granted to construct the Mackenzie gas pipeline, various alternatives should be examined to provide a basis for comparison.[36]

Most reports assume that the government will require that the pipeline be 51 per cent Canadian-owned. There are questions concerning both the attainability and the desirability of this objective. Unless majority ownership were achieved by normal market forces or by government investment, it would be necessary to improve artifically the returns to investment in the pipeline by Canadians. But it is not clear how the improved returns could be limited to Canadians for the Canadian investors might sell their shares to foreigners at a later date. It would also be difficult to justify providing such a subsidy to Canadian investors. One way of achieving control by Canadians would be to establish a second corporate entity which would hold a majority of pipeline voting equity and would itself be Canadian-owned.

Some writers have argued that Canadian ownership is not necessary because NEB regulatory control could be used to realize the same objectives as could be achieved by Canadian ownership.[37] This view, however, implies a great deal of faith in the ability of regulatory authorities to prevent such abuses as the channeling of pipeline profits outside Canada by transfer-pricing techniques. Direct revenue benefits to Canadians will be less if the amount of Canadian ownership of the pipeline is less.

The Mackenzie gas pipeline is only the first of several projects for bringing petroleum resources from the Arctic. Others include pipelines (or alternative means of transportation) for bringing oil up the Mackenzie Valley and gas from the Arctic Islands.[38]

CONCLUSIONS

The foregoing survey has disclosed a substantial amount of government regulation of the gas industry. Alberta has used its regulatory powers aggressively; the federal government has been more passive. As an illustration of the contrasting approaches consider the difference in responses by the two levels of government to the discovery that gas export prices are too low.

The proliferation of regulation should be guarded against because regulation can be very costly. The exportable surplus policies are a case in point. Given that the NEB's policy automatically protects Alberta requirements, Alberta's policy would appear to be redundant. But there are difficulties with the NEB's policy as well. While it has successfully protected Canadian requirements, it has failed to obtain maximum prices and benefits on export sales. It is desirable to consider alternatives to this policy. One alternative that has the advantage of reducing the amount of regulation is an export tax. If set high enough the tax would be an improvement over the NEB's approach to the three price guidelines; it would give TransCanada and Westcoast the protection and incentive needed to obtain adequate supplies of gas for domestic consumers, and it would replace regulatory expenses and uncertainties for exporters with a source of revenue for the federal government, which could, if desired, be shared with producing provinces. If it is felt that an export tax would not do enough to provide for future Canadian requirements, or to raise export prices, another alternative is a federally operated marketing board entrusted with a monopoly to buy gas for interprovincial and international sales.[39] This board would not need to acquire any pipelines, but because of its position as the dominant buyer and seller of gas it would have sufficient power to allocate consumption over space and over time in order to fulfill conservation objectives, and it could insist on high export prices.

An important conclusion reached in the preceding discussion is that Canadian governments have been over-generous towards the gas industry. Evidence for this conclusion was found in the discussions of income tax provisions, royalty and lease arrangements, and in the NEB's approach to export price policies. Resource industries have clearly been favored by federal income tax laws relative to manufacturing industries. Such over-encouragement runs the risk of the country losing rent to foreign shareholders of companies operating in Canada; it distorts the economy in favor of capital-intensive, export-oriented activities, and it probably results in excessively rapid depletion of natural resources.

Even more important is the finding that existing policies will be much more inappropriate in the changed circumstances of the future. Now that world energy prices seem to be entering a period of large and continual increases attention

Richard E. Hamilton

should be directed towards finding ways of obtaining rent which are responsive to increases in prices but which have minimal adverse effects on production at the margin.[40] Royalties and lease arrangements should be revised. Serious consideration should be given to eliminating the depletion and expensing provisions for producing companies as recommended by the Carter Commission.[41] A tax on gas flowing through the Mackenzie pipeline should be implemented in order to recover government expenses and the costs of maintaining environmental quality directly related to the project. This tax would be in addition to the export tax on Canadian gas. Vigorous efforts should be made to increase Canadian participation in producing companies. If these suggestions were carried out, there would be much less need to be concerned about embarking on projects such as the Mackenzie gas pipeline. These changes may appear to be drastic, but without them profits of foreign-owned producing companies could increase to levels far above those which these companies would have found quite acceptable only a few years ago, and Canadians would be deprived of very large benefits to which they have legitimate claims.

Apart from the introduction of an export tax there is little need to consider policies to subsidize domestic gas consumption. Alberta's failure to attract much industry with gas prices one-third as large as those in Ontario suggests that subsidized gas prices are unlikely to provide much incentive to Canadian manufacturing industry. Increased taxation of gas production, by allowing taxes to be reduced for manufacturers, would probably have more effect. Quite possibly a major program to reduce air pollution could result in greatly expanded domestic consumption of gas in all sectors (including even buses, trucks, and automobiles). But it would probably be better to encourage this process by intervention on the demand side. It would even be preferable to tax other fuels than to subsidize gas since the tax would do more to economize on fuel consumption.

NOTES

Helpful comments on the first draft were provided by E.H. Shaffer, H. Schwartz, L. Waverman, and W.E. Zieman.

1 D.M. Fraser, House of Commons, *Minutes of Proceedings and Evidence of the Standing Committee on National Resources and Public Works,* 13 March 1973. The NEB's concept of 'established reserves' includes 100 per cent of proven reserves plus a varying percentage, not exceeding 50, of probable reserves. Its concept of probable reserves exclude proven reserves. The estimate for established reserves of 60.3 Tcf as of 30 June 1971 does not include any estimate for reserves in frontier areas such as the Arctic and offshore areas. The discrepancy between Mr Fraser's figure for domestic requirements of 1.4 Tcf in 1972

and the figure given above of 1.146 Tcf is probably due to the inclusion in Mr Fraser's estimate of pipeline fuel and losses.

2 Advisory Committee on Energy, *Energy in Ontario: The Outlook and Policy Implications,* vol. 2 (Toronto 1973), p. 46

3 American Gas Association, *Gas Facts 1971* (Arlington VA)

4 For details of contracts with Alberta producers see Energy Resources Conservation Board, *Report on Field Pricing of Gas in Alberta* (Calgary 1972), pp. 4-1 to 4-19.

5 Thomas Kennedy, *Globe and Mail,* Toronto, 12 Dec. 1972. One reason why these investments have been so large is that the Federal Power Commission has permitted companies to work these payments into their rate bases. For Canada the resulting exploration is beneficial, but such large investments give the gas companies proprietary rights to gas which is discovered, and policy-makers will be under some obligation to respect these rights when applications are made for export licenses and for permits to construct pipelines.

6 Stanford Research Institute, *The Market Price for Natural Gas from Sources in Western Canada, 1972-1990* (Menlo Park CA 1972), vol. I, pp. 222-3. That there are more than a few producers is not, of course, sufficient to prove the existence of a high degree of competition.

7 Based on data from Statistics Canada, *Corporations and Labour Unions Returns Act, Report for 1970, Part I - Corporations,* March 1973, p. 144, Table 2.44. This table gives the value of profits by industry for each of several classes of companies: those with 95-100 per cent foreign ownership, those with 75-94 per cent foreign ownership, ... those with 0-4.9 per cent foreign ownership. I calculated an average of the class midpoints after weighting each midpoint by the value of profits in the class. I included the petroleum and coal-products industry as well as the mineral-fuels industry since Statistics Canada assigns some integrated oil companies to the former industry.

8 A.P.H. Van Meurs, *Petroleum Economics and Offshore Mining Legislation* (Amsterdam, London, New York 1971), chap. VI

9 Government of the Province of Alberta, *The Mines and Minerals Act,* 1962, and associated *Regulations.* See also the paper by Bucovetsky and Hyndman, 'Rents, Rentiers, and Royalties' in this volume.

10 E.H. Shaffer, 'Energy Conservation Boards,' in *Performance of Selected Independent Regulatory Commissions: Alberta, Saskatchewan and Manitoba,* G. Reschenthaler, ed. (Ottawa 1972)

11 Energy Resources Conservation Board, *Conservation in Alberta, 1971* (Calgary 1972), p. 13

12 Ibid.

13 Oil and Gas Conservation Board, Report 69-D, *Report and Decision on Re-*

Richard E. Hamilton

view of Policies and Procedures for Considering Applications under the Gas Resources Preservation Act, 1956 (Calgary 1969)

14 Energy Resources Conservation Board, *Report on Field Pricing of Gas in Alberta,* pp. 11-19. The 'field value' was defined as the price at the field which corresponds to the 'commodity value,' which in turn was defined as 'the maximum price that could be obtained in a specific regional market having regard for the mix of end uses and the prices of competitive fuels in the area,' p. ii.

15 *Oilweek,* 20 Nov. 1972, p. 6

16 Ibid., 5 Feb. 1972

17 Pan-Alberta is a subsidiary of Alberta Gas Trunk Line Company Limited, which was originally established by the Alberta government (but with private shareholders) with a monopoly right to transport from fields within the province all gas intended for export. The main reason for Trunk Line's establishment was to forestall federal regulation of field prices by inserting a provincially regulated link in the chain between producers and consumers. In any event, the federal government has never attempted to regulate field prices.

18 Stanford Research Institute, *Market Price for Natural Gas,* p. 5

19 All these estimates were made prior to the imposition of a federal export tax in Canada. See Bucovetsky and Hyndman. The parameters used in the calculations are as follows: old royalty rate, 9 per cent of the field price; new royalty rate, 22 per cent; income tax, 14 per cent of profits; foreign share of after-tax profits, 76 per cent, of which one-third is repatriated; withholding tax on dividends sent aboard, 10 per cent; costs of production unchanged. The income tax percentage is the average paid in 1970 (see below). Its use assumes that companies can avoid paying the full income tax rate during the mid 1970s by undertaking exploration and development in Alberta and frontier areas of Canada.

Distribution of a 24 cent increase in price

1 Royalties (22% of 40 cents less 9% of 16 cents) = 7.36¢
2 Income taxes (14% of 16.64 cents) = 2.33¢
3 Net profits accruing to Canadian shareholders (24% of 14.31 cents) = 3.43¢
4 Withholding tax (10% of $\frac{1}{3}$ of 10.88 cents) = 0.36¢
5 Net profits accruing to foreign shareholders = 10.52¢
Government take = 42%
Canadian shareholders = 14%
Foreign shareholders = 44%

20 *Report on Field Pricing of Gas in Alberta,* pp. 3-33

21 The assumptions used to make the calculations for part II production differ in important respects from those used for part I production. Since the pro-

duction is new, the increase in revenue is the entire price of 40 cents per Mcf. Costs of production must be at least 14.6 cents per Mcf (the old price of 16 cents less the old royalty), for otherwise the gas would have been produced at the old price. Marginal costs would probably be over 30 cents. An average cost of 20 cents is assumed for part II production. An arbitrary three cents is allocated for lease bonus and other land payments necessary to bring about part II production. Income and withholding taxes are excluded from the Canadian gain. These would be earned in any event on the resources used to bring about part II production, since these resources would otherwise be employed elsewhere in Canada.

Distribution of 40 cent gain

1	Cost	20.00¢
2	Royalty (22% of 40 cents)	8.80¢
3	Lease bonus and other land payments	3.00¢
4	Income tax (14% of 8.20 cents)	1.15¢
5	After-tax profits of Canadian shareholders (24% of 7.05 cents)	1.69¢
6	Withholding tax (10% of $\frac{1}{3}$ of 5.36 cents)	.18¢
7	After-tax profits of foreign shareholders	5.18¢

The Canadian gain is equal to 2 + 3 + 5, the gain by foreign shareholders is equal to 7. The gross gain to Canada from part II production is equal to the net gain. Since some exports were included in part I production, Canadian requirements were in effect assumed to be completely covered out of part I production. Hence all of part II production would be exported.

23 The calculation is made by adding the dollar gain for part I production, plus the dollar gain for part II production times .30 times 40/24 and dividing the sum by 1.50. The .30 weight reflects the fact that part II production is 30 per cent of part I, while the 40/24 weight reflects the fact that additional revenue per Mcf is greater for part II production.

24 Alberta's gross gain from part I production would consist of royalties and 11 per cent of income tax payments for a total of $32 out of every $100 of revenue. From this is subtracted $16 because of higher costs to Alberta consumers. (*Report on Field Pricing of Gas in Alberta*, p. 3-33). The gain from part II production would be $30 out of every $100 of revenue, in the form of royalties and land payments. Section 6 of the *Report on Field Pricing* presents some estimates of the multiplier effects.

25 Statistics Canada, *Corporations and Labour Unions Returns Act, Report for 1970, Part I - Corporations*, March 1973

26 *Territorial Lands Act, Public Lands Act, Canada Oil and Gas Lands Regulations*, PC 1961-797, 6 June 1961, and amendments in subsequent years. See also A. Thompson, M. Crommelin, 'Canada's Petroleum Leasing Policy – A

Cornucopia for Whom?' (unpublished paper presented to the Canadian Arctic Resources Committee, Ottawa, 22 March 1973

27 W. Kilbourn, *Pipeline* (Toronto 1970). In 1966 the NEB approved a plan by TransCanada to export gas at Emerson, Manitoba, and reimport it near Sarnia, Ontario, after transporting it south of the Great Lakes through a line to be constructed and operated jointly with the American Natural Gas Company. At first the federal cabinet rejected the board's recommendation but later reversed its decision on the condition that 50 per cent (60 per cent by 1976) of western gas reaching eastern Canada must move through the much more costly all-Canadian route.

28 It is significant that the NEB did not regulate rates on domestic sales by Canadian pipeline companies until after 14 August 1969, when TransCanada requested the board to disallow its existing rates and establish new higher ones. The board recently fixed new rates sufficient to yield the company a 9 per cent rate of return on an historical cost rate base (TransCanada had asked for 9 per cent on a current value rate base). National Energy Board, *Reasons for Decision, In the Matter of the Application under Part IV of the National Energy Board Act (Rates Application – Phase I) of Trans-Canada Pipe Lines Limited,* December 1971; National Energy Board, *Reasons for Decisions ... (Rates Application – Phase II) ...* May 1973

29 L. Waverman, *Natural Gas and National Policy* (Toronto 1973), p. 66. This cost was about 6 cents per Mcf, approximately 18 per cent of the delivered price. However, it was partly offset by a gain to western producers of $12,417,000. See p. 81

30 The evolution of these policies is described in a series of National Energy Board 'Reports to the Governor in Council' dealing with individual applications made between 1960 and 1971. The changes have tended towards greater liberalization. For example, prior to 1970, the board excluded all deferred reserves and all reserves categorized as beyond economic reach. As the titles of the reports indicate, the NEB's decisions on export licenses are not final, but are recommendations to the cabinet. See also B.D. Fisher, 'The Role of the National Energy Board in Controlling the Export of Natural Gas from Canada,' *Osgoode Hall Law Journal,* vol. 9, no 3

31 For a theoretical discussion of the exportable surplus policy see R.E. Hamilton, 'Canada's "Exportable Surplus" Natural Gas Policy: A Theoretical Analysis,' *Land Economics,* Aug. 1973

32 The Royal Commission on Energy, *First Report* (Ottawa 1958)

33 See pp. 11-17

34 National Energy Board, Part VI, *Regulations,* Regulation 11A, added by PC 1970-1706, *Canada Gazette* Part II, vol. 104, no 20, 28 Oct. 1970

35 *Minutes of Proceedings and Evidence,* 13 and 20 March 1973
36 See the companion piece by John Helliwell in this volume.
37 L. Waverman, 'Transportation and Communications in the Seventies,' in Toronto Stock Exchange, *1972 Review, Canadian Economy and Equity Market,* Feb. 1973, p. 13
38 R. Rohmer, *The Arctic Imperative* (Toronto 1973)
39 R.E. Hamilton, 'A Marketing Board to Regulate Exports of Natural Gas?' *Canadian Public Administration,* spring 1973
40 An interesting suggestion is a windfall profits tax. See C. van de Panne, *Oilweek,* 10 July 1972
41 *Report of the Royal Commission on Taxation* (Ottawa 1966), vol. IV, chap. 23

Larrett Higgins provides some interesting insights into the development of electricity in Canada and the international sale of power between countries. In 1969, electricity provided 15 per cent of Canadian domestic demand for energy. Industrial users account for over 50 per cent of total Canadian energy consumption, varying from 70 per cent in British Columbia to 40 per cent in the Prairies. The various provinces have developed their hydro capacities to different degrees, ranging from a high of 84 per cent for Ontario to 12 per cent for Western Canada.

Hydro and nuclear capacity have similar characteristics – low operating costs and high capital costs – making them ideal base-load power. Fossil fuel plants have opposite characteristics, making them ideal for peak usage. Because of hydro's attributes, intensive development of storage capacity is called for. In the one clear example in energy of an American-Canadian joint venture, Higgins argues that Canadians undervalued the storage capacity of the Columbia River. His discussions of the economic issues surrounding that project, the internal wrangling within Canada, and the benefits and costs of the project provide a fitting context for today's issues.

As complementary pieces read Waverman on Canadian-American relations and Chapman on American electricity.

LARRETT HIGGINS

Electricity and Canadian policy

The emphasis today is upon the accelerating rate of change and how to cope with its impact. It is helpful to examine some of the profound changes in the light of Alfred Marshall's dictum 'natura non facit saltum' rather than as discontinuous steps. This is particularly true of the electricity supply industry which is just entering into its third major technology, as it attempts to keep abreast of exponentially growing demand which shows no signs or prospects of abatement.

This paper deals with some aspects of electricity in Canada, and begins by providing a quantitative sketch of its place in the Canadian energy picture and indicates the structural changes which are taking place. Next it concerns itself with some of the problems of resource and cost allocation as mixed systems evolve, and finally it touches upon some aspects of trade in electric energy.

SOME QUANTITATIVE
OBSERVATIONS AND INFERENCES

To provide some quantitative perspective of electricity within the context of energy in Canada, data from recent publications of the government of Canada[1] is presented in Tables 1-5.

Table 1 shows the dimensions of Canadian energy during the period 1958-69. The table is presented in a crude input-output format which omits intermediate transactions (or arbitrarily includes many of them in final industrial demand). This is a useful way to relate inputs to outputs and (with the intermediate table) to trace the conversion transactions. The period was one of transition for Canada from a net energy importer to a balanced position in 1969 – following which the

171

TABLE 1

Canada: total energy inputs and final demand, BTU $\times 10^{12}$

	1958	1959	1960	1961	1962	1963	1964	1965	1966	1967	1968	1969
Production	1941.6	2133.9	2316.0	2463.9	3081.7	3272.3	3558.0	3783.0	4085.0	4387.2	4759.6	5271.6
Imports	1167.3	1259.8	1264.8	1262.6	1290.1	1436.8	1494.4	1640.4	1755.0	1834.6	2017.9	2001.2
Stock depletion	44.2	-15.0	-.7	26.1	17.2	-45.5	1.1	-62.0	-85.1	-34.4	-55.5	-31.7
Other	5.1	5.7	1.8	3.4	1.5	.5	.5	.6	.5	.5	1.6	1.7
Total input	3158.2	3384.4	3581.9	3703.8	4390.5	4664.1	5054.0	5362.0	5755.4	6187.9	6723.6	7269.8
Road	496.3	515.2	541.2	554.1	584.4	620.7	653.6	694.7	739.1	779.4	833.4	870.6
Rail	127.1	101.9	78.1	73.7	71.6	70.2	86.2	85.9	85.1	86.7	82.9	84.4
Air	40.2	40.7	44.8	46.9	49.1	51.5	51.0	55.4	63.5	74.6	81.5	90.1
Ship	72.0	85.0	81.5	85.1	89.9	94.0	93.1	102.4	111.8	110.1	107.1	100.7
Total transport	735.6	742.8	745.6	759.8	795.0	836.4	883.9	938.4	999.5	1050.8	1104.9	1145.8
Residential & farm	639.2	700.7	713.7	724.7	762.9	802.2	842.6	866.2	867.8	905.1	944.4	990.1
Commercial	186.4	224.1	247.5	272.8	295.0	340.3	375.5	425.8	480.9	529.8	600.9	658.4
Industrial	766.4	845.6	869.6	886.0	927.3	945.1	1028.5	1105.6	1159.9	1211.0	1265.5	1333.6
Non-energy	17.0	17.5	21.2	18.5	18.2	18.6	20.0	24.0	27.2	26.4	27.5	32.2
Total non-transport	1609.0	1787.9	1852.0	1902.0	2003.4	2106.2	2266.6	2421.6	2535.8	2672.3	2838.2	2960.3
Domestic demand	2344.6	2530.7	2597.6	2661.8	2798.4	2942.6	3150.5	3360.0	3535.3	3723.1	3943.2	4160.1
Export	306.6	333.6	418.1	624.2	927.1	972.0	1085.5	1125.6	1272.1	1503.6	1703.8	1997.8
Total demand	2651.2	2864.3	3015.7	3286.0	3725.5	3941.6	4236.0	4485.6	4807.4	5226.7	5658.0	6157.9
Distribution loss	138.5	131.2	132.7	153.5	161.6	182.0	181.9	180.6	186.2	162.8	179.9	182.0
Conversion loss	368.5	388.9	433.5	264.3	503.4	567.5	636.1	695.8	761.8	798.4	885.7	929.9
Net imports	860.7	926.2	846.7	638.4	363.0	464.8	408.9	514.8	482.9	331.0	303.1	20.4

SOURCE: Statistics Canada Catalogue 57-505 OCC, Nov. 1972

TABLE 2
Electricity: Canada, BTU X 10^{12}

	1958	1959	1960	1961	1962	1963	1964	1965	1966	1967	1968	1969
Hydro	308.8	331.1	361.3	354.6	355.1	354.6	387.2	399.8	443.5	453.4	463.4	510.9
Import	.8	1.7	1.2	4.7	9.5	9.8	10.6	12.2	11.0	14.3	15.2	9.3
Coal	45.1	41.0	47.1	55.2	89.0	128.5	153.8	189.0	190.6	219.8	263.5	279.4
Coal production	1.5	1.6	1.9	2.0	1.4	1.3	2.2	2.2	2.4	2.3	2.6	2.2
Heavy oil	15.6	17.6	22.7	25.5	26.2	28.1	38.5	73.5	79.5	75.5	99.7	92.7
Natural gas	34.2	44.6	45.1	48.5	52.0	56.5	54.5	52.9	56.5	81.1	93.9	83.0
Other	1.5	2.0	2.3	2.5	3.0	4.6	4.7	5.1	7.6	9.7	9.3	11.5
Thermal	97.9	106.8	119.1	133.7	171.6	219.0	253.7	322.7	336.6	388.4	469.0	469.0
TOTAL INPUT	407.5	439.6	481.6	493.0	536.2	583.4	651.5	734.7	791.1	856.1	947.6	989.2
Residential & farm	59.0	64.9	69.6	75.0	80.8	86.4	93.1	101.5	109.6	119.4	128.9	138.0
Commercial	36.1	41.0	43.1	49.2	55.0	63.4	73.1	81.4	99.2	106.6	116.5	131.5
Industrial	194.1	203.8	226.4	219.6	233.5	226.9	248.0	263.7	278.2	288.4	303.9	322.2
Sub-total	289.2	309.7	339.1	343.8	369.3	376.7	414.2	446.6	487.0	514.4	549.3	591.7
Export	13.9	15.7	18.8	14.2	14.0	12.3	14.2	12.6	15.0	13.6	13.6	14.7
TOTAL DEMAND	303.1	325.4	357.9	358.0	383.3	389.0	428.4	459.2	502.0	528.0	562.9	606.4
Distribution loss	30.5	33.5	33.8	34.8	36.9	37.8	42.8	45.3	48.4	51.3	54.1	54.9
Conversion loss	73.9	80.7	89.9	100.2	116.0	156.6	180.3	230.2	240.7	276.8	330.6	327.9
% total conversion loss	20.0	19.1	20.7	37.9	23.0	27.6	28.3	33.1	31.7	34.7	37.3	35.0
Thermal efficiency	.245	.244	.245	.251	.324	.285	.289	.287	.285	.287	.295	.301

SOURCE: Statistics Canada Catalogue 57-505 OCC, Nov. 1972

Larrett Higgins

TABLE 3
Electricity: Canada 1969, BTU $\times 10^{12}$

	Atlantic	Quebec	Ontario	Prairies	BC & NWT	Canada
Hydro*	24.4	222.4	138.6	40.2	85.3	510.9
Import	.1		7.6		1.6	9.3
Purchase			15.6			
Coal	26.2	.7	193.9	58.6		279.4
Coal production	1.1		1.0			2.2
Crude & heavy oil	36.9	38.8	5.7	4.9	6.3	92.7
Natural gas		.1	5.4	66.2	11.5	83.2
Other	2.2	1.3	3.3	1.1	3.6	11.5
Thermal	67.2	40.9	209.3	130.8	15.4	469.0
TOTAL INPUT	91.7	263.3	371.1	171.0	102.3	989.2
Residential & farm	7.5	39.4	56.4	20.1	14.6	138.0
Commercial	7.2	39.8	52.6	20.2	11.6	131.5
Industry	21.9	123.5	92.5	25.1	59.2	322.2
Sub-total	36.6	202.7	201.5	65.4	85.4	591.7
Export	1.7	.1	9.8		3.1	14.7
Sales	.4	15.2			.1	
FINAL DEMAND	38.7	218.0	211.3	65.4	88.6	606.4
Distribution loss	3.0	17.4	19.4	8.9	6.2	54.9
Conversion loss	50.0	27.9	140.8	96.7	7.5	327.9
* % of potential	18	21	84	12	12	20

Totals do not add due to rounding and omission of interprovincial transactions.

SOURCE: Statistics Canada Catalogue 57-505 OCC, Nov. 1972

trend has continued to net export. The table also shows the major segments of final demand and gives an indication of their various rates of growth.

Table 2 is a similar summary of the electricity sector, which includes some intermediate transactions involving other forms of energy. It shows final demand by market types which can be compared to Table 1. As before, many of the sales to the industrial sector in particular are really intermediate inputs. Of particular interest is the changing structure of inputs to the industry, which show a shift from hydro to fossil fuel and hence the change in technology that this implies. Hydro represented 76 per cent of inputs in 1958, but only 52 per cent in 1969, coal which was 12 per cent of input in 1958 was 28 per cent eleven years later. Of marginal significance as an input in 1969, nuclear power is expected to provide 56 per cent of input sources in 2000 (see Table 5).

174

In the tables hydro and import inputs are shown at 100 per cent efficiency and therefore the conversion losses relate to thermal outputs which are equal to fossil fuel inputs minus conversion losses. The resulting efficiencies, though low, can be seen to have increased, largely because of the installation by utilities of large, more efficient units. (The figures shown include both utility and industrial generation.)

Table 3 shows the regional breakdown of electricity imports and final demands, and serves to show the variety of mix of inputs in the different regions in 1969. It also gives an indication of the inter-regional balances of trade. Of the regions shown, Ontario is the most mature, evidenced by the great variety of inputs and the large size of residential and commercial demand relative to industrial. Ontario is also a net importer of energy when interprovincial trade is included. Its volume of trade with the United States makes it the most significant region in this respect. In the table, inter-regional transfers are shown as net purchases or sales but, even so, the flows are mostly one-way, which is not so much trade in a mature sense as simply the export of staples from underdeveloped regions, and therefore likely to change into exchange as these regions develop.

Table 4 shows the annual detail for Ontario, and illustrates the shift from emphasis on hydro to a mixed hydro-thermal system. For example, in 1958 fossil fuel inputs were 16.1 trillion BTU or 17 per cent of hydro and increased to 209 trillion BTU in 1969, which was 151 per cent of hydro and over half the total input.

Some indication of the reason for Ontario's shift in technology emerges when hydro output is compared to estimated streamflow potential.[2]

BTU $\times$ 10^{12}

	Output 1969	Potential*	Per cent 1969 potential
Atlantic	24.4	135	18
Quebec	222.4	1065	21
Ontario	138.6	165	84
Prairies	40.2	342	12
BC & NWT	85.3	722	12
Canada	510.9	2530	20

*At median flows

The coefficient of annual variation of hydro energy output (CV) is about 5 per cent in Ontario, which derives the bulk of its energy from the Niagara–St Lawrence system. For other provinces, a higher CV (depending upon the amount of perennial storage) would be appropriate.

TABLE 4

Electricity: Ontario, BTU × 10^{12}

	1958	1959	1960	1961	1962	1963	1964	1965	1966	1967	1968	1969
Hydro	95.6	110.5	119.2	115.1	105.5	99.7	103.4	112.9	126.8	129.9	133.9	138.6
Import	.8	1.6	1.0	4.6	9.2	9.7	9.9	9.9	8.0	8.6	8.9	7.6
Purchase*	20.4	19.2	19.8	18.7	19.4	16.9	23.0	15.7	21.0	18.1	15.7	15.6
Coal	14.5	11.6	10.2	14.1	45.2	82.0	92.7	115.9	114.1	141.7	175.0	193.9
Coal production	1.8	.8	.9	1.0	.3	.2	.9	.8	.8	1.1	1.3	1.0
Heavy oils					.3	.4	.3	.5	.7	1.5	2.7	5.0
Natural gas	.8	1.0	1.1	1.1	1.7	1.0	1.4	2.4	3.4	1.7	3.3	5.4
Other		.1	.4	.4	.1	.7	.9	1.0	1.1	1.5	2.4	3.3
Thermal	16.1	13.5	12.6	16.6	47.6	84.3	96.2	120.6	120.1	147.5	184.7	209.3
TOTAL INPUT	132.9	144.8	152.6	155.0	181.7	210.6	232.5	259.1	275.9	304.1	343.2	371.1
Residential & farm	27.9	30.0	31.8	33.7	35.8	38.1	40.2	43.2	46.2	49.5	53.1	56.4
Commercial	15.4	17.8	19.6	21.7	24.0	26.8	30.4	33.8	37.7	41.0	45.4	52.6
Industrial	53.3	59.1	61.0	60.4	62.7	64.6	69.3	75.1	81.7	85.2	90.9	92.5
Sub-total	96.6	106.9	112.4	115.8	122.5	129.5	139.9	152.1	165.6	175.7	189.4	201.5
Export Sales*	11.6	13.2	16.2	12.0	12.1	11.3	13.1	10.6	11.1	10.6	8.6	9.8
FINAL DEMAND	108.2	120.1	128.6	127.8	134.6	140.8	153.0	162.7	176.7	186.3	198.0	211.3
Distribution loss	12.7	14.7	14.4	14.7	14.4	14.1	15.5	16.0	18.1	18.1	19.3	19.0
Conversion loss	12.0	10.0	9.6	12.5	32.7	55.7	64.0	80.4	81.1	99.7	125.9	140.8
Import + export	12.4	14.8	17.2	16.6	21.3	21.3	23.0	20.5	19.1	19.2	17.5	17.4
Export – import	10.0	11.6	15.2	7.4	2.9	1.6	3.2	.7	3.1	2.0	-.3	1.2

* Interprovincial net

SOURCE: Statistics Canada Catalogue 57-505 OCC, Nov. 1972

TABLE 5

Forecast: Electricity Canada, BTU $\times$ 10^{12}

	1980	1990	2000
Hydro	802	1057	1174
Coal	785	1238	1392
Oil	282	653	1005
Gas	127	103	176
Nuclear	510	1919	5037
Other	12	40	80
Thermal	1716	3953	7690
INPUT	2518	5010	8864
Residential & farm	276	472	773
Commercial	423	908	1568
Industrial	530	810	1250
Sub-total	1229	2190	3591
Distribution loss	122	190	270
Conversion loss	1167	2630	5003
Thermal efficiency	.3199	.3346	.3494

SOURCE: *An Energy Policy for Canada: Phase 1* (Ottawa, Department of Energy, Mines & Resources, 1973), vol. 2, pp. 16-21

The effect of random streamflows on hydro production can be inferred from the table. In 1963-4 Great Lakes levels reached an all-time low with the effect that St Lawrence and Niagara flows were also low. By the end of the period shown, levels had recovered and were heading towards the record high levels of 1972-3. Note that Ontario's volume of trade with the United States did not appreciably change during the period, but it came closer to balance after 1962.

Tables 2 and 4 show the growing significance of conversion losses with the shift to fossil-fuel technology. With increments to demand largely being provided from fossil fuels in Ontario (in Quebec, British Columbia, and Newfoundland, hydro is still being developed), the demands for primary inputs are tending to grow rapidly, and the demand for electricity itself is growing more rapidly (about 7 per cent per annum) than all forms of energy consumption in Canada which is growing at 5.6 per cent. However, total energy demand with the rapid growth in exports grew at about 8 per cent in the period 1958-69. The tables show hydro inputs at 100 per cent efficiency or 3412 BTU/Kwh.[3]

177

Larrett Higgins

SOME PHYSICAL AND ECONOMIC
CHARACTERISTICS OF MIXED SYSTEMS

The use of fossil fuel to generate electricity is not new. It just happens that the Canadian evolution has for the most part been from hydro systems to mixed systems. Systems elsewhere are tending to evolve from thermal systems to mixed systems by adding hydro or pumped storage peaking capacity. The economic and physical characteristics of the two technologies are quite different, and this creates interesting problems for an economist, not only in optimal capacity allocation but also in rate making. The physical differences between the two technologies are that hydro systems are energy limited in that they depend upon (random) streamflows for energy but are relatively stable in short term peak capacity, while thermal systems are capacity limited (assuming a satisfactory fuel inventory policy). From an economic point of view, hydro systems (and nuclear) tend to have high capital and low operating costs, while it is just the reverse for fossil-fuel systems. The rate of demand for energy is subject to hourly, daily, weekly, and annual periodic variation, as well as random variation of both high (weather) and low (the business cycle, strikes) frequencies. For this reason, the different types of capacity complement rather than compete with one another. For peaking capacity it is generally desirable to minimize fixed costs, while for base load plant there exists a tradeoff between operating and fixed costs. Thus one would suppose that hydro would be used for base load, because of its low operating costs, with fossil-fuel plant used for peaking. This is in fact what happens in hydro systems as they *begin* to move into mixed systems.

The first thermal plant is simply insurance against a dry reservoir, but this use is subject to rapidly diminishing returns as the quantity of thermal capacity or storage increases. Moreover, the cost of additional hydro capacity (once the dam is built) is quite low, and for physical reasons it is ideally suited for peaking. In more mature systems one sees intensive investment in hydro capacity located close to load centres, with an attendant rise in the value of storage because, while the energy cost is not important for peaking plant, availability of that energy is vital. It is the minimum availability of streamflow that determines the intensity of development, and this can be altered by providing storage to increase the minimum assured energy supply. Thus, storage increases energy cost but makes possible more intensive development of capacity for peak use.

As the potential capacity of hydro is approached, additional thermal capacity adds higher proportionate fuel and operating costs to the system – costs which in today's and tomorrow's prices are increasing rapidly. The desire for nuclear capacity is similar to the desire for hydro – low operating costs, making it the ideal base load power.

INSTITUTIONAL ASPECTS
OF THE CANADIAN INDUSTRY

In Canada natural resources are a matter coming under provincial jurisdiction. As regards electricity, the response has varied from province to province, but there has been an underlying tendency towards public ownership. During the 1960s both British Columbia and Quebec nationalized the industry, leaving Alberta as the only province in which ownership remains in private hands.

The pioneer in the process is Ontario, which created the Ontario Hydro-Electric Power Commission in 1906. Originally, Ontario Hydro, as it is now known, was created as an enterprise for the transmission of electric power from Niagara Falls to fourteen municipal systems and acted as a co-operative. It was not created by nationalization, but very soon went into the business of generation for itself with the construction of a plant at Queenston which was completed in 1917. In due course, it acquired privately owned plants by purchase. The advent of hydraulically-generated power rendered primitive steam plants in such places as Toronto obsolete, and a great deal of political heat was generated at the time over compensation.[4]

The Hydro-Electric Power Commission of Ontario was conceived by a Conservative government, and this may explain in great measure why there has been no continued ideological debate over the issue of public versus private power as in the United States. The concept underlying the enterprise has been one of providing 'power at cost.' Because of indivisibilities and high costs of entry, the industry tends to be a natural monopoly. Increasing returns to scale tended to drive prices lower still as consumption expanded. While this might have justified marginal cost pricing involving a subsidy, the proposition of power at cost was enough of a revolutionary concept for the time, and it is difficult to believe that a subsidy would have significantly accelerated the rapid development which took place. This development was enhanced by the attraction to the Niagara Falls area of significant amounts of high load factor industrial load. A subsidy was used to extend distribution to submarginal rural areas, especially after World War II, which was justified on social rather than commercial grounds. The 'power at cost' principle imposed a budgetary constraint and resulted in a reasonable approximation to the maximization of consumer surplus, while at the same time avoiding the exchange rate problems of converting public funds to consumer surplus on the one hand and converting monopoly profits on the other.

The result of this policy has been a low rate of return on capital employed in the business. This has led to complaints of unfair competition from other energy suppliers, and to criticisms from academics and others of misallocation of resources.[5]

This is a curious argument. From Ontario Hydro's point of view, too low a rate of return would lead to financing difficulties, since the enterprise's external financing is done entirely by debt sold in competitive capital markets. The fact that its debt is guaranteed by the province may in fact lead to some subsidy. But even if this specific guarantee were to be withdrawn, the market would probably continue to regard Ontario Hydro debt as a contingent liability of the province, and so there may be something of a credibility problem.

The other grounds upon which too low a rate of return leads to misallocation of resources is that electric energy prices are 'too low' and therefore the consumption of electricity is 'too high.' In order to pin such a statement down to quantitative terms, it is necessary to have some fairly specific information on the elasticity of demand with respect to the price of electric energy and prices of other fuels. One would then calculate the consumption appropriate to any desired rate of return. This, however, still does not resolve the problem of what that rate of return should be.

Rates of return are affected by risk and the degree of monopoly power, among other things. Other regulated industries showing higher rates of return may reflect inadequate regulation of their monopoly power. On the other hand Ontario Hydro's rate of return exceeds that of the Department of Highways. This casts doubt upon the validity of the rate of return except perhaps as an upper limit to price in regulated industries.

A related problem is that of pricing in the capital-intensive service industries under conditions of inflation. Under these circumstances, all industries tend to look as though they were increasing cost industries. Marginal cost pricing under such circumstances is liable to result in a massive transfer of consumer surplus to monopoly profit, especially since the demand for electric energy (at least in the residential sector) tends to be price inelastic. The relative price prospects for other forms of energy such as oil and gas seem at present to portend an accelerated shift to electric energy, especially for heating purposes. Average cost pricing, in contrast, tends to distribute economic rent from old plants to consumers. Sustained inflation simply means that average prices have a time lag built into them; the power-at-cost principle means that they will eventually catch up. Under deflationary circumstances, the reverse is true – real unit costs will rise, and demand inelasticity implies that an increased proportion of the budget will be allocated to electric energy.

Until 1974 control of electricity prices in Ontario was largely vested with the Hydro-Electric Power Commission which set the bulk rates on an average cost basis. Retail rates in municipalities were controlled by the commission, and generally set to produce a rate of return of 10 per cent, largely for the purpose of internally financing expansion of distribution plant. Strong legislation and supervision by the commission has operated to keep the retained earnings of municipal electric utilities segregated from general municipal use with the result that municipal distribution plant is in a good state of repair. In contrast, problems have arisen with waterworks and sewers in some municipalities where this approach has not been taken.

Starting in 1974, Ontario Hydro's wholesale rates are to be subjected to a review process by a board of the Ontario Energy Board which has been set up for that purpose. While the board will not have the power to set rates directly, it will be able to make comments and recommendations regarding Ontario Hydro's rate proposals to the Ontario minister of energy.

The review process provides for intervenors to put witnesses on the stand and to cross-examine Ontario Hydro witnesses in public hearings. Its aim is to give the public greater access to the rate-making process than has hitherto been the case. It is not possible to predict what impact this will have on the rate-making process. It seems likely that it will promote lively debate upon the merits and applicability of marginal cost pricing to the peak load problem. One can only hope that the process will not degenerate into the traditional return-on-rate-base type of regulation that has led elsewhere to substitution of capital for other factors of production.

This part of the discussion has been confined to the Ontario experience, not only for reasons of greater familiarity on the part of the author, but also because the Hydro-Electric Power Commission of Ontario is in many ways a progenitor of similar institutions in other countries – notably the Tennesee Valley and Bonneville Power administrations in the United States, and some of the state power authorities in Europe.

INTERNATIONAL TRADE IN ELECTRIC POWER

The evolution of trade between Canada and the United States is a story of evolution from mercantilist notions based on balance-of-trade considerations to the more sophisticated use of comparative advantage for the purpose of optimally allocating resources.

The mercantilist position terms exports as 'good' and imports as 'bad.' Canada found, much to its discomfiture, during both world wars that firm exports of electric power could not be repatriated in spite of the fact that Canada was at war (in each case before the United States came in). This was in large part because the United States had no alternative means of supply; in effect the Canadian suppliers were acting as American utilities, creating an unhealthy dependence. Moreover, many of these firm contracts were not only long term, but at fixed prices. One of these carries a price of 1.6 mils per kilowatt-hour (compared to the going rate of 8 mils which is currently rising at 10 per cent per annum), and expires in 1999.

It is probably worth noting that major one-way transfers of firm power are characteristic only of remote or otherwise undeveloped areas such as the Churchill Falls project or the Nelson River project and do not contribute to the emergence of a power grid. In such transactions, the balance of trade is identical with the volume of trade. It is worth noting that the benefits of trade come from its volume; the problems stem from its imbalances.

The risks involved in long-term one-way export transactions are substantial, and the Canadian record in this respect has been unfortunate. Many of the early export contracts were fixed-price, long-term, firm contracts which were soon engulfed by inflation. They were, in fact, so unfortunate as to lead to the passage of the Export of Power and Fluids Act.[6] This act was superseded by the National Energy Board Act in 1958. For some unaccountable reason, the lessons were entirely ignored by the Columbia River Treaty, which is a fixed price contract running a minimum of sixty years to provide benefits to the United States the magnitude of which was not even comprehended by the Canadian negotiators. Witness the astonishing statement: 'The benefits purchased are unknown, while alternatives in the United States would have produced a known amount of power.'[7]

THE COLUMBIA RIVER TREATY

There is no doubt today that Canada has lost vast sums of money (real and opportunity cost) in the terms of the Columbia River Treaty. How did this happen? The major problem lay in the incorrect value attributed to additional storage capacity.

The amount of storage required to serve a fluctuating demand over a given time span t is an indeterminate variable. If the demand rises, the demand for storage will also rise. As the timespan t increases the range of demands and therefore the requirement for storage also increases. However, for large timespans (1 year) substitutes such as fossil-fuel energy become feasible. There is also need to provide storage for seasonal variation in streamflow. As t decreases (and it will with load growth and fixed quantum of storage), the demand for and hence the value of storage increases.

It is the existence of the foregoing paradox that lies at the root of one of the technical objections to the terms of the Columbia River Treaty. Krutilla[8] has correctly pointed out that water storage is subject to diminishing returns to incremental quantities for both flood control and power production under static demand conditions or limitless streamflow. The framers of the Columbia Treaty took this to mean that the value of storage declines over time.[9] While this is true in the initial stages of the transition to a mixed system, it is false in the mature stage – storage increases in value for electric energy as for flood control.

In the mature stage, the availability of seasonal storage permits more intensive development of hydro capacity and reduces the amount of thermal capacity that is required to meet a given demand. The thermal capacity which remains is able to operate at a much higher capacity factor than would be the case without seasonal storage, with lower unit costs as a result. The same considerations also operate in favor of nuclear capacity. Thus, the benefits of seasonal storage to electric energy production are to substitute cheaper hydro peaking capacity for thermal capacity, and this benefit increases as development proceeds. Failure of Canada to comprehend the values involved led to loading the basin to the maximum extent with storages at the lowest possible elevation in Canada where it would be of minimum use to Canadians on the grounds that delay would decrease the values.[10]

The price offer by the United States incorporated Krutilla's principle of diminishing benefits to added quantities for flood control. Thus, the price offer was 69.5 cents per annum for the first 8.5 million acre feet of flood control dropping to 5.2 cents for additional storage capacity. For power benefits, a similar declining price offer was made, but, in addition, the benefits were assumed to decline over time. Since the values increase rather than decrease over time, the result is a transfer of benefit from Canada to the United States. It is significant that, in the Terms of Sale Agreement,[11] the United States receives the right to determine the actual power benefits for purposes of resale.

The Canadian reaction was to provide as much storage as physically possible – at the lowest possible altitude where it would be of minimum value to Canada and therefore minimize obstacles to its control by the United States. The inexplicable Canadian attitude can perhaps be described in the words of Dr H.L. Keenleyside (who was co-chairman of BC Hydro) on 10 February 1964: 'There is good reason to believe that the cost of nuclear energy will continue to decline and that ... nuclear power will make most other installations uneconomic.' If this was the Canadian view, then it would appear that we thought we were pulling a fast one on the Americans.

The results in any event have amounted to a disaster for Canada. The power benefits were sold for a thirty-year period for a lump sum payment of $250 million, of which $200 million were invested in US treasury bills yielding $4\frac{1}{4}$ per cent maturing annually in amounts of $30 million until November 1971. Meanwhile, inflation and other costs escalated in Canada so that the expected surplus of $52 million over and above the cost of structures (out of which operating costs for thirty years must be paid) became a deficit. The true result is not known with

183

any precision because many of the Columbia costs were 'reallocated' in a manner which has not received public scrutiny. Testimony by Mr G.M. McNabb[12] indicates that the $52 million 'surplus' has become a loss of $120 million.

The Canadian architects of the Columbia Treaty failed to distinguish between two types of hydro projects – those near load centers in which the Columbia is perhaps unique, and the more usual use of remote sites such as Churchill Falls in Labrador, the James Bay project in Quebec, the Nelson in Manitoba, and the Peace River in British Columbia. These remote sites must necessarily supply base load, because the high capital costs of transmission disqualify them from eligibility as peaking plants of low capital cost. Their minimum economic capacity factor is high. In New York City, a Churchill Falls project must compete with base load thermal or nuclear – both would require the Storm King Mountain pumped-storage plant to help them meet a fluctuating daily load. But the Columbia River runs through a heavy load center and because costs of transmission to the Bonneville grid are almost negligible, it is ideally situated for peaking service and can tolerate progressively higher energy (storage) costs. But as the Columbia River is developed intensively (as a result of Canadian storage), the benefits payable to Canada decline.

The Columbia River Treaty experience throws useful light on the present oil conflict between the federal government at Ottawa on the one hand and the provincial producers on the other. Under the British North America Act, which forms the bulk of the written constitution of Canada, ownership of resources is vested in the provinces, but foreign and interprovincial trade are federal responsibilities. The original Columbia River Treaty was signed by Prime Minister John Diefenbaker and President Dwight Eisenhower on 17 January 1961, just three days before the Kennedy administration took office, and without the support of Premier W.A.C. Bennett of British Columbia who had written to the federal minister of finance on 14 December 1960: 'The financial proposals put forward by the government of Canada are regrettably unacceptable to British Columbia.' On 13 January 1961 he reiterated: 'I must tell you that British Columbia entertains serious doubts that power returned from the United States ... can in fact be returned to Vancouver at a cost of 3.77 mils so often quoted by your colleagues.'

The government of Canada wanted electric energy from the Columbia; the province wanted cash. A deadlock developed when Bennett took over the privately owned BC Electric Company and thus assumed control of the market for power in British Columbia (at the same time he completely outwitted his socialist opposition). The impasse was only broken by a new federal administration under Lester Pearson which acceded completely to British Columbia's demands. This cleared the way for the treaty to be ratified on 16 September 1964. This complete surrender by Ottawa to provincial demands, with no serious consideration of the defects of the treaty itself, have led to over-reaction in the current dispute over oil between Ottawa and the producing provinces. Ottawa seems to be more concerned with asserting its power than in finding a solution. In the Columbia case Ottawa under-reacted; it was concerned more with getting rid of the problem than in finding a solution. And it is Ottawa, not the United States, which is resisting a reopening of discussion.

The United States is reacting as predicted to its Columbia windfall with intensive development at Grand Coulee. A logical sequel to the third powerhouse there is to develop balanced discharge capability under power at the downstream plants in cascade as the Pacific Northwest load grows and as the Bonneville system becomes mixed within the next decade or two. The Columbia Treaty remains in force until at least September 2024.

An interesting variant of the Columbia example is the group of plants developed on the Moose River near Hudson Bay in Ontario. These are peaking plants linked to Toronto by some 450 miles of 500 Kv transmission line. The reason for their existence and development as peaking plants lies in the location of a northern load center in Ontario. While the reservoirs of these plants are refilling in the off-peak period, base load energy from thermal plants in Southern Ontario flows north to Sudbury and Timmins and so the line is in use for a high proportion of the time. The arrangement is, in effect, an internal trade-off of capacity for energy.

There are still firm contracts being signed for exports, but for the most part they are for limited periods and contain provisions for repatriation and price renegotiation. They recognize the situation as a temporary expedient. The unhappy experiences in electricity may have some relevance for natural gas developments which are pending. In particular, with shifting sources of supply, gas pipelines may have an opportunity to operate as a grid as opposed to a network.

POSSIBILITIES FOR A NORTH AMERICAN GRID

In modern interconnections, electric utilities operate much as sovereign states. They are monopolists within their defined territory, their primary purpose is the welfare of their consumers, and they form a policy unit which determines the level of acceptable risk. Their expenditure on reserve capacity is analogous to the defense budget of a nation state. They make treaties with one another, called interconnection agreements, which include provisions for commerce and mutual security. They recognize the necessity for sovereignty which is the power to act independently in a crisis (with the paradoxical exception of the Columbia Treaty which was negotiated by nation states as opposed to utilities). That is to say, mutual assistance is conditional upon the ability to provide it without threat to one's own customers.

Forced outages occur randomly and therefore unpredictably. Because of this, there are economies of scale in pooling reserves for mutual assistance by trade in emergency capacity. Also because of the randomness of the risk, it is not possible to predict where the comparative advantage will lie at any particular time. If the reserves of two adjacent systems are in balance, then the risks are balanced. If one utility has ample reserves and its neighbor is just scraping by, either for policy reasons or some other chronic cause, then the former is rendering a valuable service to the latter simply by providing a standing albeit conditional offer to trade. Trade is imbalanced not only in terms of transactions, but because the second utility would improve the security of the first if its reserves were to be brought to a better position. There is no comparative advantage in the traditional sense because the technology is mobile. There may be comparative advantage in an external sense if utility A can tolerate higher external costs such as environmental degradation to a greater extent than utility B. Reserve capacity is a joint product, and therefore poses pricing problems. The mean marginal cost formula cannot be applied objectively since the marginal costs of the reserve-deficient utility are the subjective costs of interrupting load, which are generally considered to be very high. Alternatively an arbitrary price could be set so that the expected annual costs of purchased reserve assistance would exceed the annual cost of providing and operating reserve capacity. A penalty price for such transactions is irrelevant in the case of balanced trade or risk; it provides a necessary incentive to bring the risks into balance. Otherwise a problem of mutual dependence (as opposed to interdependence) is likely to arise, and this poses political problems stemming from vested interests which restrict the independence of both utilities in a way that interdependence under conditions of balanced risk does not.

Where a number of utilities are interconnected, a competitive market for reserve capacity may arise, producing lower prices. The result is suboptimization in the short run, and possibly an unstable long-run situation such as the inventory conflict problem where each supplier in the distribution chain seeks to force others to carry the inventory, resulting in an unstable equilibrium.[13] However, forced outage is not the only source of requirement for reserve capacity; demand forecast error over lead period is important, and, unlike forced outages, it is likely to affect adjacent utilities in the same direction at any given time. Moreover, it is a low frequency phenomenon. Consequently, utilities cannot plan on being able to buy reserves if the need arises from booming demand; they need to plan their own. A high price for trade in reserves gives an incentive to provide adequate reserves.

Once the capacity is available, trade can proceed generally on a market basis. There is no centralized or over-riding control, although the amount of coordination required increases with the timespan of the transactions. This ranges from the spot transaction which concerns the disposition of spinning capacity on an hour-to-hour basis by dispatchers of adjacent utilities to scheduled flows planned in advance, not only between adjacent utilities but between members of power pools. The longer the scheduling period, the more coordinating of planning is required. Thus a scheduled interchange for tomorrow involves scheduling the starting of units; seasonal interchange may involve a changed maintenance schedule. Still more complex are joint planning arrangements by which small but adjacent utilities will alternately build larger units than could be accommodated by either's system alone in order to take advantage of economies of scale.[14] While the trade in this instance may balance in the long run, the flow may not change direction for years at a time. Moreover, these transactions require agreements for use in the case of contingencies. If the unit fails under circumstances where reserves are inadequate to carry the load of both systems, whose customers are interrupted, and in what proportions?

The foregoing transactions are of types that had led to the creation of what is essentially a North American grid, which has been formed by the interconnection of adjacent utilities into power pools, and the pools into a continental grid.[15] They are built upon the foundations of mutual security, the opportunity to trade, and recognition of the over-riding priority of supply to the customers of each individual utility.

The emergence of a continental grid in electricity has been evolutionary. From the early, and generally unfortunate experiences involving one-way flows from primitive to metropolitan areas, it has developed into a multilateral pattern of generally balanced trade in energy under conditions of shifting comparative advantage. There are also collective benefits of mutual security, but with them the possibility of major blackouts of which the Northeast power failure of November 1965 is an example. The lessons of that experience are twofold and paradoxical:
a/ the interconnections need to be stronger so that the combined system can withstand larger shocks; and
b/ there is an increased need to be able to split the grid into its component utilities to isolate trouble and prevent a major crisis.

This paradox will lie at the heart of any desire for increased interdependence among North American electric utilities, combined with the lessons Canadians see in the Columbia River Treaty.

NOTES

1 Statistics Canada, *Detailed Energy Supply & Demand in Canada 1958-1969*, Cat. #57-505 (Ottawa, Nov. 1972); Department of Energy, Mines and

Resources, *An Energy Policy for Canada,* vol. 2 (Ottawa 1973), Table 9, pp. 16-21

2 *Electric Power in Canada 1967* (Ottawa 1968). Estimates of total potential derived from Table 3, page 10 on the assumption of median flows and operation of installed capacity at 70 per cent load factor at 95 per cent flows, converted to BTUs/yr at 3412 Kwh/BTU.

3 These figures could be adjusted by using 3967 BTU/Kwh which would increase them by 16.3 per cent to reflect the conversion efficiency of falling water to electricity of 86 per cent. Alternatively a figure of 10,000 BTU/Kwh could be used to indicate fossil fuel equivalent. Another problem exists at the utilization end. The conversion of electric energy to heat is generally considered to be at 100 per cent whereas for gas or oil it is considered to be in the order of 40-70 per cent depending upon the installation and the time of year. Insulation levels also play an important role in overall efficiency of utilization. Thus, in oil and gas there are significant losses within the final demand category while for electric energy these are incurred at the production point. Consequently great care is needed in making judgments about overall efficiency.

4 Dennison, M., *The People's Power* (Toronto 1960), Chap. 9

5 Task Force Hydro, *Report* no 4, pp. 21-9; Gilbert, Robert A., 'No Shining Light,' *Barron's,* 5 Nov. 1962, p. 9

6 Revised Statutes of Canada 1955, Chap. 14. Repeated by National Energy Board Act, 18 July 1959 (RSC 1959), Chap. 46

7 *The Columbia River Treaty and Protocol: A Presentation,* issued by the Departments of External Affairs and Northern Affairs and National Resources (Ottawa, April 1964), p. 93

8 Krutilla, J.V., *The Columbia River Treaty: The Economics of an International River Basin Development* (Baltimore 1967), Chap. 3, pp. 31-43

9 *The Columbia River Treaty and Protocol: A Presentation,* p. 94

10 Higgins, Larrett, 'The Columbia River Treaty: A Critical View,' *International Journal,* autumn 1961

11 *The Columbia River Treaty Protocol & Related Documents,* issued by the Departments of External Affairs and Northern Affairs and National Resources (Ottawa, Feb. 1964), p. 78. See also Terms of Sale (B4), p. 120 for a curious redefinition not binding on the US.

12 House of Commons, Committee on National Resources and Public Works, Ottawa, 29 May 1973, pp. 21:13-21:14

13 Borch, K.H., *The Economics of uncertainty* (Princeton 1968), pp. 143-7

14 See *Submission to the Ontario Energy Board,* vol. 3: *System Expansion Program* (Ontario Hydro, Toronto, 20 Dec. 1973), section 3.2

15 The 1970 National Power Survey, Federal Power Commission (Washington 1971), part I, chap. 17

R. M. HYNDMAN AND M. W. BUCOVETSKY

The taxation literature until recently stressed the question of whether oil and gas production should be treated as any other industry. To the extent that, in North America, oil and gas producers received certain tax advantages unavailable to other industries, government policy suggested that indeed oil and gas were special. Against this academic back-drop of the 'neutrality' of tax instruments, OPEC nations were using taxes to extract revenue or rent from these same producers. The governments of Canada and the US have learnt from the governments of OPEC, and questions of neutrality have died in academic and government circles. The question now is how can the tax system be used to extract the most possible money out of these firms?

Hyndman and Bucovetsky address the question of why oil and gas producers have been favored. They dismiss the notion that oil and gas exploration are uniquely more risky than other industries. Even if it could be proven that exploration is more risky than, say, widget production, the authors suggest that depletion allowances are not the most appropriate means of encouraging risk-taking. The security-of-supply argument for encouraging exploration is also analyzed; while today we would want even more domestic self-sufficiency, it is not obvious that the existing tax advantages to the industry are the best means to self-sufficiency.

The authors examine in detail the corporate income tax, depletion allowance, immediate expensing, royalties, lease payments, and bonus arrangements under present Canadian federal and provincial legislation. The yields of these taxes are estimated. Export taxes and increased royalty schemes are discussed.

This paper should be read in con-

189

junction with Debanné on Canadian
oil, Erickson & Spann on American oil,
Millsaps and Erickson on American tax
laws. McDonald's paper has a section
on taxation which is of opposite persuasion from Hyndman and Bucovetsky.

It is the editors' opinion that the entire tax treatment of resource industries
must be reorganized. Now is the time.
Give the industry the right to raise
prices (since we feel rationing is inefficient), but at the same time ensure
that the public purse appropriates a
major share of all profits. Use the
energy crisis constructively as a time
to deregulate as well as to remove all
the special advantages enjoyed by the
industry.

R. M. HYNDMAN AND M. W. BUCOVETSKY

Rents, rentiers, and royalties: government revenue from Canadian oil and gas

In the past half dozen years the taxation of Canadian oil and gas resources has moved to the very centre of the political arena. A complex and once esoteric subject has become the stuff of daily newspaper headlines. This newfound Canadian interest has largely been conditioned by external events peculiar to world energy markets. But it also has been stimulated by the internal legacy of the Canadian tax-reform debates of the 1960s; there is a new awareness that the tax system is a legitimate instrument for increasing national welfare. In the fall of 1973, the subject has created an apparent impasse within the Canadian federal system. It is not the purpose of the present paper to judge the validity of conflicting governmental rights, nor can we forecast the outcome of the struggle. Our concerns, rather, are the background to current developments, the basic issues involved in taxing the revenue from oil and gas production, and the methods of taxation actually adopted in Canada.

BACKGROUND

In the period before 1973, the Canadian market for crude oil was dominated by major policy choices made by two national governments: United States import quotas and the National Oil Policy (NOP) in Canada. Although Canadian oil was exempt from the mandatory American import quotas of 1959, refineries which imported Canadian crude were penalized by reduced entitlements to (cheaper) offshore crude. In 1967 Canadian imports into the United States were more explicitly restricted by informal controls, followed in 1970 by formal ones.[1] Under the NOP, adopted by the government of Canada in 1961, Canadian markets west of the Ottawa valley were reserved for Canadian crude and products.[2]

Wellhead prices of Canadian crude oil are determined by price leadership on the part of one or another of the major integrated oil companies. During the period under discussion, pricing decisions by the 'majors' were probably restrained by their reluctance to compel a price of Canadian crude in the protected Ontario market which was too obviously in excess of the landed price of imported crude east of Ontario. Eastern Canadian prices were directly tied to prices outside North America. Given Canadian wellhead prices set according to these considerations, and given transportation costs, the landed price of the restricted US imports of Canadian oil was lower than the price of competing domestic oil in the US.

Excess capacity for oil production had developed in Canada in the 1950s and was accentuated by restricted access to the United States market. The excess capacity, however, was prevented from depressing prices because output prorationing was adopted by the Alberta government; provincial production was restricted to the level demanded at the set wellhead price.[3]

Despite the excess capacity, the ratio of Canadian reserves of conventional oil to annual production declined in the late 1960s as new discoveries failed to keep pace with production. More crucially, with imports restricted the older American oil fields were increasingly incapable of meeting a rising United States demand.

The quota system in the United States was dismantled early in 1973.[4] With the removal of quotas, US imports from all sources have risen dramatically. The increase in Canadian exports has pushed Canadian production to near full capacity and Canadian pipelines to full-capacity limits. Wellhead prices in Canada, though still set by the majors, are now influenced more directly by prices in the Chicago area market, where the pressure is for equalization of landed prices of Canadian, offshore, and American crude. Confronted with this pressure, and a Canadian wellhead price which had risen by some 95¢ a barrel in less than a year, the Canadian federal government, on 4 Sept. 1973, applied moral suasion to freeze Canadian oil prices at their existing levels until 30 Jan. 1974.[5] This action was followed by imposition of a federal export tax on crude oil set at 40¢ a barrel for the month of October 1973.[6] The tax was meant to reinforce the domestic price freeze by raising the export price of Canadian oil to the level of the Chicago market price, thus safeguarding a lower price to domestic refiners. However, between announcement of the export tax and its implementation, the Middle East war of October 1973 intervened to cause an acute acceleration in the world price rise. Consequently, the tax applying to December exports from Canada was increased to $1.90 a barrel.[7]

Turning to Canadian natural gas, its production and disposition has been subject to a different set of controls, some imposed by the federal government and some by the producing provinces. Natural gas prices at the wellhead have been determined by bargaining between the producer and a purchasing pipeline. In most fields this means that there is only a single bidder. Much of the gas is sold under long-term contracts at fixed or marginally escalating prices. It had become obvious that these prices were low in the light of rising world energy costs and of a severe shortage of natural gas in the United States largely induced by regulatory control of gas prices by the US Federal Power Commission.[8] At the request of the government of Alberta, that province's Energy Resources Conservation Board held hearings in 1972 and issued a report on natural gas pricing in Alberta. The board concluded that Alberta gas was being sold at bargain prices which it attributed mainly to lack of competition among buyers.[9] In the board's opinion, the then average field price of 16¢ per mcf should have been at least 10¢ higher. The premier of Alberta endorsed the report and announced a 'two-price' policy for natural gas, with lower prices for provincial utilities and strong positive action to raise the price of gas exported from the province.[10] As part of this policy Alberta has refused further sales to Trans-Canada Pipelines pending renegotiation of existing contracts to the province's satisfaction; this has raised the possibility of shortages of gas in central Canada and led to direct conflict with the government of Ontario[11] [Editors' note: for a more detailed scenario read Hamilton's paper on Canadian natural gas. At the point of writing (26 Nov.) the issue is still far from resolved].

Canada is unique among the developed countries in that it has a net current self-sufficiency in crude oil and natural gas. It has been suggested, however, that whenever the price of these energy sources increases, Canadians in the aggregate are net losers because of the large degree of foreign ownership of the industry.[12] To the concern felt in Canada, as elsewhere, over the long-term availability and cost of petroleum and natural gas is added a concern that Canadians must receive the maximum benefit from the disposal of these resources. To that end the way in which the industry is taxed can play a significant role. This is the main theme of this paper, to which we now turn.

ISSUES IN THE TAXATION
OF OIL AND GAS PRODUCTION

From an economic viewpoint the basis on which the debate over oil and gas taxation – indeed the taxation of all mineral extraction – is conducted has perceptibly improved since the appointment of the federal Royal Commission on Taxation in September 1962. Until that time there was very little serious discussion of the ends and almost none of the means of mineral tax policy. The arguments before the commission and more particularly in the infighting which followed publica-

193

tion of the commission's report[13] and the federal government's own White Paper on tax reform,[14] centered on the commission's insistence on as neutral an income tax system as could be devised (i.e. one which does not alter relative inducements to invest in, or produce, different goods) and on two main industry counter-arguments for continuing tax favor. The two counter-arguments were the extraordinary risks of oil and gas production, particularly in the exploration phase, and the international competition for the necessary investment funds. In the upshot, the federal tax reform eventually enacted in 1971[15] did not significantly alter the existing concessions to the oil and gas industry under the corporation income tax.

One aspect of government sharing in the profits from oil and gas which tended to be overlooked by the would-be reformers was that in the provinces there existed a collateral apparatus, in the form of bonus bidding, rentals, and royalties, for appropriating some of the potential profits of extraction. The effect of federal policy, tax and non-tax, was to enhance the yield from these devices. For hard reasons of revenue, as well as for more nebulous reasons of local 'prestige,' the provincial premiers vociferously opposed the proposed tax reforms; their opposition to tax reform in oil and gas and other minerals assumed a catalytic role in dismembering the broader designs of the royal commission report and the White Paper.

With the election of new provincial governments in Alberta, Saskatchewan, and British Columbia in 1971 and 1972 and more significantly with the increased perception of an energy crisis as US reserves dwindled and as OPEC turned the screws, the provinces were moved to increase their royalties. At the same time the federal government had committed itself to defining a coherent new national energy policy. A conflict between federal and provincial policies became apparent with the federal government concerned about low-cost, secure sources of energy for all Canadians, and the Alberta government concerned with maximizing the amount of rent it can collect for Albertans. Notably, the focus of the energy tax debate has shifted from emphasis on risk and neutrality of taxation to the maximization of government revenue. Objectives are now couched in terms of appropriating economic rent. The conflict between the federal and Alberta governments arises over the distribution of the rent between the Alberta government, the federal government, and the Canadian consumer. From the various debates, we identify the two basic issues which should underlie tax (or other) policy regarding oil and gas production as, first, the distribution of the economic rent which arises from oil and gas extraction and, secondly, the optimal use over time of Canadian energy deposits.

Distribution of rent
Economic rent is the excess return accruing to a scarce resource over the return necessary to attract it into use. Since oil and gas deposits have value only through exploitation, the rent arising from their production is the difference between the

market value of the crude oil or gas (at the wellhead) and the total real costs of exploitation. The total real costs of exploitation include those of labor and materials and the opportunity-cost of capital invested in exploration, development, and production. Those payments are real costs because they are required to draw the necessary inputs into oil and gas extraction. Properly excluded from the real-cost reckoning are payments made to the legal owners of the mineral rights (government or freehold landowners); these payments are residuals determined by output values and are therefore themselves an allocation of rent.[16] For any deposit, given the market value, the rent per barrel of crude oil (or per mcf of gas) produced will vary with the productiveness of the deposit, with finding costs,[17] and with costs of transportation from the wellhead to the market. The lower the unit cost of discovery, production, and transportation, the greater is the economic rent per unit of output.

Public appropriation of the economic rent will have no distorting impact on production decisions. Indeed, as we argue below, if the total rent can be identified and captured by governments, the rate at which the resource is depleted will also be optimal.

The rent element from oil and gas may accrue to a private landowner, to a government, to the producer, or to consumers. To the extent that the return on potential oil-bearing land is anticipated at the time the landowner yields his mineral rights, the capitalized value of future rents will enter into the price of the land; i.e. it will be appropriated by an advance payment to the landowner. The landowner may also retain a right to a portion of an uncertain future return by stipulating an over-riding percentage royalty on future production income. Any residual rent not so captured or taxed away generally remains in the hands of the producer.

It is possible, however, for some of the rent to accrue to a class of consumers. This would be the case if the output were sold at less than its market value. As we noted above, prices of natural gas to both domestic and American consumers have not kept pace with alternative energy prices. There seems to be little reason for subsidizing a particular set of consumers, especially foreign ones. An economic rent to domestic consumers also arises from the recently announced federal export tax on crude oil (or a proposed alternative export marketing board). Where domestic wellhead prices are determined by export prices net of transportation costs, an export tax reduces the wellhead price below what it would otherwise be. As the tax applies only to exports, it is equivalent to a production tax combined with an equal subsidy to domestic consumption. That part of the population which makes intensive use of domestic oil or oil-dependent products has received an income transfer, unless the rent is dissipated by incurring higher transportation costs and displacing imports of equal price.

Governments may appropriate some or all of the rent in their role as landowners, through taxation, or by direct participation in the industry.[18] Traditionally, the provincial governments have relied on crown land holdings as their main instrument for raising revenues from oil and gas.[19] Federal government revenues from oil and gas production have derived mainly from the corporate income tax (in which the provinces also share), which potentially could capture some of the rent besides being a tax on the return to capital.

The revenue raised from crown land ownership, from the corporate income tax, and from export taxes or their equivalent, are mutually interdependent. Since what interests the exploration and production company is its return after all expenditures, including taxes, there is a trade-off among these revenue sources; for example, preferential corporate tax treatment permits higher royalties, rentals, and lease-bonus payments without reducing the net corporate rate of return, and hence the rate of exploitation.[20] While different mixes of taxes, royalties, and so on may affect the efficiency of production and alter the rate of exploitation, the principal effect is to alter the distribution of revenues among the various claimants, including the two levels of government.

The optimal use over time
Since there is a fixed, though unknown, total amount of oil and gas deposits in Canada (and in the rest of the world), current exploitation involves forgone future use.[21] This raises the question of determining the optimal use over time of a depletable resource. The optimal pattern of domestic oil and gas exploitation over time depends on a great many factors. Among them we may list the total potential stocks of oil and gas available and current and future costs of exploiting them, the stocks and costs of depletable substitutes (e.g. coal and uranium), the costs of non-depletable substitutes (e.g. solar power), the reliability of foreign deliveries, current and future populations and incomes, technological change as it affects energy demand, alternative energy sources and non-energy uses of petroleum and gas, and, finally, the rate at which future values are discounted.

Most of these influences are subject to pervasive uncertainty. It follows that in estimating the optimal rate for exploiting domestic reserves, policy makers and their critics can never make more than an educated guess. Expectations concerning total domestic deposits and production costs are continually adjusted as the rate and nature of new discoveries change. Similarly, changes in technology, world demand, and security conditions of foreign supply, cause continual adjustments in the estimated future demand for Canadian oil and gas. While reasonable and well informed people may disagree on what the optimal rate of domestic exploitation would be, there are also differences which arise among those with different interests in the decision, especially when the distribution of rent differs with the different patterns of exploitation (for example, if the government or landowner fails to capture all the economic rent or is expected to capture an increasing share of the rent, the producing sector will have an incentive for more rapid exploitation).

The appropriate royalty[22]

Because production reduces the stock of deposits (discovered plus undiscovered), greater current production leaves a lower stock for future production. The real cost of current production thus includes the forgone value, or opportunity-cost, of the oil (and gas) in future production and use. That opportunity-cost per barrel is the discounted value of what another barrel of reserves would be worth in the future, i.e. it is the discounted present value of the difference between the future price per barrel (assuming price = marginal value) and future input costs of exploitation per barrel.

Suppose all industries were competitive and the corporate income tax were neutral across industries. Then a royalty or production tax equal to the opportunity-cost of forgone future use of deposits would result in an optimal allocation of factors of production among industries, an optimal pattern of exploitation of deposits over time, and a corresponding optimal pattern of prices.[23] Such a pattern is one with price changing over time in such a way that the margin between price and real cost rises at the discount rate.[24] By the time the price equals the cost of the substitute for the last use of oil (or gas), all deposits for which costs of production are less than or equal to that price should have been exploited.[25] The optimal royalty for any deposit is equal to the maximum rent which arises from exploiting it; the maximum rent varies among deposits according to their productivity and transport costs from the wellhead to the market.

In reality, however, prices are set internationally in an uncompetitive industry in which there are many forces operating both to speed up and to slow down the rate of exploitation. While the monopoly power of OPEC enables the exporting countries to raise the price of oil continuously by slowing down the rate of exploitation relative to growth in demand, it is not clear whether the current rate of exploitation of the world's deposits of oil is above or below the optimal rate.

If the rate of exploitation in the rest of the world were too high, current prices would be below the full cost of these resources including the opportunity-cost of forgone future use. Canadian demand should then be met to a greater degree by imports, saving domestic deposits for the future when production would be of greater value due to the then much higher world prices.[26] Conversely, if the rate of exploitation in the rest of the world were too low, current prices would be above optimal. If the lower rate of exploitation were due to a monopolistic restriction of output (e.g. by OPEC) which is expected to continue indefinitely,

R.M. Hyndman and M.W. Bucovetsky

Canadian production taxes and royalties can be set to capture both the rent attributable to the monopoly restriction and that representing the opportunity-cost of forgone future use. If the restriction of output were judged to be temporary, price-cost margins would be expected to fall in the future or to rise at a rate lower than the discount rate. In that case, maximum rents would arise from exploitation during the temporary restriction; Canadian production and exports should then be increased to take advantage of the temporarily high price. In any event, the minimum royalty, which will apply to the marginal deposit and determine the over-all rate of exploitation, should be no less than the opportunity-cost of forgone future exploitation of that marginal deposit.

Although policy makers cannot be at all certain about what is the optimal royalty and rate of exploitation, or about what rate of exploitation would result from any set of royalties, the principles outlined above are the ones that should guide their guesses. If the maximum present value of rent could be captured by governments, the rate of exploitation would be socially optimal.

The appropriate corporate income tax treatment
Suppose the appropriate royalty (or production tax) is set. What is the appropriate corporate income tax treatment of oil and gas production relative to the treatment of other industries? Petroleum industry spokesmen frequently claim that preferential tax treatment of the return to capital in oil and gas production is necessary to offset the extraordinarily high risk associated with that activity, implying that resource allocation would thereby be improved. The claim is based on three assertions: first, that oil and gas production involves very high risks; second, that given the high risk there is a need to encourage more risk-taking; and third, that the tax system contains an anti-risk-taking bias due to its incomplete loss offset.

Risk involved in oil and gas production
Like other economic activity, oil and gas production involves risk in the sense that, while a firm may anticipate earning some average rate of return on its investment, its actual rate of return will fluctuate above and below that average over time and among projects, with the possibility both of very large returns and of bankruptcy.

To measure the risk involved in oil and gas exploration and production[27] it is inappropriate simply to consider the probability of any single well turning out to be a 'dry hole.' While a high probability of a dry hole (and hence a low probability of discovering a commercially exploitable oil or gas deposit) for any single well would make drilling a single well risky, it would not in itself make oil and gas production risky.[28] If, on average, one well in ten is a success,[29] the cost of

198

finding a deposit includes the cost of drilling nine dry holes as well as the one successful well. The larger the number of wells drilled, the more certain will be the costs of discovery. For firms engaged in oil and gas exploration and production, then, it is the probability distribution of the outcome of total operations rather than of a single well which is relevant in measuring risk.

Through pooling the drilling activities of individuals or small firms,[30] and through large-scale operations of large firms, the risk involved in exploration and development is greatly reduced. The more dispersed geographically the drilling operations of a firm, through pooling or large-scale operations, the closer would its success ratio be to the industry average, i.e. the closer would its cost of finding oil be to the industry average.

If the mean outcome of exploration declined, if for the whole industry, oil and gas became harder to find, the cost of finding oil and gas would increase. On average, the cost of discovery may increase from say the cost of drilling ten wells, nine of which are dry holes, to the cost of drilling eleven wells, ten of which are dry holes. This would indicate an increase in costs but not necessarily in risk. For large-scale operations, risk would change only if the dispersion or skewness of outcomes changed, if, for example, rather than a fairly stable success ratio of say 10 per cent for the whole industry, the success ratio over a number of years varied between 5 per cent and 15 per cent, though the average over those years remained at 10 per cent. The skewness might also change, particularly over time as the probability of large fields in accessible areas remaining undiscovered diminishes.

Though in oil and gas production (and perhaps in other industries as well) small firms face greater risk than large firms, it remains to be shown whether oil and gas production is more or less risky than other industries. Oil and gas production is certainly less risky than is implied by simplistic arguments citing the probability of any single well turning out to be a dry hole. Whatever a comparison of risk by industry would reveal, there remains the question of whether encouragement of risk-taking in general would improve the allocation of resources.

The appropriate treatment of risk

To a risk-averse individual, variability of return is a real cost. He is willing to forgo a certain amount of income on average in order to receive a more stable income. For an optimal allocation of resources, prices of output should reflect the real social costs of their production. In a society of risk-averse individuals, risk-taking by them involves real social costs which should be reflected in relative prices of goods. If institutional arrangements such as diversification of ownership of firms and diversification of income sources by individuals reduce the costs of risk, relative prices of goods should reflect those reduced costs.

However, if the costs of risk are not reduced in the above manner, there is no economic-efficiency basis for subsidizing risk-taking any more than there is for subsidizing the use of certain inputs. The traditional argument for subsidizing risk-taking has not been backed by sound economic reasoning.[31]

Anti-risk-taking bias in the tax system
This leads us to the third assertion on which the argument for preferential tax treatment of the return to capital in oil and gas production is based, namely that the tax system contains an anti-risk-taking bias.

The anti-risk-taking bias arises from the lack of a complete loss-offset in the corporate income tax. Assuming a corporate income tax rate of 50 per cent, the government takes one-half of all taxable income of a firm but rather than refund one-half of tax losses, it permits only a limited carry-back of losses (in which case there would be some refund) and a longer carry-forward of the remainder. The carry-forward would result in a deferred 'refund' unless the company goes bankrupt. If the company goes bankrupt, it loses that 'deferred refund.' However, merger of the company incurring losses with a profitable company may permit the owners of the company incurring losses to get a refund indirectly.

Because the loss-offset in the corporate income tax is incomplete, the mean return and the dispersion of positive returns are reduced by a proportion equal to the tax rate while the dispersion of negative returns is reduced by a smaller proportion. Thus, because the mean return is reduced relative to the over-all dispersion of returns, the tax system contains an anti-risk-taking bias.

For large profitable firms, though, the loss-offset for each additional project is complete unless the project could cause the company to incur a loss on its total operations. Thus, with a complete loss-offset there is no anti-risk-taking bias for individual projects undertaken by large, profitable firms. In fact, Musgrave has shown[32] that risk-taking by risk-averse investors is stimulated by a proportional tax with a complete loss-offset.

The corporate income tax might thus discourage risk-taking by small or newly established firms, and perhaps should, for resource allocation reasons, include a better loss-offset or some provision to offset the anti-risk-taking bias in the absence of a complete loss-offset.

That might be an argument for preferential tax treatment of oil and gas production if the industry were uniquely risky and also composed predominantly of small firms. However, that the industry is uniquely risky has not been proved and large firms account for a significant proportion of the total activity.

Security of supply
Current concern about the long-term availability of imported crude oil and pet-

roleum products stems from two related uncertainties over the reliability of international supply. One of these is the effect of political events on the rate of world output expansion, especially by the Arab countries. The other is a concern that the price mechanism might be prevented from allocating global production among the various national markets. As to the first, while the restricting of supply for political reasons may raise the price in the same way as does restriction of supply for economic (government revenue) reasons, the political reasons are an additional and probably less predictable factor and thus cause supply to be less certain than otherwise.

If the allocation of oil supplies among consuming nations were not determined by the price mechanism, but rather if much of global production were pre-empted by specific countries under long-term agreements, those countries without direct access would face narrow markets in which oil was unavailable or else prices which were greatly in excess of long-run equilibrium prices. This would also be the fate of countries faced with outright refusal of sale by the major producing nations. Government policies in importing nations are thus legitimately concerned with the security of supply, i.e. with insurance against uncertainty, a concern which may over-ride the otherwise optimal use of their own reserves over time.

The extent to which it is desirable to turn to more secure supplies from less secure ones, in other words the proportion of total supplies rendered 'secure,' depends on the extra cost of the more secure supplies, the extra security achieved, and the extent of the risk associated with less secure supplies.

A popular fallacy which should be dispelled is that in general the more a country relies on domestic production the more secure is its supply over the long term. In fact, the more a country relies on domestic production the sooner its resources will be depleted and the less secure its supply will be in the long term. Greater security lies in holding greater domestic reserves available for emergency rather than in increasing domestic production. This, perhaps, is an argument in favor of oil sands development in Canada at a time when lower-cost conventional reserves are available. If the supply constraint is not the amount of mineral deposits but rather the time required to bring them into production, accelerated development could increase long-term security of supply.

If preferential tax treatment were necessary to encourage accelerated development, such tax treatment for oil sands production might be justified on grounds of security of supply. However, if preferential tax treatment of conventional production has encouraged more rapid development and depletion of reserves, it would have reduced long-term security of supply in the absence of oil sands development. Moreover, preferential tax treatment is not the only form of subsidy available, nor is it necessarily the most efficient in terms of ready reserves per dollar of cost.

R.M. Hyndman and M.W. Bucovetsky

To summarize our observations on the optimal use of Canada's oil and gas deposits, the rate of exploitation is affected by the royalties charged and the taxation of corporate income. The appropriate royalty on each deposit depends on costs of discovery, of production, and of transportation to the market. It should be at least as large as the opportunity-cost of forgone future exploitation of the deposit. Where there is international monopolistic restriction of output the royalty should be large enough to capture the additional monopoly rent. In examining the theoretical reasons for preferential corporate tax treatment of oil and gas production, we find no significant case for preferential treatment of the whole industry based either on efficiency of resource allocation or on security of supply. Nonetheless, dependence on insecure supplies must be balanced against the virtues of the correct exploitation rate as determined by maximum present valued royalties. Thus there may be a security-of-supply case, or initially an infant-industry case, for subsidizing oil sands or Arctic production where new technology must be developed, but preferential tax treatment would not necessarily be the best form of subsidy even if one were justified. With this theoretical background we turn to an examination of taxes and royalties on oil and gas in Canada.

CANADIAN TAXATION OF OIL
AND GAS PRODUCTION

Corporate income tax
The federal government and all ten provinces levy a tax on 'taxable' income of corporations. The definition of taxable income used by the provinces is that of the federal government except in Ontario and Quebec where there are a few minor differences.

There are two distinctive aspects to the taxation of corporate income in oil and gas production (and mining) which afford very favorable treatment to that industry relative to other industries. First, corporations in oil and gas production are allowed to treat as current expenses, for purposes of determining taxable income, most expenditures of a capital nature related to future Canadian production. Eligible expenditures now include land acquisition costs, purchased royalty interests, geological and geophysical expenses, and drilling costs – essentially all the capital costs of productive or abortive wells except above-ground production equipment.[33] In other industries, expenditures on capital assets can only be included in costs for tax purposes gradually over the life of the income producing assets (capital cost allowances are spread over the life of the asset) and, though capital-cost allowances are generally accelerated relative to the true rate of depreciation, the tax saving they confer falls well short of that afforded by immediate 'expensing.'[34] The expensing of capital costs delays tax payments until the

202

TABLE 1

Corporate income taxes and adjusted* book profit, 1966–70 (millions of dollars)

	Mineral fuels	Petroleum and coal products	All manufacturing	Total non-financial
1966				
Adjusted book profit before taxes (PROFIT)	174.2	246.3	2794.4	5302.9
Corporate income taxes (TAX)	17.5	55.8	973.7	2122.8
Corporate tax/book profit (TAX/PROFIT)	0.100	0.227	0.348	0.400
1967				
PROFIT	290.4	156.9	2405.7	5158.1
TAX	58.8	28.0	976.9	1922.2
TAX/PROFIT	0.202	0.178	0.406	0.373
1968				
PROFIT	279.3	206.0	2756.2	5702.9
TAX	39.8	41.3	1264.7	2285.5
TAX/PROFIT	0.143	0.200	0.459	0.401
1969				
PROFIT	269.5	219.7	2989.7	6076.0
TAX	27.6	48.2	1384.8	2487.6
TAX/PROFIT	0.102	0.219	0.463	0.409
1970				
PROFIT	213.2	250.5	2306.2	5449.3
TAX	33.2	72.1	1182.5	2384.3
TAX/PROFIT	0.156	0.288	0.513	0.438
1966–70 average				
PROFIT	245.3	215.9	2650.4	5537.8
TAX	35.4	49.1	1156.5	2240.5
TAX/PROFIT	0.144	0.227	0.436	0.405

*Book profit before taxes less net capital gains, non-taxable dividends received, and prior years losses applied

SOURCE: Statistics Canada, *Corporation Taxation Statistics,* 1966, 1967, 1968, 1969–70

future (indefinitely if the company grows at a sufficient rate) and thereby greatly reduces the burden of taxation.

Second, taxable income in oil and gas production is further reduced by $33\frac{1}{3}$ per cent by the depletion allowance. Under the new Income Tax Act, what is now an automatic one-third reduction of the profit subjected to tax, will become a maximum reduction in any year after 1976. In the future, depletion will have to be 'earned' on the basis of $1.00 of allowance for every $3.00 of exploration and development spending (essentially the expensible capital expenditures mentioned above, with the exception of property acquisition costs). However, the cumulative bank of eligible expenditures that may be tapped for depletion claims after 1976 includes all the relevant spending incurred since 7 November 1969. Subject to timing considerations, the combined effect of expensing and earned depletion will be similar to an allowable write-off of $133\frac{1}{3}$ per cent of pre-production costs.

An indication of the effect of the special provisions on corporate tax revenues for oil and gas production is given by comparing the ratio of corporation income taxes paid to book profit, adjusted to remove inter-corporate dividends and other untaxed accruals, in industries producing crude oil and gas and in other industries. Although we are unable to isolate all production revenue from oil and gas, Table 1 does show that the special provisions for taxing oil and gas production substantially reduce the corporate income taxes paid by the affected industries.

It has been aptly observed that the Canadian tax system (here referring primarily to the corporation income tax) 'is not designed to capture a very high percentage of the economic rent.'[35] On the contrary, the differentially lighter burden of the corporation income tax on oil and gas production has encouraged greater financial commitment to this industry than would have been the case if all corporate capital bore the same rate of tax. Although it has encouraged an accelerated rate of exploration, development, and production,[36] as noted above, the principal effect was probably to enhance the rents paid to landowners, including provincial governments.[37]

Land revenues

It is apparent that in the past the principal public rent collection device in Canada has been through the tenure system on crown-owned oil and gas lands. In this respect, the province of Alberta has been both the pace-setter and the chief beneficiary. The province's revenue from its oil and gas holdings runs consistently at over 50 per cent of its net general revenue (excluding federal government conditional transfers).

The methods by which Alberta draws revenue from public ownership may be roughly summarized as follows. In the general case, reservations of petroleum and natural gas rights (essentially prospecting licenses granting the holder the right to explore a tract of not over 100,000 acres) are disposed of under sealed tender bid. The applicant must pay a fixed fee and an adequate bonus (a cash sum that presumably reflects his evaluation of the land), and submit a plan for exploration. Reservations may be retained only for short, renewable periods, with a $6\frac{1}{2}$-year maximum in any event.[38]

If a commercial deposit is found (or otherwise at the explorer's discretion), the reservation must be converted to lease. This means that the explorer may retain control of only 50 per cent of the land in each township in his original reservation.[39]

Production from crown lands requires a lease, granted now for 10-year periods and renewable provided certain drilling requirements are met. Lease rights may be obtained by conversion from a reservation (as just described) or other form of exploratory right. They are also allocated through competitive bonus bidding on partially proved acreage relinquished to the crown. As long as a lease is retained an annual rental based on acreage must be paid.

Once a property starts to produce it is obliged to contribute monthly royalty payments. Literally, the royalties are stipulated as an in-kind fraction of the real output of each well on crown lands. In practice, they take the form of a percentage tax on the value of output. Before 1973, the royalty on oil was on a sliding scale, 8 per cent on wells producing up to 750 barrels a month, rising to $16\frac{2}{3}$ per cent on those with monthly production of 2,700 barrels and up. On natural gas the rate is $16\frac{2}{3}$ per cent.

Amounts that the province of Alberta has collected from bonus bidding, acreage rentals, and royalties are shown in Table 2. The other petroleum-producing provinces have adopted variants of the Alberta system, but their revenue potential is not nearly as great. Total crown-land oil and gas receipts for all four western provinces are summarized in Table 3.

The federal government, too, to the extent that it has custody of mineral rights within the province of Alberta, has adopted the method of bonus bidding and royalties. In contrast, rights to explore and produce on federally administered acreage in the Territories and offshore require no bonus bidding and entail future royalties of only 5 per cent in the first three years of production and 10 per cent thereafter.[40] The relevant federal statute is now being reviewed; no new federal permits have been granted since March 1972.[41] However, it has been observed that the review and ban have no meaning unless the federal government is prepared to abrogate its existing commitments.[42] Some 80 per cent of the land with oil and gas potential (presumably the 80 per cent with the best probabilities) is already under permit, and existing permits, converted to lease, can remain valid for a total of thirty-three years.

TABLE 2

Revenue to the province of Alberta from disposition of crown petroleum rights, 1947 to 1972 (thousands of dollars)

Year	Sale of crown reserves						Rentals	Royalties				Total revenue
	P&NG Leases	P&NG reservations	Drilling reservations	Natural gas licences	Natural gas leases	Sub-total sales		Oil	Gas	Gas products	Sub-total royalties	
1947 to 1959 inclusive	360,515	85,346	56,987	6,394	1,176	510,418	231,876	212,780	5,124	443	218,347	960,641
1960	39,564	1,469	9,227	3,649	56	53,964	31,992	25,613	1,783	144	27,540	113,496
1961	31,421	479	10,660	1,165	907	44,631	30,861	32,062	2,537	832	35,432	110,924
1962	16,049	3,312	11,212	2,515	67	33,154	38,476	40,889	4,761	2,340	47,990	119,620
1963	26,131	1,444	18,777	179	117	46,647	37,792	43,457	7,435	4,247	55,139	139,519
1964	59,516	1,573	23,660	—	71	84,820	42,771	47,060	8,063	5,731	60,854	188,445
1965	79,427	—	39,804	397	35	119,662	57,408	51,058	9,015	7,898	67,971	245,041
1966	76,363	391	21,568	721	77	99,120	53,220	56,788	9,343	9,135	75,266	227,606
1967	67,268	62	18,692	1,688	12	87,721	53,507	70,683	10,035	11,997	92,714	233,943
1968	59,753	1,408	30,977	1,205	49	93,391	55,235	75,956	11,659	13,706	101,322	249,948
1969	42,980	14,077	44,565	558	—	102,180	61,224	87,396	14,004	11,819	113,219	276,623
1970	15,462	193	8,069	1,952	12	25,688	56,111	106,009	17,537	12,871	136,417	218,216
1971	14,254	255	6,714	2,662	37	23,922	68,844	131,788	20,990	14,944	167,721	260,487
1972	10,368	534	12,688	2,113	23	25,727	74,502	156,828	22,013	17,442	196,284	296,513
26-year total	899,069	110,541	313,602	25,197	2,638	1,351,046	893,821	1,138,370	144,298	113,546	1,396,214	3,641,081

SOURCE: Province of Alberta, Department of Mines & Minerals, *Alberta Oil and Gas Picture 1947-1972*. Totals may not add, due to rounding.

TABLE 3

Revenue to the western provinces from disposition of crown petroleum rights, 1947 to 1972 (thousands of dollars)

Year	Manitoba			Saskatchewan			British Columbia			Total, four provinces, incl. Alberta			
	Land sales	Rentals	Royalties	Land sales	Rentals	Royalties	Land sales	Rentals	Royalties	Land sales	Rentals	Royalties	Total revenue
1947 to 1959 inclusive	991	1,380	1,641	42,751	34,387	20,598	19,094	29,429	1,584	573,254	297,072	242,170	1,112,496
1960	5	199	315	2,080	5,016	6,929	6,187	6,709	1,207	62,236	43,916	35,991	142,143
1961	134	93	306	1,319	4,081	8,102	7,642	6,545	1,479	53,726	41,580	45,319	140,625
1962	26	90	298	3,747	2,408	9,599	11,356	7,183	3,634	48,283	48,157	61,521	157,961
1963	33	47	276	5,313	2,480	11,545	7,092	7,723	5,506	59,085	48,042	72,466	179,598
1964	110	35	307	8,304	2,935	14,535	13,094	8,445	5,190	106,328	54,186	80,886	241,400
1965	93	62	344	11,311	3,228	14,206	18,161	8,304	5,473	149,227	69,002	87,994	306,223
1966	87	60	353	7,110	3,535	16,341	15,839	10,209	7,768	122,156	67,024	99,728	288,908
1967	78	56	370	9,343	4,006	15,708	14,298	10,357	9,607	111,440	67,926	118,399	297,765
1968	54	39	411	5,150	4,218	15,125	15,077	10,622	10,945	113,672	70,114	127,803	311,589
1969	82	31	405	4,872	4,480	14,553	21,646	10,340	12,797	128,780	76,075	140,974	345,829
1970	10	26	376	3,820	3,903	14,241	16,340	9,174	13,405	45,858	69,214	164,431	279,511
1971	34	21	373	2,473	3,819	14,666	22,185	9,428	14,668	48,614	82,112	197,428	328,154
1972	– e	22e	370	4,691e	3,900e	15,000	20,496e	10,000e	15,500	50,914	88,424	227,154	366,492
26-year total	1,737	2,161	6,145	112,284	82,396	191,148	208,507	144,468	108,763	1,673,574	1,122,846	1,702,270	4,498,690
Provincial 26-year totals from all sources	10,043			385,828			461,738						

e estimate by *Oil Week*

SOURCE: Table 2 and *Oil Week*, Annual Review Issues

Provincially-owned lands have been a far more lucrative source of government revenues than has the corporate income tax. An exact comparison of yields cannot be made because it is not possible to identify corporation taxes paid on production profits alone, excluding those on refining and marketing profits. It may be noted that all oil companies with some production income paid total corporation taxes of $81 million in 1969 and $119 million in 1970.[43] This is considerably more than would be their tax liability on production income alone, but still it represents only 25 per cent and 40 per cent, respectively, of land-based revenue to the four western provinces in the same years.[44]

The weaknesses of the traditional collection devices are that they apply only to crown lands, and that they provide for no public share of a rising annual rent on the land. If the future were known, competitive bonus bidding could, in principle, capture 100 per cent of the rent.[45] If bonus bidding is absent or if it falls short of capitalizing the anticipated rent, we may predict premature pre-emptive occupation of the public lands. Percentage royalties on output provide an additional means of capturing part of the uncertain future return; they allow some sensitivity to the richness of individual deposits, to the extent that royalty rates vary with the rate of flow. Their main shortcoming is that if prices rise over time, as we predict they ought to do under an optimal pattern of use, a fixed fraction of output value represents a continuously smaller proportion of the rent element. The traditional output royalties are also unable to tap any additional windfall rents due to (unanticipated) monopoly restriction of world output.

Recent tax developments

As this paper is being written, the future tax system with respect to oil and gas extraction is very much in flux. For 1973, the Alberta government implemented a new tax on the assessed value of crude oil reserves, applicable to freehold land and to holders of crown land who did not 'voluntarily' increase their royalty rates. The optional new royalty schedule is on a scale rising from 5 per cent to 25 per cent of monthly oil production; it is expected to average at 21 per cent. Expected to yield the province an additional $70 million in 1973 if wellhead prices were unchanged, by August the added taxes were indicated to be some $103 million.[46] British Columbia has increased its royalty rates on both crude oil and natural gas, with effect from 1 June 1973. Royalties in BC on oil now range from 10 per cent to 40 per cent of gross production, representing, on average, an increase of about 30 per cent over the former schedule. Saskatchewan, too, in its 1973 budget, indicated that its royalty rates would rise.

Another 1973 innovation is the announced method by which Alberta will tax profits on the proposed oil sands operation of Syncrude Limited, now scheduled for a 1978 start of production. Here, Alberta has adopted a method formerly prevalent in the Middle East: the 'royalty' will be a 50 per cent interest in the net profit of the operation.[47]

Several possible future directions have been indicated. The newly created BC Energy Commission made two proposals to the provincial government in September 1973. One was that the province set up a crown agency to market natural gas. The other was that the traditional royalty system on natural gas be abandoned in favor of a price-per-mcf formula based on current 'competitive value.'[48] Early in October, the Alberta government announced it would scrap its existing royalty schedules and its newly-implemented oil reserves tax. Instead, the province would tax both oil and gas on a 'world commodity basis.'[49] The province, in other words, would adopt the method, favored by OPEC, of altering royalties by specifying a fixed percentage of a national 'posted price' determined by the government. In late November, Alberta was talking in terms of establishing its own monopoly marketing board with authority to buy and re-sell the oil produced on crown-leaseholds.[50]

In a year in which the swift pace of world events has been matched by dramatic shifts in Canadian oil and gas policy, the domestic tax innovation with the most far-reaching repercussions was the federal export tax on crude oil, mentioned at the beginning of this paper. We noted there that the purpose of the tax, 40¢ a barrel on October and November 1973 exports and $1.90 in December, was to bolster a 'voluntary' price freeze on domestically marketed oil. We also observed that, where wellhead prices are determined by export prices net of transportation costs, an export tax is equivalent to a production tax combined with an equal subsidy to domestic consumption of Canadian oil. The same result could be achieved by a monopoly marketing board which paid domestic producers a price equal to the export price net of transportation costs, less an amount equal to the displaced export tax. The export tax or its equivalent is thus a means of rent collection with a particular distribution among the federal government and domestic consumers.

With current exports running at over one million barrels a day, an export tax at the $1.90 level would yield total revenues of about $60 million in a month. If a share of 40 per cent[51] were paid to the producing provinces, the Alberta government would be compensated for all royalties lost at the current royalty rate on both exports and domestic sales through a failure of the wellhead price to rise by $1.90 a barrel. Alberta's share of the December export tax receipts would be some $20 million, an amount that very nearly duplicates the direct monthly yield of its own royalties and reserves tax. On the other hand, the December export tax also implicitly subsidizes domestic consumers of Canadian crude to the extent of about $41 million. If the wellhead price were to rise by the full $1.90, it would be possible in principle for the provinces to pre-empt the entire additional rent, in which case, the Alberta government alone could receive some $84 million in extra revenues in December. There are, however, strong indications that the province means to share the windfall from any near-term price increase with producers in the province.[52]

An export tax, however, may also play a role in regard to security of supply. Suppose, for example, that it were determined that for security-of-supply reasons, Canadian oil must supply a larger portion of the eastern Canadian market still subject to competition from imports. An export tax could then be set equal to the excess of the Chicago area price (the export market price) over the price of imports landed in Montreal, plus the excess cost of transporting Canadian oil to Montreal over the cost of bringing Canadian oil to Chicago. The net-back to Canadian producers would then be the same whether the oil were exported or sold domestically as far east as Montreal. Moreover, domestic oil would be competitive with offshore imports in the Montreal market.[53]

Apart from security-of-supply reasons, holding domestic prices below long-run equilibrium export prices is an inefficient means of capturing rent for Canadians. The lower domestic price encourages the use of oil where it is less valuable to consumers than the amount a barrel of oil could earn if switched to export. Further, to the extent that new Canadian markets are served by supplies diverted from export, the higher transportation costs involve an additional efficiency loss. If, as apparently planned by the federal government,[54] the Canadian price is not to be held below international levels, the export tax or equivalent price discrimination by a marketing board would primarily be part of a security-of-supply policy, rather than serving as a major rent-collection device.

SUMMARY

From our examination of the basic issues which underlie tax and royalty policies we concluded that for an optimal pattern of exploitation over time (excluding consideration of security of supply) land payments, royalties, and taxes combined should capture the economic rent from oil and gas production. Some adjustment might be justified on security-of-supply grounds, but it would not necessarily be a reduction in taxes or royalties. The principal effect of altering the mix of taxes and royalties is to alter the distribution of rent among provincial governments, other resource owners, producers, and the federal government. An export tax is equivalent to a production tax combined with a subsidy to Canadian consumption of domestic crude.

The proportion of the economic rent that the provincial governments can capture without reducing the rate of exploitation is increased by the preferential corporate tax treatment of oil and gas production but reduced by the export tax. A question left unanswered in this paper is whether combined present taxes and royalties result in a rate of exploitation above or below the optimal rate.

NOTES

1 For details, see K.W. Dam, 'Implementation of Import Quotas: The Case of Oil,' *Journal of Law and Economics,* XIV, April 1971, esp. pp. 28-35
2 An exception to the NOP rule was made for fuel oil purchased in bulk.
3 Output restriction by a single province, Alberta, created a protective umbrella over all Canadian production because proved reserves in Alberta are over 85 per cent of the Canadian total.
4 Both mandatory quotas and tariffs were removed and replaced by a fee system. In 1973, fees apply to imports in excess of the former quota. The volume of fee-free imports is to be phased out by 1980. The Secretary of the Interior has authority to abrogate fees on Canadian imports.
5 *Globe and Mail,* Toronto, 5 Sept. 1973
6 Ibid., 14 Sept. 1973
7 Ibid., 2 Nov. 1973
8 See P.W. MacAvoy, 'The Regulation Induced Shortage of Natural Gas,' *Journal of Law and Economics,* XIV, April 1971, pp. 167-99
9 *Report on Field Pricing of Gas in Alberta,* Calgary, Energy Resources Conservation Board, August 1972
10 Province of Alberta, Hansard, 16 Nov. 1972
11 A further current natural gas problem stems from 'coning' (the blockage of gas flow from the reservoir due to the irregular flow of water) in a major British Columbia gas field, raising the spectre of a gas shortage in that province in the winter of 1973-4, unless Alberta gas fields are connected with the pipeline serving BC and the US northwest.
12 F. Roseman and B.W. Wilkinson, 'Who Benefits? The Alberta Energy Price Increases,' *The Canadian Forum,* LII, June-July 1973, pp. 48-52
13 Royal Commission on Taxation, *Report,* Volumes 1-6, Ottawa, 1967
14 Hon. E.J. Benson, *Proposals for Tax Reform,* Ottawa, 7 Nov. 1969
15 *Canadian Income Tax Act, Chap. 63, S.C. 1970-1*
16 To the extent that payments to landowners are compensation for income forgone from an alternative use of the land, these payments do represent a real cost and not a residual rent.
17 While there may be practical and perhaps even conceptual problems in associating exploration costs with specific deposits, the principle is our main concern here.

R.M. Hyndman and M.W. Bucovetsky

18 Direct government participation is a new phenomenon in Canada. In 1969, the Quebec government incorporated SOQUIP as a crown-owned explorer. In 1973, the Saskatchewan government organized a similar company, SASKOIL, and the Alberta government announced its formation of the Alberta Energy Company, a company to be owned half by the government and half by the Alberta public, to share in the profits of Syncrude Limited's operations in the Athabaska oil sands. The federal government has a 45 per cent interest in Panarctic Oils Limited which is exploring in the Canadian Arctic Islands. In the fall of 1973 rumors had it that the federal government would shortly establish a government-owned integrated oil company (or buy out an existing company).

19 Title to mineral-bearing lands in Alberta is divided approximately as follows: provincial government 81 per cent, federal government (National Parks and Indian Reservations) 9 per cent, freehold 10 per cent. Freehold lands are more significant in the other western provinces, particularly Manitoba (see Royal Bank of Canada, Oil and Gas Department, *Oil and Gas in Canada,* Calgary, 1972).

20 Interaction with foreign tax laws must also be considered, especially the US foreign tax credit.

21 There is a possibility that technological change might render some currently profitable deposits unprofitable in the future, in which case current exploitation does not imply forgone future use.

22 The term 'royalty' is used in two senses in this paper. In the present section it is used as a generalized term to cover any 'rent-capturing device' imposed by a government. In the following section, where we describe existing Canadian levies, the term is used more conventionally to describe a proportional share of output reserved to the landowner.

23 If the cost per barrel of exploiting all deposits were equal, the optimal tax or royalty would be the same for all deposits. Since costs vary, the optimal royalty will also vary.

24 This is a relative price rise, i.e. one in addition to a general rate of inflation.

25 This is obviously a simplification abstracting from transportation costs, differing production costs for differing rates of exploitation, etc.

26 This statement is tempered by the security-of-supply question, discussed below.

27 'Production' is used in this section to refer to all activity up to and including the production stage: exploratory geological and geophysical work, drilling of wildcat wells, development drilling, and production.

28 Oil and gas exploration involves not only risk but also uncertainty. Following the distinction made by Frank H. Knight, risk arises from the unknown out-

212

come of an activity when the distribution of outcomes is known, while with uncertainty neither the individual outcome nor the distribution is known; the distribution must be inferred (F.H. Knight, *Risk, Uncertainty and Profit*, London, 1933).

29 The term 'success' is obviously a simplification since commercially exploitable deposits may range from small pools which are just worth being produced to large pools in a new oil field of 100 million barrels or more.

30 There seems to be specialization according to size of firm within oil and gas production so that the alternatives facing large and small firms differ. See J.W. McKie, 'Market Structure and Uncertainty in Oil and Gas Exploration,' *Quarterly Journal of Economics*, 74, Nov. 1960, pp. 543-71, and R.S. Shearer, 'Nationality, Size of Firm, and Exploration for Petroleum in Western Canada 1946-1954,' *Canadian Journal of Economics and Political Science*, 30, May 1964, pp. 221-27.

31 The discussion above is a simplification of the argument in K.J. Arrow and R.C. Lind, 'Uncertainty and the Evaluation of Public Investment Decisions,' *American Economic Review*, LX, June 1970, pp. 364-78.

32 R.A. Musgrave, *The Theory of Public Finance*, New York, 1959, pp. 312-22

33 Costs of fixed production assets not explicitly covered by immediate write-off are recoverable under ordinary capital allowance provisions, but at favorable rates.

34 A major exception is the two-year write-off of machinery and equipment for use in manufacturing and processing, in effect from 9 May 1972 to 31 Dec. 1974.

35 Minister of Energy, Mines and Resources, *An Energy Policy for Canada – Phase I*, Ottawa, 1973, Vol. 1, p. 147

36 In the presence of output controls, by prorationing, favorable taxation of capital invested in oil and gas may merely have fostered waste in the form of a larger stock of capital than was necessary to remove the product efficiently.

37 To the extent that some oil lands are not crown-owned, but freehold, there is some irony in the fact that royalty income was eligible for a 25 per cent gross depletion allowance under the old Act. Far from appropriating these rents, they were taxed more lightly than other income. After 1976, royalty income will come under the general 'earned' depletion provisions.

38 As noted, the description in the text above covers the general case only. Alternative methods of disposition apply in tightly held areas (Drilling Reservations), to the southeast corner of the province (Permits), and to exclusively natural gas rights (Natural Gas Licences). All of them involve bonus bidding, and allow for eventual conversion to lease.

39 Spacing of retained lease blocks must be chosen in a checker-board pattern.

40 North of 70 degree latitude, the 5 per cent royalty applies for five years. One restriction on federal land grants is that the lessee must be a Canadian citizen or a corporation classed as 'Canadian.'

41 *An Energy Policy for Canada*, Vol. 1, p. 148

42 Andrew Thompson and Michael Crommelin, 'Canada's Petroleum Leasing Policy – A Cornucopia for Whom?,' *The Canadian Forum*, LII, June–July 1973, pp. 22-26. The authors contrast federal policy in Canada with that in the state of Alaska and in United States offshore lands, where, for example, royalties are 20 per cent and $16\frac{2}{3}$ per cent respectively.

43 Statistics Canada, *Corporation Taxation Statistics, 1970*, Cat. 61-218, pp. 152-3

44 We estimated total corporation taxes paid on Alberta production income only, using the numbers available in *Corporation Taxation Statistics* and a number of proportionality assumptions. It was found that in both the 1969 and 1970 taxation years provincial land revenue to Alberta was between 10 and 11 times higher than the applicable corporation tax paid, federal plus provincial.

45 The present value of rent depends on the rate of discount applied to future earnings. If the private rate of discount, for example, exceeded society's rate of time preference, then even with complete knowledge private bids would fall short of the full value of the rent.

46 *Globe and Mail*, Toronto, 2 Aug. 1973. The new plan also contains some very powerful incentives for rapid exploration drilling.

47 It is still unclear whether a royalty based on profit may be deducted by a corporation from the income which is subject to corporate income tax; a royalty based on output is expensible for income tax purposes.

48 *Oilweek*, 1 Oct. 1973

49 *Oilweek*, 8 Oct. 1973 and *Globe and Mail*, Toronto, 5 Oct. 1973

50 *Globe and Mail*, Toronto, 20 Nov. 1973

51 Ibid., 9 Nov. 1973. The Canadian Press reported that the federal government did offer the provinces 40 per cent of export tax receipts.

52 Ibid., 22 Nov. 1973

53 Let Chicago price be p_c and price of offshore imports in Montreal be p_m (where $p_c > p_m$). Let transportation cost from Canadian wellhead to Chicago be t_c and transportation cost from Canadian wellhead to Montreal be t_m (where $t_m > t_c$). Then, if an export tax is set at $(p_c - p_m) + (t_m - t_c)$ on sales to the Chicago market, the net Canadian wellhead price is p_c minus t_c and minus the tax as above, an amount equal to $p_m - t_m$. This is also the net wellhead price for Canadian production sold in Montreal.

54 *Globe and Mail*, Toronto, 23 Nov. 1973

PART ·THREE

Policy Overlaps

The degree of interdependence in Canadian-American energy relationships is large and complex – Canada exports half its natural gas and oil production to the US while importing half its coal requirements from the US. American companies own a large share of Canadian oil and gas reserves, pipelines, and refining capacity. Together the two countries have jointly planned a large hydro electric system – the Columbia River Project. Amid these relationships, is calling for a continental energy policy merely asking for a formal label?

Waverman points out that despite these extant relationships, the two countries have viewed each other as reluctant marriage partners. Both countries have vetoed numerous export and import contracts in the past. The one case of clear joint planning – the Columbia River Project – has turned out to be detrimental to Canada.

The evidence today suggests the end to these interrelationships. Canadians are concerned about the degree of foreign domination of industry. Canadian 'Project Independence' will come about before Nixon's 1980, reducing the flow of energy products across the border. Americans cannot rely on Canadian energy in the future: Canadian reserves (except for the tar sands) are probably limited and are earmarked for future generations of Canadians.

The papers by Debanné, Helliwell, Chapman, Starratt *et al.*, and Spann and Erickson in this volume are complementary, as are those by Steele, Adelman, and Homet in the first volume.

216

LEONARD WAVERMAN

The reluctant bride: Canadian and American energy relations

In 1973, amid chaotic world energy markets, the United States and Canada independently moved towards self-sufficiency in energy. President Nixon's 'Project Independence' was designed to make the US independent of imported oil and gas by 1980. Under Project Independence, Canada is placed in the same category as Libya and Saudi Arabia. Later in 1973, Canadian federal government officials moved to ship oil to Quebec temporarily until a domestic oil pipeline could be built to the east coast. When that pipeline is constructed, Canadian oil exports to the US will fall by at least 50 per cent.

These policies mark a watershed in American-Canadian relations. While a continental energy policy has never been simultaneously considered by both countries ('continental' meaning joint planning of energy production and shipment without regard to borders), strong ties exist between the two energy economies. American capital, management, and skilled labor developed the initial Canadian oil and gas fields and largely built Canada's two major domestic pipelines. Today, foreigners (largely American) own 83 per cent (by book value of assets) of Canadian petroleum-refining capacity,[1] 77 per cent of the entire Canadian petroleum industry,[2] 40 per cent of domestic Canadian pipelines,[3] 60 per cent of coal, and 25 per cent of uranium mining.[4] At the same time, much of the revenue from oil and gas sales in Canada comes from exports to the US. In 1972, 45 per cent of Canadian oil production was exported to the US, as was 40 per cent of natural gas production.[5] This oil amounted to 8 per cent of US consumption in 1973. The links between the two countries also include international flows of electricity, since some ability exists to borrow peak generating capacity from the other country. Both countries developed Columbia River projects. From large

217

Leonard Waverman

Canadian hydro projects, 10 to 20 per cent of the annual electricity generated is anticipated to be exported for a short time to the US, from whom Canada imports 50 per cent of its coal requirements.

The prospective Gas Arctic Pipeline which would bring gas from Prudhoe Bay and the Mackenzie Delta areas of the North Slope will increase Canadian exports of natural gas to the United States. While the two countries have developed different types of nuclear generating capabilities, in the past a significant portion of American uranium consumption has been filled by Canadian production.

Analyzing these statistics might suggest that a 'need' for a continental energy policy is simply semantic – what more could be done to cement the two countries together? Yet continentalism in the true sense of the word does not hold in North American energy relations. Each country has suggested a continental policy, though at separate times, since policies developed by each country, based on self-interest, have tended to hurt the other. Indeed both countries have been reluctant brides to any possible energy marriage. The future does not hold any remote possibility of a continental energy policy. Indeed on 15 November 1973 President Richard Nixon stated: 'Our Canadian friends – they are pretty tough on us at times too, you know, when they are looking down our throats ...'[6]

In this paper, I propose to summarize briefly Canadian energy reserves, production, and consumption. I will then suggest the themes which have governed the development of policies in the two countries since 1950, showing alternative probes for a continental energy policy. Finally, I hope to present a brief critique of evolving Canadian policy and to suggest a scenario for the future – not marriage but mutual respect and trade.

NORTH AMERICAN ENERGY: FACTS AND POLICIES

Oil

In Table 1 appear recent Canadian data for oil reserves, production, consumption, exports, and imports. All exports go to the United States; 30 per cent of imports come from the Middle East, the remainder from Venezuela. The Canadian theme against which all Canadian energy policy must be played is the Canadian National Policy enunciated in the 1870s. Canada is a diverse land, with clumps of settlement mainly spread out on the long border with the US. To promote political unity, economic integration was required. The cheapest trade routes run north-south. Afraid that political units on an east-west axis would break up under north-south flows with the US, east-west economic flows were to be encouraged.

With the expansion of the oil industry in Alberta, the decision was made to ship that oil east as far as the Ottawa Valley. Three conflicting goals had to be reconciled. First, the oil industry was to be promoted. But Canadian oil is rela-

TABLE 1

Crude oil reserves, production, exports, and imports – Canada (million barrels)

Year	Remaining at beginning of year	Total additions	Net production	Remaining at end of year	Net change in reserves during year	Imports	Exports
1951	1,202	221	47	1,376	173	88	0.3
1952	1,376	363	60	1,679	302	82	1.4
1953	1,679	246	80	1,845	165	82	2.5
1954	1,845	457	95	2,207	362	77	2.3
1955	2,207	429	127	2,509	301	87	16.7
1956	2,509	509	169	2,849	339	106	42
1957	2,849	206	181	2,874	25	112	55
1958	2,874	457	166	3,165	291	103	30
1959	3,165	514	183	3,497	331	116	34
1960	3,497	372	191	3,678	181	127	41
1961	3,678	716	221	4,173	495	133	67
1962	4,173	552	244	4,480	307	135	86
1963	4,480	657	256	4,881	400	147	91
1964	4,881	1,566	270	6,177	1,296	143	102
1965	6,177	825	291	6,711	533	143	108
1966	6,711	1,396	316	7,791	1,080	158	127
1967	7,791	721	344	8,168	377	163	151
1968	8,168	584	371	8,381	212	177	169
1969	8,381	631	393	8,619	283	190	203
1970	8,619	377	438	8,558	-60	208	245
1971	8,558	254	480	8,333	-225	244	274

SOURCE: First five columns: Canadian Petroleum Association, *Reserves of Crude Oil, Natural Gas Liquids and Natural Gas in the United States and Canada* (published jointly with the American Petroleum Institute and the American Gas Association), May 1972. Last two columns: Canadian Petroleum Association, *1971 Statistical Yearbook*

tively high cost. Mid East oil at cost (not at world cartel prices) could be transported and undersell Albertan oil almost as far west as Alberta. To develop the oil industry, it was guaranteed a market. Why not all Canada? Quebec might balk at paying very high prices to the west in order to aid Canadian nationalism. How could Quebec develop if it were at a disadvantage because of high fuel costs? Moreover, the multinational oil companies had to be pacified since they would have preferred the more lucrative export market. They agreed to a compromise. Canadian National Oil Policy (NOP) retained the area west of the Ottawa Valley as the exclusive preserve of domestic producers.[7] Imports were freely allowed into the eastern remainder of the country. This compromise may well have maximized the profits of the multinationals. To ship this oil east and export it to the US, a pipeline was constructed which runs through the US south of the Great Lakes.[8]

As early as 1949, excess capacity had appeared in western oil fields. Prorationing began in the early 1950s; the Alberta Oil and Gas Conservation Board deciding how demand should be divided among wells – demand, of course, at the going price. Price competition was not considered. With excess capacity and a small domestic market, Canadian producers looked to the American export market. Canada was, of course, subject to the import controls affecting all foreign oil suppliers to the US.

In 1955, a US Cabinet committee advised that oil imports be voluntarily restricted to maintain the 1954 ratio of imports to domestic production. That committee report raised the issue of national security – excessive imports were harmful both to 'orderly industrial growth' and to 'incentives for exploration.' National security by definition excluded America's best ally – Canada (and also Venezuela whose subsequent entry into OPEC may have been the ultimate factor in strengthening OPEC). After the breakdown of these voluntary restrictions, the Mandatory Oil Import Program began in 1959.[9] Canada, of course, vehemently objected and in 1961 received overland exemptions. In effect, Canadian imports into US District V (west of the Rockies) was treated as American oil; Canadian imports into the other US districts were exempt from the quota until 1967. After 1967, Canadian crude imported into Districts I to IV, was subtracted from the allowed import quota. Since the tickets for allowed quotas were sellable, while Canadian crude had no such monetary advantage to refineries, this 1967 decision tended to limit Canadian crude. Furthermore, in that year an intergovernmental agreement between the two countries set rising limits on Canadian crude imports. With no enforcement provisions to the agreement, Canadian imports each year were above the 'voluntary' quota. As a result, objection to Canadian oil imports continued through 1970, and as late as 1971 Canadian oil fields were operating at 68 per cent of capacity.

An important point must be noted: *if* the United States had had no controls on oil imports throughout the post-war period, and *if* the world oil industry had been competitive, it is unlikely that Canada would have sold as much oil as it actually did to the US. It is clear that Middle East oil under these circumstances would have supplanted Canadian oil in US markets.

The discussions of limiting Canadian oil imports and measuring the cost in US markets of Canadian crude versus Mid East crude became an academic exercise in 1972. By mid 1972, Canadian producers were at full capacity and exporting record volumes of oil to the US. In June 1972, the Canadian government, feeling that additional exports of oil might come at the expense of domestic Canadian consumers, limited exports and introduced legislation requiring export permits for oil. Americans who had forgotten about the American limits on Canadian imports in previous years were outraged at this cut. The Canadian officials went further. The Arab cutback had affected oil supplies into Quebec and the Maritimes (by an unknown and uncertain amount). The Canadian government began to ship Alberta oil via tanker from British Columbia through the Panama Canal to Montreal via Portland, Maine. (The major pipeline to Montreal goes from Portland since the St Lawrence River freezes in the winter.) In addition, two tankers have been making weekly trips from Sarnia, Ontario, to Montreal, carrying some 220,000 bd. These shipments, of course, must be curtailed in the winter. To create a permanent link to Quebec, the Canadian government announced in December 1973 a $200 million pipeline from the Great Lakes to Montreal. This pipeline cannot begin operation until 1976 at the earliest and is no solution to Quebec's present difficulties. The exact diameter of the pipeline is unknown at this time, but it will carry 350 to 900 million bd, oil which would have been exported to the US.

At the time these decisions were being taken, Canadian officials froze the prices of refined products west of the Ottawa Valley and have allowed price increases east of that line, limited to the increased costs of refineries. In order not to extend the domestic price freeze to foreigners, nor to allow the oil companies to acquire extra profits, the Canadian federal authorities slapped on an export tax. At first, this tax was $.40 per barrel; it is now $6.40.

Reactions in the United States to these moves have been varied and mostly uninformed. For example, Professor Houthakker called for a retaliatory tax on the Canadian oil pipeline which passes through the US.[10] Such a view is nonsense. It is immaterial to American consumers whether they pay $5.50 for a barrel of Canadian crude – all of which goes to a Canadian oil company or part of which goes to the Canadian government. It is clear that the Canadian companies would have raised the price themselves, had the government not intervened. A case can also be made that the export tax benefited Americans, and that the price increase is lower than the price private companies would have set.[11]

221

Canada, it is clear, is heading for a policy of self-sufficiency or autarky in oil. The US now wants increased Canadian oil, at a time when it is clear that far less will be available than at any time in the past. The two countries are moving apart in oil policy. While Canada would have been willing to discuss a continental oil policy in the late 1950s, the US was unwilling; it was then the reluctant bride, but today the suitor has changed and it is Canada who is reluctant to commit her resources.

Natural gas

The picture in natural gas is similar. The two countries have followed divergent policies. Canadian gas policy has, since 1950, required that all imports and exports of gas be approved by the National Energy Board. Gas is not allowed to be exported until the board is convinced that Canada's domestic requirements have been adequately provided for. There must remain in Canada proved reserves equal to 25 times the domestic requirements, four years after the export project begins. In the mid 1950s, the Canadian government refused to allow imports of natural gas into Ontario, using the auspices of the Navigable Waters Protection Act to limit the construction of a pipeline across the Niagara chasm. The next year, the Canadian government subsidized the construction of a west-east gas pipeline to Montreal. Indeed the government had to aid the pipeline because of the inefficiencies resulting from the policy decision to build through the rock and muskeg north of the Great Lakes, rather than through the Prairie soil which lay in that foreign country south of the lakes.[12] It is remarkable that in 1956 Canada would fear building a pipeline through American lands. This fear was natural in 1867, when the British vetoed the cheapest rail route to the Maritimes because it traveled through Maine. The fear was American takeover of a vital national unifying link. But how could Canadians in 1959 fear American takeover of a natural gas pipeline? The fear remains and grows!

In 1963, the original Canadian gas pipeline to the east was at capacity; looping was required. In 1966, the National Energy Board approved a plan to build a second link, south of the Great Lakes. On 25 August 1966, Prime Minister Pearson, speaking for the cabinet, announced the rejection of the southern route: 'The government does not believe it is to be in Canada's best interest that the future development of facilities for bringing western gas to its Eastern Canadian market should be located outside Canadian jurisdiction and subject to detailed regulation under the laws of the United States, which are naturally designed to protect the interests of the United States citizens.'[13] Although the Cabinet later reversed the decision, it is important for future policy that such fears still existed in 1966.

TABLE 2

Proved natural gas reserves in Canada (billion cubic feet)

Year	Remaining at beginning of year	Gross additions				Net change in underground storage	Net production*	Remaining at end of year	Net change in reserves during year	Exports
		Revisions	Extensions	Discoveries	Total					
1955	12,628	1,641		514	2,155	3	145	14,641	2,013	
1956	14,641	2,156		650	2,807	4	192	17,260	2,618	
1957	17,260	515		699	1,214	2	243	18,234	973	16
1958	18,234	2,155		431	2,586	2	334	20,488	2,253	87
1959	20,488	2,662		695	3,358	34	438	23,422	2,934	85
1960	23,422	3,785		255	4,040	5	474	26,994	3,571	91
1961	26,994	2,690		545	3,235	0	693	29,535	2,541	169
1962	29,535	2,124		393	2,517	0	836	31,217	1,681	343
1963	31,217	-43	1,537	1,159	2,653	25	903	32,992	1,775	360
1964	32,992	3,153	3,668	486	7,308	27	1,009	39,319	6,327	392
1965	39,319	-471	1,978	623	2,130	-7	1,087	40,354	1,034	405
1966	40,354	2,158	1,532	512	4,202	17	1,125	43,450	3,095	432
1967	43,450	1,572	1,268	603	3,443	4	1,216	45,682	2,231	513
1968	45,682	230	2,867	282	3,380	-1	1,394	47,666	1,984	604
1969	47,666	2,043	2,690	1,104	5,838	2	1,556	51,950	4,284	680
1970	51,950	493	2,516	193	3,203	20	1,799	53,375	1,424	779
1971	53,375	983	2,280	775	4,039	0	1,953	55,461	2,086	911

*Preliminary estimate

NOTE: Marketable gas reserves prior to 1963 have been derived by statistical conversion of the original estimates of 'recoverable' gas reserves.

SOURCE: Canadian Petroleum Association, *Reserves of Canada Oil, Natural Gas Liquids, and Natural Gas in the United States and Canada* (published jointly with the American Petroleum Institute and the American Gas Association) 26 (May 1972). Last column: Statistics Canada, *The Canada Petroleum and Natural Gas Industry*, years 1957 to 1960, *Trade of Canada, Exports*

Leonard Waverman

The oil pipeline to Montreal announced in December 1973 has two possible routes – north and south of the Great Lakes. Based on historical decisions and in view of today's oil neuroses, the line will likely go north at an additional cost of some $90 million.

Canadian authorities have refused export permits for natural gas, first in 1953 and again in 1971. No new gas exports have been permitted for the last two years.

In the early 1950s, the Federal Power Commission, the guardian of American national security for natural gas, refused *both* export and import licenses. In 1951, the FPC refused to allow Tennessee Gas Transmission to export gas to Ontario, on the grounds that the gas was needed in the US. The FPC reversed its decision in 1953 only to find Canadian authorities refusing to allow imports.

In October 1950, a Canadian company, Westcoast Transmission, applied for permits from Canadian and American authorities to provide gas to the northwestern United States. In June 1954 the FPC denied Westcoast permission to build a 400-mile pipeline. Instead, Pacific Northwest Pipeline Corporation was permitted to build a 1400-mile line to the San Juan Basin in New Mexico and Colorado, a natural gas reserve which even in 1954 was inadequate to serve California and Washington.

This decision to restrict imports of gas into the US has been interpreted in a number of ways. Several authors (including a Canadian royal commission) have concluded that this decision was based on national security grounds. Since natural gas is difficult to store, the FPC attempted to rely as little as possible on foreign suppliers over which it had no jurisdiction. But although there was some note of protectionism in this policy, it is likely that Canadian authorities were more responsible for the American decision.[14] Not only had a royal commission been instituted in Canada to conduct an inquiry into the role of imports and exports, but elected representatives were making public statements as to the need for export controls.[15] This was not an atmosphere conducive to trade.[16] Furthermore, Westcoast Transmission had received neither explicit governmental approval nor confirmed gas supplies before applying to the FPC.

Westcoast Transmission began negotiations to bypass the Pacific Northwest market and build a pipeline to California. The resulting map would have shown parallel pipelines carrying gas in opposite directions, the Canadian line delivering gas to California, the US line delivering gas to Washington. The negotiations had reached the point where a price had been established between the companies involved when, in 1955, the FPC permitted Westcoast Transmission to act as a supplementary supplier to the Pacific Northwest. In October 1957, several years after the initial plan and five years after Westcoast had received approval from the Alberta Oil and Gas Conservation Board, the line was completed.

224

Today, the two countries have two conflicting applications to carry Arctic natural gas to North American markets. The Gas Arctic Company will likely apply to Canadian and American authorities to construct a pipeline to carry both Prudhoe Bay (American) and Mackenzie Valley (Canadian) gas to North American markets via an overland route through Canada. El Paso has applied to the FPC to carry Prudhoe Gas via tanker from Alaska to continental US markets. One of these applications dooms the other. Yet, they will likely be studied separately in each country. How much more sensible for the two countries to set up a body which would analyze both projects at the same time!

Coal[17]

Coal, which represented 60 per cent of energy consumption in Canada in 1900, represents 6 per cent today. Today's consumption is concentrated in two sectors: metallurgical coal, used as coke in steel production; and steam coal, used as boiler fuel in electricity generation. Note the decrease in coal produced and consumed from 1958 through 1971 (Table 3). Production peaked at 17.6 million short tons in 1952 and reached a trough of 10.2 million short tons, 10 years later.

Three shocks hit the Canadian coal industry – the oil and gas discoveries in Western Canada; the availability of low-cost foreign oil imported into eastern Canada; and the availability of Appalachian coal to central Canadian markets. The resurgence of the industry, at least in the west, is due to export demand for metallurgical coal. Because of this resurgence, subsidies to the industry have been curtailed. The subsidy program which began in 1928 in order to keep the price to domestic consumers competitive with imported coal yielded $250 million to Nova Scotian coal producers and $50 million to Albertan producers.

In 1972, 19.3 million short tons of coal were imported into Canada, chiefly bituminous. These imports represented over 66 per cent of Canadian coal consumption in 1972 (on a BTU basis). In that same year, Canada exported 9.5 million short tons, chiefly to Japan. These exports represented nearly 50 per cent of Canadian production. The ties between Canada and the US in coal are then the reverse of other forms of energy – Canada is a large net importer.

However, these last years have seen increased supply constraints and rapidly rising prices for Appalachian coal; from $11.60 per ton (delivered) in 1968 to $18.70 per ton in 1972.[18] Moreover, this imported coal is of a high sulfur content (4 per cent), necessitating costly stack-gas scrubbing to meet Ontario's air emission standards.

Western Canadian coal reserves are of low sulfur content. Given the supply constraints in Appalachia, the rapidly rising prices for imported coal, and the premium likely payable for low-sulfur coal, it seems only a matter of time (probably

TABLE 3
Canadian coal

	Millions of short tons			Domestic consumption* (%)			
	Production	Exports	Imports	Residential	Commercial	Industrial†	Transport
1958	11.6	0.4	13.4	20	5.5	64.5	10
1959	10.5	0.5	13.6	18.4	7.4	66.3	5.9
1960	10.8	0.9	12.3	17.3	7.4	70.8	4.0
1961	10.3	1.0	12.1	15.8	6.9	71.6	3.0
1962	10.2	0.9	12.3	13.3	6.6	75.6	2.7
1963	10.5	1.1	14.7	10.9	5.3	78.8	2.4
1964	11.2	1.3	14.7	9.2	4.6	81.5	2.3
1965	11.5	1.2	16.3	7.0	4.1	85.0	2.1
1966	11.2	1.3	16.4	6.0	3.5	84.7	2.3
1967	11.1	1.4	15.8	4.7	3.2	88.1	1.8
1968	11.0	1.4	17.3	3.4	2.6	91.0	1.1
1969	10.7	1.4	17.2	2.9	2.4	91.4	1.3

*BTU Basis, does not add to 100 per cent because of losses and adjustments
†Includes coal used for thermal generation of electricity plus coal used for coking purposes
SOURCE: Statistics Canada, *Detailed Energy Supply and Demand in Canada*, 57-505

TABLE 4

Uranium production and exports

	Production (short tons U_3O_8)		Canadian exports of uranium (millions of dollars)		
	Canada	US	to US	Britain	Total
1961	9641	17399	174	18.3	192.7
1962	8430	17010	149.2	16.6	166.
1963	8352	14218	96.6	40.5	137.5
1964	7285	11847	34.9	39.6	74.6
1965	4443	10442	14.7	38.9	53.7
1966	3932	9587	13.7	22.6	36.4
1967	3738	9125	1.0	22.8	23.9
1968	3701	12338	–	26.1	26.1
1969	3854	10934	.5	15.	24.5
1970	4104	12768	17.0	9.	26.0
1971	4100	12800	5.9	11.4	17.9

SOURCE: *Department of Energy, Mines and Resources*, Canadian Minerals Yearbook, Ottawa 1971

three to five years) before a serious effort is made to ship Albertan coal into the Ontario market supplanting American coal. These shipments (possibly by slurry pipeline) will *not* be for national unification purposes but simply for cost minimization. Given the large American coal reserves in the fields in Oklahoma, Utah, and Idaho (southern extensions of the Western Canadian fields), Canadian coal will not be shipped to the US.

Coal is therefore another energy source which will see diminished trade between Canada and the US in the future.

Uranium

The Canadian uranium industry began as a government corporation (Eldorado) which had a monopoly on exploration and production until 1947. The great military demand for uranium in the United States and Britain led to the lifting of the ban on private prospecting in 1947; the introduction of subsidies to help encourage production and the eventual establishment of twenty-three mines and nineteen treatment plants by 1959.

Export demand ceased abruptly in 1959, all purchase options beyond 1963 were dropped with one exception (see Table 4). The Canadian federal government buttressed the industry with stockpiling arrangements (at a cost to date of

227

Leonard Waverman

TABLE 5

Estimates of future nuclear capacity and demand for uranium concentrate

| | Estimated world nuclear capacity (MW) | | | | |
	1970	1975	1980	1985	1990
Canada	480	2,500	7,000	16,000	35,000
US	6,850	64,000	16,500	300,000	500,000
Western Europe	10,000	30,000	92,000	197,000	320,000
Japan	1,290	7,000	27,000	60,000	120,000

| | Annual demand for uranium at the mill head assuming above nuclear generating capacity (tons $U_3 O_8$) | | | | |
	1970	1975	1980	1985	1990
Canada	200	550	1,400	3,000	6,000
US	7,800	20,000	42,000	71,000	108,000
Western Europe	2,700	12,000	23,000	39,000	57,000
Japan	500	28,500	6,600	16,000	27,000
Other		1,300	4,000	12,000	21,000

SOURCE: H.B. Merlin, 'Nuclear Capacity, Its Growth and Impact,' Canadian Nuclear Association, mimeo, June 1971

$101 million) among other policies. Shipments in 1972 were only 30 per cent of 1959 shipments and only three firms remain in operation. Interest rekindled in 1966 as nuclear generation appeared to be a dominant technology; prospecting began again and new reserves were found. By 1970, the future role of nuclear generating capacity was bleak and activity ceased once again. With the recent (December 1973) signing of a major twenty-year purchase agreement with Japan, prospecting will likely be heavy in the summer of 1974.

Given the estimated growth in world nuclear capacity and the resulting demand for uranium (Table 5), Canadian exports of concentrates to the US may well be the *major* energy flow across the border in 1980 and years beyond.

Electricity

In Table 6 are summarized the changing distribution of imports to Canadian electricity production and the international trade in that commodity. The future holds two divergent tales – provinces who have developed only a minor part of their hydro capacity are planning hydro projects. The James Bay and Churchill

228

TABLE 6

Canada: electricity

	Million KWH				Domestic consumption (%)		
	Production	Exports	Imports	% thermal	Domestic	Commercial	Industrial*
1958	90,509	4086	245	7.7	18	12	70
1959	97,040	4593	512	8.0	19	10	71
1960	105,885	5512	357	8.0	19	11	70
1961	103,919	4157	1394	9.4	20	14	66
1962	104,073	4112	2779	12.8	20	14.5	65.5
1963	103,919	3613	2884	17.6	20.6	14.9	64.5
1964	113,485	4159	3121	18.8	20.1	15.5	63.4
1965	117,183	3684	3575	23.0	20.7	16.8	62.5
1966	129,995	4397	3218	21.7	20.3	19.2	60.5
1967	132,890	3994	4181	24.6	21.0	19.0	60.0
1968	135,831	3988	4451	30.0	21	19.7	59.3
1969	149,741	4320	2740	27.6	21.3	21.9	57.8

*includes energy supply industries

SOURCE: Statistics Canada, *Detailed Energy Supply and Demand for Canada,* 57-505

Falls projects will make Quebec 90 per cent hydro-dependent in 1980. The Nelson River project will have similar effects in Saskatchewan. Ontario, having developed 85 per cent of its hydro potential, is concentrating on nuclear developments; 5000 MW of nuclear power is now on stream and 7000 MW will be added by 1980.

The Canadian and American governments sole coordinated energy project – the Columbia River project – turned out to be an unmitigated disaster for Canada.[19] While something less than 30 per cent of the waters of the Columbia River are in Canada, its rise in the Canadian mountains meant that effective flood control and hydro development of the river in the US required Canadian cooperation, since dams on the Washington state side of the border could not adequately control the river. The constitutional division of power within Canada essentially gave the BC government the authority to write the contract – which it did. The US would build all the treaty dams on the river (three in BC) in exchange for all the power generated on the US side, made possible only because of Canadian dams. For $400 million, equal to the ultimate cost of the dams to BC, the US got all the power for thirty years, at a price one-fifth of today's price.

The vast James Bay project, adding 8.3 million KWH to Quebec's generating capacity, will add significantly to Canadian electricity exports in the short term.

Leonard Waverman

However, these exports will diminish as domestic Quebec demand increases. Therefore, the existence of increased electricity exports is due solely to the lumpiness of the James Bay project (similar to the prospective Gas Arctic pipeline).

CONTINENTALISM?

As the proceeding portions of this paper have shown, little coordination has occurred between governments in the United States and Canada on energy matters. At times when it appeared that Canada was willing to contemplate a continental energy policy, US federal officials were reluctant to place special emphasis on Canadian resources. Now that the US would have more interest in a continental policy, Canadians are not at all interested. Nixon's much-touted 'Project Independence,' to make the US self-sufficient in energy by 1980, has its parallel in Canada. In fact, it is quite likely that a Canadian 'Project Independence' will be completed well before 1980.

Two questions arise. First, how distant are the countries from a continental energy policy? In reality, have companies effectively set a continental energy market despite government rhetoric? If continentalism is not now present or forseeable, what are the costs and benefits to Canadian and Americans of 'Project Independence?'

In the introduction to this paper, the degree of interdependence in energy flows between Canada and the US was detailed. Given the amount of government restrictions on trans-border flows, there is no presumption that these actual flows are optimal. Several studies have examined the costs to consumers of government restriction on trans-border energy flows between Canada and the US. A study of Waverman indicated that the artificial restrictions on natural gas flows could cost some $200 million, incurred almost entirely by eastern Canadian consumers.[20] These costs are accounted for by the additional costs of inefficient east-west transportation routes when compared to cheaper north-south routes. These costs then are then part of the costs of 'Project Independence.'

Besides creating artificially expensive transportation routes, the restrictions which involve exports and imports have a number of other costs. The Canadian authorities have apparently decided to maintain a single price of oil across Canada. Besides maintaining this price below the world price (or opportunity cost of oil), the decision necessitates subsidizing Canadian consumers east of the Ottawa Valley for their higher cost oil imports, some $1.2 billion per year.

Let us examine some of the implications of maintaining a domestic price below the world price and thus directly and indirectly subsidizing Canadian consumers. If a barrel of oil is worth $10.00 in Chicago, let's say, and $6.00 in Toronto, what effects occur? First, under free trade, it is obvious that the barrel of oil would be

230

exported, yielding $10.00. Proponents of the domestic price freeze suggest that the additional $4.00 earned by producers in Canada is illusory – producers are largely foreign-owned, and therefore the $4.00 (or the $10.00) flows out of the country.

If these producers are taxed on grounds identical to all other Canadian producers, a large proportion of the additional revenue flows to governments. A great deal is made of the issue that oil and gas producers are treated better than other industries. If this is the case, remove their tax benefits rather than attempting to rectify an anomaly in the tax structure by a second anomaly in pricing. If the only reason for maintaining a domestic price below the world price is to prevent windfall gains from accruing to foreign entrepreneurs, the tax and withholding systems should be improved.

Canadians view the energy crisis with some mystery and anger. If Canadians are self-sufficient in energy, why should domestic prices be ruled by embargoes and misappropriate policies elsewhere? While this argument has an emotional appeal, its logic is misplaced: a domestic price-freeze policy will *cost* Canadians a great deal of money.

The costs of domestic price freezes on oil

Decisions undertaken by domestic Canadian producers or consumers should be based on a price of $10.00 per barrel. Looking at consumers first, since the opportunity cost of oil is $10.00, not $6.00, *all consumers* are being subsidized. It is easy to see that consumers east of the Ottawa Valley are being subsidized since the rest of Canada directly gives them $1.2 billion per year. Similarly, all other Canadian oil consumers are being subsidized – by oil producers, shareholders in oil firms, and all those who would have benefited from a rise in the price of oil to $10.00. Since the government revenue from such a price increase could be very large, offsetting tax revenue from other sources, Canadians are *worse* off due to the price freeze in terms of the higher income and sales taxes now being paid. Specifically, non-oil-users and those with interest in oil property are subsidizing oil users. To some extent this subsidy is being borne by foreigners. However, the domestic freeze does involve a shift in the income distribution towards those who consume oil. I know of no study which examines the equity of tax subsidies which are based on the volume of oil consumed – the higher the volume, the greater the subsidy. It is not obvious *a priori* that this subsidy is progressive (i.e. benefits low-income groups more than it benefits high-income groups); for this to be so, low-income families must spend a greater proportion of their income directly and indirectly on oil. Various studies which examine gasoline consumption indicate that high-income groups spend at least as great a proportion of their incomes on gasoline as do low-income groups.[21] In the case of gasoline, the subsidy is either proportional or regressive, but surely not progressive.

Note that the problem of this subsidy is the exact opposite of the problem faced in the US today. There, the question is whether to eliminate the supply shortage in gasoline through a market mechanism (tax or price increase) or through rationing. If American authorities are convinced that rationing is superior to a market on income distribution grounds, that a tax on gasoline would fall proportionately more on the poor (i.e. would be a regressive tax), this then is a case for a subsidy in Canada, since that subsidy (a negative tax) would go proportionately more to the poor.

Canadian consumers paying $6.00 for a barrel of oil compared to a world price of $10.00, will consume more oil than is optimal. Assuming, for the moment, a constant supply of oil, this higher use will deplete our reserves faster than if the price is allowed to rise. We cannot be concerned about both the high price of oil and the low volume of reserves. In opting for a low price of oil, we are implicitly suggesting that conservation is not a real issue.

In all other parts of the world, assuming a $10.00 per barrel price of oil, consumers will be readjusting their consumption to become more efficient in oil use. Large cars will be traded in on small cars. Better insulation will be used in construction. Producers who use oil as an input will be substituting other inputs – labour and capital – for energy. Canadians will, on average (accounting for differences in income etc.), drive bigger cars, use less insulation, and produce goods with more energy input per dollar of output. Canada will be a more energy-intensive economy than other economies.

While every argument for the subsidy discusses the extent of foreign control in energy production in Canada *ad nauseam*, few discuss the foreign content in energy consumption. *The subsidy will flow to foreigners, if the more energy-intensive industries are foreign-owned or if they export their products.*

Some suggest that Canadian energy-intensive exporting industries will be better off because of the low price of oil in Canada. Certainly, they will be as well off as if all Canadians chipped in to give them a cash subsidy. In subsidizing export industries, we are subsidizing their consumers – the readers of the *New York Times*, for instance. If government officials really wish to subsidize newspaper readers in the US, let us see a campaign platform based on that issue!

I do not mean to be flippant. The measure of the distribution of gains and losses of an indirect subsidy are difficult to make and, from what I can determine, has never been seriously attempted. *Keeping the price of oil low is not a zero-cost benefit to all Canadians, it involves taking from some Canadians and foreigners and giving to other Canadians and foreigners.* Such a subsidy policy may have 'incorrect' income distribution effects, i.e. may subsidize the rich Canadian or the foreigner more than the poor domestic Canadian. Moreover, the policy is inefficient in consumption – it encourages the use of energy at a time when we are supposed to be concerned with discouraging that use.

Producers will also be acting on the $6.00 signal if they expect the Canadian price always to be kept there. At least some uncertainty must be added to their actions. The volume of oil found is clearly a function of the price it will command in the market. There are areas of the country, depths of drilling required, types of deposit (tar sands), which are economic to varying degrees according to the price of oil. If the price is maintained at $6.00, rather than $10.00, less oil will be found. This is not because producers are malicious or evil, but simply because drilling activity is a function of the price.

Other inefficient production decisions will be made. There are many forms of energy: oil, natural gas, nuclear energy, hydro, etc. Imagine two different electric generation projects available, nuclear and thermal (oil-burning). The thermal generating plant is cheapest when oil is $6.00 per barrel but is more expensive when oil is $10.00 per barrel. The nuclear plant has a comparable cost on a BTU input basis of $7 per barrel. Because the Canadian price is maintained below the world price of $10.00, oil-burning electric plants are installed. However, the oil burned in these plants could have been sold outside the country for $10.00 per barrel. It clearly would have increased Canadian welfare to install a nuclear plant and export the oil. This is a simple example. Consider the range of investments, available to consumers and producers, which depend on the price of fuels, prices relative to each other and relative to all other inputs. All these investments are biased when the price of one input is artificially kept below its opportunity cost.

There is one specific investment which requires a more complete discussion. Until the spring of 1972, consumers in Ontario were paying roughly 30¢ per barrel more for oil than consumers in Quebec. With the rise in the world price last year, Quebec consumers began to pay more for their oil, at the moment (January 1974) something on the order of $10.50 per barrel (Venezuelan 32°). The government has decided to extend the Interprovincial Pipeline running from Alberta to Ontario at least as far as Quebec at a cost of some $200 million. The pipeline diverts a substantial part, if not all, of present oil exports to the US.

The pipeline is necessary in government eyes to enable all Canadian consumers to enjoy a single price of oil. Until now this single price was never a part of oil policy. As mentioned earlier, this will involve the construction of the pipeline, an explicit subsidy of $1.2 billion per year until construction, and an implicit annual subsidy of that amount after construction (assuming that the oil shipped to Quebec could be sold in the US at $10.00, rather than $6.00).

Leonard Waverman

A CALL FOR COHERENT POLICY

The oil market is now in profound disequilibrium. The prices obtained in spot markets for participation oil in the region of $22.00 do not indicate the long-run price towards which we are aiming. We do know that: a/ there is no physical shortage of oil; b/ the costs of production in the Persian Gulf are 10¢ to 20¢ per barrel; c/ OPEC consists of strange bedfellows – Libya, Nigeria, Iran, Saudi Arabia, Venezuela, etc.

None of us are fortune tellers, but suppose that some economists, like Adelman, are correct: competition breaks out and in 1976 the world price settles at $3.00 per barrel? At that point, in Canada, we are sitting on the world's longest most uneconomic oil pipeline. Quebec will insist on free imports. Alberta will demand that its guaranteed markets stay guaranteed. The US will not want expensive Canadian oil. One can imagine the rounds of discussions concerning the extent to which producers will be subsidized.

Short-run market disequilibrium conditions should not dictate long-run economic policies. This is an easy statement for an academic to make, but the political life of a minority government is also short-run. And it is politics which dictates economics, not vice versa.

If I had the capacity to make energy policy for Canada and the US, what would I do? First, I would remove the domestic price ceilings on oil and natural gas in both countries as well as eliminating inequities in the taxing of energy producers. I would not opt for more rules, more regulations, and subsidies. Government regulatory bodies have shown a great ability to bring about market disequilibria and little ability to solve problems. Using the carrot of higher prices and the stick of removing inefficiencies in tax structures, the market would be allowed to find the equilibrium price and output. And if my economist friends convinced me that this rapid rise in price was unequitable, I would subsidize those who are inordinately hurt.

Washington is confused about Canadian intentions in energy policy. The angry outbursts at the Canadian export tax, culminating in the Senate resolution of 29 January, condemning the Canadian tax and implicitly suggesting retaliation, seem to most Canadians sheer hyperbole. Because the US cannot control Middle East production or world prices, some uninformed officials strike out at the one nearest – Canada. Canadians are not taking advantage of Americans in setting an export tax. Why should Canadians subsidize Americans by selling them oil at below world prices? Americans are not subsidizing Canadian computer buyers or offering to rewrite the Columbia River treaty provisions. Canada is a minor producer in the world; it cannot affect the world price; and it would be foolish to sell at less than that price.

234

Words have power. Canadians fear Americans; they fear their overwhelming size, they fear the longest unguarded border in the world; they fear economic and political domination. This fear is only heightened by threats of retaliation which emanate from senior American politicians. These threats suggest that Canadians do not have the power to control their own resources.

In this paper, I have shown how this fear of American domination has controlled some aspects of Canadian energy policy. World events have made self-sufficiency an important policy for other reasons – basically, the ability to maintain an independent foreign policy.

In fact, the world events of the last six months have had one severe repercussion – it has made the Canadian policy for some self-sufficiency appear to be one of the wise decisions of the post-war period. This is most unfortunate. Viewed from 1960, the Canadian policy of limiting imports and exports appeared far too costly compared to the benefits. Viewed from 1974, the benefits of the policy appear to far outweigh the costs. But policy decisions cannot be judged on their merits weighed at that point in time when exogenous world events have turned the world on its head. Moments of short-run disequilibria are not the time to make long-run irrevocable decisions.

What could go wrong with 'Project Independence' in the US and Canada? First, the policies have high costs; they create inefficient transport networks; they tend to give signals to develop the wrong resources at the wrong time; if accompanied by import controls and/or price controls, markets and production and consumption decisions are distorted. Remember we are comparing the *costs* of independence with the *price* of the imported rival Middle East oil. That price can fall by 80 per cent overnight; those costs cannot. The benefits of independence cannot be minimized. These benefits are: *some probability* of a lower price of oil than the world price and insurance against blackmail.

There is also, however, some probability that the world price will fall, say to $6.00 per barrel. Suppose that by 1984 Nixon's 'second Manhattan project' has yielded new reserves of liquid fuels at costs of $10.00 per barrel. Canada has a pipeline stretching from Alberta 3200 miles to Halifax, distributing tar sands oil at a delivered cost on the east coast of $11.00 per barrel. In that future year, OPEC crumbles; Britain finds the world's largest oil reservoir under Birmingham; and the world price falls to ten times cost – $2.50 per barrel. North American projects independence have developed the highest-cost oil in the world. Imports of these low-cost foreign reserves are not allowed. One cannot really trust the British. Officials quote 1973 as the only past year of any value to 1984 decisions. Consumers and manufacturers plead for low-priced imports to make North American industry competitive with European industry which has access 'to low-cost oil.' Subsidies are paid to industries and automobile drivers in North America to lower their price to the world average ...

What possible role can Canadian energy play in US requirements? With respect to coal, no role is likely. In natural gas, a decreased role is likely. In uranium, the role depends on expected nuclear capacity in all countries. In oil, the role is limited, unless tar sands deposits are being considered. In electricity, again, the role is minor. Large-scale Canadian hydro projects will provide some interim electricity.

Therefore, except for high-cost tar sands oil, Canada is unlikely to provide a large proportion of American energy needs. This is not to say that Canadian energy will be unimportant in American markets – to some markets, like Wisconsin and Michigan, it will be crucial, and over-all it will be important as a secure marginal supply. Just as Americans demanded the best terms in helping to build Canada's energy sector, so Canadians will demand the best terms for their exports. To expect anything else would be naïve at both ends.

Continentalism in energy cannot be an important ingredient of joint North American energy development. This is not simply because of political forces, but because, apart from the tar sands, Canadian energy reserves are too small to be very important in the US. This does not mean that coordination of policies is unimportant – it is vital for two reasons. First, the marginal secure supplies keep the wolf from the door. Second, uncoordinated irrational policies will increase the costs to both countries, something which neither can afford in the long run. Therefore, Canadians should not consider hoarding their energy – a growing American economy is important to Canada. Moreover, the hoarded energy may be fool's gold if technology makes it so. Americans should not cast covetous eyes on Canadian energy – those reserves will not help them very much. Canada is a collection of resources looking for an identity. Canadian self-consciousness is real and must be understood by Americans. The Canadian drive for self-sufficiency will require policy decisions to be made in the US – chiefly how the border states now relying on Canadian oil will be supplied. It is essential that the two governments consult to ensure that the longest lead time is available for changes in supply. Mutual trade, respect, and consultation is the only form of continentalism available.

NOTES

1 Estimate made from Statistics Canada, *Corporation and Labour Unions Returns Act,* 1971 Report
2 Ministry of Energy, Mines and Resources, *An Energy Policy for Canada* (1970), 2, appendix B

3 *Ibid.,* 219
4 *Ibid.,* 220
5 *Ibid.,* 230
6 Quoted in *New York Times,* 30 December 1973
7 Debanné argues that this policy merely formalized the policy desired by the multinationals. See his paper below.
8 See W. Kilbourn, *Pipeline* (Toronto 1970).
9 Proclamation 3279
10 H. Houthakker, Data Resources Inc., computer memo, Dec 1973
11 When the export tax was raised to $1.90, I phoned Ed Erickson, who said, 'A bargain – we'll take all we can get.' Americans who are shareholders in Canadian oil companies are hurt by the export tax to the extent that share prices do not reflect the opportunity costs of the reserves.
12 The company was lent $80 million interest-free. The government itself built the 696 most difficult miles of the pipeline and leased it to the company for five years. L. Waverman, *Natural Gas and National Policy* (Toronto 1973), on which parts of this section are based.
13 As quoted in *Montreal Gazette,* 27 Aug. 1966
14 The Royal Commission on Energy placed sole responsibility for the decision with the FPC. They stated that the US would never depend on imports from a foreign country 'without some intergovernmental agreement assuring the continued adequacy of supply' (*First Report,* 1958, 6-23).
15 'The policy of the Canadian government is to refuse permits for moving natural gas by pipeline across an international boundary until such time as we are convinced that there can be no economic use, present or future, for that natural gas in Canada.' So said C.D. Howe to the House of Commons, 13 March 1953, as quoted in Kilbourn, *Pipeline.*
16 This is the view of H.G.J. Aitken, 'The Midwestern Case: Canadian Gas and the F.P.C.,' *Canadian Journal of Economics and Political Science,* 25, 2 (May 1959), 129-43.
17 This section and those on uranium and electricity are partially based on the Ministry of Energy, Mines and Resources, *Energy Policy for Canada.*
18 *Ibid.,* 2, 270
19 See Larrett Higgins, 'Electricity and Canadian Policy,' below.
20 Waverman, *Natural Gas and National Policy.*
21 For a summary of these studies and some extensions, see P. Verleger Jr, 'A Dynamic Model of Gasoline Demand,' Data Resources Inc., mimeo. (1974).

Professor Houthakker reiterates some of the central themes of these volumes. The 'energy crisis' is policy-induced. There is not in fact an imminent physical shortage of fossil fuels, particularly oil. The world energy economy can be expected to be primarily fossil-fuel dependent for the balance of this century, at least. The recent price increases in the world oil market reflect effective monopoly power exercised by the producing country cartel, together with either capitulation or concurrence, especially on the part of US policy makers. There are sound reasons to believe that the producing-country international oil cartel may be subject to severe destabilizing forces in the future. There are not inconsequential price elasticities of demand and supply for energy production consumption – in total and among alternative fuels – and simply projecting current production and consumption patterns without taking into account the likely effects of prospective price changes will give increasingly erroneous results. Current energy policy must be integrated with future energy policy through a rational approach to research and development.

These are ideas that appear again and again in various chapters of these volumes. Policy formation must begin with the facts and the likely responses to various policy variables before the consequences of alternative policy strategies can be assessed.

Professor Houthakker's chapter on the energy problem should be compared to the chapters by Roberts, Kellogg, and Barnett. Although Houthakker does not spend a great deal of time discussing the subjects dealt with by these authors, it is clear that his perspective is similar. In addition, there is no doubt that his views are similar to those expressed by Ms Starratt and Professor Spann. Finally, Professor Houthakker's chapter must be compared to the chapters by Professor Adelman, Dr Collado, Mr Homet, and Professor Nye. If Mr Homet is prescient and we are in fact embarking on 'Project Interdependence,' we must agree on what the lessons of these chapters are.

H. S. HOUTHAKKER

The energy problem

There is no unanimity on the real nature of the energy problem. There are some who, as is fashionable nowadays, attribute to it some cosmic significance as yet another harbinger of the end of the world as we know it. According to this view the world has almost run out of all conventional sources of energy so that we have to make a drastic switch to unconventional sources. Among scientists, who are especially prone to this view, each has his own favorite theory - solar energy, nuclear fusion, the fast breeder, magneto hydrodynamics, and a few even more exotic ones.

It is true, of course, that we should be exploring whatever new ideas on energy production appear to be promising, and that a moderate investment in some of them may well be rewarding. In fact, I shall suggest later an important tactical reason why considerable research in new sources of energy might be to our advantage even if the payoff is remote. Nevertheless, we should not blindly accept the view that conventional energy sources are so close to exhaustion that nothing short of a revolution in technology will bring us over the present difficulties. We are not going through at the moment the beginning of the end of the world, but simply an adjustment in our energy supply pattern. Such adjustments have occurred frequently over the years, though they have not usually drawn much public attention. Only a century ago most energy used by man was drawn either from his own labor, or from draft animals and firewood, supplemented by a little coal and falling water. The petroleum industry is barely a century old, and the electric power industry is younger still. The natural gas industry is of even more recent origin. These forms have gradually displaced the traditional sources of energy which are no longer of any importance. If we take a longer view, the only thing that is constant in the energy picture is change. Perhaps the readjustment we are going through now is a little more rapid than earlier ones, but of cosmic significance it surely is not.

All this does not mean, of course, that there is no energy problem. We are indeed going through a period of adjustment, and what we do or do not do during this period will have consequences for years to come. New patterns of supply (and perhaps also of demand) are being established. These new patterns will be with us for at least a decade, possibly until the end of the century. Government policies are being reconsidered, and large investments in research, exploration, and equipment have to be planned. Exaggerated notions about the magnitude of the energy problem can easily lead us into unduly costly solutions, such as last year's plan for buying natural gas from the Soviet Union at about twice the likely cost of alternative supplies. Dispassionate projections of future developments are needed if these policy changes and investment decisions are to be made with confidence, though we should remember that even the most careful projections are likely to go astray.

THE BASIC FACTS

Our greatest need is a clear conception of the basic facts in the current energy situation. Let me enumerate what I see as the basic facts:

1 There has been a steady increase in energy consumption, usually at a rate somewhat less than the growth rate of real GNP, although in recent years somewhat above it, possibly because of environmental restrictions. Such fluctuations in rates of growth are far from unusual in economic relations, and are just one of the hazards of facing the economic forecaster. [Editors' note: See the chapter by Barnett. Professor Houthakker does not develop the argument in detail, but the brief view expressed here is consistent with the consensus opinion of the contributors to these volumes. Economic growth and environmental protection, at some cost, are not mutually inconsistent.]

2 Petroleum production in the United States has started to decline. Efforts to find more petroleum in the 'lower 48' have not been very successful in recent years and exploration has declined. The large discovery in Alaska, made in the late 1960s, has so far remained useless. There is considerable potential for additional oil finds not only in Alaska but also in offshore areas adjoining the Pacific, the Gulf, and the Atlantic. More onshore production in the 'lower 48' can also not be excluded because higher crude prices stimulate secondary recovery, deeper drilling, and new exploration.

3 Natural gas production has failed to keep up with the growing demand, primarily because of price controls. Since these controls have now been relaxed

considerably, an increase in production can be expected, but not immediately. There is probably a great deal of gas in offshore areas; important finds have already been made in the Canadian Arctic, while the importation of liquefied gas over long distances has become commercially feasible.

4 We still have vast reserves of coal, but low-sulfur coal is found mostly in the Mountain states, resulting in high transportation costs to principal markets. It may be necessary to gasify the coal to send it East by pipeline rather than transport it by rail. Lack of water and restrictions on strip mining may also affect the cost of this coal adversely.

5 The potential for new hydroelectric power is limited, while nuclear power has so far been something of a disappointment, because of the many breakdowns in nuclear stations. The period of construction is also inordinately long, in part because of the delays involved in obtaining construction and operating permits. Nevertheless, many nuclear stations are under construction or planned.

6 The petroleum refining industry in the United States is operating close to its present capacity. Until the president's energy message of a few months ago, the industry was planning very little expansion, but now that crude supplies are being made easier to obtain, several large firms have announced sizable construction plans. Even so, it is likely that the possibility of importing refined products, envisaged in the energy message, will be used during the next few years.

7 The above supply and demand factors make it likely that we shall have to import more petroleum during the next few years, though this depends also on how strongly rising prices discourage consumption. Of any additional imports a large part will come not from our traditional suppliers, Venezuela and Canada, but from the Persian Gulf and other remote areas. This means increased transportation costs, aggravated further by the inability of nearly all our ports to accommodate large tankers.

8 The oil-exporting countries have gradually built up a comprehensive cartel organization which has been effective in securing large price increases and a share in the ownership of local petroleum operations. There can be little doubt that the cartel will try to proceed further along these lines, and that it will attempt to restrict supplies if this is necessary for the achievement of its aims. However, the ability of OPEC to control the output of its members is largely untested. [Editors' note: In late 1973, those countries participating in the Arab oil embargo were publicly dissatisfied with Iran's policy of maintaining production and selling to all sources.]

9 The cost of energy from unconventional sources is for the most part conjectural and the necessary technology is not fully developed. Among domestic sources, the production of oil from shale and the gasification of coal would probably become commercially feasible if the price of crude oil rose to $5 or $5.50

per barrel from its present level between $4.00 and $4.50. [Editors' note: 'Present level' was as of 20 November 1973.] Synthetic oil from the Canadian tar sands can be produced at a lower price, but is subject to control by the province of Alberta. Prospective breakthroughs in nuclear technology, such as the fast breeder and fusion, are still in the laboratory stage and are not likely to become commercially available until the late 1980s at the earliest.

10 The increased imports of petroleum and natural gas necessary during the remainder of this decade will have an important but not overwhelming impact on our balance of payments. In 1972 mineral fuels accounted for about $8\frac{1}{2}$ per cent of our imports. This percentage is likely to rise to about 12 per cent in 1973, and could be as high as 15 per cent in 1980, depending in part on what policies we pursue in the meantime. The impact of this increase in imports on our balance of payments as a whole will be minor since it is likely to be offset, at least in part, by an increase in US exports and by earnings from invisible transactions. Some of the oil-producing countries will control an increasing share of the world's monetary reserves unless they find better outlets for their earnings.

This is the medium-term energy situation as I see it. In the short run the situation has been aggravated by the successive price control programs, which upset the delicate mechanism by which the supply of refined product adjusts to the everchanging patterns of demand and thus caused shortages of gasoline and heating oil. The Arab embargo has made the situation even more acute.

ESSENTIALNESS AND ELASTICITY

The energy picture is complicated and a great deal depends on the relative strength of its various interacting elements, which can only be estimated by detailed econometric analysis. The many energy projections now circulating are usually based on simple trend extrapolation, occasionally with some modification to allow for exceptionally favorable or unfavorable developments. Most of them do not allow for the influence of prices on supply or demand, and this is their principal weakness. There is a great deal of loose talk about energy being 'essential,' which presumably means that without energy our life would be entirely different from what it is now. This may be true, but it is also irrelevant. Energy is subject to the marginal principle, just as are other supposedly 'essential' commodities such as food. At the margin neither food nor energy is essential; both are subject to price elasticity, which may be low, but is almost certainly not zero. In fact, for some important energy products, particularly gasoline and electric power, the price elasticity appears to be quite considerable after enough time for adjustment has elapsed.

CARTELIZATION AND CAPITULATION

The most serious policy problems for the next few years will result from the cartelization of the supply side. Lacking effective substitutes at anywhere near current price levels, the consuming countries are vulnerable to monopolistic exploitation and political embargos. This is not a new situation; we have been net importers of petroleum for several years, and other areas, especially Western Europe and Japan, are almost entirely dependent on imports. Until recently, however, the petroleum-exporting countries were not sufficiently coordinated to achieve higher prices, especially in the face of rapidly increasing supplies. Their big opportunity came around 1970, when a number of developments both enhanced and demonstrated the vulnerability of the importers, particularly of the US. The great Alaskan discovery was virtually nullified by opposition to the pipeline. The Administration had failed to prevent two successive increases in the domestic crude price despite considerable overcapacity. The proposal for a tariff made by the Cabinet Task Force on Oil Import Control would have kept foreign suppliers in check, but it was set aside for reasons of domestic politics. Finally, some supply interruptions in the Mediterranean served to show that the importing countries were quite prepared to pay the higher landed prices that had resulted. The OPEC countries consequently saw the time ripe for higher revenues.

The importing countries had relied mostly on the bargaining power of the major oil companies, the traditional intermediaries in the world petroleum market. During the Teheran negotiations of early 1971 they turned out to be a weak reed. The American majors obtained an antitrust exemption enabling them to bargain jointly with the producer cartel, and thus hopefully to achieve a better deal for consumers. No sooner had the antitrust exemption been granted, however, than the companies capitulated to OPEC and passed on the resulting price increase to their customers.

Whatever determination to hold out for a better deal they may have had was in any case undercut by the State Department. In an intervention that was as unnecessary as it was unprecedented, the department sent its Under Secretary to tell OPEC that, in effect, oil is our lifeblood. The assembled OPEC negotiators were undoubtedly surprised by this novel approach to bargaining, rarely practised in the bazaar, but it did not take them long to realize that victory was being handed to them. The Texas Railroad Commission, no stranger to producer control over oil prices, further strengthened the hands of OPEC by refusing to allow an increase in domestic production.

This uninspiring sequence of events is history now. It has been argued that the producers had the whip hand and no other outcome of the Teheran negotiation was possible. If so, we need not have given an antitrust exemption to the oil companies and could have kept the Under Secretary of State at home. The cost of the Teheran agreement to consumers consists not only in that particular increase in prices, but also in the justifiable conviction it gave OPEC that the importers are unwilling to stand up in defense of their interests. On one pretext or another, the Teheran agreement has already been superseded by even more onerous retreats and the end is not in sight.

How to deal with OPEC will probably be the key policy problem in the energy area for the next few years, once the immediate problem of the embargo is overcome. Two opposing views on the future of OPEC have been expressed by leading experts on the world petroleum market. One is Professor Morris Adelman of MIT, who has long emphasized that the world supply of petroleum is increasing at a rapid rate and that the cartel therefore is likely to break down if it is not actively supported by the importing countries. The principal proponent of the other, and more widely accepted view, is James Akins of the State Department, now our ambassador to Saudi Arabia, who has argued strongly that the market power of OPEC cannot be broken and that consumers will have to live with higher prices. I am simplifying their respective positions somewhat, but the essential conflict is clear. [Editors' note: This section of Professor Houthakker's chapter is a very apt condensation of much of the argument in Professor Adelman's chapter. It could be used as a road map for the detailed account of events, circumstances, and rationalizations chronicled there.]

On Adelman's side there is the unquestioned fact that large discoveries of petroleum and natural gas are being made all the time. In the last few years there have been major finds in Alaska, in the Canadian Arctic, in the North Sea, in Indonesia, and not least in the Middle East itself. Contrary to Adelman's predictions, however, the world price of petroleum has increased, not decreased. [Editors' note: It must be noted that Adelman's basic prediction is the long-run pressure of supply upon price. Adelman has correctly predicted the consequences of policy actions taken early in the 1970s to increase price.] Recent price increases would seem to be a strong point in Akins's favor, but it also has to be recognized that the higher price of crude oil is partly the result of government policy, whether by omission or by commission. As mentioned earlier, the US State Department in effect encouraged the importers' capitulation at Teheran in early 1971, and Akins can hardly be credited for predicting a development he himself helped bring about. So far the importing countries have been reluctant to let market forces operate in the world petroleum markets, so Adelman may yet be vindicated if different policies are adopted. This does not mean, incidentally, that I support Adelman's suggestion of forcibly curtailing the role of the international oil companies, though such curtailment may come about in any case as a result of increased participation of producing countries' governments in local and downstream operations.

LONG-RUN PROSPECTS
AND PROBLEMS FOR THE CARTEL

The history of producer cartels in other commodities also tends to support Adelman's view. There have been many such attempts, ranging from wheat to rubber, but very few successes. In several of these attempts, consuming countries were formally or informally involved, but that has not necessarily prevented a breakdown. Usually one or two countries, whose economic fortunes are closely tied to a single commodity, take the lead on the producers' side; the role of Brazil in the successive coffee agreements is an example. With some concessions the leading country or countries can usually get the cooperation of most of the minor producers in a scheme to raise prices by reducing supplies, but to obtain such cooperation the leading country or countries frequently have to consent to a reduction in their market share. Even so, the minor producers tend to be unenthusiastic. Since their interest in the commodity is not as dominant as that of the leading countries, they are less willing to cut their production in order to maintain the agreed price level. Sometimes a few small producers will not cooperate at all and use the opportunity of higher prices to expand their output. The resulting surpluses tend to bring commodity agreements to an end.

The experience in other commodities suggests, therefore, that in the longer run the success of a commodity cartel depends on its control over the minor producers, especially those for whom the commodity is not particularly important. It is instructive to look at OPEC from this point of view. The two largest exporters are Saudi Arabia and Iran. The former's exports consist almost entirely of oil, but Iran has gradually diversified its activities. The other countries in the Persian Gulf are dependent almost entirely on petroleum and therefore would have a strong interest in preservation of the cartel; this is also true of Libya, but less so of Algeria, Nigeria, Venezuela, and Indonesia, all of whom have substantial varied exports. Some of these countries are likely to be recalcitrant if OPEC tries to curtail production in order to sustain prices, a practice known in the petroleum industry as market demand prorationing. So far OPEC has not had to resort to prorationing by mutual agreement, although some member countries have curtailed production on their own account, partly for noneconomic reasons. The real test for OPEC will come when countries such as Iran and Indonesia are asked to cut back production. Iran, for instance, has an ambitious development program which depends on a steady flow of foreign exchange. Up to a point this need could be met by credits from other OPEC members in the Persian Gulf, provided the state of politics in that area is sufficiently stable to make this palatable. Iraq may also be a problem for OPEC. Although it is an Arab country heavily dependent on oil, it also has expensive development plans and counts on increased oil production to pay for them.

Another difficulty that OPEC may face in the next few years has to do with transportation. Since crude oil has a very low value per unit of weight, freight charges are a large part of the landed price. Exporters that are close to consumer markets can generally command a premium over their most distant competitors, but the size of this premium depends on the level of tanker rates. The tanker market is notoriously volatile and frequent adjustments of relative prices are therefore required. This problem has already come up in the case of Iraq, which in 1971 obtained a considerable premium for its crude because of its direct access to the Mediterranean through pipelines. When freight rates fell sharply after the Teheran agreement, the premium effectively priced Iraq out of the market. Iraq reacted in the time-honored way by expropriating the foreign companies operating on its soil, but this does not appear to have fully solved the problem, even though in the meantime the rates have again risen sharply. It is not at all clear, in fact, what kind of mechanism OPEC can develop for adjusting export prices to changing tanker rates.

These are some of the reasons that may lead to a breakdown of OPEC even without active opposition from consuming countries. The circumstances described are clearly hypothetical, so we cannot and should not count on OPEC breaking up. Since the consuming countries cannot be reasonably certain of Adelman's prediction being realized, they clearly have to look to alternative strategies. One proposal is to form a consumer cartel. Unfortunately a consumer cartel could easily raise more problems than it would solve. Even if the consumer countries were prepared to act in unison, a bilateral monopoly is likely to be unstable, long stalemates being punctuated by sharp clashes. The resulting instability would, no doubt, spill over into the political sphere. Moreover, the prospects of keeping the consuming countries together are not very bright. Some importing countries such as Italy have a long history of going it alone, while several others are automatically suspicious of anything the United States is thought to want. The role of the major oil companies in a bilateral monopoly would also be hard to define. These companies will continue to be needed because of their expertise, their equipment, and their marketing organization, but even though they are domiciled in consuming countries they have rarely taken the consumer's point of view. There are also difficult technical problems which a consumer cartel would face; an example is the geographical pattern of prices and its dependence on changing freight rates.

Another possibility would be for individual consuming countries to make special deals with individual producing countries. There is ample precedent for this; the US has so far given preferential treatment to oil from Venezuela and Canada. France has made special arrangements with Algeria and Iraq, while a Japanese company recently made a deal with Abu Dhabi. Such leading producers as Iran and Saudi Arabia have long expressed a desire for a special relationship with the United States, which might involve foreign investment in US refining facilities as a token of good behavior. This idea deserves further exploration, especially in the case of Iran; after the Arab embargo of October 1973 it would be foolish to rely too much on Saudi Arabia. It should be realized, however, that consuming countries who go this route may have to pay a high price for rather dubious advantages, as France discovered in Algeria and Iraq.

ALTERNATIVE SOURCES OF FOREIGN SUPPLY

For the consuming countries a more promising alternative to making special deals with OPEC is to develop alternative sources of supply, a policy which the high price of crude encourages in any case. Several countries, of course, have been doing this already; I shall discuss efforts in the US below. Britain and other European countries are pushing ahead in the North Sea and Canada in the Arctic.

Perhaps the most intriguing possibility in this area is the Soviet Union. Several large-scale projects for obtaining crude oil and natural gas from Russia have advanced beyond the planning stage and are now being negotiated by the US and Japan on the political level. It is ironic that our fear of being held to ransom by the Arabs, with whom we have on the whole had fairly good relations, should drive us into the arms of the Russians with whom our experience has been considerably less favorable. Although political factors have certainly not been absent, our oil trade with the Middle East has generally been determined by commercial considerations. This would hardly be the case in transactions with the Soviet Union. While we can be happy with the improved atmosphere between the US and the Soviet Union, we should also remember that in the last 20 years Soviet leadership has changed a number of times with little or no warning. Another somewhat disturbing aspect of the proposed deals with the Soviet Union is that they call for enormous investments by the exporting countries with very little participation on the Soviet side. These deals would have a better prospect of continuity if the Soviet Union itself had invested large resources in them. In other recent transactions, especially in grain, the Russians have shown themselves shrewd bargainers, eager to exploit the weaknesses of their trading partners; some of the natural gas transactions discussed in 1972 would apparently have resulted in exhorbitant prices to the US. It can be argued that low-cost exports of grains and high-cost imports of energy resources are part of the price of a relaxation of tensions between the superpowers. If so, they may be worthwhile, but some caution is in order with respect to large investments in territory where our influence is uncertain at best. It should also not be forgotten that the Soviet bureaucracy, with whom foreign companies would have extensive dealings, does not appear to be very efficient in its domestic operations.

Despite these cautions, it is clearly in the interest of both the importing countries to have as many sources of supply as possible, provided the costs from each of them is reasonable. The consuming countries are temporarily in a weak position, but in the long run their prospects are much better if they have substitutes for crude oil from OPEC countries. If OPEC continues to be effective in raising crude prices, we may also have to give thought to schemes for discouraging investment by American and Japanese companies in the member countries, concentrating more on countries that are not under OPEC's control.

ALTERNATIVE SOURCES OF DOMESTIC SUPPLY

Turning now to the US, let us recall that we were the first to develop petroleum and natural gas on a large scale, and as a result the lower 48 states have been exploited and explored so thoroughly that few large discoveries have been made in recent years. In fact much of our petroleum production is obtained by secondary recovery techniques that are inherently expensive; in a free market crude oil produced by such techniques could not compete with oil from new reservoirs. The cost of extracting crude from large new wells is frequently very low when compared to the cost per barrel of oil from old small wells which must be pumped. Since many of our wells are in the latter category, the federal government imposed import controls to keep these high-cost wells in production, and some states until recently limited the output of the larger wells. Needless to say these restrictive practices represented a considerable loss of real resources and a burden on consumers. The recent replacement of the import quota program by a tariff was an important step in the right direction; however, it could have prevented many problems if taken three years ago when it was first recommended by the Cabinet Task Force on Oil Import Control.

The producers of low-cost oil have naturally looked with envy at the high price of crude prevailing in the US, and at the even higher prices of petroleum products prevailing in other countries. Assisted by rising demand the producing countries have succeeded in raising crude to a point where its landed price in the US now exceeds the price of domestic crude. Since the major industrial countries are all dependent on petroleum imports, OPEC could no doubt go further in increasing

248

crude prices in the short run. [Editors' note: The effect of such price increases would be to increase non-OPEC supply, which in turn would tend to have adverse effects upon cartel stability.]

I have already argued that the emergence of a strong producer cartel is the crux of the energy problem. The problem is not, as is widely believed, a physical shortage of fossil fuels. These fuels already exist in abundant quantity and they will be used somehow and sometime; the only question is at what price.

It is here that energy research and development come into the picture. In the extensive literature on the subject there is a tendency to assume that the price of crude in 1980 or 1985 will be at some given level, and to evaluate alternative sources of energy against this assumed price. This procedure is erroneous and likely to lead to a serious misdirection of energy research. The price of crude petroleum in 1980 to 1985 cannot be taken as given since it depends critically on what we ourselves do in the meantime, and especially on what we do in energy research and development. For instance, if we decide to go for oil from shale and establish a large capacity for producing syncrude at, say, $5 a barrel then we can be pretty sure that the equivalent price of foreign crude will stay below $5 a barrel. [Editors' note: A price of $5 a barrel is used primarily for purposes of example. A price of, say, $10 a barrel could have been used instead. What a price of $10 a barrel would mean would be: more development of high-cost, marginal domestic supplies of both conventional oil and syncrude; larger lease bonuses for offshore drilling, large windfall profits on old reservoirs; a landed foreign oil price of $10 a barrel; and a higher self-sufficiency ratio.] Conversely if we do not develop shale oil or other substitutes the equivalent crude price could easily go above the six or seven dollars a barrel often used as an assumption. Similarly, if we continue to concentrate our research on such far-out possibilities as the nuclear breeder, then we will remain defenseless against OPEC until such time as nuclear breeders come into widespread operation, which is not likely to happen before 1990. Even by that time there will probably still be plenty of fossil fuel, so that the nuclear breeder may be a white elephant. Successful development of a breeder reactor will reduce the value of oil in the ground and would therefore be helpful in accelerating crude output, but the present value of this benefit would seem to be small.

THE INTEGRATION OF RATIONAL R&D AND ENERGY POLICIES

If we want to plan our energy R & D rationally we should not ask what fraction of our energy supply can be economically supplied by a new source in the future, for the answer is likely to be zero and largely irrelevant anyway. We should ask, rather, what development of a new source will do to the price of fossil fuels, which are likely to remain the bulk of our energy supply in the foreseeable future. It is true that we could go the way of a self-fulfilling prophecy and decide to use the new sources of energy we develop regardless of their comparative costs, on the grounds that we have already paid for the research. This would not be a rational use of energy R & D, and I hope we will not take that direction.

To avoid any misunderstanding, let me repeat that the above analysis does not mean we should not undertake energy research on a sizable scale. The scattergun approach of a 'Manhattan project' is probably not justified, but it would be well worth our while to stimulate the development of the more immediately promising new sources of energy. Without claiming any expertise in energy technology, it appears to me that there are three areas in particular which warrant support under appropriate formulas, namely oil from shale, gas from coal, and cryogenic transmission of electric power. There appears to be general agreement on the promise of the first two sources; in my opinion the third also merits support because it may lead to a more competitive structure of our electric power industry, resulting in large gains in efficiency and environmental impact. I also favor moderate funding of the more remote prospects, but not on a scale of billions of dollars per year. We have better ways of using both the taxpayers' money and our scientific manpower.

The analysis I have sketched also has important implications for the form in which support for the development of new energy sources is to be given. This applies particularly to shale oil and gas from coal. The main deterrent to the private development of these industries is price risk. If my analysis is correct, the price of crude will remain below the cost of syncrude. Nevertheless we probably need the potential of oil from shale if we are to keep the price of crude petroleum down. This can be done by allowing potential producers of shale oil to bid on options to sell syncrude to the government at a fixed price. As an example, the government could invite bids on options to sell syncrude, of given specification and location, at a price of say $6 per barrel. Since it will probably cost less than $6 to produce a barrel of syncrude, such an option would have a positive value and there would be bidding among potential producers. Under this system producers would have an incentive to keep costs as low as possible, since their profit is inversely related to that cost. Also, since they would have to pay something to buy the option, they would have an incentive to stay in production. If syncrude could be sold in the open market at $6 a barrel or more the options would not be exercised.

The cost to the government would be the difference between the option price of $6 (in this example) and the market value of the syncrude produced, less the initial proceeds from the sale of the options. Financing and management of the syncrude plants would remain entirely in the private sector. I do not have an exact estimate of the cost to the taxpayer of this policy, but my impression is that it would cost at most a few hundred million dollars to provide sufficient incentives for the establishment of a shale oil industry with a capacity of a million barrels a day. The savings to consumers resulting from the lower price of crude petroleum would be at least one billion dollars and possibly much more than that. More precise estimates depend on the elasticities of supply and demand for the commodities involved; research on these numbers is now underway. One effect of encouraging shale oil production, for instance, might well be to get more syncrude from the Alberta tar sands; the provincial government is unlikely to leave this material in the ground forever.

The above discussion of new energy sources does not mean we should neglect the possibility of obtaining more fuel of conventional types. Let me mention a few examples. The Navy Department has recently estimated reserves in Naval Petroleum Reserve No. 4 in Northern Alaska at no less than 33 billion barrels, equal to at least five years of consumption and not much less than the proved reserves in the rest of the United States. This reserve and the smaller one in California appear to be no longer needed for military purposes, and therefore should be brought into production as soon as possible. According to the geologists there are excellent prospects of finding oil and gas in the Gulf of Alaska, in the Pacific, and perhaps in the Atlantic. And, of course, we have huge reserves of coal.

On the demand side there are also certain things that could be done. We need not go all the way with those who would rebuild our cities or invest tens of billions of dollars in mass transit to save on gasoline; such measures should be evaluated on broader grounds than energy alone. Taxes on selected energy resources or energy consumers are a more practical possibility, though at this point I am not prepared to either endorse or oppose them. Calculations at Data Resources, Inc. have shown, for instance, that the demand for gasoline has a considerable price elasticity, amounting to about minus 0.75 in the long run (that is, after about 3 years). [Editors' note: If a 10 per cent *increase* in price yields a 7.5 per cent *decrease* in quantity demanded, the price elasticity of demand is minus 0.75.] This elasticity represents two effects: when gasoline is more expensive people drive less, and they tend to buy cars with higher fuel efficiency. A moderate tax on gasoline would therefore have a noticeable effect on petroleum consumption and thus make us less vulnerable to OPEC's price policies. What such a tax would amount to, in effect, is that consumer surplus otherwise likely to be captured by OPEC is pre-empted by the US Treasury. It would also reduce our reliance on foreign refining capacity. On the other hand, an additional tax on gasoline would be somewhat regressive, with an income elasticity in the long run of about plus 0.75. Its effects may also be too small in the short run to deal with current shortages, and the revenue generated may not fit in with our overall fiscal policy.

CONCLUDING PERSPECTIVE

We should avoid looking at saving energy as an end in itself. For instance, some gasoline could apparently be saved by lowering highway speed limits but this would also mean that some time would be wasted in longer trips. It is by no means evident that in the long run the marginal amount of energy is more valuable that the marginal amount of time, though in the short run there may be no alternative to such measures. We are now going through a difficult period of transition in which arbitrary decisions are needed to prevent hardship to some consumers and dislocation of the economy. Once we survive this period we should be able to regain a sense of proportion, and view energy as our servant rather than our master.

FRANKLIN M. FISHER

This is the most technical chapter in these volumes. This is because Professor Fisher addresses a very specific problem in a very rigorous manner. The problem that Professor Fisher examines is the real cost of drilling oil and gas wells (both productive and dry) in the United States. Real drilling costs (the value of other goods and services one must give up to drill an additional well of a given depth in a given area) did not appear to increase in the United States in the years examined by Professor Fisher. In fact, there appeared to be a decrease in real costs. For example, over the period 1960-66, the real costs of 10,000 foot depth oil wells decreased about 8-9 per cent. Real gas well costs at 10,000 feet appeared to decrease about 14-16 per cent.

These depth-favoring cost changes are very important. They indicate that incremental technological change do-minated other factors over this period. There were no astounding technological breakthroughs (such as the rotary drill) in this period. Rather, the progress made in turning back the tendency for costs to increase was the result of technically competent people solving day-to-day problems in drilling rig management. Although we popularly think of technological progress in terms of 'revolutions' or 'breakthroughs,' most real technological advance is the result of the cumulative effects of the piecemeal solution of many small specific problems. As with the industrial economy at large, so too with the oil industry.

The technological progress in drilling wells, however, does not necessarily mean reduced real costs per barrel of oil or mcf of gas found. If the volume of reserves found per well has decreased more rapidly than real costs per well, then real costs per unit of reserves may have increased. Recent drilling statistics do indicate that findings per foot of hole drilled have decreased. But these statistics must be treated with caution. If real drilling costs at depth have decreased, then it is possible to drill smaller, deeper wells at a profit. Thus, at approximately constant real prices, simple statistics which show decreased finding rates per foot of hole drilled are not inconsistent with Professor Fisher's results. Rather, they may be consistent with a continued decrease in the trend of real drilling costs that more than offsets shifts in drilling activity to higher cost areas and deeper horizons.

The behavior of real drilling costs per unit of reserves found discussed above must be regarded as a tentative hypothesis. Professor Fisher's data covered only the period to 1966. But extension of the systematic trends he discusses to more recent years is consistent with more fragmentary evidence from the post-1966 period. The data can be extended and improved. It must be if we are to have an accurate and national discussion of national energy policy. Discussion of real drilling costs per unit of reserves discovered must take into account the effect of cost changes to induce changes in the size distribution of prospects accepted at any depth. Professor Fisher's specific findings should be compared to the more general conclusions of Professor Barnett and Dr Kellogg. They are also relevant to the overall policy questions addressed by Professor MacAvoy. Since many of the same companies using the same technology drill in both the United States and Canada, Professor Fisher's results may also be applicable to the Canadian experience with real drilling costs.

FRANKLIN M. FISHER

Technological change and the drilling cost-depth relationship 1960-6

INTRODUCTION

In an earlier work,[1] I examined the relationship between well depth and drilling costs in the extraction of crude petroleum and natural gas in the United States and considered the question of whether and how that relationship had been altered by technological and other change in the period 1955-9. The principal results of that study were as follows:

1 The relationship between well-depth and drilling cost can be very closely represented by an equation of the form

$$Y = K(e^{\alpha X} - 1) \tag{1}$$

where Y denotes costs in dollars, X, depth in feet, e is the base of the natural system of logarithms, and K and α are parameters to be estimated. Estimation of that relationship for different areas in the United States at the same period of time shows a consistent pattern in which a definite trade-off is observed between areas with relatively high costs for shallow wells and relatively low rates of increase of costs with depth (high values of $H = \alpha K$ and low values of α) and areas with relatively low costs for shallow wells but a relatively high rate of increase of costs with depth.[2]

2 The *Joint Association Survey of Drilling Costs* (JAS),[3] which is the source of the data, is sadly defective. It makes very inefficient use of its ample information from a statistical point of view and the published results are an inextricable mixture of actual figures and curve-fitting with no reliability estimates. Use of an only relatively slightly processed sample for 1959 suggests strongly that the often

very great curvature of the drilling cost-depth relationship is understated by JAS procedures.

3 Ignoring this (as one unfortunately must if one is to proceed at all) and examining changes in the relation (1) as estimated from the JAS published data for 1955-6 and 1959, there is evidence of systematic change in the drilling cost-depth relationship due both to technological change and to the slow movement to higher-cost areas as lower-cost ones get drilled up. In particular, while costs increase very sharply with well depth and while well depths are increasing over time, the evidence for the 1955-9 period suggests pretty strongly that technological advance more than kept pace with this and with the slow drift toward high-cost areas. Costs (in real terms) at the end of the period tended to be lower than at the beginning. The exception to this was the costs of very deep wells (beyond 15,000 feet) and, indeed, the changes during that period tended to be 'shallowness-favoring,' that is, cost reduction tended to be greater at smaller depths than at greater ones.

The present study carries the previous work forward by examining annual data for the period 1960-6. As far as the first two of the matters discussed above are concerned, the conclusions are essentially unchanged. The relationship (1) continues to fit the published data quite well and, as far as one can tell, those data themselves are unfortunately still open to the serious criticisms already summarized.[4]

Turning to the evidence as to the effects of technical and other change, as in the earlier period, it seems clear that technical advance more than kept pace with the drift toward higher cost areas and the increases in well depths. The picture which predominates is clearly one of reduction in real costs. Whereas in the earlier period, however, changes tended to be shallowness-favoring, in the 1960-6 period, changes were overwhelmingly depth-favoring on the average, except in the cost of dry wells where they were approximately neutral with regard to depth. Such depth-favoring change on the average is caused by its predominance in the mid-continent region together with more or less depth-neutral change in other regions. In short, on the average, wells in given areas and depth classes cost less to drill (in real terms) at the end of the period than at the beginning, and the most substantial reductions on the average occurred in the costs of drilling (and equipping) relatively deep productive wells. Such reductions (adjusting for inflation) were roughly (for gas wells) on the order of 15-17 per cent at 10,000 feet but were still roughly 3 per cent near the surface. For oil wells, there may just possibly have been an average increase near the surface of 7-10 per cent if the least favorable year is chosen, but even then reductions of roughly 9 per cent were experienced at 10,000 feet on the average. For dry wells, a general reduction of 11-15 per cent was involved.

INTERPRETATION OF PARAMETERS

An extensive discussion of the relationship (1), the interpretation of its parameters, and its properties was given in my earlier study and will not be repeated here. A summary of that discussion is required, however, in order to examine the results discussed below.

The two basic parameters of (1) are α and $H = \alpha K$. Defining 'marginal cost' for purposes of this paper as the rate of increase of drilling cost with depth[5] and denoting it by MC, differentiation of (1) yields:

$$MC = He^{\alpha X} \tag{2}$$

so that H is interpreted as the limit of marginal cost as depth goes to zero. From (2)

$$\mathrm{d}\log MC/\mathrm{d}X = \alpha \tag{3}$$

so that α is the percentage increase of marginal cost per foot increase in depth. It is also the limit of the greater percentage increase of total cost for a foot increase in depth as depth becomes very large.

Some idea of what is involved can be obtained by observing that for a value of α of 2.0×10^{-4}, which is roughly representative of the order of magnitude of the estimated values, marginal cost doubles approximately every 3300 feet, while total costs at 7400 feet are double what they are at 5000 feet, at 13,000 feet are double their value at 10,000 feet, and at 18,200 feet are double their value at 15,000 feet.

Over-all increases in costs are reflected in increases in K, while changes in α determine whether changes are depth-favoring (a downward change) or shallowness-favoring (an upward change).

Finally, while the validity of (1) ultimately rests on its ability to fit the data, it can be interpreted in a heuristically appealing way. If one assumes that the difficulty of going a foot deeper is best measured by the difficulty of already drilling to a given depth, then marginal cost is a function of total cost. The simplest form for such a functional relationship is that of proportionality, but this is ruled out by the fact that the total cost approaches zero with depth (set-up costs are not included) but marginal cost does not. The simplest admissible form is linearity and this leads directly to (1) since:

$$MC = He^{\alpha X} = H + \alpha K(e^{\alpha X} - 1) = H + \alpha Y. \tag{4}$$

The fact that (1) is non-linear in its parameters makes estimation thereof somewhat difficult. A full explanation of the methods used is given in appendix A of my earlier study; here we need only discuss such matters as are required for an

257

TABLE 1

Average values of α and H for United States: 1960-6, all cases

Year	Number of wells[1]	Average value of α (10^{-4} omitted)	Average value of H (current dollars)	Average value of H (1964 dollars)
DRY WELLS				
1960	17,392	2.1483	4.3712	4.5382
1961	16,935	2.2805	4.0094	4.1034
1962	16,545	2.3575	4.0624	4.1726
1963	16,302	2.1610	4.9675	4.0369
1964	17,456	2.3045	3.7574	3.7574
1965	15,846	2.3558	3.6016	3.4676
1966	14,490	2.2353	4.2836	4.0139
PRODUCTIVE WELLS				
1960	26,843	2.1381	6.3376	6.5797
1961	26,855	1.9977	6.4599	6.6113
1962	27,202	2.0627	6.5159	6.6926
1963	25,370	2.0505	6.1084	6.2153
1964	25,833	1.8362	6.5862	6.5862
1965	23,582	1.8502	6.9374	6.6847
1966	19,901	1.7485	7.4928	7.0210
OIL WELLS				
1960	21,219	1.7430	7.0618	7.3316
1961	21,168	1.8370	6.8503	7.0108
1962	21,360	1.7341	7.2519	7.4485
1963	20,690	1.7564	6.6136	6.7293
1964	20,978	1.6950	6.8850	6.8850
1965	18,813	1.6633	6.9610	6.7075
1966	15,840	1.4488	8.6095	8.0674
GAS WELLS				
1960	5,248	1.9713	7.3436	7.6242
1961	5,650	1.8956	7.5003	7.6761
1962	5,815	2.0998	6.8371	7.0225
1963	4,754	1.6226	6.7803	6.8990
1964	4,834	1.5958	7.6003	7.6003
1965	4,750	1.7862	7.6612	7.3822
1966	4,028	1.6472	7.9658	7.4642

1 Number of wells in areas with sufficient degrees of freedom for regressions

TABLE 2

Average values of α and H for United States: 1960-6, straight-line cases excluded

Year	Number of wells[1]	Average value of α (10^{-4} omitted)	Average value of H (current dollars)	Average value of H (1964 dollars)
DRY WELLS				
1960	16,683	2.2396	4.3399	4.5057
1961	15,304	2.5235	3.8325	3.9223
1962	15,535	2.5108	3.7667	3.8688
1963	15,477	2.2761	3.9105	3.9789
1964	16,815	2.3923	3.7299	3.7299
1965	15,208	2.4546	3.5762	3.4459
1966	14,176	2.2848	4.1114	3.8525
PRODUCTIVE WELLS				
1960	26,483	2.1381	6.3376	6.5797
1961	26,855	2.0246	6.4449	6.5959
1962	27,202	2.0763	6.5125	6.6891
1963	25,370	2.0641	6.0858	6.1923
1964	25,833	1.8658	6.4113	6.4113
1965	23,582	1.9074	6.9005	6.6492
1966	19,901	1.9158	7.2319	6.7765
OIL WELLS				
1960	19,806	1.8666	6.9292	7.1939
1961	20,436	1.9028	6.7137	6.8710
1962	20,808	1.7801	7.1424	7.3361
1963	20,437	1.7695	6.6116	6.7273
1964	20,578	1.7279	6.8322	6.8322
1965	18,108	1.7281	6.8554	6.6057
1966	14,298	1.6050	8.2295	7.7113
GAS WELLS				
1960	5,190	1.9933	7.0099	7.2777
1961	5,589	1.9163	7.3547	7.5271
1962	5,804	2.1038	6.8294	7.0146
1963	4,699	1.9617	6.6630	6.8437
1964	4,404	1.7516	7.2459	7.2459
1965	4,519	1.8775	7.4888	7.2160
1966	3,673	1.8064	7.4878	7.0163

1 Number of wells in areas with sufficient degrees of freedom for regressions

Franklin M. Fisher

understanding of the results as presented in Tables 1 and 2. [Editors' note: Professor Fisher's detailed results are not presented here. These results are summarized in Tables 1 and 2. The detailed results consist of four tables of the joint distribution of the estimated values of H and α for each category of well (oil, gas, dry, productive) for each of the seven years 1960-6. In addition, a fifth table contains the actual drilling cost regressions. These tables are available from E.W. Erickson.]

A clear pattern emerged from the estimations, matching that already found in the earlier study. Areas with relatively low values of H are areas where drilling costs of shallow wells are relatively low. Areas with relatively low values of α are areas in which the rate of increase of drilling costs with depth is relatively low. Other things equal, we would not expect to find many areas in which both parameters are low, for these are low-cost areas which it pays to drill first. Nor would we expect to find many areas with high values of both parameters, for these are high-cost areas which it pays to drill last. Of course, among the 'other things equal' is the probability of finding oil or gas, so that such statements can only be read as general tendencies, but there is clear evidence of an efficient α-H frontier along which most observations lie. It is the movement of that frontier over time which shows what is happening to drilling costs. The drilling up of low-cost areas tends to shift the frontier into higher cost regions; technical improvement tends to mitigate, cancel, or reverse such shifts. To an evaluation of such effects we now turn.

CHANGES IN THE DRILLING-COST FUNCTION, 1960-6

Because of the number of years involved, comparisons of parameter shifts in individual areas are omitted. Instead, we proceed by computing the average values of α and H for each year and type of well, where the parameter estimates for each area are weighted by the number of wells of the given type drilled in that area in the given year. The result is a composite picture which can not truly be said to represent the drilling-cost function in any one area. However, since that function in fact represents a relationship of costs to depth, taking into account the different nature of the formations drilled at different depths within a given area, the average parameters for the United States as a whole can be thought of as showing much the same thing on a more aggregate level. From this point of view, it is perhaps not too important whether a downward shift in the aggregate drilling-cost function comes about from downward shifts in each component area or from a general shift in drilling activity toward low-cost areas. Either one shows up in terms of what it cost, on the average, to drill wells of a given depth. In fact, however, the existence of the efficient α-H frontier and the fact that the relative importance of different areas in drilling did not change radically shows pretty clearly that most of the observed average effect came from real-cost reduction on individual areas rather than through a shift in activitȳ.

Tables 1 and 2 give the average values of α and H for the United States for the years 1960-6. The final column gives H in 1964 dollars (α, the percentage increase in marginal cost per foot increase in depth, is unaffected by price level changes), where the deflator is the Independent Petroleum Association of America index of drilling costs adapted for this purpose.[6] The two tables differ in that Table 1 includes a small number of cases in which the sum of squares being minimized fails to have a minimum (the likelihood function – assuming normality and independence – fails to have a maximum) as α goes to zero and K goes to infinity. These are cases in which it can be shown that the best estimate of (1) is the limiting case of a straight line through the origin. In such cases, H is the slope of that line. Table 2 does not include such cases. Those cases, if reflective of reality ought to be included, but they are somewhat suspect. Not surprisingly, the general picture is much the same whichever table one considers (for example, less than 5 per cent of the wells drilled in 1960 in areas with enough observations to allow estimation were drilled in such straight-line areas).

And that general picture is very clearly one of cost reduction. We begin by examining changes in H (in real terms). These reflect changes in the cost of drilling a marginal foot near the surface and, therefore, in total cost for very shallow wells. For a constant value of α, moreover, a downward percentage shift in H corresponds to the same downward percentage shift in K and therefore to a cost reduction of the same percentage, uniform as to depth. A downward shift in H together with a downward shift in α indicates a cost reduction of the same percentage as the reduction in H near the surface but a greater reduction at depth.

Clearly, the over-all trend for all types of well is for H to fall, the reductions being as much as 10 per cent over the period. The only exception to this is the sharp rise in H which occurs in 1966 for oil wells and thus for productive wells also. So very sharp a change in a single year appears to be an aberration, which is quite possible given the nature of the data, but if it is not, then, on the average, the cost of drilling and equipping relatively shallow oil wells rose sharply in 1966 and was higher than in 1960 (although, as we shall see, the cost of relatively deep oil wells was lower). Aside from this, however, the costs of relatively shallow wells clearly declined over the period.

As far as dry wells are concerned, the situation was much the same for deep wells as for shallow ones. While H declined over the period, α remained relatively constant so that the same percentage change in costs applied to all depths. For oil wells and gas wells (and thus for productive wells), however, cost reductions at depth were greater than indicated by the percentage reductions in the appropriate values of H. For such wells, there is a clear and unmistakable downward

Franklin M. Fisher

trend in α strongly indicating that technical and other change tended to be depth-favoring.

Nor is the magnitude of that effect by any means negligible. To take just two examples, comparison of the figures for gas wells in 1966 with those for 1960 shows a reduction in real costs of about 2.1 per cent near the surface, but a reduction of about 16.8 per cent at 10,000 feet. For oil wells, comparison of the figures for the same two years shows an increase in real costs of about 10.1 per cent near the surface (although, as explained above, this may be misleading) but a *decrease* of about 8.4 per cent by 10,000 feet.[7]

Moreover, an examination of the detailed results for individual areas shows that the depth-favoring phenomenon in the averages is not principally due to any shift in drilling activity toward lower-α areas. Depth-favoring cost change is clearly the predominant tendency in the mid-continent region, with changes elsewhere being roughly depth-neutral.

Why should depth-favoring changes predominate on the average? Since more oil and gas tends to be found at depth than in relatively shallow formations, and since costs increase so very sharply with depth, the incentive toward technical improvements which will be effective at great depths is clear. Moreover, as experience with very deep wells accumulates, we should expect some reduction in their costs. Hence, it is not a surprise to find change which is in no case shallowness-favoring on the average and, for most well types, depth-favoring. The difference between dry and productive wells in this respect is harder to understand, however, as is the difference between the mid-continent region and the remainder of the country.

What accounts for such strongly depth-favoring change on the average in the case of productive wells but neutral change in the case of dry ones? I do not know, but here are some possibilities (not in any particular order):

1 There was technical progress in equipping as well as in drilling. Progress in equipping was depth-favoring while progress in drilling was depth-neutral.

2 Equipping costs became relatively more important over the period. Since these costs tend to go up rather more linearly with depth than do drilling costs (which is shown by the generally lower values of α for productive than for dry wells), an increase in their importance shows up as a decrease in α. The trouble with this argument, however, is that the relative increase in the importance of such costs would have to have been very substantial to account for the observed effects and that it would imply that over-all reductions in costs were lower for oil and gas wells than for dry ones, which does not appear to have been the case.

3 Since dry wells are mostly wildcats while productive ones are mostly drilled on proven fields, the general tendency (in the absence of technical change) for drilling to move to increasingly costly formations affects dry wells more than oil

and gas wells. This, by itself, would mean that technical change would show up as less cost reduction for dry wells than for productive ones, but would say nothing about depth-favoring versus depth-neutral change. If we also observe, however, that because the discovery of more oil and gas requires deeper drilling, formations which are relatively inexpensive to drill at depth will get drilled first, then we can see that the drift to more expensive formations *may* in itself be a shallowness-favoring drift. If so, then depth-favoring technical change would show up as such in oil and gas wells but might be offset by this phenomenon in dry wells.

The trouble with the first two of these possibilities is that it is hard to see why they should have had different effects on costs as between the mid-continent and the rest of the country, although it is at least possible that they did. The third possibility clearly could have different effects in different regions as its action depends very much on the types of formations found.

In any case, the existence of cost reduction of at least a depth-neutral and, for oil and gas wells, a predominantly depth-favoring character is unmistakable. As in the 1955-9 period, the real costs of well drilling in the United States went down in the early sixties. There is some evidence that this trend may have continued through the sixties and into the seventies, but the data have not yet been systematically evaluated. As these long-run real-cost trends become a more important element in the determination of national energy policy, it is to be hoped that the data collection and processing effort keeps pace.

NOTES

This study was supported by a grant from Resources for the Future, Inc. I am indebted to Martin Neil Baily, Alan Marin, Susan Oman, and especially, Nancy R. Greene for computational assistance.
1 'Measuring the Effects of Depth and Technological Change on Drilling Costs,' Study II in Franklin M. Fisher, *Supply and Costs in the US Petroleum Industry* (Baltimore 1964). All references are to this study unless otherwise noted.
2 These matters and the properties of (1) are explored at somewhat greater length below.
3 New York: American Petroleum Institute, Independent Petroleum Association of America, and Mid-Continent Oil & Gas Association, various years; 1955-6 and 1959 were used in the previous study. The survey has been annual since 1959.
4 New analysis is not possible here since I do not have available a sample such as that for 1959 which was used in the previous study. The published descriptions of methods by the JAS do not suggest any very substantive change. I now leave this disheartening matter, but the industry should not.

5 Note that in a cross-section study in which the observations are different wells, this is the difference in cost between two wells which differ slightly as to depth, not the cost of drilling a given well a little deeper. In that sense, it is a long-run rather than a short-run marginal cost.

6 The index of items purchased by operators, unadjusted for depth, was combined with the index (or indices) of contractor rates using the 1964 weights.

7 These comparisons use the figures which include all cases (Table 1). If the figures excluding the straight-line cases (Table 2) are used instead, the reduction in costs for gas wells is about 3.6 per cent near the surface and about 14.3 per cent at 10,000 feet. For oil wells, there is an increase of about 7.2 per cent near the surface and a decrease of about 9.2 per cent at 10,000 feet.

JOHN HELLIWELL

This coming year will see several applications in Canada and the US to transport Arctic gas to North America markets. Professor Helliwell discusses the criteria which should be used in assessing the social viability of these projects.

Debate has already begun in Canada on whether the $5 billion Mackenzie Valley gas pipeline should be built. Much of that debate has centered around the impacts on the economy of the construction and financing of the pipeline project. Professor Helliwell and a number of other faculty members and students at the University of British Columbia have developed a model to study these impacts.

Helliwell discusses these macro impacts and correctly dismisses them as largely irrelevant to the issue of whether the pipeline should or should not be constructed and the timing of con-

struction. Certainly, the government has a range of policies available to counteract any harmful impact which the pipeline may have on the economy. The real issue is whether the Mackenzie Valley pipeline, now or later, maximizes the welfare of Canadians. The real test is whether the resources devoted to the pipeline are best allocated here or elsewhere.

This paper examines this crucial question – at what stage in Canadian energy development would such a pipeline maximize the benefits less the costs to Canadians. Helliwell *et al.* find that the pipeline should not, as its proponents suggest, begin operation as soon as possible, carrying Prudhoe Bay gas and some Canadian gas to American markets and some Canadian gas to Canadian markets. Rather, the study finds that benefits to Canadians are maximized if the pipeline is delayed a number of years until it is needed entirely to serve the Canadian market.

Obviously, analyzing the project before application is made involves a number of assumptions. Still, the paper represents a significant increase in the level of sophistication in analyzing the social welfare of the project and provides a real contribution to the debate.

JOHN HELLIWELL

Economic consequences
of developing Canada's Arctic gas

A number of faculty and students at the University of British Columbia have been studying the national economic effects of various plans for developing Canada's Arctic energy resources. This paper contains a summary of earlier results and reports on more recent extensions.[1] The first section was originally prepared as part of a conference paper (Helliwell, 1973 b), and the remaining sections contain more recent calculations of the costs and benefits of alternative uses of Canada's Arctic gas. The focus of the analysis is on the natural gas resources in the Canadian Mackenzie Delta region because the first proposal to come forward from the industry is for a pipeline to move gas from the Mackenzie Delta, and from Prudhoe Bay in Alaska, to Canadian and United States markets. The proposal, being made by a consortium of about thirty Canadian and US firms, involves a 48-inch pipeline to be built as soon as possible to carry 4 billion cubic feet per day (Bcf/d) of Alaskan and Canadian gas to southern markets, primarily in the US Mid-West and West. The project itself is very large, and deserves careful assessment in its own right. The significance of the project is greatly increased by the fact that it is the first of a whole chain, each part of which depends on the first step. Whatever the rhetoric, the substance of energy policy is defined by the sequence of government responses to changing circumstances. The Canadian government's approach to the Mackenzie Valley pipeline proposal will influence strongly the procedures and results of subsequent decisions.

The two types of economic study described in this paper by no means cover all the ground for economic analysis of major energy projects. The first type is concerned with the economic impact of the construction and operation of an

267

John Helliwell

Arctic pipeline and the related facilities for gas production in the Mackenzie Delta. The second type of study bypasses the project's short-term impact on income, employment, and the balance of payments. Instead, we ask the broader question: Does the project make better economic sense than any of the obvious alternatives? The most obvious alternatives involve deferred development of the Mackenzie Delta, consequently avoiding Canadian exports of Delta gas and, possibly, trans-shipment of Alaskan gas. By simulation methods, it is possible to test separately the various facets of the proposed project to see what better alternatives are lurking unseen. No study is as broad as it should be. To keep our project to a manageable scale, we have skirted the problems of fitting natural gas into a comprehensive forecast of Canadian energy supply and demand. Neither have we considered the relative advantages of pipeline, rail, dirigible, and so on, as means of transporting gas to southern markets, although such studies must at some time be done. Instead, we give top priority, as reported in the later parts of the chapter, to assessing the urgency of the matter. If, as the proponents argue, the proposed Mackenzie Valley pipeline is an opportunity that must be seized immediately, or else deferred at great cost, then the decision process must be truncated accordingly. But if, as we have tentatively concluded, there is no advantage in proceeding immediately, then the way is clear for a more comprehensive range of alternatives to be considered before a final decision is made.

ECONOMIC IMPACTS OF PIPELINE
CONSTRUCTION AND OPERATION

Economic impact studies using econometric models (sets of estimated equations depicting the evolution of the economy) are becoming increasingly common for the evaluation of investment projects and government policies. The method is fairly straightforward. First, it is necessary to find or develop an econometric model whose equations describe the economy in sufficient detail. Then the model is used to derive a base or control solution as far into the future as desired, constrained only by the decreasing accuracy of the model's structure and information, and the consequent weakening of the model-builder's nerve. The control solution for our economic impact experiments is a simulation of the Canadian quarterly model[2] RDX2 running from 1973 to 1985. For the base solution, the 300-odd exogenous variables, for which the values must be determined outside the model, were classified into groups and given mutually consistent growth rates. These values, plus the historically estimated coefficients and the 1972 initial conditions, determine the paths to 1985 of the 260-odd endogenous variables of the model.

268

For the analysis reported in this chapter, the model is supplemented by eighty new variables, fifty-five coefficients, and sixty equations outlining the construction and operation of a Mackenzie Valley pipeline, the production of gas in the Mackenzie Delta and non-frontier regions, and the distribution of costs and benefits among the various participating groups. The exogenous variables, the coefficients, and the structure of the equations are based on announced features of the pipeline proposal being prepared by the Gas Arctic consortium,[3] a variety of cost and demand information, and the tax, royalty, and tariff-setting procedures expected to apply to northern pipelines and gas production. The new equations comprise an additional sector of the model. Links between the new sector and the rest of the model are provided by inserting certain employment, expenditure, and financing variables relating to the pipeline and gas production into the relevant parts of the main model.

When all this preparation was complete, the model, including the pipeline and gas production sector, was started in 1973 and run through 1985, and the results compared with the control solution. What of the results, and of the economics behind them? During the construction phase, there are increases in activity and investment expenditure in other industries, and increases in imports of goods and capital, directly and indirectly due to the pipeline. The direct material, labor, and import requirements for the pipeline, and the pattern of foreign and domestic financing for the project, are embodied in the information read into the model. The model itself contributes the estimates of the indirect or induced effects of the project. The induced responses follow a cyclical pattern, because of the so-called 'accelerator principle.' When firms in other industries face a rising demand due to the project, they increase their output and attempt to increase the size of their own facilities in order to meet the higher level of demand at least cost. When the project is over, other industries find themselves with excess capacity, and cut their investment below what it would have been had the pipeline never been constructed.

RDX2 has a very detailed dynamic structure that shows vigorous cyclical responses to a large investment project. In assessing the likely effects of pipeline construction, we have dampened these responses in two ways. The material demands for a large pipeline ought to be carefully enough planned that their timing and temporary nature would be well known to governments and suppliers alike. Recognizing the temporary nature of the demand, many suppliers would choose to produce beyond normal capacity rather than expand their plants. A substantial reaction of this sort was built into the model, thus lessening the induced boom-and-bust investment cycle. Policy-makers, using RDX2 and other similar models, are already assessing different mixes of monetary and fiscal policies that

TABLE 1: Part A

Direct trade and capital account impacts of Mackenzie pipeline and gas production 1975-85 (in millions of current dollars)

Year	Capital account* inflows (New issues-retirements) FBALP&G$	Balance of trade effects (XBALP&G$)** under various export assumptions			
		Case 0 50% Prudhoe gas 50% Delta exports	Case 1 50% Prudhoe 50% Delta exports	Case 2 50% Prudhoe 50% Canadian use	Case 3 100% Canadian use
1975	597	-623	-623	-623	-679
1976	927	-641	-641	-641	-697
1977	905	-507	-507	-507	-598
1978	857	-233	-265	-296	-427
1979	329	220	77	-65	-242
1980	-101	612	339	65	-264
1981	-222	766	445	125	-260
1982	-235	775	456	137	-248
1983	-136	706	389	72	-309
1984	-136	702	387	73	-304
1985	-136	738	406	74	-298

Part B

Direct plus induced effects of Mackenzie pipeline and gas production[†] 1975-85
(based on 50% Prudhoe, 25% Delta exports; includes policy offsets)

Year	Trade balance XBAL$ mill. of current $	Balance of payments UBAL	Price of foreign exchange PFX $Can/$US	Business output (excluding pipeline output) UGPP millions of 1961 $	Unemployment rate RNU %	Total employment NE millions
19751	-916	-389	.005	635	-.241	.029
1976	-1067	-89	.008	1076	-.631	.075
1977	-907	339	-.001	685	-.479	.074
1978	-548	582	-.012	182	.213	.041
1979	125	395	-.021	-886	.923	-.017
1980	767	-35	-.010	-1276	1.012	-.061
1981	1072	-91	.006	-1021	.637	-.070
1982	638	-35	.000	-488	-.096	-.047
1983	-390	-273	-.017	-159	-.589	-.017
1984	-971	-586	-.022	-137	-.498	.002
1985	-840	-393	-.020	-573	-.060	-.005

*The direct capital account inflows contain all foreign capital used for the pipeline, plus interest-free loans from US gas purchasers to Delta producers. To simplify comparison, interest-free loans were kept at values compatible with case 1. Other foreign capital for gas production is treated as an induced rather than a direct flow. Results are trucated to millions of dollars.

**The direct trade account effects include pipeline tariff receipts, gas export revenues based on prices in existing contracts for future sale, and foreign interest and dividends on pipeline financing. Foreign interest and dividends on gas production are treated as induced flows.

†All these results are in the 'shock minus control' format. The base case solution values are subtracted from the model solutions including pipeline and gas production in order to obtain the numbers in the table.

John Helliwell

could be used to smooth the transfer of real resources in to and out of the project during the construction phase.

The operations phase is a different matter, as the pipeline would be working for more than thirty years. Thus there is no point in trying to shield the rest of the economy from the effects; the choice of this long-term project over others implies a willingness to substitute gas and pipeline service exports for other net exports in the balance of payments. Quite naturally, effects on balance of payments and the exchange-rate change required to make room for the gas project increase as gas exports increase. Most of our simulations have been done using the proponents' plan to use one-half of the pipeline's 4 Bcf/d throughput capacity to trans-ship Alaskan gas to Canada's southern border, one-quarter to export Mackenzie Delta gas to the United States, and the remaining one-quarter to ship Delta gas to Canadian markets. Part A of Table 1 shows the direct effects on the trade account (XBALP&G$) and capital accounts (FBALP&G) of pipeline and gas production under varying assumptions about the quantity of gas exported. During the construction phase, the direct trade account deficit (−XBALP&G$) is usually smaller than the capital account surplus (FBALP&G) by an average of about $300 million per year. This assumes 51 per cent of the equity and one-third of the long-term debt to come from within Canada. The net direct balance-of-payments effects (XBALP&G$ + FBALP&G) during the operations phase depend very much on how the pipeline is used. Four alternative series for XBAL&G$ are shown in part A of Table 1. Case 0 shows the biggest trade surplus, with all of the pipeline used to ship Alaskan and Canadian gas to US markets. Cases 1, 2, and 3 involve increasing concentration on Canadian use. In case 3 there are no export receipts at all, and XBALP&G$ is made up entirely of foreign interest and dividends on the pipeline, once construction is complete. The net balance-of-payments impact during the mid-1980s ranges from a positive amount of $600 million in case 0 to a negative amount of over $400 million in case 3. Using the RDX2 estimates of the effects of exchange-rate changes on other trade flows, the required long-term changes in the price of foreign exchange would be such as to raise the relative value of the Canadian dollar by less than 4 per cent in case 0, and to lower it by less than $2\frac{1}{2}$ per cent in case 3. For case 1, the plan now likely to be proposed by the Gas Arctic consortium, the indicated increase in the value of the Canadian dollar is about $1\frac{1}{2}$ per cent. In all likelihood, the prices contemplated by existing export contracts for Delta gas, which are the prices used in the Table 1 calculations, are unrealistically low. Higher prices, such as those assumed in the second half of the chapter, would increase the export surplus in cases 0 and 1.

Part B of Table 1 reports a few of the results showing the direct plus indirect effects of pipeline construction and operation using the assumptions of case 1.

272

The first two columns show the changes in the overall trade balance (XBAL$) and the total net balance of payments (UBAL). The simulations are done using a flexible exchange rate version of RDX2, so that changes in the balance of payments and in the price of foreign exchange (PFX, expressed as the number of Canadian dollars exchanged for one US dollar) are mutually determined. Subject to lags, positive values for UBAL lead to a lower PFX (a higher value for the Canadian dollar) while lower values for PFX eventually reduce UBAL. But in the shorter term, trade flows are influenced more by activity levels than by relative prices, so that the exchange rate does not move directly towards a new equilibrium level.

The three right-hand columns of part B in Table 1 show the net effects on aggregate activity and employment. Because of its extreme capital intensity, the pipeline is treated as a separate sector. Thus the constant-dollar business output series UGPP excludes value added by pipeline operations, although it naturally does include, during the construction phase, all the components of the pipeline that are manufactured in Canada. The unemployment rate is down during construction, up afterwards, and then down again in the mid 1980s, relative to the control solution. Total employment is up during construction by a maximum of 75,000 jobs, about ten times the direct labor requirements for pipeline construction. The subsequent cyclical loss of jobs is almost as large, so that the average net employment effect between 1975 and 1985 is about zero. The results for total employment do not match exactly with those for the unemployment rates. This is because there are induced changes (subject to lags) in labor force participation and net migration – the total population is almost 100,000 higher than control in 1979, and equally as much lower in 1983.

Our numerical results are intended to demonstrate some of the economy's main adjustment mechanisms, and are not offered as forecasts. The particular numbers resulting are very dependent on the initial conditions and on the assumed policies. In a very real sense, the numbers could be anything we chose, depending on the extent to which offsetting policies are employed. But if policies can be so adjusted, how can the results be used to justify a project?

Now, at last, we have reached the main point of this section of the chapter – that from the national point of view, job creation as such cannot be the justification for a project, because there are many fiscal and monetary policies that could in principle be used to generate the same jobs on as permanent a basis as desired. If a project is worthwhile on other grounds, then macroeconomic impact simulations of the sort reported in this section can help in the design of policies to ease economic adjustment.

To find out whether the Arctic pipeline scheme proposed by the Gas Arctic consortium makes economic sense from the Canadian point of view, we need to compare it to other uses of Canadian resources. This is the purpose of the rest of this paper.

273

John Helliwell

ESTIMATING COSTS AND BENEFITS

In this section we consider the several types of economic beneficiary of natural gas development. This will set the stage for subsequent sections, in which we ask whether the Gas Arctic proposal makes the best use of the gas reserves in the Mackenzie Delta. We assume, for the purpose of our calculations, that the economy could digest such a project, and that the services of the pipeline would be priced so that all costs, including a return on capital, were fully covered without surplus. This is, of course, the intent of the National Energy Board (NEB) rules for regulating pipeline tariffs. There are some doubts about the procedures actually used by the NEB, but our current estimates are based on the assumption that the goal of NEB regulation is achieved – to have each user pay his share of the costs. Thus the pipeline-builders and owners obtain no 'economic rents' – a term used to denote an excess of revenues over all costs, including a normal return on capital. If there are any economic rents generated by the pipeline, they accrue to the gas producers, to gas users, or to governments acting as resource owners or fiscal agents.

The latest version of the model contains equations for eight different classes of economic rent. These classes, and the relevant sources of economic rent, are as follows:

1 Rents to Canadian provincial governments from non-frontier gas production. More than 90 per cent of Canada's ultimate non-Arctic onshore potential natural gas reserves are in Alberta and BC, split about three to one in favor of Alberta. These provinces gain economic rents from natural gas by levying royalties on the well-head prices (we assume an average rate of 25 per cent and by receiving a share (about one-quarter) of the corporation tax paid by gas producers, against which is offset the amount of tax that would have been generated were the capital invested in an industry with average profits.

2 Rents to the Canadian federal government from non-frontier gas production. Based entirely on the corporation income tax, these rents can be negative if the pre-tax profits in the industry are not enough above average to cover the cost of the depletion allowance and other tax incentives to gas production, and also the tax yield that would have been generated were the capital invested in another industry. The federal share is also reduced by the fact that provincial royalties are allowed as a tax-deductible expense.

3 Rents to producing firms from non-frontier gas production. The producing firms as a group obtain economic rents if their total returns, after all exploration and development costs, processing costs, royalties, and corporation taxes, are greater than the available return on capital invested elsewhere.

4   Rents to Canadian governments from Mackenzie Delta gas production. The Mackenzie Delta region is entirely in the Northwest Territories, so that all taxes and royalties accrue directly to the federal government. The corporation income tax rules are the same as in the non-frontier regions, but the royalty rates are much lower. The currently established rates on the producers' selected parcels are 5 per cent for the first three years of a pool's production and 10 per cent thereafter. The rates applicable to crown acreage are in abeyance, as are the rules governing the producers' ability to put together lease blocks covering the richest production areas. In our latest calculations, we are assuming that an average 25 per cent royalty rate would apply on the acreage reverting to the crown, and that 20 per cent of total production would come from that acreage.

5   Rents to producing firms from Mackenzie Delta production. The calculation procedure is similar to that used for rents accruing to non-frontier producers. Our current estimates are mainly based on well-head prices that are derived by subtracting pipeline tariffs from assumed city-gate prices in the Great Lakes region. Thus, if exploration, production, and processing costs were the same in the Delta and in non-frontier regions, the rents per unit of production would be smaller in the Delta because of the much greater transportation costs.

6   Rents to Canadian gas users. Most of our rent estimates are based on the assumption that Canadian domestic purchasers of gas have to pay as much as they would for an equally preferable alternative energy source. Under these conditions, there are no economic rents accruing to Canadian gas users as such. For some experiments, however, we assume an element of price regulation, in which the city-gate price is held below the cost of alternative energy sources. An upper-bound estimate of the flow of user rents is obtained by multiplying the gap between the regulated price and the value of gas by quantity used.

7   Rents to US producers and users of Prudhoe Bay gas shipped through Canada. Our calculation of these rents is based entirely on the difference between the estimated costs of transporting Prudhoe Bay gas to Chicago via a Mackenzie Valley route and a guess (50¢/mcf, in constant 1973$) at the cost of moving it to California by pipeline across Alaska, liquification, and tanker shipment down the West coast. This flow of rents provides no measure of the total economic rents from Alaskan gas, nor is it intended to. For assessing possible benefits of a Mackenzie Valley pipeline, what is needed is a measure of the cost savings provided by the Mackenzie Valley route over the next best alternative.

8   Rents to US purchasers of Mackenzie Delta gas. If gas were to be exported at the prices set out in the export contracts already negotiated by the major producing firms in the Mackenzie Delta, our earlier computations show that more than 95 per cent of the economic rents from Delta Gas production would be

received by the gas purchasers. Subsequent sharp increases in oil prices have made the gas contract prices still more unrealistic, therefore subject to upward revision, either through 'most-favored nation' clauses in the contracts or by NEB regulation. Because of the unrealism of the contract prices, we now make the assumption that well-head gas prices are set so as to leave no rents for Canadian gas users in Toronto. These well-head prices do leave some rents in the hands of US purchasers in the Chicago area, however, because it is substantially cheaper to move gas from Alberta across the plains to Chicago than across the rugged Canadian Shield to Toronto.

Each of the eight classes of economic rent described above is represented by an equation that accumulates the relevant flows, using an assumed annual rate of social time preference (the social discount rate) of 8 per cent (4 per cent in real terms) to the year 2021, which is the end of the career of the longest-deferred of the pipelines assessed here. The cumulated values in 2021 are then discounted back to give a total present value in 1973, measured in millions of 1973 dollars.

It will be apparent that the latter five of the eight rent classes described above are necessary elements in an assessment of the amount and distribution of the net economic benefits from various plans for using the potential gas reserves in the Mackenzie Delta. But why do we bother to calculate the first three classes of rent, all of which relate to non-frontier gas? The reason is that most of the proposals envisage using at least some of the pipeline's throughput of Delta gas to serve Canadian markets. If the high-cost Delta gas arrives when the available flows of lower-cost non-frontier gas are still sufficient to serve Canadian needs, then the present value of total rents will be lower as a consequence. To find out how much lower, it is necessary to calculate total Canadian demand and the cost and quantities of gas available from non-frontier sources. These computations are also necessary to find out when the available flow from non-frontier supplies would start to fall short of Canadian domestic requirements.

Enough in the way of background. The next step is to report and explain some of the results.

ASSESSING THE FEATURES OF THE PROPOSED PIPELINE

The Gas Arctic consortium is proposing to construct a 48-inch pipeline, with a throughput of 4 billion cubic feet per day, to be used 50 per cent to carry Prudhoe Bay gas to US customers, 25 per cent to export Mackenzie Delta gas to US customers, and 25 per cent to carry Delta gas to Canadian markets. In our cost-benefit calculations, which are now cast in annual terms, the Gas Arctic plan has gas starting to flow in 1979, with 1981 as the first year of full capacity use. The Gas Arctic plan is compared here with two deferred alternatives. The first alternative involves a five-year deferral and no exports of Delta gas. Thus half the pipeline is used to ship Delta gas to Canadian users and the other half to ship Alaskan gas to US users. The second alternative involves a ten-year deferral, with the entire pipeline capacity used to ship Delta gas to Canadian markets. Earlier results indicated that total Canadian rents were as high in the deferred cases as in the Gas Arctic proposals. The Gas Arctic proponents have, however, argued that Canadian arctic gas would be needed for Canadian use by 1980, and that the pipeline's capacity was so large that 25 per cent exports and 50 per cent use for Prudhoe Bay gas were essential to make the pipeline feasible at all. Our earlier calculations served to give contrary results on all these points, but the 'package' nature of the alternatives considered made it difficult for readers, and for ourselves, to assess the separate importance of deferral, exports, and the transshipment of Prudhoe Bay gas.

In this paper the model is used to help disentangle the issues. A number of the model's assumptions and features have been revised, as described in Appendix A. The most important change is in the estimated market value of gas, which is almost sure to reach higher levels in 1974 and 1975 than we had previously assumed. The 1972 and early-1973 city-gate price of natural gas in Toronto was in the neighborhood of 40-45¢ per thousand cubic feet (mcf).[4] Our earlier studies assumed a 1973 value of 60¢ (which is now turning out to be about right), with the price rising at 11 per cent per year to $1.00/mcf in 1978, and at 6 per cent from 1979 to 2000, thereafter growing at the assumed general rate of inflation. The unprecedented increases in crude oil prices in the fall of 1973 have led us to increase our price estimates for the rest of the 1970s, but not beyond the year 2000, when the value will be set more by the cost of energy from tar sands, oil shales, coal, and substitutes for hydrocarbons than by the supply and demand for crude oil. In the shorter term, however, natural gas values will follow crude oil markets rather closely. We are currently assuming a city-gate price of 82¢/mcf in 1974, rising at 10 per cent per year to $1.20/mcf in 1978 and thereafter at 5 per cent to the year 2000. The 1974 price of 82¢/mcf corresponds to a crude oil price of about $5 Canadian per barrel.

The effect of these new prices is to increase the economic rents available from early extraction and sale of gas reserves.[5] If the stream of rents from development grows at a rate that is smaller than the rate of interest used in calculating present values, then more rapid development of the resource will appear advantageous. Our model includes a number of complicating features, but this underlying principle retains some force. Some important qualifications will be noted later. Part A of Table 2 shows the rents to each of the participating groups, along with sums

TABLE 2

Net rents from exploitation of Canadian Arctic gas
(present values of all future rents are reported in millions of 1973 dollars)

Part A: Comparison of Gas Arctic plan with two deferred alternatives

	Impact on rents from non-frontier production			Rents from Mackenzie Delta production					
	Provinces	Federal gov'nt	Producing firms (23% Canadian owned)	Canadian gov'nts	Producing firms	Total rents to Canadians	Rents to US shippers of Prudhoe Bay gas	Rents to US purchasers of Delta gas	Total rents going outside Canada
	1	2	3	4	5	6	7	8	9
Case 1	-174	20	-187	1840	1601	2043	1471	649	3177
Case 2	-184	37	-197	1628	1546	1823	1215	0	2223
Case 3	-6	-4	-10	1545	1505	1909	0	0	1121

Part B: Comparison of cases with various starting dates, with trans-shipment of Prudhoe Bay gas in all cases, but no exports of Delta gas. Increments to non-frontier exports used to avoid temporary excess capacity.

Pipeline to start operation	Provinces	Federal gov'nt	Producing firms (23% Canadian owned)	Canadian gov'nts	Producing firms	Total rents to Canadians	Rents to US shippers of Prudhoe Bay gas	Rents to US purchasers of Delta gas	Total amount of non-frontier exports, in Tcf
1979	-397	-9	-422	1840	1601	1737	1471	0	.14
1986	-112	32	-110	1556	1492	1824	1125	0	.29
1987	-77	31	-68	1519	1464	1823	1080	0	.27
1989	0	0	0	1443	1402	1793	1003	0	.55

Case 1 50 per cent capacity to carry Prudhoe Bay gas to USA, 25 per cent to export Mackenzie gas to USA, 25 per cent to carry Mackenzie gas to Canada. Full operation begins in 1980.
Case 2 Five-year deferral, no exports of Mackenzie gas.
Case 3 Ten-year deferral, all capacity for Canada

of Canadian and non-Canadian rents, from the Gas Arctic proposal and the two deferred alternatives described above. The Canadian total comprises government rents in Canada plus the Canadian share of producers' rents in the Delta (25 per cent) and the non-frontier (23 per cent) producing areas. The non-Canadian total comprises the rents to US producers and users of Prudhoe Bay gas, to US purchasers of Delta gas, and to foreign (mainly US) shareholders in producing firms. There is no element of domestic gas price regulation in Table 2, so that no column is required for rents to Canadian gas users.

The entries in the first three columns of Table 2 show the amount by which the present value of economic rents in the non-frontier producing areas is altered by development of Mackenzie Delta gas. The amounts are calculated by subtracting from total non-frontier rents the amount that would be generated if the Delta deposits were not developed. With few exceptions, the entries are negative, because of the costs of temporarily excess capacity in non-frontier production when the Delta pipeline comes on stream, and, in the case of the two earlier pipelines, because of the cost of deferring non-frontier production in favor of Delta production. The 'base case' rents are large – estimated to have present values of $11,660 million (1973) for the provincial governments, $4400 million for the federal government, and $12,330 million for the producing firms. These cover 97 trillion cubic feet (Tcf) of marketable gas estimated to remain in the non-frontier regions, 53 Tcf of which were in proven form at the end of 1972.

The rents from Delta gas production shown in columns 4 and 5 of Table 2 are based on one-half the amount of gas delivered by a 4 Bcf/d pipeline over a thirty-three-year life. Potential gas reserves in the Delta are estimated to be large enough to use an entire 48-inch pipeline. By late 1973, however, proven reserves are only 7 Tcf, enough to provide for little more than one-eighth of the gas required to fill the pipeline.[6] In cases where the whole pipeline is used to transport Delta gas, the rents are calculated for the full amount and divided by two for presentation in the Table. Delta gas rent calculations in Table 2 relate to about 24 Tcf of gas delivered to a southern terminus of the Mackenzie Valley pipeline. The average rents per Tcf of gas are thus about twice as high for non-frontier as for Delta gas.[7] [Editors' note: To paraphrase Helliwell: with the objective of maximizing rents, why develop now high-cost reserves (Arctic) when low-cost reserves, yielding higher rents, are still available?]

The results from the comparison of alternative packages confirm our earlier conclusion that there is little economic reason (there was even less using gas price estimates made before the 1973 Mid-East war) for early development of Mackenzie Delta gas, taking the Canadian viewpoint and assuming no major changes in government policy. The next steps are to explain the differences among the cases, and then to consider some policy options that might increase the Canadian bene-

279

John Helliwell

fits from the various alternatives. The best way of unravelling the package plans might be to attempt answers to key questions that must be in the forefront of the mind of anyone assessing the current Mackenzie Valley pipeline proposal.

1 What additional exports are required to ease the digestion of the Mackenzie Valley pipeline? The answer to this naturally depends on how much of the pipeline is used for Canadian gas and when the pipeline is built. The answers in this paragraph relate to cases where half the pipeline is used for Alaskan gas, and measure the effects of different starting times. Table 2, part B shows the rents generated, and the amount of incremental non-frontier exports required to avoid any excess capacity when the Mackenzie Valley pipeline comes on stream. The amounts, measured in Tcf of cumulated exports, are very small. The reader may be surprised at the smallness of the indicated amount of exports, especially for the more immediate pipelines, which are being constructed before they are required. The reason is that, in the current version of the model, new investment in non-frontier capacity can be cut to zero at any time, thus making way quite quickly for Delta gas. In addition, we have used the Ontario (1972) forecast for gas demand, which has domestic requirements rising at 8 per cent per year to 1980, 4 per cent to 1990, and 2.5 per cent thereafter. Exports under present contracts are also dropping off unevenly in the late 1980s, to further complicate matters. However, the results indicate that the maximum Canadian rents occur with starting dates between 1984 and 1987, with further deferral being less costly than more rapid development. The results for a 1984 start are found as 'case 2' in Part A of Table 2 (.27 Tcf of additional non-frontier exports are indicated). All of these numbers are approximate, and subject to future revision, but the main answer to question 1 is clear – no substantial amounts of exports are required for the purposes of digesting a large Mackenzie Valley pipeline. The largest amount in any of the cases is .55 Tcf, less than 5 per cent of the quantity of Delta exports proposed by the Gas Arctic consortium. The export of natural gas on a short-term basis is not usual in Canada, but is likely to become increasingly practical as more US gas users fill their requirements from a number of sources, including liquified gas and gas from coal.

2 What are the consequences of not using half of the pipeline for transporting Prudhoe Bay gas? The proponents of the Gas Arctic pipeline proposal have suggested that deferral of the project would mean loss of the Prudhoe Bay trans-shipment, and consequently much larger costs of gaining access to Delta gas for Canadian use. The first point to note in this regard is that under the Gas Arctic plan there is no mechanism whereby Canadians share in the economic rents arising from the trans-shipment of Alaskan gas. On the contrary, the route now preferred by the consortium on account of the interests of US customers is almost 300 miles longer than the alternative route from the Mackenzie Delta to central

Canadian markets. Because of this, the total Canadian rents for case 3, in Part A of Table 2, are more than 100 million dollars higher than those for a pipeline starting up in the same year (1989) with Prudhoe Bay gas filling 50 per cent of its capacity. The effect of the shorter route is a cost-saving of closer to $200 million, but it is offset somewhat by the higher costs of digesting a 4 Bcf/d pipeline. Some accommodating non-frontier exports are assumed in case 3, subject to the rule that the total flow of non-frontier exports should never exceed the 3 Bcf/d maximum flow achieved under presently approved export contracts.

Although there is a net gain to Canadians in not shipping Alaskan gas in case 3, the capacity-sharing would become more important if construction were to start earlier. With a five-year deferral, Canadian rents would drop by $200 million if the whole of the pipeline were put to domestic use, even with some cushioning non-frontier exports, subject to the rule mentioned above. If the available supply of additional lower cost non-frontier reserves is smaller than the 44 Tcf we have supposed, then the cost disadvantage of earlier starts would be lessened. In any case, if the pipeline were deferred until needed for Canadian use, it could readily be digested for that purpose, despite its 4 Bcf/d capacity. This result would become even stronger if we adjusted the pipeline cost estimates to spread the investment in compressor stations over a longer period, thus postponing a substantial amount of investment until the throughput capacity was required.

3 How soon does Canada need Delta gas for Canadian use? Our calculations indicate, as shown in Appendix B, that the available flow from existing reserves and 44 Tcf of potential would satisfy projected Canadian requirements until 1989, without exceeding extraction limits set to achieve the maximum present value of total recovery. Such calculations are obviously subject to change, as cost, demand, and geological information alter. Because of the three- or four-year lead time required for an Arctic pipeline, it is appropriate to build in some safety margin in gas supply, possibly by building gathering systems and processing plants with some excess capacity, to permit above normal extraction rates if necessary.

4 What are the advantages of exporting Delta gas? The calculations in Table 2 indicate that Delta gas exports are not necessary for logistical reasons, but can produce increased economic rents if the export prices are sufficiently high. The model used for our simulations is not complete enough to provide a firm numerical answer to the question. It is tempting to look at existing export contracts, their prices, and the past tax and royalty arrangements, and conclude that the Canadian interest would have been better served without those exports. But the question to be answered now is whether, at *some* price, and, if so, at *what* price, it would be worth while to export Delta gas. To get the answer to this question, it will be necessary to develop a more solidly based model forecasting energy values in different forms, at different times, and at different locations. This last

281

factor is especially important for natural gas, because transport is more expensive for gas than for most other energy sources, especially oil and coal. In general, this factor mitigates against export, unless the future substitute is available in or near the same regions. But such analysis is beyond the scope of this chapter.

5 Some Policy Options: It is apparent from the results in the previous section, from the review of Canadian natural gas policy elsewhere in this volume (see the paper by Richard Hamilton), and from the energy policy review of the Department of Energy, Mines, and Resources (1973), that Canadian policies in the past have not been very effective in collecting economic rents from natural resources. To do better in the case of Arctic gas, at least three separate types of policy would be required. For Canadians to gain a share of the transportation-based rents from the Mackenzie Valley route for Prudhoe Bay gas, a throughput tax or some equivalent would be required. An export tax, or sales through a publicly-owned sales agency (as is now being done in British Columbia), would serve to obtain a Canadian share in the transport-based savings accruing to US purchasers of Delta gas. If a two-price system were introduced to place some rents in the hands of Canadian gas users, a matching export tax of a size equal to the difference between the regulated price and the market value would be required to ensure equal treatment of producers for domestic and export consumption.

Finally, there is the key matter of collecting the large rents that accrue at the well head. Our base case calculations for the next 97 Tcf of non-frontier gas production, although rough, suggest that over $12 billion (1973) of economic rents will remain uncollected, assuming existing tax and royalty provisions, and that prospective further increases in gas value are fully reflected in well-head prices. In the Arctic, the Canadian rent-collection provisions are ever less adequate, but the high transport costs mean that rents per unit of production will in any case be less. The calculations in Table 2 indicate uncollected producers' rents in the Mackenzie Delta with a present value of about $1.5 billion (1973). This covers 26 Tcf of gas, so that the uncollected rents on the potential reserves of 55 Tcf amount to about 3.0 billion.

Economic rents are defined as amounts in excess of payments required to discover, produce, process, and deliver the resource in question. The goal of public policy should therefore be to collect all of such rents on behalf of the public at large, as owners of the resources. The trick is to collect the rents while leaving intact all available incentives for least-cost methods (see Hyndman-Bucovetsky chapter). A detailed analysis of the possible methods is obviously beyond the scope of this paper. All that I shall attempt here is a rough translation of the measure of total collectible rent into an equivalent royalty rate for Delta gas production.

TABLE 3

Effects of example changes in federal tax and royalty policies

	Non-frontier rents			Rents from Mackenzie Delta		Rents to US shippers of Prudhoe Bay gas	Rents to Canadian governments, as % of total rents
	Provincial gov'nts	Federal gov'nts	Producers	Canadian gov'nts	Producers		
Base case recalculated with federal tax revisions	13165	8914	6310				77
Case 2 recalculated with federal tax revisions (compare with case 2 in Part A of Table 2)	−231	−102	−10	2000	1175	1215	41 (compared to 37% for case 2 in Part A of Table 2)
Case 2 with federal tax revisions plus Delta royalties at 25% plus $6\frac{2}{3}$% throughput on Prudhoe Bay gas	−231	−102	−10	3337	473	579	74

John Helliwell

If it is granted that resource rents ought to be collected by governments on behalf of the ultimate resource owners, there remains the difficult question of dividing them between the levels of government. In Canada the provinces clearly have priority over resources in the non-frontier regions, but there are intersecting federal claims through the income tax.

In this constitutional situation, the straightforward solution is for the federal government to tax the resource industries as other industries are taxed, and for the provincial governments to collect the remaining resource rents via royalties, regular auctioning of production leases, or some combination of methods. Table 3 shows a partial approach to this situation by removal of the percentage depletion allowance and by treating royalties as charges against after-tax rather than before-tax corporation income, because of the increasing use of royalties as collectors of economic rents. The first figure in Table 3 shows the recalculation of the base-case rents on non-frontier gas, assuming non-frontier royalty rates unaltered at 25 per cent (the base case is non-frontier production only). The two changes combine to provide a notable increase in rent-collecting efficiency. The share of the non-frontier rents collected by governments rises from 57 to 78 per cent, an increase, in terms of present value, of about $6 billion.

The second result in Table 3 shows case 2 from Table 2 recalculated using the revised base-case rents and the revised tax structure. The case involves a pipeline coming on stream in 1984, used half to carry Delta gas to Canadian markets and half to ship Prudhoe Bay gas to US markets. The results show a 30 per cent increase in the amount of Delta rents collected by the federal government, but the bigger government stake in non-frontier rents means a larger cost in terms of deferred collection of non-frontier rents.

The third result in Table 3 supplements the revisions in tax structure by two further changes. The first is an increase in the royalty rate for Delta production to 25 per cent. The second measure is a throughput tax levied by the Canadian federal government as a means of obtaining a Canadian share in the transportation-based rents generated by the use of the Mackenzie Valley route for Prudhoe Bay gas. The tax is applied only to the Prudhoe Bay throughput, as the purpose is to obtain a Canadian share in the transportation rents. The tax is set, for example purposes, at $6\frac{2}{3}$ per cent of the city-gate value of gas, about equal to 8¢ per mcf in 1978. This rate was chosen to give a roughly equal sharing of the transportation rents between the United States and Canada. Each of the two policy measures has the effect of adding about $650 million (1973) to the present value of economic rents collected by Canadian governments, bringing the rent collection ratio up to 75 per cent. The effect of the increase in royalty rates is substantially more than it would have been if the income tax had not been previously revised to make royalties non-deductible.

The combined effect of the two revisions in the tax structure, the increase in Delta royalty rates, and the throughput tax on Prudhoe Bay gas, is to increase by about $7.5 billion the present value of rents collected from 97 Tcf of non-frontier gas and 26 Tcf of Delta gas. The amount would be over $9 billion for 97 Tcf of non-frontier gas plus the estimated Delta potential reserves of 55 Tcf. Similar striking results can be obtained from policy changes applied to other plans for a Mackenzie Valley pipeline and development of Delta gas. These large results from fairly modest changes in the tax and royalty structure are a direct consequence of the high and increasing value of natural gas, which has generated very large potential rents.

CONCLUSIONS AND QUALIFICATIONS

Three distinct types of experiment have been reported in this paper. Macroeconomic simulations of the whole economy to 1985 were used to judge the aggregate repercussions of a Mackenzie Valley pipeline and Mackenzie Delta gas production. The conclusion was that the potentially destablizing effects of pipeline construction could probably be contained with appropriate monetary and fiscal policies. The pipeline plus offsetting policies generated a cyclical response, with no net effect on average income and employment.

Following from the conclusion that macroeconomic impact would not serve either to qualify or disqualify a Mackenzie Valley pipeline proposal, the second type of experiment concentrated on the costs and benefits of the Gas Arctic proposal and some deferred alternatives. The conclusion from these experiments is that neither exports of Delta gas nor trans-shipment of Prudhoe Bay gas is necessary to make a pipeline feasible. This is especially so if construction is deferred until non-frontier production has expanded to the point when, a decade or more hence, the marginal costs of non-frontier production reach the cost of producing and transporting frontier gas. The differences among the cases, in terms of rents to Canadians, were quite small, indicating that the timing has considerable flexibility. If, for example, deferral appeared advantageous in terms of obtaining better arrangements for cooperation with northern Eskimos and Inuits, or if further research promised to improve the environmental or cost consequences of pipeline construction, then these other considerations should probably be allowed to govern.

Finally, experiments were undertaken to test the effects of some policy changes intended to increase the efficiency and equity of the tax and royalty system used to collect resource rents. The results were striking. In the base case, the removal of percentage depletion, and the recognition of provincial royalties as a device for collecting economic rents, rather than a tax-deductible expense, increased the present value of rents collected by about $6 billion. In an example case of development of Delta gas, the amount of Delta rents collected was increased by about $500 million. Two further changes – an increase of the Delta royalty rate to 25 per cent, and the levying of a throughput tax designed to share Prudhoe Bay transportation rents equally between the United States and Canada – each increased the present value of Delta rents collected by a further $600-700 million. Thus it would seem that large increases in the equity and efficiency of rent collection are possible. When these results are compared with the earlier results, it is apparent that it would be a great mistake, in these times of high and rising resource values, to approve any Mackenzie Valley pipeline proposal without first making substantial improvements in the tax and royalty system.

What qualifications ought to be made? First, that much of the data underlying the calculations will be subject to continuing change, so that at least the details of the conclusions will continue to shift. Second, the fifty-year time horizon of the analysis of costs and benefits means that there is much uncertainty about many of the results. If and when the model is expanded to include a more comprehensive treatment of energy supply and demand, and if the consequences of guesswork are tested by means of sensitivity tests, the results will still have to be used with caution. Despite the many problems of depicting the future in quantitative terms, there seems little alternative, if natural resource policy is to be taken seriously.

NOTES

1 The research has two main parts – estimation of aggregate economic effects and analysis of costs and benefits of alternative uses of the natural gas in Canada's Arctic. The study of macroeconomic impact originated with a group of fourth-year undergraduates, who presented the results to a UBC extension course on Arctic energy. A revised and more complete version appears as Chapter 10 in Pearse, ed. (1974). A summary of the results was presented as the first part of Helliwell (1973 b), and appears unchanged in the present paper. The study of costs and benefits is presented most fully by Helliwell, Pearse, Sanderson, and Scott (1974), and in summary form as the second part of Helliwell (1973 b). The second part of the present paper contains results based on a variety of revisions and extensions to the model. Appendix A describes the main revisions that have been made. In preparing this chapter, I have received helpful advice from several UBC colleagues, research assistance from Chris Sanderson, and programming assistance from Robert McRae.

2 RDX2 is an aggregate quarterly model of the Canadian economy. Its structure and properties are described in Helliwell *et al.* (1971).

3 The Gas Arctic consortium is represented at present by Canadian Gas Arctic Study Limited, whose officers have given numerous addresses outlining the features of the proposed project. A view of the plans as they stood in mid-1973 may be found in Gray (1974).

4 The recent energy policy paper issued by the Canadian (federal) Department of Energy, Mines, and Resources (1973) records the 40–45¢ figure on page 94 of Volume I.

5 Even though the value of gas rises at a rate well below the rate of social time preference, the rent total, or some components of it, can rise faster, because most elements of production cost rise only at the lower general rate of inflation. In Table 2 only the flow of federal government rents from non-frontier production grows faster than the rate of discount, thus increasing in present value as extraction is deferred. The federal government rent stream is smaller and faster growing than the provincial stream, because it is based only on corporation income tax, while the provinces also collect royalties based directly on the well-head price.

6 In late 1973 the Gas Arctic consortium announced the results from two consulting firms commissioned to assess the drilling results to date. The firms apparently agreed that the potential reserves in the Mackenzie Delta are 55 Tcf, but that only 7 Tcf was in the fields that had been discovered to date. See Horte (1973).

7 The costs of discovering and producing new non-frontier reserves are assumed to rise almost four-fold as the next 44 Tcf of reserves are added. It appears, from our data, that the rents per marginal unit of production in the non-frontier regions become less than the Delta rents slightly before 44 Tcf more have been discovered. Thus the rents on existing non-frontier reserves are much more than twice as high as Delta rents. These figures are highly subject to change. Recent work by Russ Uhler at UBC suggests that discovery costs in the more established regions of Alberta may be rising very steeply indeed. The recent reports (see note 6) of unexpectedly poor exploration results in the Delta suggests that costs there may be higher than we have supposed.

REFERENCES

Canada, Department of Energy, Mines, and Resources (1973), *An Energy Policy for Canada: Phase 1*, Ottawa, 2 volumes

Gray, Earle (1974), 'Why Canada Needs the Arctic Gas Pipeline,' Ch. 2 in P.H. Pearse, ed. (1974)

Helliwell, John F., H.T. Shapiro, G.R. Sparks, I.A. Stewart, F.W. Gorbet, and D.R. Stephenson (1971), *The Structure of RDX2,* Bank of Canada Staff Research Studies, no 7, Ottawa

John Helliwell

Helliwell, John (1973 a) 'More on the National Economic Effects of Arctic
Energy Developments,' Appendix AA, *Minutes of Proceedings and Evidence,*
House of Commons Standing Committee on National Resources and Public
Works, Issue no 22, 5 June 1973, pp. 41-80
Helliwell, John (1973 b) 'Estimating the National Economic Effects of Arctic
Energy Development,' Proceedings of the Royal Society of Canada, *Sympo-
sium on Energy Resources,* Ottawa
Helliwell, John (1974), 'Impact of a Mackenzie Pipeline on the National
Economy,' Ch. 8 in P.H. Pearse, ed. (1974)
Helliwell, John, Peter Pearse, Chris Sanderson, and Anthony Scott, 'Where Does
Canada's National Interest Lie? – A Quantitative Appraisal,' Ch. 10 in P.H.
Pearse, ed. (1974)
Horte, V.L. (1973) 'Energy Resources and their Dependence on Price-Natural
Gas,' Proceedings of the Royal Society of Canada, *Symposium on Energy
Resources,* Ottawa
Ontario, Advisory Committee on Energy (1972), *Energy in Ontario: the Out-
look and Policy Implications,* Toronto, 2 volumes
Pearse, P.H., ed. (1974) *The Mackenzie Pipeline: Arctic Gas and Canadian Energy
Policy,* Toronto

APPENDIX A

Recent revisions to equations and data
This appendix summarizes the main changes that have been made to the model
presented in the appendices to Chapters 8 and 10 of Pearse, ed. (1974).

Some of the more important changes are:
1 To cut computation costs, an annual version of the model is being used for
the cost/benefit simulations extending into the next century. This has involved
converting many of the coefficients and numerical constants, and the refining of
some approximations that became too rough on an annual basis.
2 In earlier versions, we treated non-frontier reserves and discoveries as initial
reserves, of which only 95 per cent was recoverable. Our present accounting is
entirely in terms of marketable gas, and makes use of the estimates of existing
and potential reserves from the Federal Department of Energy, Mines, and Resources (1973, p. 88).
3 The accounting for government rents from non-frontier production has been
improved. There are new equations for taxable producer income, income tax, the
rate of depletion allowance, and the separate accumulation of provincial and federal rents.

4   Higher royalty rates are used for Delta production, making some allowance for some part of production to be subject to (as yet undetermined) rates higher than the 5 per cent and 10 per cent rates applicable to the leases selected by the permit holders.

5   As described in the text of the chapter, the assumptions about gas values have been increased, especially during the 1970s, because of the unforeseen increases in crude oil prices in the last months of 1973.

6   The most recent Gas Arctic choice of route for the Mackenzie Valley pipeline involves a longer route from the Mackenzie Delta to Central Canadian markets. The new route better suits the interests of the US gas purchasers, and presumably would be dropped in favor of a shorter route if the whole pipeline were used for Canadian purposes. The saving of 300 miles of prairie pipeline decreases the pipeline tariff by 3 cents (in 1973 prices) in the appropriate cases.

The complete annual version of the model, including all equations, coefficients, and data assumptions, is available in a University of British Columbia Department of Economics Discussion Paper, 'A Model for Calculating Costs and Benefits of Alternative Uses of Canada's Arctic Gas.' Copies are obtainable from the Department of Economics, University of British Columbia, Vancouver, BC.

APPENDIX B

Required production from Canadian gas reserves
Estimated flows required for export and domestic consumption,
and available non-frontier supplies, 1973–2021 (billion cubic feet per day)

Year	Requirements[1] for exports (EXGASNF)	Domestic[2] requirements (DEMAND)	Total requirements (DEMAND + EXGASNF)	Requirements minus non-frontier supplies[3] (DEMAND + EXGASNF − GASMAX)	Post-72 discoveries brought into production (in Tcf) (GASADD)
1973	2.8	4.10	6.90	0.0	0.0
1974	2.8	4.43	7.23	0.0	0.0
1975	2.9	4.78	7.68	0.0	0.0
1976	2.9	5.16	8.06	0.0	0.0
1977	3.0	5.58	8.58	0.0	0.0
1978	3.0	6.02	9.02	0.0	1.10
1979	3.0	6.51	9.51	0.0	5.15
1980	3.0	7.03	10.03	0.0	5.10
1981	3.0	7.31	10.31	0.0	3.63
1982	2.7	7.60	10.30	0.0	1.44
1983	2.6	7.91	10.50	0.0	3.67
1984	2.6	8.22	10.82	0.0	4.82
1985	2.5	8.55	11.05	0.0	4.92
1986	2.3	8.89	11.19	0.0	4.57
1987	1.9	9.25	11.15	0.0	3.40
1988	1.9	9.62	11.52	0.0	6.07
1989	1.7	10.00	11.70	0.78	0.15
1990	0.6	10.40	11.00	0.73	0.0
1991	0.4	10.66	11.06	1.30	0.0
1992	0.2	10.93	11.13	1.90	0.0
1993	0.2	11.20	11.40	2.72	0.0

1994	0.2	11.48	11.68	3.45	0.0
1995	0.0	11.77	11.77	4.32	0.0
1996	0.0	12.06	12.06	5.41	0.0
1997	0.0	12.36	12.36	6.16	0.0
1998	0.0	12.67	12.67	7.17	0.0
1999	0.0	13.00	13.00	8.05	0.0
2000	0.0	13.31	13.31	8.81	0.0
2001	0.0	13.65	13.65	9.79	0.0
2002	0.0	13.99	13.99	10.86	0.0
2003	0.0	14.34	14.34	11.65	0.0
2004	0.0	14.70	14.70	12.36	0.0
2005	0.0	15.06	15.06	13.17	0.0
2006	0.0	15.44	15.44	13.92	0.0
2021	0.0	22.36	22.36	22.36	0.0

1 Assuming no new export contracts beyond commitments in 1973. Flows derived from terms of existing contracts. Extensions or renewals of some expired contracts were assumed for our simulations of cases 2 and 3. In case 2 exports were restored to 2.9 Bcf/d for 1984 and 1985, returning to the base numbers in 1986. In case 3, exports were restored to 2.7 Bcf/d in 1989, 3.0 in 1990 and 1991, 2.3 in 1992, 1.5 in 1993, .8 in 1994, and zero thereafter.

2 As forecast by the Ontario Advisory Committee on Energy (1972).

3 GASMAX is the maximum available flow from non-frontier reserves. Studies by the Alberta Energy Resources Conservation Board and the BC Department of Mines and Petroleum Resources for the BC Energy Commission indicate that end-1972 reserves are producing at substantially below well-head capacity. If the proven but unconnected reserves are brought on stream as required, our calculations indicate that new reserves would not be needed until 1978. Thereafter, new reserves (GASADD) are brought into service as fast as required to meet the gap between the growing demand and the declining flows available from end-1972 reserves. Removeable reserves (measured on a marketable pipeline basis) of .0526 per year for fourteen years, declining thereafter by 15 per cent per year for eight years, then level again at the diminished rate until the reserves are fully depleted. Recent contracts have generally involved initial minimum flows of 1 million cf/d per 7.3 Bcf of reserves, equal to a proportional rate of .05. Maximum flows may be as much as 25 per cent higher, so that .0526 may well be an underestimate of the appropriate annual average.

Transportation is a major user of energy. Cars, trucks, buses, railroads, pipelines, ships, and aircraft together accounted for over one-quarter of the energy consumed in North America in 1972. Canada, because of its lower population densities, spends a higher percentage of its energy on transportation than the United States.

In this chapter, Dewees examines each of the separate energy-using modes. He details the relevant energy cost for moving people and freight for the different types of transportation services. Highway vehicles predominate; gasoline alone is nearly 75 per cent of all the fuel used for transportation services. Trends are examined in both intra- and inter-urban transportation markets to see if there is a movement towards using more energy-intensive means of moving individuals and goods. The lowest energy use in moving people within the city is rapid transit; be-tween two cities it is a bus. The highest energy use in moving people within a city is the private automobile; between two cities, the airplane. For goods, rail traffic uses least energy per ton/mile. Trends are, however, to the most intensive energy use.

Dewees argues that changing modal choice can best be done by letting prices determine individual behavior, rather than legislating how traffic should move. A significant rise in the price of gasoline, for example, would have a number of effects: people would drive less, switch to urban transit, and purchase smaller cars. Each of these effects will significantly reduce gasoline consumption.

For the environmental consequences of transportation, see the papers by Dewees in Volume I and by Stoel and Waverman in this volume. For a discussion of gasoline see the Erickson & Spann and the Debanné chapters.

292

DONALD N. DEWEES

Transportation energy demand

Direct energy consumption by the transportation sector of the economy accounts for almost one-quarter of all domestic North American energy consumption.[1] It is therefore natural that when people worry about future supply and demand of energy, they worry about transportation. Because of the 'energy crisis' people want transportation to be more energy-efficient, and perhaps even to be reduced in total. In particular, there is concern about the vast energy appetite of the automobile. Yet transportation trends since the Second World War generally show increased relative use of transport modes with high energy consumption rates.

The projection of transportation energy demand and the evaluation of policies to modify that demand require some perspective on the present and projected use of different transportation modes, and their energy consumption per unit output. We can then estimate the effect of changes in relative energy prices or of specific governmental policies regarding energy and transportation. We can examine the implications of rising energy prices for growth of various transportation modes, and see what effect future transportation projections will have on total energy demand.

Almost all energy directly consumed by the transportation sector comes from petroleum. While coal is a significant fuel for marine operators, almost all air and land transportation runs on gasoline, diesel oil, jet fuel, or close relatives of these fuels. The largest single use is for automobiles, accounting for 60 per cent of all transportation fuel consumption (see Table 1). The next largest fuel category is gasoline used by buses and trucks, which include small delivery vans and school buses. The third is aviation jet fuel, at a little under 10 per cent of total transportation energy, while diesel oil for highway vehicles and railroads accounts for 6.4

TABLE 1

US transportation fuel consumed by mode and fuel, 1970

Mode	Fuel	Gallons ($\times 10^9$)	BTU ($\times 10^{12}$)	Per cent of transport fuel	Modal totals (BTU $\times 10^{12}$)	Per cent of transport fuel
Automobiles	Gasoline	65.6	7,610	60	7,610	60
Buses and trucks	Gasoline	20.8	2,413	19	3,230	25
	Diesel oil	6.33	817	6.4		
Pipelines	Oil	.55	66	1	66	
Railroads	Diesel oil	3.8	490	4	490	4
Airlines (1969)	Gasoline	.032	3.6		1,216	9.6
	Jet fuel	10.1	1,212	9.6		
Marine	All oil	.55	74	1	74	1
Totals	Gasoline	86.4	10,027	79		
	Diesel and other	11.2	1,447	11		
	Jet fuel	10.1	1,212	10		
	Transport fuel	107.7	12,686	100		

SOURCES: Motor Vehicle Manufacturers Association, *1972 Automobile Facts and Figures* (Detroit 1972), p. 52; US Federal Aviation Authority, *Statistical Handbook of Aviation* (Washington 1971), Table 6.28; Interstate Commerce Commission, *Transportation Statistics in the United States* (1970), Parts I, V.

TABLE 2

Canadian transportation fuel consumed by mode and fuel, 1969

Mode	Fuel	Barrels ($\times 10^6$)	BTU ($\times 10^{12}$)	Modal total (BTU $\times 10^{12}$)	Per cent of transport fuel
Highways	Gasoline	158.7	828.6	870.6	76
	Diesel	7.2	42.0		
Railroads	Diesel oil	12.3	71.7	84.4	7.4
	Light & heavy oil	1.6	9.7		
	Other		3.0		
Airlines	Gasoline	1.6	8.2	90.1	7.8
	Jet fuel	15.1	81.9		
Marine	Light & diesel oil	5.9	34.1	100.7	8.8
	Heavy oil	9.6	60.5		
	Coal		5.9		

		Barrels ($\times 10^6$)	BTU ($\times 10^{12}$)	Transport use as per cent of total by fuel	Per cent of transport fuel
Totals	Gasoline	160.4	836.8	99	73
	Diesel	25.2	147.8	55	13
	Light	.4	2.7	.5	.2
	Heavy	10.9	68.5	11	6
	Jet fuel	15.3	81.9	99	7.8
	Total petroleum	1,137.9		45	100.0

SOURCE: Statistics Canada, 'Detailed Energy Supply and Demand in Canada 1958-1969,' Ministry of Energy, Trade and Commerce, Nov. 1972.

and 4 per cent respectively. Marine oil consumption is almost negligible. Gasoline is the most important single fuel type, supplying almost 80 per cent of total transportation energy.

Somewhat different patterns are observed in Canada, as shown in Table 2, where highway vehicles consume 76 per cent of all transportation fuel compared with 85 per cent in the United States, with the remaining share almost evenly divided between railroads, airlines, and marine uses. Gasoline comprises 73 per cent of total transportation fuel and diesel oil, 13 per cent. Looked at from another point of view, Canadian transportation consumes 99 per cent of all gasoline produced, 55 per cent of all diesel oil, and 99 per cent of all jet fuel. At the same time, transportation uses less than 1 per cent of all light oil consumed in the country, and only 11 per cent of the heavy oil. Direct energy consumption for transportation accounts for 45 per cent of all Canadian domestic petroleum consumption. The only other significant transportation fuel is coal for marine operators. It is clear, then, that in North America transportation runs on petroleum, and over half of the transportation petroleum goes to automobiles.

TRENDS IN TRAFFIC MODES

During the last thirty years, there have been substantial shifts in the share of traffic carried by several modes, with increases in the use of modes of high fuel consumption rates. Before analysing future transportation energy use and policies to change it, we must see how these shares stand now, and what can be expected in the future. While few hard estimates of future modal traffic exist, we can make some extrapolations from changes in shares, technology, costs, and prices of the modes and their inputs.

Domestic intercity freight
Total intercity freight in the United States has grown at about 3 per cent per year since 1950. The railroads have shown modest increases in total traffic during these two decades, but the rail share of intercity freight has declined from 63 per cent in 1940 to only 40 per cent in 1970 (see Table 3). The lost rail traffic has been diverted to trucks and oil pipelines, each of which has doubled its share of total traffic since 1940, and doubled or tripled total traffic since 1950. In the future, the rail share of traffic should continue to decline until they have specialized in carrying bulk commodities like coal and long-distance carriage of piggyback, container, and carload general traffic. The truck share will increase correspondingly, while pipeline traffic will depend on total oil shipment. While air freight has been growing rapidly both in absolute tonnage and percentage of the

TABLE 3

Share of transportation markets by mode (Domestic US, 1970)

INTERCITY FREIGHT	Ton miles $\times 10^9$	Per cent of total
Railroads	770	40
Truck	410	21
Waterway	310	16
Pipeline	430	22
Airlines	3	.18
Total	1920	100.
INTERCITY PASSENGER	Passenger-miles $\times 10^9$	Per cent of total
Railroads	11	.9
Auto	1026	87
Bus	25	2.1
Waterway	4	.3
Airlines	119	10.0
Total	1185	100.
URBAN PASSENGER	Passenger-trips $\times 10^9$	Per cent of total
Bus	4.1	4
Rapid transit	1.7	2
Auto	98	94
Total	104.	100

SOURCES: US Department of Commerce, Bureau of the Census, *Statistical Abstract of the United States 1972* (Washington 1972), p. 536. Bus and electric railway data are from the American Transit Association, *Transit Fact Book,* Table 6. Auto travel is from the Motor Vehicle Manufacturers Association, *1971 Automobile Facts and Figures,* pp. 52, 57. Passenger trips are total urban vehicle miles divided by 9 miles per average trip times 1.9 passengers per average trip.

total, its share is still insignificant compared to the others, and should remain so for a decade at current growth rates.

Domestic intercity passenger traffic
Total intercity passenger travel has grown more rapidly than GNP since 1950, at 4.8 per cent per annum, spurred by rising incomes and declining real prices of road and air travel. Railroads fell from 6.4 per cent of the intercity passenger market in 1950 to under 1 per cent in 1970, losing traffic to the airlines, whose share rose from 2 per cent to 10 per cent (see Table 3).

Given continuing increases in income, and technological development in air transportation, the airlines' share of intercity passenger travel should continue to grow rapidly for the foreseeable future. The percentage share of the automobile may continue its recent decline, although absolute auto travel will probably continue to grow. The slow increase in absolute bus travel may continue, although its share will probably decline under present conditions, since there seems little room for technological advance, and the major short-haul competitor, the railroad, has already yielded up most of its passengers.

The precipitous decline in rail travel will continue inexorably until only a few specialized services remain. The price of bus, automobile, and long-distance air travel is generally less than railroad, yet railroad passenger fares do not generally cover average costs. Except in the Boston-Washington corridor, railroad speed has not increased since the early 1900s; the bus and automobile are now equally fast, the plane many times faster. Increasing railroad speeds involve staggering expenditures on roadbed and rolling stock, which could be justified, if at all, only on the most heavily travelled lines. It may be worthwhile to maintain high performance rail passenger service in a few short densely populated corridors such as Washington–New York or Washington-Boston. It may be desirable or even economic to maintain one or two long-distance tourist trains. Aside from these special situations, long-distance rail travel is uneconomic[2] and it is both inevitable and desirable that the nostalgia which continues to support a network of long-distance railroad passenger service yield to economic reality.

Urban passenger traffic
Urban passenger travel, even more than intercity passenger travel, is dominated by the automobile. Less than 10 per cent of all passenger trips are by any other mode, and less than 5 per cent of passenger miles are by other modes, since the automobile tends to be used for longer urban trips (see Table 3). Over two-thirds of the urban transit travel is by bus, which has declined 50 per cent in total passenger trips from 1950 to 1970. One-third of transit travel is by electric railway, which includes street-cars, subways, and elevated trains. The street-car has, of course, almost vanished, while rapid transit travel appears to be essentially constant since 1955. Commuter railroad travel, outside of New York City, Chicago, and Philadelphia, is trivial. No mode of urban transportation except the automobile shows any growth between 1950 and 1970.

While analysis of past transit investment does not suggest that significant numbers of cars will be taken off the highways simply by constructing rail rapid transit, it may be that some future growth in travel will be attracted to new systems now under construction. In this event, the absolute and percentage share of rapid transit may grow somewhat, while the auto's share may decline. It would be optimistic to forecast that within a decade rail rapid transit would double its share of urban passenger trips. But even if this occurred, and if all the additional transit passengers had previously been auto passengers (a highly unlikely assumption), the reduction in motoring would be about 2 per cent. Bus travel may be expected to continue its decline, especially as new rapid transit lines will gather most of their passengers from existing bus lines. Thus, even a substantial urban rapid transit construction program by itself would reduce urban motoring by negligible amounts. Unless other policies are undertaken which would specifically restrict motoring, or increase its cost, we may expect motoring to continue to account for over 90 per cent of urban passenger travel for the foreseeable future.[3]

Implications of modal trends for energy use

The general predictions about relative growth of different transportation modes can be used with specific fuel consumption rates to determine the directions of future transportation energy use. Table 4 shows the average energy use per unit of output for each of the major transportation modes. Waterways and railroads get better than 200 ton-miles per gallon of oil. Pipeline fuel use estimates vary by a factor of 10, from 180 to 1850 BTU (British thermal units) per ton-mile carried. These estimates cannot be reconciled, nor can any be conclusively rejected. However, the Mooz figure seems high for an admittedly low-cost mode, so it will be assumed here that pipeline fuel use is about that of railroads and waterways.

Since trucks require three and one-half times as much energy per ton mile as railroads, shifting rail traffic to trucks increases fuel consumption per ton mile. The most rapid expected growth rate for freight traffic in percentage terms is for air cargo, and as the fuel consumption figures in Table 4 show, this will vastly increase the energy required per ton-mile carried. If air cargo achieves several per cent of the intercity freight market, its high energy consumption should begin to raise total intercity freight energy use; at 10 per cent of total intercity freight ton-miles it would consume over half of all intercity freight fuel.

The lowest energy consumption per intercity passenger mile is achieved by intercity buses, with railroads requiring approximately twice as much energy. Thus railroads are not only more expensive than buses, they have no advantage in energy efficiency.

Automobiles use up to two and one-half times as much energy per passenger mile as do railroads, and three to four times as much fuel as buses, indicating that significant energy savings could be achieved by a diversion of automobile passengers to buses. Aircraft use more than twice as much fuel per passenger mile as do automobiles on the average, and up to eight times as much as buses. Thus the projected large increases in air travel will mean substantial increases in total energy consumed per passenger mile, depending in part on whether passengers are being diverted from automobiles or buses. A large part of the growth in air

299

TABLE 4
Energy use by mode

	Ton-miles/gallon (from Rice[1])	BTU/t-m	BTU/t-m (Mooz[2])	From fuel & traffic totals[3] ton-miles/gallon	BTU/t-m
INTERCITY FREIGHT					
Pipeline	300	450	1850	730[4]	180
Waterway	250	540	500	540[5]	240
Railroad	200	680	750	210[5]	610
Truck	58	2340	2400		
Aircraft	10	13,600	63,000		
	Passenger-miles/gallon	BTU/p-m		Passenger-miles/gallon	BTU/p-m
INTERCITY PASSENGER					
Railroad	80	1700		36[5]	3640
Bus	105	1300		89[6]	1400
Automobile	26	5230		29[7]	4020
Airline	21	6480		13[8]	9430
URBAN PASSENGER					
Bicycle[9]		180			
Walking[9]		300			
Bus	110	1240		32–80[6]	3950-1580
Rapid transit	75	1810			1970-790[10]
Automobile	26	5230		23	5090

1 See R.A. Rice, 'System Energy as a Factor in Considering Future Transportation' (paper presented to the American Society of Mechanical Engineers, Dec. 1970). Gallons/t-m from Rice; BTU/t-m assume a uniform 136,000 BTU/gallon of fuel

2 W.E. Mooz, 'Energy Trends and Their Future Effects upon Transportation,' *Proceedings, Transportation Research Forum*, XIV, 1, 1973, pp. 703–15

3 Generally obtained by dividing total fuel use for a recent year by total traffic. Sources of fuel and traffic data are noted individually,

4 In 1969 pipelines carried 411 billion ton-miles of oil, consuming 13.5×10^6 barrels in the process. *Statistical Abstract of the United States*, p. 536

5 In 1969 Class I railroads moved 774×10^9 ton-miles of freight. Freight trains used 3.3×10^9 gallons of diesel fuel, plus 10 per cent for switching locomotives, and 428×10^6 kwh of electricity. They also moved 12×10^9 passenger-miles on 320×10^6 gallons of diesel fuel and 740×10^6 kwh of electricity. Inland waterways moved 308×10^9 ton-miles of freight on 13.3×10^6 barrels of oil. See *Transportation Statistics in the United States*, for the year ended 31 Dec. 1969 (83rd Annual Report, Interstate Commerce Commission 1970), Part I, Railroads; Part V, Waterways

6 Buses moved 25.3×10^9 passenger-miles in intercity travel in 1970. Commercial buses used 644×10^6 gallons of fuel, but much of this was for urban, not intercity, travel. Deducting 361×10^6 gallons of urban fuel gives 89 passenger-miles per gallon in intercity service. Some fuel is gasoline, some diesel oil, so an average of 125,000 BTU per gallon is used. For urban service, with 5.7×10^9 passengers and 361×10^6 gallons of fuel, passenger-miles per gallon range from 32–80 depending on whether the average urban bus trip is 2–5 miles. See American Transit Association, *Transit Fact Book*, and Motor Vehicle Manufacturer's Association, *1972 Automobile Facts and Figures*

7 Autos average 13.6 miles per gallon. If this is split as 12 mpg for urban driving and 15.2 in rural areas (long trips), then with 1.9 persons per car the auto averages 29 passenger-miles per gallon on trips, and 23 passenger-miles per gallon in the city. See MVMA, *1972 Automobile Facts and Figures*, pp. 35, 52

8 Domestic airlines carried 125×10^9 passenger-miles on 9.8×10^9 gallons jet fuel in 1969 for domestic and international service. See US Federal Aviation Authority Statistical Handbook of Aviation (Washington 1971)

9 From E. Hirst, 'Energy Consumption for Transportation in the US,' Oak Ridge National Laboratory, Report ORNL-NSF-EP-15, March 1972, p. 13

10 Rapid transit used 2194×10^6 kwh of electricity for 1.9×10^9 passenger trips. This is 1970–790 BTU/passenger-mile depending on whether the average trip is 2–5 miles. ATA, *Transit Fact Book*, 1968, pp. 6, 11

travel, however, may come from increases in total travel, since incomes are rising and the price of air travel has been declining. Intercity transport energy per capita may therefore increase even more rapidly than energy per passenger mile. Because air travel is already 10 per cent of the intercity market, the effects of further air growth are already being felt in total energy use.

For urban transportation the lowest energy consumption per passenger mile is achieved by bicycle riders (see Table 4). Of the widely used transportation modes, rapid transit achieves the lowest energy consumption per passenger mile. Buses consume approximately twice as much energy per passenger mile as rapid transit, and automobiles are twice as high as buses. Thus the anticipated substitution of rapid transit for some bus travel will tend to reduce energy consumption per passenger mile in those urban areas where transit is installed. Should there be a substantial shift to bus or rail transit from the automobile, great economies could be achieved in urban energy consumption. And, of course, if large numbers of people could be induced to ride bicycles for serious transportation, enormous decreases in total energy consumption would be achieved. If it becomes too expensive to buy fuel for the family car, North Americans can hop on their bicycles, and maintain their mobility while improving overall national health.

One other major factor affects future energy consumption: auto pollution controls have since 1970 significantly reduced automobile fuel economy. Reductions in compression ratios increased fuel consumption by as much as 10 per cent for 1973 cars over pre-1971 vehicles. More stringent controls in the near future may lead to further decreases in fuel economy[4] not shown in the tables above, although in the long run we may develop technology which allows low emissions and good fuel economy. Also, future regulations may induce the use of catalysts in the exhaust system, thus demanding unleaded gasoline. Abandonment of tetraethyl lead means that the amount of gasoline which can be produced from a barrel of crude oil will decline somewhat. Total BTUs of crude oil necessary to produce an automobile passenger-mile will thereby increase.

EFFECT OF RISING PETROLEUM
PRICES ON TRANSPORTATION

It has been suggested that we are entering a period of short-run, and perhaps even long-run, increases in the price of energy relative to other items in the economy. If these increases occur, and in particular if they affect the price of petroleum products, we can expect them to have some impact on the transportation sector of the economy. These effects would include reductions in total transportation, changes in allocation of traffic among the modes, and changes in the techology for energy use within each mode.

TABLE 5

Petroleum input per dollar output by mode[1] ($/$)

Mode	(Sector)	Direct input[2]	Direct & indirect input[3]
Railroads	65.01	.029	.038
Buses	65.02	.057	.069
Trucks	65.03	.037	.047
Waterways	65.04	.026	.035
Airlines	65.06	.088	.104
Pipelines		.020	.025
Automobiles		.15[4]	

1 Dollar value purchased from sector 31.01 (petroleum refining and related products) per dollar output of each transport sector. Producers' prices are used, so sales taxes are not included. From *Input-Output Structure of the United States Economy, 1963,* vols. I, II, III (Washington, DC). The direct input column is from vol. II *Direct Requirements for Detailed Industries,* and the direct & indirect column from vol. III, *Total Requirements for Detailed Industries.*
2 Direct purchases of petroleum products by the mode.
3 Direct purchases of petroleum products by the mode plus indirect use of petroleum products by all other industries which provide input to the mode.
4 Since motoring is a final consumer good, not an intermediate good, its coefficient is not available in the input-output table. The figure entered here is the average pretax expenditure on gasoline by the typical motorist as a percentage of total motoring costs. This is only roughly comparable with the other elements in the table.

Suppose, for example, that over a short period, perhaps a few years, the wholesale price of all petroleum products were to double, all other prices in the economy remaining constant. The delivered price of most fuels would rise by less than 100 per cent, because that price includes taxes (which are considerable for highway fuels) and includes distribution costs. For example, state and federal taxes total approximately 11¢ per gallon on gasoline, so that if gasoline retails for 40¢, doubling the pre-tax price would only increase the retail price by 75 per cent. The percentage change in retail fuel price by mode will be less than 100 per cent and will vary from one mode to another, with automobiles bearing perhaps the lowest percentage burden.

The effect of such a price increase on average cost also varies considerably by mode. Table 5 shows expenditures on petroleum per dollar of output by mode.

This does not cover all energy costs, of course – only petroleum-related costs. It is clear from Table 5 that even a doubling in the wholesale price of petroleum products would lead to small increases in average costs for most modes, since petroleum-product costs average between 5 and 10 per cent of output value. Automobiles would be seriously affected since gasoline accounts for 15 per cent of total automobile operating costs even without gasoline taxes. Airlines would also be seriously affected since fuel accounts for 10 per cent of all airline output value.

If we assume that the price elasticity of demand (the percentage change in quantity consumed with respect to a percentage change in price) for all transportation is unitary, then it is clear that doubling the wholesale price of petroleum products will reduce total transportation less than 15 per cent, probably much less. We do not have accurate price elasticities of demand among the various transportation modes which could be used to evaluate the transport price changes resulting from a uniform price increase in petroleum products. It seems safe to assume, however, that there would be little reallocation of freight traffic among waterways, pipelines, and railroads since their petroleum coefficients are quite similar and small. Trucking would tend to suffer somewhat, with traffic being diverted to railroads, although this effect would probably be small. Air cargo would probably be seriously affected. Automobile vehicle-miles which would experience a cost increase of 15 per cent, would be reduced by about 15 per cent if we can accept a unitary demand elasticity. Finally, air passenger traffic would probably suffer a 10 per cent decrease in the face of cost increases approximately 10 per cent. Thus, in the short run, significant savings in energy consumption could be achieved through decreased use of some modes by doubling the wholesale price of petroleum products. The fuel savings could hardly be expected to exceed 15 per cent, however.

In the medium and long run, further adjustments could be expected. Not only would traffic decrease, but the technology used by each mode to produce transportation could be adapted over a period of years. Doubling the wholesale price of petroleum products would lead to development of more efficient engines for propelling all modes of transportation. Since the diesel engine achieves higher fuel economy at the cost of greater capital investment than a gasoline engine, we could expect, judging from European experience,[5] that those buses and trucks which are currently powered by gasoline engines might in the future tend to be built with diesel engines. In this way increased capital intensity could be applied to conserve the more expensive energy resource. We could also expect that both gasoline and diesel engines for commercial operations would be maintained better than they currently are to the extent that maintenance can affect fuel economy. For diesel engines this would have the incidental benefit of reducing air pollution since diesels produce more pollution when poorly maintained than when they are well adjusted.

It is not clear what technical change might take place with aircraft, other than reducing cruising speed, since lower speeds use less fuel per aircraft mile. The use of faster aircraft with higher energy consumption rates, particularly the supersonic transport, would be delayed by fuel price increases.

The most substantial technological change to arise from increased fuel prices would undoubtedly occur in automobiles. It has been clearly demonstrated that both engine size and vehicle weight have a substantial effect on automotive fuel consumption.[6] While the current fuel consumption for cars in North America averages under 14 miles per gallon, some subcompacts can average between 25 and 30 miles per gallon. The owner of a full-sized North American car of 3600 pounds with a medium sized v8 engine of approximately 350 cubic inches could save two or more miles per gallon by reducing engine size 100 cubic inches to that of a medium-sized six-cylinder engine, and could save another two miles per gallon by reducing vehicle weight 1000 pounds to that of a compact car. Since doubling wholesale gasoline prices would increase consumer prices by 75 per cent, and raise total motoring expenditures by 15 per cent, we could expect substantial changes to lighter vehicles and smaller engines. Power-consuming options such as air conditioning might become less popular, or be designed for greater efficiency. The diesel engine might even appear in automobiles in North America as it has in Europe. Thus, while motoring might decrease only 15 per cent from this fuel price increase, fuel consumption per passenger mile could decline by 25 per cent or more, depending upon responses of both consumer and manufacturer. Total gasoline consumption could fall by one-half. Consumer willingness to sacrifice vehicle size and performance for fuel savings would permit greater economies here than anywhere else in the transportation sector.

It should be noted that the substantial price increases contemplated here would significantly alter the capital equipment produced for the transportation industry, particularly automobiles. Some of these changes could be made very rapidly, simply by increasing production of some models and reducing production of other models. Engines and vehicles would take several years to redesign and several years to get into production. Accelerating these time tables is likely to be quite expensive both in high costs for rapid development, and in the opportunity cost of scrapping or leaving idle capital equipment designed for previous production mixes. Thus the more rapid are energy price changes, the greater the losses or inefficiencies in adapting transportation equipment to them. This suggests that an appropriate element of government policy might be to forecast future price changes, and avoid taking action which would artificially accelerate or exacerbate those changes.

D.N. Dewees

POLICIES FOR REDUCING
TRANSPORTATION ENERGY USE

The visibility of transportation energy consumption to the layman, and the current concern over energy supply, have led to numerous proposals for direct regulation of the transport sector to reduce its energy consumption. It has been suggested that automobile engine size be limited or taxed, that total motoring be limited, that air passenger traffic be limited, and that railroads be revived, subsidized, and otherwise better treated. We have noted that if a true energy shortage emerges, and is allowed to reflect itself in higher energy prices, this will tend both to reduce total transportation consumption, and reduce energy consumption per ton-mile or passenger-mile travelled. The policy question, then, is whether any further action is necessary other than that resulting automatically from the price mechanism. Possible policies will be considered in two categories: reducing energy consumption per transportation output unit, and reducing total transportation output.

1 / *Reducing energy consumed per transportation output*
When considering policies to alter energy consumption per unit of transport output, we must first ask whether there is any reason to believe that the various transportation modes are not currently using technology which is efficiently designed to balance capital costs and performance against energy use. This is a difficult question to address empirically, but if we look at the non-automobile sectors there seems to be little reason to believe that current designs are not optimal given current (or recent) prices. The major transportation modes all include large firms with sufficient resources to gather the information necessary to allocate efficiently their own resources.[7] Large airlines, railroads, trucking companies, and bus operators all have the capability for evaluating alternative technologies, and selecting that which maximizes their own profits. If all prices are correct (other papers in this volume consider whether petroleum prices are economically 'correct'), this should lead to the socially optimum combination of resources for producing transportation; there is no justification for government intervention to force such firms to purchase any other combination of factors or technology.

Furthermore, equipment suppliers to the transportation industry are in general both technologically sophisticated and reasonably competitive. US aircraft manufacturers are acknowledged world leaders in development of efficient and profitable aircraft. Trucking companies can choose from a bewildering variety of engines, cabs, bodies, and frames made by many manufacturers. And whatever criticisms may be levelled at corporate giants such as General Motors, no one has successfully argued that they have failed to produce efficient and low-cost buses,

306

trucks, and railroad locomotives. Should North American manufacturers fail at some point to offer a satisfactory variety of equipment, there are experienced manufacturers of buses, trucks, locomotives, and other transportation equipment in Europe and other countries ready and waiting to fill the gap. In the absence of restrictive governmental policies (which have occurred in the field of transit vehicles), there seems no reason to fear that the variety of technology offered by manufacturers will not exhaust current technological capabilities and provide efficient transportation given current prices.

The above comments refer to equilibrium conditions. It is possible that, if energy prices are now in a period of substantial increase, this may not have been adequately forecast by transportation companies or their suppliers. If these price changes were not adequately anticipated, then a time lag may occur before equipment is available which will be efficient given new relative prices. Thus a reasonable role for government might be to forecast relative price changes, and when significant shifts are anticipated, pass this information to the affected parties. If the present shift was not anticipated, the government might support research and development for new technology, and research into selection of technology for various factor price possibilities. Since these are activities which need not be undertaken with great intensity during long periods of constant prices, the established firms may not perform them satisfactorily.

To justify intervention more direct than that just suggested requires that we assume either that current factor prices are not socially optimal, that serious externalities exist, or that the government knows more about the operation of a transportation industry than do members of that industry themselves (which is inconceivable). Thus the government role should be limited to providing information, correcting prices which do not adequately reflect social costs, and controlling externalities when these arise. Any more detailed intervention can only lead to massive government bureaucracies, great delays in decision-making, and the introduction of substantial inefficiencies into the transportation industry.

The automobile case may be significantly different from commercial transportation activities because of the different information gathering abilities of private motorists as compared to large transportation companies. It is quite possible that motorists do not know the relationship between vehicle parameters such as engine size and vehicle weight and fuel consumption. They may not be able to estimate accurately fuel costs for a vehicle over its entire life. They may, therefore, not be in the same position to choose efficiently equipment that best meets their needs, as are major transportation companies.

Here again a useful government function would be to provide consumers with better information. For example, it might require that all automobile sales brochures specify the expected or average fuel consumption rates of all automobiles under specified typical conditions. This would give consumers the information they need to make efficient choices among alternative makes and models of cars. Furthermore, consumers are less likely than industry to anticipate future price changes. The government might also provide a service by forecasting future gasoline prices, and perhaps including these with automotive fuel consumption estimates.

Proposed limitations on automobile weight and horsepower are more difficult to defend than the simple information policies. If we believe in consumer choice, and that individual tastes are not affected by what the neighbors own, then specific regulation of vehicle attributes must be less efficient than changing the prices of some inputs such as fuel. In fact, the typical proposals for limiting automobile design are generally not well suited to reducing fuel consumption. Reducing engine displacement alone does not guarantee lower fuel consumption. If fuel consumption is the variable of interest, it would be better to regulate it directly, and best simply to change its price.

It may, however, be argued that an individual's tastes are affected by the actions of others. For example, I may care little about the absolute horsepower or power to weight ratio in my car, but be quite concerned that it is the fastest in my neighborhood. I may care little for long automobiles other than to ensure that mine is no shorter than any of my neighbors. If demand for automotive attributes is significantly affected by this kind of interdependency, then it is possible that true efficiency gains, and improvements in social welfare, may be achieved by specific limitations on some automotive attributes. It is difficult, however, to determine the extent of such interdependencies or to set reasonable limits on either engine size or vehicle weight. If there is any justification for intervening directly in the purchase of automotive attributes, it would seem better to change their prices, perhaps taxing engine size, horsepower, or weight, rather than setting absolute constraints. In this way those for whom the attributes are especially important can still purchase them while the average level of each attribute will be reduced.

Finally, timing is important. The average age at scrapping of automobiles in North America is almost ten years, while buses, trucks, aircraft, and railroad locomotives endure substantially longer. Thus, even if automobiles built next year were to consume 10 per cent less gasoline per vehicle-mile, they would travel just over 10 per cent of all vehicle-miles, and reduce total fuel consumption by only 1 per cent in that year. It would be ten years before the design change was fully reflected in all automobiles on the road. Thus, changes in transportation capital equipment will affect total transportation energy use only gradually. If a short-run crisis lasting one or two years were anticipated, changing new car designs would be worthless to combat that crisis.

2 / *Changing modal choice*

It is sometimes suggested that we should engage in active policies to promote 'energy-efficient' modes of transportation and restrict less efficient modes. For intercity freight, this would presumably mean curtailment of air cargo and trucking, with encouragement to railroads, waterways, and pipelines. Once again, however, we must ask whether any intervention would be necessary if all prices in the transportation system were socially correct. Just as we concluded that no such intervention could be justified in choosing technology within a mode, so it would appear that no intervention could be justified in allocating traffic among modes. It is true that airlines use far more fuel per ton mile than do railroads. It is also true, however, that air cargo is many times faster than railroad, and handles cargo quite differently. There are some goods of high value or of a perishable nature which can be shipped by air cargo but would not move at all by rail. For the shipper of perishable commodities or high value commodities time is money. Every day that a valuable shipment is delayed costs its owner interest or inventory costs. Every day that a perishable shipment is delayed costs it owner for loss and spoilage.[8] The shipper who chooses air cargo presumably has considered these factors and the relative prices of air cargo and other modes, and concluded that he saves more by using a faster mode than he gives up by the increase in price. In this situation any restriction on air cargo would mean that we lose more in interest costs, loss, and spoilage than is gained in savings of fuel and other factor inputs. If the prices of all modes accurately reflect their social costs, such intervention is inefficient, meddlesome, and undesirable.

If factor prices and transport prices do not adequately reflect their costs, then this itself may be a justification for some intervention. It is argued, for example, that railroads are a declining cost industry, so that charging the efficient marginal cost price will lead to deficits since marginal costs are below average. To the extent that this is true, and that deficits are not recouped by discriminatory pricing against high-value commodities, railroads may be unable to charge the efficient marginal cost price. Here one solution is government subsidy which would enable the railroads to charge marginal costs although they incur average costs. The justification for such policy, however, is not that it saves energy, but that it saves all resources by promoting an efficient mode of transportation.

Whether such a policy should be embarked upon would depend upon the gains in efficiency which might reasonably be achieved, the increased traffic that could be diverted to railroad through subsidized operation, and the probable decrease in rail efficiency which might result from the knowledge that losses could be paid up out of the public purse. Experience in subsidizing the US maritime industry is so depressing as to make one highly sceptical about the desirability of subsidizing another form of transportation.[9] If railroads would gain only small amounts of traffic as a result of an efficient subsidy, then it may not be worth the cost. Thus, any subsidy proposals must be examined carefully, and the predicted social gains measured most cautiously.

It is also argued that existing regulation restricts some carriers, including railroads, in uneconomic ways, so that they carry less traffic than if allowed to compete freely. Such regulations should be re-examined and relaxed unless they have some more important purpose to fulfil.

Another justification for altering the current allocation of transportation resources would be reducing pollution and noise externalities. One could justify reducing automobile travel because automobiles produce air pollution, noise, and highway congestion for which motorists do not pay. While an optimal pollution price might be on the order of a few cents per vehicle mile, it has been estimated that an optimal congestion toll in urban areas could run as high as 10 cents per mile.[10] If we impose charges to reflect these externalities or if we restrict motoring because of them, we will at the same time save gasoline. If we use a price elasticity of demand for motoring of approximately -.8,[11] then tolls of 5 cents per mile would reduce motoring by 40 per cent. Not only would urban congestion and pollution be reduced, but there would be the happy side effect of substantially reducing gasoline consumption.

There is, however, the practical problem of assessing such tolls. We do not have the technology for monitoring every automobile's operation and charging accordingly. We might possibly record total miles per year regardless of location, and apply a uniform charge to all cars, or all cars registered in a particular area, but the ease of disconnecting the odometer or resetting it could lead to massive evasion. We might levy tolls on expressways, although this would miss the worst congestion on city streets. If we use parking charges, we discriminate against short-trip drivers by charging per trip rather than per mile. If we levy a gasoline tax we discriminate against large cars as compared to small cars, although the contribution to congestion is almost independent of vehicle size; with present pollution laws the pollution rate is completely independent of engine size and vehicle weight.

Furthermore, to collect 5 cents per mile through a gasoline tax would require additional taxes of approximately 70 cents per gallon at the current fuel consumption rates. Since this would nearly triple the price of fuel, it is certain that a primary consequence of such a tax would be to shift people to smaller cars with smaller engines. Thus, a still greater tax would be necessary to achieve the desired total motoring reduction. The political problems of levying a new tax approaching one dollar per gallon of gasoline should be obvious.

Large price increases would be necessary to reduce motoring significantly. Furthermore, subsidy of substitutes to automobile travel is a weak policy for reducing motoring. It has been estimated that providing current transit services free of charge would increase transit usage in cities by only 30 per cent, reducing motoring by less than 4 per cent.[12] Removing large numbers of commuters from their automobiles would require paying people to take public transportation.[13] Significant reductions in motoring will only come if we simultaneously improve transit services and impose severe restrictions on the automobile, including prohibitions in limited areas, priority for transit vehicles in other areas, and very substantial price increases for each mile of motoring.

CONCLUSIONS

Recent transportation trends have included increases in per capita passenger travel, a rapidly increasing airline share of the intercity passenger market, increasing automobile dominance of the remaining passenger market, and a diversion of rail freight to trucks and to air freight. All of these changes contribute to an increase in per capita energy use for transportation. Increases in per capita transportation energy use should not be regarded as undesirable per se, however, since they generally produce better performance which has a positive economic value. Opposition to such changes could be justified only if they are associated with other undesirable conditions such as noise or pollution, or if we can foresee substantial increases in the cost of producing petroleum fuels in the near future. The former is likely and the latter is dealt with at greater length elsewhere in this volume.

This increase in per capita transportation energy use can probably not be reversed solely by promoting or subsidizing more energy-conserving modes such as intercity bus or railroads or urban mass transit, although a rail freight subsidy might have some impact. The deterrent to using the less energy-intensive modes has more to do with performance than with price, and for some the performance cannot be substantially improved except at enormous costs. Success in reducing transportation energy use will depend upon increasing the price of all transport modes, particularly automobile vehicle-miles and flying. Introducing pollution and congestion charges would be one way to effect such increases; increasing the price of petroleum products would be another. Large increases in both would undoubtedly have a substantial effect.

If energy shortages do appear and the price of petroleum products is allowed to rise, this will naturally tend to reduce the use of energy by the transportation sector. Combined with controls on congestion and pollution, this would reduce total transportation activity, but if all these changes reflect corrections in an imperfect economic system, the reduction in transportation should be regarded favorably, not unfavorably.

Proposals that we regulate in great detail a variety of forms of energy consumption bring to mind our experience in regulating private and industrial activity over the last century. If we have learned anything, it is that the best regulation is simple regulation. Attempts to control minute operating details of complex firms or industries have introduced inefficiencies into those industries, or made it possible for the industry to capture the regulatory agency, since it must provide the experts so essential to adequate regulation. Aside from the automobile, there is no reason to believe that the transportation industry as a whole, or any major sector of it, has not efficiently allocated resources including fuel, given current prices. If it is using too much energy, the best solution is also the simple solution: increase the price. Doubling the wholesale price of petroleum products would probably reduce total transportation output less than 10 per cent, but could reduce transportation energy use by 25 per cent or more.

In the case of the automobile, it is more likely that resources are not currently allocated efficiently, because of pollution and poor information. The latter problem could be attacked by providing information to consumers regarding fuel consumption of alternative vehicles and future fuel prices. The former can be improved by pollution controls and restrictions on auto use. These restrictions should include substantial increases in the marginal cost of motoring, elimination of automobiles from selected urban streets, provision of exclusive bus lanes on other streets, and avoidance of parking subsidies. If these policies are pursued with vigor, and combined with some further support of mass transportation, they could result in significant reductions in total motoring and thus fuel consumption.

A combination of fuel price adjustments and motoring and aircraft regulation policies could be designed to achieve any desired reduction in transportation energy consumption. Nothing could be more foolish than to embark upon an extensive program of tampering in the internal operation of a variety of firms which make up the transportation industry in an attempt to conserve what is conceived to be a single scarce resource. It would be easy to exhaust our national energies in such regulatory activity, and find that we had not saved fuel but had seriously misallocated many resources in many ways such that total fuel consumption had actually increased.

NOTES

1 Transportation accounted for 24.4 per cent of all domestic energy consumption in the United States in 1970. US Department of Commerce, Bureau of the Census, *Statistical Abstract of the U.S. 1972* (Washington DC 1972), p. 506. This

is more energy than was consumed by households and commercial units, but less than that consumed by industry. That figure includes only direct energy consumption, and thus ignores energy used to produce transportation equipment, construct transportation facilities, and supply other indirect transportation uses, inclusion of which would substantially raise the percentage.

2 This view has been eloquently advanced by George W. Hilton, 'The Basic Behaviour of Regulatory Commissions,' *American Economic Review,* vol. 62 (May 1972), pp. 47-54.

3 For an analysis of urban transportation, see J.R. Meyer, J. Kain, and M. Wohl, *The Urban Transportation Problem* (Cambridge, Mass. 1966).

4 *Report by the Committee on Motor Vehicle Emissions,* National Academy of Sciences (Washington DC 1973), pp. 62-5

5 See R.U. Ayres and R.P. McKenna, *Alternatives to the Internal Combustion Engine* (Baltimore 1972)

6 See D.N. Dewees, *Economics and Public Policy: The Automobile Pollution Case* (Cambridge, Mass. 1974), Appendix A

7 In 1972 five airlines and six railroads had annual operating revenues over one billion dollars. Six airlines and ten railroads had assets over one billion dollars. And at least five trucking companies had revenues over $200 million and assets over $100 million. 'The 50 Largest Transportation Companies,' *Fortune* (July 1973), pp. 130-1

8 See P.O. Roberts, Jr and D.N. Dewees, *Economic Analysis for Transport Choice* (Lexington, Mass. 1971), chap. 5

9 For a critical review of the US maritime subsidy program see S.A. Lawrence, *U.S. Merchant Shipping Policies and Politics* (Washington DC 1966)

10 H. Mohring, 'Relation between Optimum Congestion Tolls and Present Highway Uses Charges,' *Highway Research Record,* no 47 (1964).

11 Dewees, *Economics and Public Policy,* chap. 6

12 G. Kraft and T. Domencich, *Free Transit* (Lexington, Mass. 1970)

13 L. Moses and H.F. Williamson, Jr, 'Value of Time, Choice of Mode, and the Subsidy Issue in Urban Transportation,' *Journal of Political Economy,* vol. 71 (June 1963), pp. 247-64.

Facts and figures can be confusing. For example, most people have heard of the vast oil reserves available in tar sands or in oil shale. Such deposits occur around the world and were used in North America long ago by the Indians. A number of fortunes have been lost attempting to develop large-scale commercial exploitation of these oil-bearing sands. Still, the ultimate reserves are so vast that a major thrust is likely due to develop these reserves. Conservative estimates suggest that 300 billion barrels of such non-conventional oil exists in Canada, most of this in the Athabasca tar sands of Alberta. The US is thought to have one trillion barrels of undeveloped oil from shale, most of this in Colorado, Utah, and Wyoming.

Professor Quirin estimates the amount of reserves in these two types of strata – tar sands and oil shale – recoverable at minimum cost technology. He estimates that at $5.00 per barrel, 20 billion barrels of oil are available from oil shale. At $7.00 per barrel, 150 billion barrels are available from shale, and 30 billion barrels from tar sands. At $9.00 per barrel, 900 billion barrels of oil could be profitably extracted from shale and 300 billion barrels from tar sands.

Until last year, when the price of oil was around the $3.00 per barrel mark, no one thought seriously of developing $5.00 per barrel shale. Now that Nigeria has announced a price of $16.40 per barrel, non-conventional oil from shale and tar sands looks cheap.

The problem is two-fold. First, these non-conventional sources are profitable only if the world price remains above $6.00 per barrel. While some may feel that this is a certainty, many economists, including those writing in these two volumes, think that it is a distinct possibility that the world price could fall back to $3.00–$4.00 per barrel. Any shale plants in existence because they are profitable at $9.00 per barrel would soon close down if the price fell to $3.00. Remember that the *cost* of Mid East oil is less than $.50 per barrel (plus transport costs). Therefore, if we are to undertake crash programs to develop shale and tar sands we must be committed to high-priced oil. Secondly, with each plant producing 100,000 bd, it would take 30 plants to produce 3 mbd and 240 plants to produce 24 mbd. Since each plant costs in the order of $1 billion in construction costs and takes 3-6 years to construct, the expected supply from these non-conventional sources is limited for the next 10-15 years. Quirin doubts whether more than 1.4 mbd capacity will be available from these sources before 1985 unless a special crash program is devised. Even then it is inconceivable that annual supply could be more than 5 mbd. Natura non facit saltus (nor do large plants).

G. D. QUIRIN

Non-conventional energy sources

The purpose of this chapter is to summarize what is known about non-conventional energy sources and to evaluate their possible contribution toward the resolution of the energy 'crisis.' Our discussion is confined with one exception, to non-conventional *primary* sources of energy; novel techniques for the utilization of existing energy sources which may offer some prospects of increased thermal efficiency, such as fuel cells, total energy systems, the thermionics and magneto hydrodynamics (MHD) are ignored. These may make an important contribution to the eventual resolution of our energy problems by stretching existing fossil fuel reserves, but will not add to them. The one exception discussed is the utilization of coal to produce synthetic liquid fuels. The importance of these liquid fuels in transportation applications, particularly motor vehicles, is sufficiently great that it is necessary to consider the provision of adequate supplies as a separate subproblem; although some substitution possibilities exist, e.g., railroad and pipeline electrification.

Precisely what should be included among non-conventional energy sources is to some degree a matter of taste. Presumably it includes prospective energy sources available in significant quantity, for which some technology exists, but which are not being commercially utilized to any extent at the present time. Conceivably, such a definition could include nuclear power generation, which is still a marginal contributor to the overall energy pool. However, nuclear energy may finally be coming of age, and since it has been allotted a chapter of its own, it is excluded from consideration here. The sources of energy considered are: (a) tar sands oil, (b) oil from oil shales, and (c) oil from coal. All of these sources are either being used now or have been used at some time in the past, in various

315

G.D. Quirin

parts of the world. We are concerned with delineating the extent to which they may make an increased contribution to the supply of energy and the terms on which such an increased supply is likely to occur. The perspective is basically North American, since the ability of this market to supply its own requirements will continue to play a pivotal role in determining the availability of energy elsewhere in the world.

CONTRIBUTIONS IN THE NEAR TERM
(PRIOR TO 1980)

The question of whether unconventional energy sources will make a contribution toward the resolution of the immediate energy supply problem can be quickly answered in the negative. Apart from existing operations which are making a small contribution to the present supply, and which cannot be augmented to a significant degree, no commercial installations involving these technologies are likely to be in operation much before 1980. The reason is that the technologies are capital intensive, that engineering manpower with the requisite experience is limited, and the complexities of plant design and construction are such that it is unrealistic to expect engineering work to be completed, the necessary government approvals obtained, construction finished, and plants in operation in much less than seven or eight years. Since some of the developments, particularly the expansion of oil shale production, are likely to have significant environmental impacts, and have already begun to generate opposition from environmentalists, it is quite possible that this is a serious underestimate of the lead time required. Indeed, the impact of these sources, even assuming that energy prices stabilize at levels which make their exploitation economic, is apt to be slight until well after 1985; combined oil shales plus tar sands output by 1985 seems unlikely to be much in excess of one million bd crude oil equivalent, or approximately 3 per cent of North American requirements. They may well grow in importance subsequent to 1985 if circumstances are favorable, but the rate remains unclear at the present time.

TAR SANDS

Major economic interest in tar sands has been focused on the extensive deposit located near Fort MacMurray in Alberta, which outcrops along the Athabasca River and was in use by Indians when explorers reached the area in the 1780s. Similar deposits occur elsewhere in Alberta, in the us, in Venezuela and in other parts of the world. These deposits differ from the types generally exploited commercially in that the oil is highly viscous and does not flow to wells. The higher

316

viscosity is due to a difference in chemical composition from conventional oils. Various explanations of the difference have been advanced; the dominant current view is that the deposits were initially deposits of conventional oil that was degraded by bacterial action to its present state. Whatever the cause, the difference in composition makes it necessary for the crude product to be processed to produce a synthetic crude which can be transported by pipeline and used as a refinery feedstock. This characteristic is shared by other heavy oils, found in very substantial volumes in the Cold Lake region of Alberta, which are classified with tar sands oils for our purposes.

Attempts to recover oil from the Athabasca deposits have been made from time to time. A small quantity of the tar sands themselves were used for street paving in Edmonton in 1914. A number of attempts to recover oil from oil sands were made in California during the 1890s and subsequently in other centers.[1] Many of these attempts were successful technically, but inability to compete with oil from conventional sources prevented commercial development and bankrupted those companies which attempted commercial recovery of oil from bituminous sands in the US. Pilot plant operations in the MacMurray deposit were undertaken during the 1920s and 1930s by the University of Alberta, and a plant was erected on the site by Abasand Oils Ltd. The plant subsequently burned and interest in the project declined following the major oil discoveries in Alberta during the 1940s and 1950s. Attempts to interest investors in commercial operations were continued by the Alberta government, however, and a 45,000 bd plant was opened by Great Canadian Oil Sands Ltd. (Sun Oil Co.) in 1967. The plant cost about $250 million, and has been in operation since that time. It has been plagued with operating and other problems since opening. While these problems appear to have been resolved, the initial cost forecasts seem to have been unduly sanguine. To the end of 1972 operations had yet to show a profit and a loss of some $90 million had been accumulated to that time. It is probable that the increased crude oil prices of 1973 have finally made the plant profitable, if only marginally so.

Engineering work on two other proposed plants has been carried on since the late 1950s and negotiations with governments regarding lease terms taxation and other matters have been carried to an advanced state. One project, that of Syncrude Canada Ltd., has plans to begin construction in 1974 if certain tax matters can be cleared up satisfactorily.

The available reserves of tar sands oil are huge. Technically recoverable oil from the Athabasca deposit alone has been estimated at 300 billion barrels; other deposits in Alberta and Saskatchewan, including the heavy oils of the Cold Lake–Lloydminster area, will add an additional 100 billion barrels to the total. In all, these reserves are two-thirds as great as the recoverable reserves of all the world's conventional oil fields. Of this amount, however, only some 30 billion barrels are in portions of the formation sufficiently close to the surface to permit use of the present strip mining technology; the remainder will require the use of shallow wells and *in situ* recovery techniques, on which significant research has been done but without application on a commercial scale. Initial estimates suggest that these techniques will not be significantly more expensive than strip mining. The Lloydminster–Cold Lake heavy oil deposits have been produced in small quantities since the 1930s, using conventional recovery technologies; exploitation on a major scale will require special technology to overcome the high viscosity of the resource.

OIL SHALES

Oil shales are deposits of shale containing kerogen, organic matter that is well along in the geochemical process of being converted into oil. Oil shale deposits in Scotland and in New Brunswick were commercially exploited for many years. These deposits are small and output from them was never of more than local importance. With the reductions in shipping costs which have taken place in the last two decades, and the consequent reductions in the laid-down cost of conventional crudes, these operations have been forced to close.

As in the case of tar sands, economic interest has focused on a single group of deposits of enormous magnitude, those in Colorado, Utah, and Wyoming. There are a number of other deposits elsewhere in the world. However, they have been examined much less intensively than the Colorado deposits, and no systematic effort to search for other deposits, or even to fully delineate other known deposits has been undertaken, since this resource, like the tar sands, has been considered submarginal economically up to the present time. Consequently, the degree to which known reserves might be augmented in the event that oil shale production became economically feasible is a matter for conjecture. Oil shale reserves in Colorado are of the order of 1000 billion barrels, substantially in excess of present worldwide reserves of conventional crude oil.

There are further similarities between the oil shales and tar sands. The basic resource must be mined, the portion of the reserve accessible to open-cast mining is limited, and the crude product recovered from the source material must be processed to yield a synthetic crude which can serve as an input to the conventional refining process. At the technical level, these similarities are superficial only, but they make for economic similarity in terms of such fundamental characteristics as capital intensity, a need to exploit maximum scale economies with attendant indivisibilities and a need for high load-factor operation, and vulnerability to risk created by price fluctuations. In addition, the Colorado deposits share with the

Athabasca deposits, to some degree at least, remoteness from major consuming markets, which makes integration of the crude synthesis operation with subsequent refining stages impracticable because of the crude-products transportation cost differential. It is doubtful that the savings available from such integration would be sufficiently great to exercise a worthwhile locational influence in the long run. Once we leave the level of general economic characteristics, differences appear.

Nearly all of the Colorado deposits must be recovered by underground mining. The shale beds are relatively thick, at least in comparison with coal seams, but are overlain in many cases by mountaintops. Intensive investigations by the US Bureau of Mines have indicated that conventional room-and-pillar mining techniques appropriately mechanized offer the least costly means of recovering shales for subsequent stages in the production process. However, this process leaves a large fraction (at least 50 per cent) of the original deposit unrecovered, at the end of mining operations. Should improvement of the recovery factor become an important economic goal, alternative techniques might be developed, at higher unit costs.

Shale recovered from the mining operations must, under present technology, be subjected to destructive distillation in order to separate the lighter hydrocarbon fractions from waste material. Pilot plant studies have tested a number of retort designs and heat transfer systems for this stage in the process, which is fairly critical in determining the overall recovery efficiency from the mined material and hence unit costs. A large volume of waste material, in the form of spent shales, is produced at the retorting stage and its disposal poses major environmental problems. One solution is to return the spent shales to mined-out portions of the formation, an expedient that is relatively costly. Since 50 pounds of shale are produced per gallon of oil, a 100,000 b/d operation would generate 38.3 million tons of spent shale in a year. The entire landscape of the area would be obliterated in a few years if some expedient such as that mentioned above were not chosen.

The product from the retorts is deficient in hydrogen and different in several other respects from conventional crude oils. To produce a suitable refinery feedstock, fairly elaborate further processing is required, the end product of which is a synthetic crude that may be shipped by pipeline.

In addition to the waste disposal problem, a further environmental problem, at least as far as the Colorado area deposits are concerned, is posed by the vast quantities of water consumed in the process. The deposits occur in an area of relatively low rainfall, where the limited existing water resources are already the subject of dispute among competing claimants. In spite of this, most of the economic evaluations that have been published appear to assume that water inputs are available as a free good, and take account only of pumping costs. If adequate water is not available, the deposits cannot be developed. The processing weight shrinkage is so spectacular that relocation of the processing operations to a water-rich area is probably impracticable; water will have to be imported to the area by pipeline, or recycling procedures adopted, or both, if the deposits are to be utilized.

The effective limiting factors determining the contribution of oil shales to the energy economy of the future, at least in the next half century, will be costs, which will be increased as deeper and or leaner deposits must be utilized, the sheer magnitude of the engineering tasks involved in constructing a large number of processing plants, and environmental considerations. Reserves do not constitute an important limitation; the existing reserve could support 10 million barrels per day in output for over 250 years. Achieving this output rate would require 100 processing plants of 100,000 barrels per day capacity. Even if one plant were in operation by 1980, and the number of plants doubled every three years, this output level would not be reached until early in the twenty-first century. This is a sustained rate of growth of a magnitude which has seldom been realized for such a prolonged period in any industry; the social problems of increasing the industrial labor force in the area by the implied magnitude are staggering. The water problem alone seems likely to restrict growth rates at an earlier point, with such an output level unlikely to be achieved from the Colorado deposits until well on in the next century. Development of other known deposits will probably be postponed until the commercial exploitation of the Colorado deposits is well under way. As oil shales emerge as a significant commercial energy source, exploration for additional deposits could become an economically attractive activity, and output from other sources may be expected to expand. Even if oil shales become a major energy source by the late 1980s, major contributions from other locations seem unlikely much before the turn of the century.

SYNTHETIC OIL AND GAS FROM COAL

Interest in hydrocarbon fuels from coal as a substitute for conventional crude petroleum and natural gas has persisted because of the realization that coal reserves are at least an order of magnitude greater than petroleum reserves and that coal will still be available when its more glamorous relatives have been exhausted. Gas from coal, of course, antedates the use of natural gas in most parts of the world by several decades. While manufactured gas has virtually disappeared from the North American scene, largely within the last three decades, natural gas is still in the process of displacing it in other parts of the world – British Gas Boards hope to complete a conversion to North Sea natural gas by 1980. Natural gas has displaced manufactured gas from market after market because it is cheaper (vastly so in terms of energy content), cleaner, and more convenient in many ways. Because of transportation cost problems which were not solved until the advent of the high-pressure pipeline in the late 1940s, natural gas has been a relatively late arrival on the energy scene, and is still in the process of displacing other energy sources. Manufactured gas is, at the moment, on its way to oblivion, certain uses of coal are still disappearing, and oil is being driven from markets it only recently captured from coal.

In the US, but only in the US, the expansion of gas markets is being constrained by an artificially induced shortage created by an experiment in social engineering that has imposed price ceilings on the commodity for twenty years and has finally managed to suppress increments to supply. President Nixon's 1973 energy proposals to Congress call for a removal of these ceilings. We have serious doubts about the fate of these proposals in the legislature and suspect that relaxation of the controls is still several years away. MacAvoy and Pindyck have estimated that the resulting supply-demand imbalance could be corrected within a decade by complete decontrol, and in a somewhat longer period if 'partial' decontrols are adopted.[2] The Starrat-Spann chapter in the North American volume addresses itself to this problem of regulation-induced shortage.

Worldwide, and in the US once field price controls are eliminated, we expect to see gas markets growing, not only in volumetric terms but in market share terms, for at least another decade, and probably more. While reserves are finite, the deeper portions of sedimentary basins contain larger fractions of hydrocarbons in natural gas form to the virtual exclusion of crude oil below 15,000-20,000 feet. Exploration to date has concentrated on the shallower portions of basins and we may expect to find gas discoveries continuing in the period when oil discoveries have practically ceased, if price increases are sufficient to encourage drilling in the deeper portions of the deeper basins, such as the Sverdrup basin in northern Canada, where sediments 75,000 feet thick are reported.

Consequently, while a switch to coal-based gas remains a possibility at a time when gas discoveries are no longer able to meet growing market demands, the more immediate interest is in coal as a substitute for oil. Coal-oil conversion, using the Fischer-Tropsch process, requires a coal-gas transformation as an intermediate step; natural gas as well as manufactured gas is available as a source material, and conversion into liquids will not take place unless the price of energy in liquid fuel form is sufficiently greater than its price in gaseous form to bear the attendant conversion costs. A liquid-gas fuel price differential, favoring the former, has existed over almost all of the past century, largely because of transportation cost differentials. These very real advantages of liquid fuels are overlooked frequently by industry spokesmen and regulators who suggest pricing of crude and natural gas on a contained-BTU basis. The historical differential, however, has seldom been large enough to encourage conversion. If liquid fuel prices rise relative to coal prices, two-stage conversion may be expected to emerge as an economic means of supplying liquid fuels. In addition, of course, gas from coal may be developed to supplement natural gas supplies.

Gas-to-oil conversion processes have been known for more than half a century; the Berguis process was used in Germany during World War I, while the basic Fischer-Tropsch process was invented in 1933. Considerable development work on the process has been done not only in Europe but on this continent by the US Bureau of Mines. Commercial scale operations for the production of synthetic gasoline were undertaken in Germany from 1936 to 1945 to ease strategic dependence on conventional oils. A large plant in South Africa has been operating since the 1950s. In neither case were the installations motivated by purely commercial considerations; the South African plant operates behind a substantial tariff wall. Concern over oil supplies in North America in the 1940s, at a time when the magnitude of Middle Eastern oil discoveries was unrecognized, led to the large-scale development of natural gas reserves intended for use in synthetic gasoline manufactured in both the US and Canada, and a plant was actually built by Carthage Hydrocol Inc. The project was an economic failure, and the gas was eventually committed to the expanding pipeline network at distress prices.

While this record is not particularly inspiring, re-examination of the process is warranted in the light of rising oil and natural gas prices and the possibility of underground gasification of coal, which might provide an economic source of raw materials and avoid the environmental problems created by large-scale strip mining of the coal.

ECONOMIC EVALUATION – PROBABLE COSTS

In estimating costs of oil produced from these sources, we have attempted to estimate the price at which capital would be freely attracted into the industry and would earn a competitive return. Many of the multiplicity of cost estimates which have been published over the years and on which our own estimates are loosely based appear to have been made with somewhat different purposes in mind – either to convince potential sponsors of further research of the viability of the technology, to persuade regulatory authorities that economic feasibility requirements have been met, or in some cases simply to estimate the minimum price at which the possibility of commercial exploitation might be considered. While there is no evidence of deliberate bias, many of the studies appear to have adopted methodologies that impart an unintentional bias. For example, it is common enough in petroleum industry practice to omit consideration of interest during construction and startup costs from feasibility studies. Where construction takes a few months, and plant is sufficiently standardized that startup problems are minimal, such omissions are unimportant. Where construction takes five or six years and a single plant costs in the order of a billion dollars, which could be yielding a return much sooner if devoted to alternative investments, the omission of interest during construction ceases to be trivial. Where the technology, or a major part of it, is new, startup costs of one form or another are apt to be substantial; initial losses on the Great Canadian Oil Sands venture have added nearly 40 per cent to the original capital investment to the time of writing.

In addition, the authors of many feasibility studies have shown considerable ingenuity in devising financial structures which keep estimated capital costs and/or income taxes to a minimal level and have made optimistic assumptions about royalty arrangements. Indeed, the promoters of initial ventures in these areas have demonstrated a corresponding flair for creative finance in devising complex capital structures involving substantial use of debt (to secure tax write-offs on interest), partial public-sector participation and a number of other novel features. There is nothing wrong with this; without such arrangements the projects could not, in all probability, be financed at the present time. But implicit in such arrangements is the use of corporate credit dependent upon earnings on other operations to subsidize the new venture. This is, no doubt, necessary at present, but it will not provide a viable basis of operation when the time comes that the tub must stand on its own bottom and attract billions in new capital.

Similarly, favorable assumptions about income-tax arrangements or royalties are frequently found in the feasibility studies and even in the arrangements made by the sponsors of initial projects with the relevant governments. These can be regarded, in my opinion, as government contributions to the costs of innovation. When commercial production really gets underway, governments will expect their piece of the action, and indeed should do so if inefficient resource allocation is not to be encouraged. In Canada, percentage depletion has already disappeared, while in the US the rate has been reduced. Regardless of how initial ventures may be treated, it seems most prudent to assume that percentage depletion will ultimately be applied only to the imputed values of coal or oil shales at the point of leaving the mines, and that the resulting savings will be too trivial to bother computing at this stage.

Royalty deals made so far have also been quite favorable. It is arguable that royalties are a means of sharing economic rents, and since these resources are at the moment marginal and generate no rents, no royalty at all should be payable. No government has been willing to go this far, however, and as synthetic oils from these sources replace conventional production on which royalties have been received, it seems reasonable to assume that comparable royalties or taxes equivalent thereto will be levied on the output of synthetics, if only to maintain public revenues.

In making our evaluations, therefore, we have assumed (a) that because of the inherent riskiness of the operations, as discussed below, debt financing will be limited to 25 per cent of the total, the balance being provided as equity; (b) that plant investment will be written off over an average expected plant life of 25 years, with double declining balance depreciation used for tax purposes at a rate of 8 per cent; (c) a corporate tax rate of 40 per cent; (d) a royalty rate of $16\frac{2}{3}$ per cent on the value of synthetic crude FOB works, treated as an expense for tax purposes.

Interest or cost-of-capital assumptions are critical in any analysis of this type. Given the capital intensity of the production processes involved, almost any desired cost can be produced by making a suitable assumption about interest rates, as the protagonists of nuclear-power development have demonstrated. We assume the industry would require a 12 per cent return if financed on an all equity basis – close to the postwar average yield of NYSE stocks.[3] This required yield would be increased slightly as a consequence of the assumed leverage, but would be provided in part from the tax savings on bond interest payments. As to the assumed interest[4] rate on bonds, there is substantial agreement that current (1973) interest rates incorporate an allowance for anticipated inflation which is somewhat higher than normal. A rate of 6.5 per cent has been used in the analysis.

Capital costs have been computed on an 'equivalent annual cost' basis as the annual annuity required over 25 years to provide the desired rate of return after tax on the total capital employed.[5] Amounts required on a per dollar of investment basis are computed in Table 1.

Table 2 presents estimated costs of producing synthetic oil from shales of varying grades. These range from $5.04 for 40 gallon-per-ton material to $7.92 per barrel for 20 gallon-per-ton material. Only some 20 billion barrels of the total recoverable reserve of 1000 billion are of the highest grade. These figures suggest that the best grades of oil shales become economically exploitable at prices just above $5.00 per barrel, and that further escalation to a price in the neighborhood of $8.00 per barrel will permit the development of virtually all the reserves included in present estimates. Table 3 presents a similar estimate for synthetic crude from the tar sands. It indicates a price of approximately $7.00 per barrel for the low overburden portion of the deposit, which includes perhaps 30 billion out of the total 300 billion barrels recoverable. We have not presented estimates for costs of oil from coal. Since coal may be used independently as an energy source, its opportunity cost may be expected to rise as the costs of com-

TABLE 1

Computation of equivalent annual cost per dollar of initial investment

	$
(a) Net present value required to cover debt and equity	1.0000
(b) Additional PV required to cover corporate income tax if no write-offs permitted (40% tax rate)	0.6667
(c) Deduct PV of tax saving from depreciation tax shield[1]	0.1636
(d) Deduct PV of tax saving from write-off of bond interest[2]	0.0499
(e) Present value of receipts required to provide capital recovery plus return	1.4532
(f) Equivalent annual cost 25-year annuity whose present value at 12% is $0.18528 per dollar of investment	

1 See tables in N.E. Harlan, C.J. Christensen, and R.F. Vancil, *Managerial Economics, Text and Cases* (Homewood, Irwin, 1962), assumes 8% declining balance rate
2 Present value (at 12%) of 40% (tax rate) times annual interest of 6.5% on $.25 debt

TABLE 2

Oil shales cost estimates*

	Grade of material, gal/ton		
	20	30	40
(a) Capital cost including 20% allowance for interest during construction	860	650	540
(b) Equivalent annual cost of servicing capital (X 18528)	159.3	120.4	100.0
(c) Annual operating cost	81.6	66.1	53.6
(d) Total annual cost exclusive of royalty	240.9	186.5	153.6
(e) Royalty, $16\frac{2}{3}$% of revenues	48.2	37.3	30.7
(f) Annual revenues required $million	289.1	223.8	184.3
(g) Annual output, million bbl	36.5	36.5	36.5
(h) Expected cost per barrel	7.92	6.13	5.04

* 1973 dollars, basis plant capacity 100,000 barrels per calendar day

TABLE 3

Tar sands cost estimate*

(a) Capital cost, including 20% allowance for interest during construction	960
(b) Equivalent annual cost of servicing capital (× 18528)	177.9
(c) Annual operating cost	31.1
(d) Total annual cost exclusive of royalty	209.0
(e) Royalty, $16\frac{2}{3}$% of revenues	41.8
(f) Annual revenues required, $ million	250.8
(g) Annual output, million bbl	36.5
(h) Expected cost per barrel	6.87

* 1973 dollars, basis plant capacity 100,000 barrels per calendar day

TABLE 4

Potential availability of oil from oil shales and tar sands

			Annual volumes	
Price ($)	Source	Reserves (cumulative)	Billion bbl	mb/d
5.00	Shale	20	0.4	1,096
6.00	Shale	100	2.0	5,480
7.00	Tar sands	30	0.6	1,640
	Shale	150	3.0	8,220
	Total at $7.00		3.6	9,860
8.00	Tar sands	150	3.0	8,200
	Shale	900	18.0	49,300
	Total at $8.00		21.0	57,500
9.00	Tar sands	300	6.0	16,400
	Shale	900	18.0	49,300
	Total at $9.00		24.0	65,700

peting fuels rise. Indications are that if crude oil prices were to escalate to $7.00 or $8.00 per barrel, rising coal prices would put the cost of oil from coal above the $10.00 per barrel level. It thus seems likely that tar sands and oil shale reserves will be exploited first. The prices shown are, for the reasons explained, probably higher than those at which initial output will occur, because of special tax incentives and other benefits likely to be bestowed upon initial developers. They are believed to be representative, however, of the prices at which substantial additions to the supply will take place.

Potential output attainable on a 50-year reserve basis for operating plants, assuming complete development, may be calculated as shown in Table 4. Thus it appears that crude from these sources will be able to supplement supplies from conventional sources and ultimately to replace them, in North America at least, and that reserves in excess of 50-years' requirements will be available at rates of consumption roughly double those prevailing today. This could be achieved at a price less than double the present price.

The rate at which such supplementary supply is likely to become available is, of course, critical in terms of potential contribution to the anticipated supply shortage from conventional sources. We can only guess how soon supplies from these sources will become available; available engineering and construction skills are apt to provide some constraint on growth in the initial years at least. We doubt whether more than 1.5 million b/d of capacity will be in production before 1985 unless a crash program is instituted and special incentives provided. Even then capacity of as much as 5 million b/d seems doubtful. By the mid 90s, however, a capacity of 10 million b/d seems feasible, with 25 million b/d or more by the next decade. The volume of conventional crude likely to be available from continental sources at this time suggests continued dependence on overseas for a significant fraction of supply, unless substitutes for liquid fuels are developed and used, or the rate of growth in demand slowed by other means. The implied doubling of the real price of energy could have such an effect.

NOTES

1 On a list of over 40 attempts operated on a laboratory or pilot plant scale prior to 1924, see S.C. Ellis, *Bituminous Sands of Northern Alberta,* Mines Bureau Publ., No 625 (Ottawa 1924)

2 P.W. MacAvoy and R.S. Pindyck, 'Alternative Regulatory Policies for Dealing with the Natural Gas Shortage,' *Bell Journal of Economics and Management Science,* vol. IV, autumn 1973, 454-98

3 L. Fisher and J. Lorie, 'Rates of Return on Investments in Common Stocks: The Year-by-year Record, 1926-65,' *Journal of Business,* vol. 41, July 1968, pp. 291-316

G.D. Quirin

4 For the assumed relationships between these variables, see F. Modigliani and M.H. Miller, 'The Cost of Capital, Corporation Finance and the Theory of Investment,' *American Economic Review,* XLVIII, 1958, pp. 261-97
5 For this concept, see G.D. Quirin, *The Capital Expenditure Decision* (Homewood 1967), pp. 38-9

STEPHEN L. McDONALD

Conservation is an idea with attributes similar to those of patriotism: nearly everyone subscribes to it, but it means different things to different people. Moreover, conservation must be considered within the setting of over-all energy policy. This setting includes security of supply, free market pricing of energy sources, tax policy, environmental protection, governmental support of research and development, the rational leasing of public lands – as well as conservation. Free market pricing is particularly important. In a competitive situation with well functioning capital markets and in the absence of externalities, economists generally believe that the forces of supply and demand result in an optimal allocation of resources. Consumers are not encouraged to use too much or too little by artifically low or high prices. Profit incentives encourage producers to use the most efficient methods to create output. The distribution of resource use over time is governed by interest rates and price expectations. There may be problems of intergenerational resource use, but these are offset by the beneficial legacy which the current generation leaves for its successors through the social support of research and development.

Even when there is agreement about the ends of conservation policy, however, there may be disagreement about the means. Alternative conservation methods are not perfect substitutes, and a non-optimal set of institutions may create serious distortions of efficient resource allocation. Professor McDonald illustrates how conservation regulation in North America created such distortions. Canadian conservation regulation has not suffered as much from the most serious of these defeats – lack of oil reservoir unitization. However, even with an inefficient set of institutions, profit incentives in the United States have created powerful forces for regulatory reform to permit production of any given rate of output in the least-cost manner. Nevertheless, substantial regulatory improvements could still be made, and Professor McDonald recommends a significant additional reform, of particular importance if the United States embarks on a course of energy self-sufficiency.

Professor McDonald's discussion of self-sufficiency should be compared to those of Grennes & Winokur and Homet; his discussion of government support of research and development to the chapter by Houthakker; his tax policy discussion to that of Millsaps and Hyndman & Bucovetsky; his comments on competition and the rational leasing of public lands to that of Erickson & Spann; his discussion of free market pricing of energy resources should be compared to the Starratt &

Spann chapter; and his comments on environmental protection should be compared to those of Roberts, Dewees, Stoel and Waverman, and Barnett.

330

STEPHEN L. McDONALD

Conservation regulation and the elements of a national energy policy

The energy crisis in the United States may be defined as a present and prospective excess demand for energy, particularly for energy derived from oil and gas, which apparently cannot be eliminated without sacrifice of one or more present objectives of public policy. The crisis arises out of an increasing supply-price of oil and gas from domestic sources accompanied by price regulation, import restrictions, and growing efforts to prevent environmental damages, and is complicated in the short run by very low supply and demand elasticities. The problem of designing a policy that will facilitate our permanent escape from the crisis is essentially one of choosing components that will work together, but it is also one of assigning weights to different, in some ways conflicting, objectives. As an economist, I shall recommend a policy that derives from heavy emphasis on allocative efficiency.

By 'policy' I shall mean a general course of action reflecting some fundamental principle of behavior or broad objective. I shall emphasize policy so defined and give relatively little attention to programs necessary to implement policy. Throughout I shall assume, as I believe, that the domestic industries producing energy sources are in a structural sense reasonably competitive, and that they would behave competitively in the absence of certain public programs, such as market-demand prorationing in the oil industry. My chief concern will be with the long run – say, the next decade and beyond – rather than with the next year or two.

With these preliminaries out of the way, I suggest that there are seven essential elements of an acceptable energy policy for the United States. These elements are: (1) security of supply, (2) free-market pricing of energy sources, (3) neutral taxation, (4) environmental protection, (5) governmental support of research and

Stephen L. McDonald

development, (6) rational leasing of public lands and (7) conservation. Let us discuss them in order.

Security of supply
Three kinds of potential cost are associated with insecurity of supply of energy sources: loss of real product from fluctuations in input availability, loss of freedom in foreign policy from threatened interruption of supply, and reduced defense capability from actual or potential seizure of producing areas by an enemy. These are surely important enough to justify some sacrifice of allocative efficiency to assure steady, dependable supplies. The problem is most acute with respect to oil, although it may soon extend to gas and eventually to uranium; and as a practical matter it points to some degree of import restriction. That degree should vary directly with the proportion of imports originating in insecure areas.

There is, of course, an opposing argument based on national security: that we should import freely while we can, in order to conserve our domestic resources for use in emergencies. This argument has a certain surface plausibility and appeals to many, but on close examination it turns out to be a weak one. Consider the primary case of oil. If we allowed unlimited imports, the domestic oil industry and its service industries would shrink and a corresponding amount of the labor and capital devoted to these industries would find employment elsewhere. The oil-related skills of the reallocated workers and entrepreneurs would gradually die out. The annual growth of reserves of oil in absolute terms would be adapted to the smaller share of the domestic industry in national consumption. The pattern of refinery location would shift to adjust to new sources of oil and different modes and routes of transportation. Now, suppose that following these adjustments an emergency arises and some foreign sources of oil are cut off. The factor reallocations just described would have to be reversed. There would be shortages of skilled labor and equipment that could not be remedied in a short while. Even as adequate skills and equipment became available, it would require several years, due to the long lead-time from preliminary exploration to production in the oil industry, to develop the capacity necessary to replace interdicted foreign oil with domestic production. And only after discoveries were made could transportation facilities be built to join new domestic sources of supply with refineries. In short, the economy probably could not respond quickly enough to cope with a serious emergency; the oil resources 'conserved' would have been saved to little or no effect in a national security sense.

But, it will be asked, if we rely more heavily on domestic production now, will we not sooner run out of domestic resources and then be utterly dependent on

332

foreign sources, with all the adverse security implications of such dependence? The answer is that due to the almost infinite gradation of the quality and accessibility of natural deposits such as oil, and the very large quantity of 'poor' deposits, including those in oil fields subject to secondary or tertiary recovery, we shall not run out but shall push out the margin of domestic exploitation until the marginal cost (and price) of conventional oil equals that of some substitute, most imminently oil from shale, tar sands, or coal, and from that point the substitute will gradually displace conventional oil in domestic consumption. (Of course, consumption will be restricted by the rise in real price.) We shall not run out of oil, but at any moment we shall be poorer than we would be if free trade with security of supply were possible, for we shall be devoting more of our labor and capital to producing oil than would be required to produce goods in which we have a comparative advantage to exchange for oil in international trade. That, of course, is the price we must pay for additional security of supply.

If imports are to be restricted, it is better to limit them with a flexible tariff which can be adjusted as required to achieve the desired result under changing conditions than with a quota. Under a tariff, imports tend to be allocated to those who can use them most economically, and adjustment of the tariff to induce a given level of imports tends to produce a domestic price which calls forth a market-clearing domestic output in the long run, while in the short run allowing sufficient flexibility of imports to compensate for temporary short-falls of domestic supply.

Free-market pricing of energy sources
The current shortages of natural gas, refinery inputs, refined products, and coal give practical emphasis to the important market-clearing and rationing functions of free prices or, more important, the efficiency consequences of free prices under circumstances of reasonable competition, neutral taxation, and internalization of all social costs. As earlier indicated, I believe the industries producing energy sources in this country are structurally competitive and would behave competitively in the absence of certain forms of public regulation. In this paper I recommend the removal of such regulation and argue for neutral taxation and internalization of externalities, and therefore submit that free pricing is a legitimate and important element in any energy policy.

Since August 1971 the US federal government has to some degree regulated most prices as an anti-inflationary measure, including the prices of the major energy sources. These controls were imposed at a most inopportune time for oil (and indirectly for gas, a partial joint product with oil): a period when the domestic oil industry was approaching, for the first time in twenty years, full utilization of capacity, with excess demand in close prospect, thus a period when the relative price of oil should have risen sharply.

Stephen L. McDonald

The other problem of direct price control relates to natural gas moving in inter-state commerce, the price of which has been regulated by the Federal Power Commission since 1954. The production of natural gas, however, appears to have the structure of a reasonably competitive industry. James W. McKie, who among economists has made perhaps the most exhaustive study of the problem of gas price regulation,[1] has shown that the production of gas for interstate shipment is an industry which is less concentrated than the typical manufacturing industry in the United States. There is no evidence of collusion among producers in the negotiation of prices with interstate shippers. Moreover, the production of natural gas, unlike oil, is not subject to restriction and prorationing by state authorities in the name of conservation. There thus appears to be no valid economic reason for the regulation of natural gas prices. They should be freed, at least prospectively, on gas yet to be discovered, to perform their function of equating supply and demand for this fuel.

It should be repeated that oil and gas are partially joint products. Much gas is found in association with oil, and nonassociated gas is often found in the search for oil. Hence, the supplies of oil and gas depend partly on the prices of each other. Price policy with respect to either has a bearing on the equilibrium price of the other.

Neutral taxation
On the assumption that in the absence of any tax the allocation of resources among industries would be optimal (that is, that in each industry marginal social cost would equal marginal social utility), taxes ideally should be neutral with respect to the allocation of resources. Either each type of tax imposed should be neutral, or there should be compensating unneutrality within the tax system as a whole. Most analysis proceeds on the former norm, considering each tax individually; and it is on the basis of such procedure that with respect to the corporation income tax, essentially a flat-rate tax, most economists have condemned percentage depletion and other special tax provisions that reduce the effective rate of corporate tax on income from the production of minerals, including oil and gas, coal, oil shale, and uranium.

Stripped to its essentials, the criticism is this: consider two industries which in the absence of a corporate income tax have equal marginal private (and social) rates of return on investment. If the two industries are now taxed at different effective rates on their income, marginal social rates of return are unaffected, but private rates fall; and the fall is less in the case of the industry enjoying the lesser effective rate of tax. Resources now tend to be reallocated in favor of the latter industry until marginal private rates of return are re-equalized. But now marginal social rates of return are unequal – lower in the tax-favored industry – and it is

334

seen that society is worse off because resources have been marginally diverted from higher-yielding to lower-yielding uses. This effect could have been avoided by taxing the two industries at the same effective rate.

This argument is based on the assumption that the corporate income tax is not shifted but is borne by stockholders. On the assumption that it is shifted forward to consumers (and there is considerable evidence that it is), I have elsewhere[2] shown that equal effective tax rates are unneutral, reducing output and raising relative prices in those industries that due to high risk and capital intensity must earn an especially large profit per dollar of sales and thus must pay an especially high tax per dollar of sales. Thus, to shift a 50 per cent corporate income tax forward in the form of higher prices, an industry with a required profit margin of 20 per cent of sales would have to raise prices by that percentage, while another with a required margin of 10 per cent would have to raise prices by that lower percentage. The rise in the relative price of the former would divert consumer demand and productive resources from the former to the latter.

I offered evidence that the oil and gas industry is relatively risky and capital-intensive, and that, on the assumption of forward shifting, the lower effective corporate income tax enjoyed by that industry is only mildly unneutral in its favor. I know of no comparable study of the other mineral industries, which also receive tax concessions although nominally of different size than those of the oil and gas industry. (For example, the percentage depletion allowance is 22 per cent of gross income for oil and gas and uranium, but only 15 per cent for shale oil and 10 per cent for coal. The significance of certain exploration and development costs undoubtedly differs among mineral industries due to differences in the relative size of such expenditures in the exploration-production cycle.)

Thus I am not sure that the special tax privileges enjoyed by the several major energy sources render the corporate income tax unneutral either among themselves or between them as a group and the rest of the economy's products. It would be surprising, however, if the privileges had no allocative effects at all in these two dimensions. No doubt, if we knew more about their effects we could improve the functioning of the economy by altering them. But as long as we are uncertain, and at the same time reluctant to make an excess demand situation temporarily worse, I suggest that we keep these provisions in our tax system. If we ultimately decide that the corporate tax is not shifted, we should abolish these provisions. If we ultimately decide that it is shifted, we should abolish the tax as such by integrating it with the personal income tax, and then abolish the special tax privileges. With either of these steps, we will move toward a more neutral tax system. [Editors' note: While most papers in these two volumes show a unanimity unknown among professional economists, differences of opinion do surface. The questions of the riskiness of the oil and gas industry relative to other

Stephen L. McDonald

industries and the correct taxing policy are two areas where opinions differ. Both the papers by Hyndman and Bucovetsky and by Millsaps *et al.* disagree with McDonald on these two points. Economists will be economists.]

Environmental protection
The free price system tends to yield a socially optimal allocation of resources if, among other things, all external costs of producing goods and services are internalized and reflected in the prices of the relevant products. In connection with the production and use of the major energy sources there are potentially (and in actuality) significant externalities in the form of environmental damages – or more properly, damages to people through alterations of the environment. These range from the pollution of fresh water with waste brines produced in association with oil to the destruction of soil and scenery by strip mining; from the pollution of air with the fumes and smoke of burning high-sulfur coal to the destruction of stream life with waste heat from nuclear reactors. In all cases of environmental alteration, we should attempt to measure the cost to members of society. If no one is hurt – if the cost is nil – the environmental alteration should not be prohibited and the affected producer should not be penalized. If the cost is positive and greater than the cost of prevention, the environmental alteration should be prohibited, with the cost of prevention borne proximately by the producer and ultimately by the consumers of his product. If the cost is positive and less than the cost of prevention, then the producer should be required to compensate those damaged, either directly if they are few in number or indirectly through an appropriate tax if, say, whole communities are damaged.

The great difficulty in any rational solution lies in the problem of quantifying or evaluating environmental damages. The solution of that problem is still to be found.

Governmental support of research and development
Research and development expenditures are investments, of course; and, as with other investments, most of them are properly left to private enterprise to be made or not made depending on their prospective profitability. In some important cases, however, private enterprise cannot be depended on to make the optimum amount of R and D investments from the point of view of society as a whole. The first of these cases involves basic scientific research. Generally speaking, the product of basic research, additions to scientific knowledge and understanding, is not patentable and cannot be kept secret if put to use, and thus is not subject to appropriation for the exclusive economic benefit of the researcher. Thus a business enterprise, which maximizes profit by pushing investment to the point where the rate of return *to it* of the last investment is just equal to the cost of capital, will in

basic research stop short of the point where the rate of return *to society* is just
equal to the cost of capital, which would be optimal from society's point of view.
This is what rationalizes the fact that most basic research takes place in non-profit
institutions – universities, foundations, and government – and what justifies a continued large role of government in funding basic research in the energy industries.

Government also has a legitimate role in conducting or financing applied research in some circumstances – when projects are deemed too risky for private
capital to undertake, when the outlays involved are too large to be handled by
the typical business enterprise in the industry in question, when a problem of
great urgency requires a rapid mobilization of scientific resources, and when
there are national security aspects of the research problem. All these circumstances would seem to apply in some cases to current problems of research in the
energy industries, from the development of economical fast-breeder reactors to
coal gasification, from the use of underground nuclear explosions to loosen tight
gas-bearing formations to the development of an economical means of removing
sulfur oxides from the wastes of coal combustion. The solution of these and
similar problems will facilitate the orderly supplementation of, and substitution
for, oil and gas – the energy sources of which we domestically have the least – as
their real prices rise in the years ahead.

Rational leasing of public lands
It appears likely that a disproportionate amount of the oil and gas, and perhaps
other minerals, remaining to be found in the United States will be found on federal lands, particularly in the offshore areas. Future supplies of these minerals
therefore depend partly on the rate at which new lands will be offered for lease
by the federal government. It seems that there are two desiderata in this regard.
First, whatever the rate chosen, it should be kept as constant as possible so that
the industries involved can plan their exploration and development programs and
make financial arrangements in a systematic way. The growth of oil and gas supplies, for instance, and the financial success of lease sales will both be favored by
minimizing the uncertainty imposed on the industry as to the amount and timing
of financial requirements, exploration effort, and utilization of specialized skills
and equipment. Second, the rate at which federal lands are offered for lease should
be that which promises to maximize the present value of expected income from
federal lands. Like any rational private owner of wealth which can yield income
over an extended span of time, the government should seek to maximize the value
of its wealth. To do so is consistent with an efficient social allocation of resources.
Doing this would involve solution of a complex calculus of variations, problems
for which the data are not available. An alternative would be to develop some
rules of thumb which we would be willing to adjust as experience dictated.

Stephen L. McDonald

In this regard, in a recent energy message, the president of the United States stated that he was directing the US Secretary of the Interior to triple the rate of leasing offshore federal lands by 1979.[3] He asked Congress for legislation to extend the investment tax credit to exploratory drilling for oil and gas. He spoke warmly of 'conservation,' apparently defined as voluntary reductions of consumption. He proposed a doubling of federal expenditures on research and development in the energy field. Finally, he indicated his support in various ways for deepwater ports, a pilot program in shale-oil production, leasing for geothermal energy production, and relaxation of environmental standards to permit the burning of more coal. Thus, on several scores the president's policy messages are in agreement with the arguments presented here. In some respects, however, they are not. We disagree particularly in regard to environmental protection and conservation.

Conservation

Conservation is the optimal time path of the use of resources. As such, it requires decisions with regard to both consumption and production. All too often conservation is thought of as either a purely consumption decision, or else a strict preservation decision in the sense of not producing at all. A more meaningful definition of conservation includes not only whether we use a resource, but also how and when we use it. In this connection, conservation decisions in the production of oil and gas are especially important.

CONSERVATION REGULATION

In connection with the energy problem, we are speaking of the conservation of depletable natural resources – oil, gas, coal, and so on. By conservation of such a resource I do not mean the mere prevention of physical waste in its mining and preparation for use; nor do I mean the deliberate reduction of consumption of it below the point where marginal utility equals price. Rather, I mean by conservation a manner and time-distribution of extraction and use that promises to maximize the present value of the resource at any point in time.[4] Such a definition implies the prevention of all true economic wastes, including the extraction and use of some part of the resource at a time when its net value after extraction costs would be less than its discounted net value at some future time. It implies that conservation is a dynamic problem, with the time-distribution of use continually changing as the relationship of present to expected future costs and prices changes, and, of course, as the rate of interest changes.

In the case of solid-energy sources, such as coal or oil shale, conservation need not be a public problem if the extractive industry is reasonably competitive and the market rate of interest is taken to reflect the marginal rate of social time pre-ference. Presumably profit-motivated miner-businessmen seek to maximize the present value of their property, and they are as good at predicting future costs and prices as public officials. But there is a problem with oil and gas, which are fluid and move readily through the porous rock in which they are deposited. The problem arises out of multiple ownership of extraction rights in a given reservoir, the 'rule of capture' as the law of ownership in produced oil and gas, the fluid nature of the resource, and the pressure-differential method of production. This combination of circumstances makes it possible for one owner to capture oil or gas from his neighbor's property by drilling more wells and producing them at a faster rate than his neighbor. It means that if any given owner attempts to delay production to some future date he only succeeds in losing part of his property to his neighbors. So there is a tendency for all producers to extract oil and gas as rapidly as possible without regard to the future or to the fact that, for technical reasons too complicated to describe here, rapid extraction tends to reduce the amount of oil (but not gas) ultimately recovered from the reservoir.

The obvious solution to this problem is for the individual owners in a common reservoir to pool their interests, sharing costs and revenues *pro rata*, and operate the reservoir as a unit. Every owner knows this, but he also knows that if he holds out and makes himself an exception to the pooling of interests while others go ahead he has more to gain at the expense of his neighbors than from joining the pool. Consequently, it is very difficult to unitize a reservoir through voluntary agreement, and it is almost never done except for purposes of secondary recovery after reservoir pressures are so spent that the hold-out has little to gain from inde-pendent behavior. State and provincial regulation has been the dominant social vehicle for coping with these problems. But state regulation has not been an un-qualified success in dealing with the most critical problem – that of unitization.[5]

Regulation of crude oil production
In all thirty-two oil-producing states in the United States, the drilling for, and production of, crude oil are subjected to regulation. This is also true for the major oil-producing provinces of Canada. The nature and extent of regulation vary from area to area, but the typical aims are the prevention of damage to resources other than oil (e.g. fresh water), the conservation of oil,[6] and the protection of the cor-relative rights of owners of interests in oil deposits. 'Conservation' for purposes of regulation is generally interpreted to mean the prevention of physical waste of oil. Production control, our chief concern here, has been officially justified as a means of preventing physical waste – with substantial reason, as we shall see. How-ever, production control has also affected costs and prices; and it is through this effect that such control interacted with import restrictions.

Stephen L. McDonald

The major form of regulation has been to restrict aggregate oil production in a state or province to state-wide or province-wide 'market demand.' Quantitatively most important, such regulation has been actively practised in five states – Texas, Louisiana, Oklahoma, Kansas, and New Mexico – which together account for about three-fourths of US oil production – and the province of Alberta, accounting for 80 per cent of Canadian oil production. It is the type of regulation most commonly associated with cost-increasing spare productive capacity.

Before describing this type of regulation, however, it will be useful to note certain pertinent technical characteristics of crude oil production. The critical rate of extraction which if exceeded will result in significant losses of otherwise recoverable oil is known as the 'maximum efficient rate' or MER. Restriction of a reservoir's production rate to its MER is thus one method of preventing physical waste of oil. Of course, under such restriction the total allowable output of a reservoir must be allocated equitably among individual producers in order to protect correlative rights.[7] As a general rule, once sufficient wells have been drilled in a reservoir to reveal its areal extent, variations in thickness, potentially recoverable reserves, alternative natural drives, and other operating characteristics – knowledge essential to establishing relative property rights and determining the maximum rate of production consistent with no physical waste – the technical efficiency of oil recovery is not increased by increasing the number of producing wells.[8] Due to the fluid character of reservoir contents and the pressure-differential nature of production, the wells essential to information-gathering are usually adequate in number and location to drain a reservoir eventually. Additional wells are of use only to increase the rate at which oil may be extracted, since the feasible rate of production from a reservoir, given its degree of depletion, varies directly with the number of producing wells.

It is apparent, then, that restriction of the number of wells may be used to impose a ceiling on the rate of production from a reservoir and thus prevent a rate that would lead to physical waste. Such restriction is accomplished in the producing states by regulation of well spacing, providing for the centering of wells on drilling units of specified minimum acreage. Spacing regulation may be the primary means of controlling production and allocating it among producers (protecting correlative rights), or it may be subsidiary to control based on MER or market demand and designed primarily to protect correlative rights and prevent the installation of capacity in excess of that required for allowable output.

With regulation of well spacing and restriction of production to MER the connection between production control and physical waste prevention is simple and direct. With limitation of output to market demand,[9] however, the connection runs through prevention of discriminatory buying and price reductions, which to many producers may be objectives in their own right. Although market-demand prorationing was not extended significantly beyond the southwestern states in the post-war period, it persisted and was developed in that area. It was the dominant regulatory institution in the oil industry. The administrative apparatus for market-demand prorationing remains in place in the major producing states. Its working and economic significance are the subjects of the next two sections.

The operation of market-demand prorationing
Restrictive market-demand prorationing involved two steps; the prospective determination of the quantity of oil demanded in the state or province[10] during each month, and the allocation of this total among reservoirs and wells in the area as monthly allowables. This procedure, of course, is based on a situation where domestic supply exceeds demand at the prevailing price. This situation seems currently to be mainly of historical interest. However, as recently as 1964, the province of Alberta was producing at 40 per cent of MER.

Because the administrative apparatus for market-demand prorationing is still with us, and because it is an instructive lesson in the adaptation of institutional forms to economic pressures, the development of the system is interesting to trace (and this will be done, for discussion purposes, for Texas). With some exceptions, to be noted below, the allocations are in proportion to 'basic' allowables. The basic allowables may in some instances be reservoir MERs or other special reservoir allowables, but usually they are derived from a statewide schedule of well allowables related to well depth and acreage drained.

Two such schedules, chosen for their relative importance, are reproduced in Tables 1 and 2. They are, respectively, the Texas 1947 and 1965 onshore 'yardsticks,' the former applicable to discoveries made prior to 1 January 1965, and the latter to discoveries made on or after that date. Basic allowables in barrels per well per day are given in the body of each table, these increasing with well depth and the number of acres per well. Thus, according to the 1947 yardstick the basic allowable for a well on forty acres increases from 57 barrels per day in the 1000-1500 foot depth range to 560 barrels per day in the 14,000-14,500 foot depth range; and the basic allowable of a well in the 8000-8500 depth category increases from 103 barrels per day if the acreage drained is ten acres to 253 barrels per day if the acreage drained is 160 acres. Note that in this depth category four wells on forty acres (ten acres each) would have a total basic allowable of 412 barrels per day, while one well on forty acres would have a basic allowable of only 133 barrels per day. The 1965 yardstick has a similar general structure, but the basic allowables are proportionate to acreage in the ten-to-forty acre range and the 160-acre allowables are substantially larger than in the 1947 yardstick. Consequently, under the 1965 yardstick there is no incentive to drill wells on less than forty acres (in the 8000-8500 foot depth category four

341

Stephen L. McDonald

TABLE 1

Texas 1947 allowable yardstick (barrels per day)

Depth (000 ft.)	Acres per well				
	10	20	40	80	160
0.0– 1.0	18	28			
1.0– 1.5	27	37	57	97	177
1.5– 2.0	36	46	66	106	186
2.0– 3.0	45	55	75	115	195
3.0– 4.0	54	64	84	124	204
4.0– 5.0	63	73	93	133	213
5.0– 6.0	72	82	102	142	222
6.0– 7.0	81	91	111	151	231
7.0– 8.0	91	101	121	161	241
8.0– 8.5	103	113	133	173	253
8.5– 9.0	112	122	142	182	262
9.0– 9.5	127	137	157	197	277
9.5–10.0	152	162	182	222	302
10.0–10.5	190	210	230	270	350
10.5–11.0		225	245	285	365
11.0–11.5		255	275	315	395
11.5–12.0		290	310	350	430
12.0–12.5		330	350	390	470
12.5–13.0		375	395	435	515
13.0–13.5		425	445	485	565
13.5–14.0		480	500	540	620
14.0–14.5		540	560	600	680

SOURCE: Texas Railroad Commission

wells on forty acres would have a total basic allowable of 136 barrels per day, while one well on forty acres would have a basic allowable of 133 barrels per day) and there is greater relative incentive to drill one well to 80 or 160 acres. As these facts suggest, the 1965 yardstick was deliberately designed to encourage wider well spacing than prevailed under the 1947 yardstick. We shall have more to say on that later.

The basic allowables in the yardsticks[11] are maximum allowables. Actual effective allowables in any month are limited by the estimated market demand for that month. The typical procedure in estimating prospective market demand is as follows. Approximately two weeks before the beginning of the month for

TABLE 2

Texas 1965 allowable yardstick (barrels per day)

Depth (000 ft.)	Acres per well				
	10	20	40	80	160
0.0– 2.0	21	39	74	129	238
2.0– 3.0	22	41	78	135	249
3.0– 4.0	23	44	84	144	265
4.0– 5.0	24	48	93	158	288
5.0– 6.0	26	52	102	171	310
6.0– 7.0	28	57	111	184	331
7.0– 8.0	31	62	121	198	353
8.0– 8.5	34	68	133	215	380
8.5– 9.0	36	74	142	229	402
9.0– 9.5	40	81	157	250	435
9.5–10.0	43	88	172	272	471
10.0–10.5	48	96	192	300	515
10.5–11.0		106	212	329	562
11.0–11.5		119	237	365	621
11.5–12.0		131	262	401	679
12.0–12.5		144	287	436	735
12.5–13.0		156	312	471	789
13.0–13.5		169	337	506	843
13.5–14.0		181	362	543	905
14.0–14.5		200	400	600	1000

SOURCE: Texas Railroad Commission

which an estimate is to be made, the regulatory commission conducts a public hearing in which are received formal 'nominations' (statements of intentions to buy) from the principal oil purchasers in the state. (Purchasers' nominations make no mention of price, the implicit assumption being either that price will remain unchanged or that demand is so inelastic with respect to price in the short run that prospective price has negligible bearing on prospective purchases.) The commission also takes cognizance of the Bureau of Mines monthly forecast of demand in the state, and of the level of oil inventories, and receives any pertinent testimony from those present at the hearing, such as statements by independent producers regarding their ability to find markets for past allowable output. Then in the light of all information available to it the commission forms its judgment as to the probable quantity of oil to be demanded in the state (or area in New Mexico) during the coming month. This quantity, adjusted by expected inventory change and estimated underproduction of allowables, becomes the total nominal allowable for the state (or area) during the subject month.

If the total allowable based on market demand was less than the sum of the basic (maximum) allowables for the state (or area), as it ordinarily was in the post-war period up to 1971, then it was allocated among the fields and wells involved. The allocation was in two steps. First, the fields and wells exempt from market-demand restriction, such as water-flood fields, discovery wells, and certain low-capacity wells, were allotted their exempt special allowables or capacity rates of production as applicable. Second, the sum of exempt allotments was then subtracted from the total allowable estimated to match market demand, and the remainder was allocated to non-exempt fields and wells in proportion to their respective basic allowables. The proportionate allocation to non-exempt fields and wells in Texas, Louisiana, and Oklahoma was accomplished by means of a 'market demand factor,' a decimal fraction representing the ratio of the total non-exempt share of allowed production to the total non-exempt basic allowable, which was multiplied by each well's basic allowable to compute its actual allowable for the effective period. (Somewhat different but roughly equivalent procedures were followed in New Mexico, Kansas, and Alberta.) Thus, if the market demand factor were 60 per cent, a well whose basic (yardstick) allowable was 102 barrels per day would have an effective allowable of $.60 \times 102 = 61$ barrels per day.

The exemptions from market-demand restrictions (of the types indicated above) are quite important, especially in Texas, Oklahoma, Kansas, New Mexico, and Alberta. The proportion of total crude oil production accounted for by exempt wells in each state varies, of course, with the degree of restraint on non-exempt wells, but in 1963, when market-demand factors in the Southwest were around their post-war lows (e.g. 28 per cent in Texas), the exempt proportions were 43 per cent in Texas, 58 per cent in Oklahoma, 47 per cent in New Mexico, 61 per cent in Kansas, and 20 per cent in Louisiana.[12] The exemptions were designed to encourage exploration and secondary recovery, and to prevent the 'premature' abandonment of low-capacity wells. They undoubtedly contribute to these ends, but they add to the degree of restraint imposed on non-exempt wells when demand is depressed relative to capacity. [Editors' note: Various evidence suggests that the kind of exploration encouraged by exemptions was only a marginal source of long-run addition to productive capacity. Exemptions discriminated against low-cost, high-capacity production in favor of high-cost, low-capacity production.]

The economic significance of market-demand prorationing

The limitation of oil output in an area to the quantity demanded (implicitly at or near the going price) and allocation of the total among all wells in the state had two general effects. First, it tended to support the going price by creating disincentives for the development of any excess supply at the going price. Second, it assured each producer a share in the total market, provided only that he could afford to produce at the going price. It thus tended to prevent discriminatory buying and price reductions, and hence physical waste. In this manner market-demand prorationing contributed to conservation as conceived by legislators and regulatory officials in the affected states and provinces.

But what, then, determined the going price of oil? One popular hypothesis is that the regulatory commissions in concert determined the price of oil by deliberately manipulating supply relative to demand. Presumably in league with oil producers (who are often their political constituents, as in Texas and Oklahoma, where regulators are elected) they seek a 'high' price of oil, the hypothesis runs, such as the managers of a monopolistic cartel would try to obtain, or such as may be necessary to protect the numerous (and politically potent) high-cost producers in the industry. In the light of the origins of market-demand prorationing, in a period when raising the price of oil was an explicit objective, this hypothesis has a certain appeal; but it is difficult to reconcile with the weakness of the nominal price and steady decline in the real price of oil all during the sixties while costs were rising continuously.

An alternative hypothesis, favored by the present writer, is based on the opinion, formed after several years of observation, that the regulatory commission in each area independently and passively adjusted allowable output to quantity demanded without regard to the level of prices. If this view is correct it leaves the price level indeterminate in terms of the usual supply and demand analysis. If quantity supplied was equated continuously with quantity demanded regardless of the price, then there was no unique equilibrium price at which there was neither excess demand nor excess supply. The hypothesis is, accordingly, that the oil price was 'administered' by major integrated oil companies, acting without collusion but each in contemplation of the probable response of others, at a level determined by a number of considerations. These include the target rate of return on investment, the benefits of percentage depletion (the base of which is the wellhead value of oil produced)[13] and the effects of oil and product prices on entry and exit of independent producers and refiners. On these considerations the optimum price of oil for a given integrated firm would be one which competitors would imitate, which would yield at least the target rate of return, which would not attract so much entry by independent producers as, through the regulatory allocative mechanism, to decrease substantially the market share of the firm, and which would not create antitrust difficulties by making it impossible for independent refiners to survive. Of course, it is unlikely that a given price would be at the optimum level for several firms simultaneously, or for a given firm for more than a year or two; hence, fairly frequent changes.

Both hypotheses are consistent with the rise in the price of crude oil by stages from 1947 to 1957. In this period the prices of inputs were rising and unit costs were further increased by declining rates of capacity utilization in the non-exempt categories of production. Given these circumstances, the desire by either regulators or integrated firms to shore up rates of return in the industry would lead to higher prices. But higher prices, by simultaneously attracting imports and buttressing the domestic incentive to explore and expand secondary recovery operations, led to still lower rates of capacity utilization and still higher unit costs. This lesson was learned by 1957, and according to the second hypothesis the major integrated firms deliberately lowered the crude oil price, 1957-9, in order to break the vicious circle by discouraging domestic exploration and further rapid expansion of exempt categories of production. In combination with restricted imports after 1959 the new price policy, if such it was, proved successful. The growth of new capacity slowed, and in 1962 the rate of capacity utilization began a gradual rise which has continued to the present (1971). The crude oil price began to rise again only when, in the late sixties, the elimination of unwanted spare capacity came in sight. [Editors' note: McDonald's hypothesis of an administered price, if correct, is not inconsistent with his earlier statements to the effect that field markets for oil and gas are structurally effectively competitive. Rather, it represents constrained profit maximization through use of a regulatory apparatus which existed for other purposes. In the editors' opinion, it would be difficult to say that the state regulatory agencies had been 'captured' by the major oil companies.]

It is interesting to note that the growth of spare capacity in the fifties was confined to the areas practicing restriction of production to market demand. In the other states the development of excess supply produced a small decline in the relative price of crude oil,[14] which quickly attracted sufficient demand from the market-demand states to eliminate the excess supply. Thus, when there is excess supply at the average price of crude oil in North America as a whole, relative price flexibility in the nonmarket-demand states assures that their share in the market grows, while spare capacity increases in the market-demand areas.

Whatever the hypothesis as to price determination, it is evident that the average price of crude oil was too high for long-run equilibrium in the fifties and that market-demand prorationing made that condition possible. Without regulatory restriction of output to market demand at the going price, excess supply would have developed at the going price in the early fifties and competition among suppliers would have forced the price down. Unwanted spare capacity would then have been gradually eliminated as the lower price stimulated demand and caused marginal operations in exploration, development, and production to be abandoned. With relatively cheap imports available, the domestic price would have fallen until either imports were restricted by regulation or the price reached the level of the marginal cost of imports. [Editors' note: It must be remembered, however, that during this period the most likely sources of imports were from concessions controlled by the firms whose nominations were an important determinant of the domestic price.] Domestic production would have shrunk relative to domestic demand as the result of progressive elimination of marginal capacity. But with market-demand prorationing it was possible for the price of oil to rise in the fifties, domestic production shrinking relative to domestic demand by regulation and being allocated in such a way as to shelter marginal operations and burden otherwise relatively low-cost operations with spare capacity.

A significant element in the growth of spare capacity in the fifties and its gradual reduction in the USA in the sixties was the set of incentives created by the depth-acreage allowable schedules employed in the market-demand states. Consider again the Texas 1947 yardstick (Table 1 above). On a 160-acre tract an operator could drill one well, or two wells (80 acres each), etc., up to 16 wells (10 acres each). If all the wells should prove productive, the total allowable on the tract, assuming a reservoir at 8200 feet, would be 253 barrels per day for one well, 346 barrels per day for two wells, etc., up to 1648 barrels per day for 16 wells. Given the total recoverable oil in the reservoir beneath the tract, the period of recovery would be shorter and the present value of the oil would be greater as the number of wells was increased.[15] But, of course, increasing the number of wells increases the total investment required. So there is a conflict between present value of oil and well investment, and a comparison of these indicates some particular number of wells which would maximize the *net* present value of the tract. Presumably that is the number which a rational operator would choose.

As we increase the assumed depth of the reservoir the relative allowables for different well densities change and the necessary investment per well increases. Consequently, we would not expect the optimum well density to be the same at 14,000 feet, for instance, as at 8200 feet.

The effects of several other variables can be readily seen. As the market-demand factor is reduced the gain in total allowable from increasing well density is reduced while the increase in well cost is the same. Consequently, reducing the market-demand factor reduces the optimum well density. Increasing the price of oil has the opposite effect. It increases the gains in present value from increasing the density of wells and therefore increases the optimum well density. Increasing production costs or well costs decreases the optimum well density. Finally, increasing the total recoverable oil assumed, increases the required recovery period at any allowable rate, and due to the discount factor (at least 10 per cent after taxes in oil operations) puts a premium on a relatively high allowable. It thus increases the optimum well density.

As earlier noted, the Texas 1965 yardstick differs significantly from its 1947 counterpart. For instance, it provides for no significant increase in tract allowable if the number of wells is increased from 4 (40 acres) to 16 (10 acres). But since the well investment increases proportionately with the number of wells, there is no incentive to drill on less than 40 acres. Note also that the 160-acre allowable relative to the 40-acre allowable is increased in the 1965 yardstick, increasing the relative incentive to drill on 160 acres, especially in deep reservoirs.

Elsewhere[16] the present writer has estimated optimum well densities under different state allowable schedules, using cost and price assumptions representative of the mid-sixties. It was calculated that the Texas 1947 yardstick, assuming recoverable reserves of 12,500 barrels per acre and a 30 per cent market-demand factor, yielded an optimum of 10-acre spacing at depths up to 5000 feet, 20-acre spacing at depths between 5000 and 10,000 feet, and 40-acre spacing at depths over 10,000 feet. In contrast, under the same assumptions the Texas 1965 yardstick yields an optimum of 160-acre spacing at all depths over 2000 feet, although the net present value at 80-acre spacing is almost as great in the depth range of 2000-8000 feet. It is evident, then, that the 1965 yardstick induces much wider spacing than the 1947 yardstick, as was intended.

The Louisiana regulatory commission altered its depth-acreage allowable schedule in 1960 with a view to encouraging wider well spacing. The present writer has calculated that, assuming 12,500 barrels of reserves per acre and a 30 per cent market-demand factor, the pre-1960 schedule induced 10-acre spacing at depths up to 8000 feet, 20-acre spacing at depths between 8000 and 11,000 feet, and 40-acre spacing at depths over 11,000 feet. The new 1960 schedule apparently induces, under the same assumptions, 40-acre spacing up to 7000 feet, 80-acre spacing between 7000 and 11,000 feet, and 160-acre spacing at depths above 11,000 feet.[17] So the change apparently has the intended effect.[18]

There are two ways in which the wider spacing induced by the new allowable schedules in Texas and Louisiana is significant. First, it reduces the well cost associated with discoveries of given size and, other things equal, reduces the price at which a given quantity of oil can be supplied. Second, it reduces capacity relative to basic allowables and, other things equal, tends to reduce the growth of capacity in relation to the growth of demand and production. Undoubtedly the changes in the allowable schedules of the two principal producing states contributed, along with a declining real price of oil, to the gradual reduction of spare capacity in the industry from 1962 to 1971. Since 1971, spare capacity has been non-existent. But this has been a result of international as well as domestic factors.

The province of Alberta has, since 1969, attempted to allow the more prolific, low-cost pools to increase their production, thus reducing the social costs evident with American prorationing. The Alberta allowable formula is as follows:

$$A_p = MD_a[(U_p - P_p/2)/(U_a - P_a/2)]$$

where A_p is pool allowable; MD_a is provincial adjusted market demand (market-demand factor); U_p is pool ultimate reserves; P_p is pool cumulative production; U_a is provincial ultimate reserves; P_a is provincial cumulative production. Therefore, new high-reserve pools with little cumulative production are allowed relatively high production rates. To prevent, as in the United States, the 'early abandonment' of wells, if the formula yields a production rate which is below an established minimum allowance, the well or pool can increase its production to some stated value which is a direct function of depth (15 Bd for wells of 2400 feet to 65 Bd for wells of 15,000 feet).

CONCLUSIONS

Market-demand prorationing and imports
As earlier indicated, the rapid growth of oil imports into the United States in the fifties was associated with a rising domestic price of crude oil and growing excess capacity in the producing phase of the nation's oil industry. In a free competitive domestic market the crude oil price would have declined in the face of cheaper imports, and reduced growth of domestic production would have been at the expense of the highest-cost operations; no long-term spare capacity in low-cost operations would have arisen. The contrary behavior of price and spare capacity must be attributed to the operation of market-demand prorationing. [Editors' note: See the chapter by J. Debanné on Canadian oil for a picture of how imports were controlled there.]

Such contrary behavior made imports relatively more attractive and perhaps contributed to the speed with which imports displaced domestic production. It is doubtful, however, that it can be blamed for the ultimate level of imports, as a share of the national market, attained before mandatory import restrictions were imposed as a national security measure. In the judgment of the present writer, a purely competitive solution, with the domestic price equal to the marginal cost of imports, would have involved an even larger share for imports. Today, with no spare capacity remaining in the industry, the domestic price is below the marginal financial cost of imports. This relationship, however, is a result of the recent successes of the OPEC cartel. There is considerable evidence that the long-run marginal real resource cost of foreign oil landed in the United States is less than the current US price. [Editors' note: See the chapter by M.A. Adelman in volume 1.]

The significance of market-demand prorationing in relation to imports is not that the former caused the latter, but that the former in response to the latter imposed an inefficient allocation of production on the industry and, for a time, a needlessly high price on the American consumer. In Canada, guaranteeing the Canadian market east of the Ottawa valley plus prorationing policies in Alberta greatly increased the price of oil to Canadian consumers. As imports increased in the early fifties, the growth of demand for domestic oil slowed relative to the growth of domestic supply in the United States. To the resulting excess supply the response in the nonmarket-demand states was different from that in the market-demand states. In the former a small decline in relative price attracted sufficient demand from the latter to re-equate supply and demand. In the latter the going price was supported as output was adjusted to demand by regulation, the full burden of adjustment falling on non-exempt categories of production. Thus the total response involved a reallocation of output from market-demand to nonmarket-demand states, and from non-exempt to exempt fields and wells. [Editors' note: The domestic problems encouraged a rapid expansion into foreign exploration by the relatively smaller firms in the US industry. See, for example, Rene P. Manes, 'Import Quotas, Prices and Profits in the Oil Industry,' *Southern Economic Journal*, July 1963, pp. 13-24.]

As spare capacity grew in the market-demand states the going price proved insufficient to yield target rates of return to integrated firms, the chief owners of non-exempt productive capacity. They responded (at first) by raising the domestic price of oil. Now imports became even more attractive; the incentive to exploration, particularly outside the market-demand states, was bolstered; secondary recovery operations, largely exempt from market-demand restriction, became more profitable; and low-capacity wells, also largely exempt, received a new lease on life. Consequently, domestic supply still tended to outrun demand for domestic oil, and further restrictions on non-exempt categories of production became 'necessary' in the market-demand states; hence, higher costs, higher prices, and so on. By the time it became apparent to integrated firms that a domestic price reduction was required to break the vicious cost-price-restriction circle, the nation's oil output was seriously misallocated between the market-demand states and other areas, and between primary, flowing production and secondary recovery and other low-capacity operations. This misallocation may be regarded as the real cost imposed upon the nation by market-demand prorationing in combination with integrated firms' price policy as imports took a growing share of the domestic market in the fifties.[19]

But, as earlier indicated, neither the price policy nor the tools of market-demand prorationing proved to be immutable. Price policy was apparently reversed in 1957, and the resultant decade-long decline in the real price of oil in the United States together with changes in depth-acreage allowable schedules to induce wider well spacing gradually reduced spare capacity in the market-demand states and increased the efficiency with which production was allocated. The real cost of market-demand prorationing was probably lower at the time of the deliberations of the Cabinet Task Force on Oil Import Control than at any time since the early fifties.

A regulatory alternative

Even if future price policy continues to allow capacity rates of production from low-cost, flowing wells, market-demand prorationing along present lines will still impose an unnecessary cost on consumers. This is because the depth-acreage allowable schedules are essentially arbitrary in structure, providing an equally arbitrary set of incentives as to well spacing and hence capacity creation. If capacity in a reservoir reflects arbitrary incentives, then capacity rates of production cannot be regarded as ideal on economic grounds. There can be no assurance that such rates of production are consistent with avoiding even physical waste, much less avoiding the waste of economic value, which ought to be the aim of conservation regulation. On these grounds, the Alberta rules are superior to their counterparts south of the border.

What is needed is a system of regulation under which the operators in each reservoir would have the incentive, and would be free, to select the well density and rate of production which would maximize the value of the reservoir to society. Aside from regulation along present lines to prevent damage to resources other than oil, all that is required for such a system is mandatory unitization of all reservoirs – in the case of new ones, as soon as their areal limits are established. Under such a system private costs would be identical with social costs and, given reasonably competitive markets, profit-motivated private decisions would lead to socially desirable results.

Specifically, unitization in the early stages of development of a reservoir eliminates the incentive, which otherwise competitive operators have, to drill wells densely and produce at capacity in order to induce drainage or counter-drainage across property lines. [Editors' note: The question of density is equally important at 20,000 feet as it is at 10,000 feet. Professor McDonald's unitization suggestion removes this problem from the realm of regulatory bias.] At the same time, unitization forces each operator to bear his share of the sacrifice of such unrecovered oil as may result from the collectively chosen rate of production. The present value of this sacrifice, if any, would therefore be duly weighed in the production decision. Similarly, well costs would be weighed against the possible gains in present value from installing more capacity and accelerating production. In short, the operators collectively would bear all relevant social costs (and capture all social benefits), so that in maximizing the present value of their property, which is to say maximizing profits over the long run, they would maximize the value of the reservoir to society.

To maximize present value the operators of a unitized reservoir would balance the value of future production against that of current production. A decline in the current price relative to expected future prices would induce a lower rate of current production so as to shift recovery toward the future. A rise in the current price relative to expected future prices would have the opposite effect on current production. Thus, in contrast to a non-unitized situation, in which the competitive operator would always produce at capacity regardless of the relative current price, under universal unitization oil supply in the short run would be elastic with respect to price. Consequently, price under universal unitization would be more stable than under unregulated competitive extraction. The substitution of universal unitization and freedom as to the production rate for market-demand prorationing probably would not result in much loss of price stability.

Universal unitization would also deal with the other problem that concerns proponents of market-demand prorationing – discriminatory buying when there is excess supply at the going price. Since under a unit agreement each producer shares according to formula in the output of a reservoir, it is impossible for a buyer to discriminate effectively among producers in the reservoir. Price competition would prevent discrimination among reservoirs. An integrated buyer could not afford to favor his own production if the opportunity cost of it (reflecting expected future prices) exceeded the price of others' output. Thus, operators of reservoirs without buyers could quickly attract them with lower offering prices – a desired result in a situation of excess supply.

In conclusion, it is possible to deal with the peculiarities of oil production and achieve conservation, properly conceived, without the tool of market-demand prorationing. Moreover, the alternative of universal unitization with well spacing and production freedom would minimize the cost to the people of the United States and Canada of domestic production partially sheltered from the competition of imports.

It is clear that compulsion by the responsible public authorities is required, although the states and provinces which have jurisdiction outside the federal public domain, have chosen not to compel unitization,[20] but to regulate well spacing and production rates directly. A few major producing states and provinces, accounting for about 75 to 80 per cent of domestic North American production, restrict production to 'market demand' and allocate the allowable output among all producers. This form of regulation grew up in the United States during the Great Depression in connection with general New Deal efforts to raise prices by restricting production, and the operators in the industry, particularly the independents, still highly value the price support and market-sharing benefits of it. This regulation, however, is new to Canada, beginning with excess capacity in the early 1950s. These sentiments, together with a naïve notion of conservation as the prevention of physical waste, account, I believe, for the reluctance to compel unitization of new oil and gas reservoirs and thereafter allow the operators in reservoir groups to make their own decisions as to the manner and time distribution of production, a procedure which would tend to promote conservation as I have defined it.

As long as the states and provinces have jurisdiction (and a constitutional question is involved here), the best the federal governments can do is to exert demonstrative leadership by compelling unitization of new reservoirs discovered on lands in the public domain, including the outer continental shelf which promises to be a major source of new discoveries in the years ahead. It would help also if the federal governments would remove the basis of a fear many members of the industry profess to have, that unregulated control of production by groups of operators in unitized reservoirs would invite antitrust prosecution, by enacting a statute, as many states have done, specifically exempting unitized operations from the antitrust laws.

NOTES

1 James W. McKie, 'Incentives for Sound Growth: Gas Price Regulation,' in *Essays in Petroleum Economics,* S.H. Hanke and S.L. Gardner, eds. (Golden, Colorado 1967), pp. 144-61

2 Stephen L. McDonald, *Federal Tax Treatment of Income from Oil and Gas* (Washington 1963)

3 US House of Representatives, *Message from the President of the United States Concerning Energy Resources,* House Document 93-85, 93d Congress, 1st Session, 18 April 1973

4 For an analysis of petroleum conservation based on that definition see Stephen L. McDonald, *Petroleum Conservation in the United States: An Economic Analysis* (Baltimore 1971).

5 Unitization involves the pooling of separate property rights in a reservoir, the development and operation of the reservoir under a single plan and the sharing of costs and proceeds from production according to a prearranged formula.

6 Conservation of natural gas, often produced in association with crude oil, is also an object of regulation. However, controversies about state regulation have centered on crude oil. We shall concentrate on regulation of crude oil operations. Market-demand factors in the major producing states have been at 100 per cent for approximately two years.

7 For a fuller discussion see Stephen L. McDonald, *Petroleum Conservation in the United States.*

8 The only exception known to the author pertains to reservoirs containing unusually heavy oils.

9 The foregoing was in fact the official rationalization of restriction of production based on 'market demand.'

10 The State of New Mexico is divided into two separate market areas for this purpose.

11 The depth-acreage allowable schedules in use in the other Southwestern states differ in detail but have the same general structure as the Texas Yardsticks, specifying basic allowables that increase with depth and acreage per well.

12 US Department of the Interior, Office of Oil and Gas, *An Appraisal of the Petroleum Industry of the United States* (Washington 1965), p. 26

13 An integrated producer-refiner producing about 80 per cent or more of its refinery runs finds it in its interest to raise the price of crude oil even if product prices cannot be raised, thereby increasing the depletion allowance and reducing tax liability on a given income, up to the point where tax liability disappears or some other consideration (e.g. possible elimination of refinery competition and antitrust difficulty) contravenes.

14 Where there are independent producers and refiners, integrated firms cannot successfully administer the price unless output is limited to market demand.

15 Of course, increasing the rate of production beyond some point would reduce recoverable oil; such reduction would eventually offset the gains in present value that result from shortening the recovery period.

16 McDonald, *Petroleum Conservation in the United States,* pp. 170-82

17 For estimates of spacing incentives in allowable schedules of Oklahoma, New Mexico and Kansas, see ibid.

18 Unfortunately, data are not available to show the extent to which spacing in Texas and Louisiana has in fact been widened by the new schedules.

19 For an effort to quantify this cost at the height of misallocation, see M.A. Adelman, 'Efficiency of Resource Use in Crude Petroleum,' *Southern Economic Journal,* vol. 31, October 1964, pp. 101-22.

20 Most of the producing areas, not including Texas, have statutes under which unitization of a reservoir may be compelled for certain purposes, usually secondary recovery, if a large majority of the owners of producing interest consent.

TOM STOEL AND LEONARD WAVERMAN

Energy-related activities (mining of fuels, transportation, and consumption) are major causes of pollution. This paper details the ways in which each of the fuels, at each stage in the production-consumption link, creates harmful emissions.

Most economists agree that government intervention, at least in the form of setting up mechanisms for charging prices for air and water, is justified. Government intervention in North America has not relied on the economists' ideal of prices. Instead, regulatory standards and the banning of certain fuels are the major kinds of governmental environmental protection acts. Stoel and Waverman critically analyze the role of government and suggest certain improvements.

First written by Tom Stoel, this paper was edited by Leonard Waverman who added the sections on Canada and Canadian-American cooperative efforts.

The paper by Dewees in the first volume contains a slightly different emphasis on the ways of limiting pollution. The papers on coal, oil, natural gas, electricity, in this volume are quite complementary. Of major interest to readers of this paper are the Kneese and Carnesale & Elleman papers in the first volume.

TOM STOEL AND LEONARD WAVERMAN

Protection of the environment

Energy-related activities are major causes of air pollution, water pollution, damage to land, and destruction of natural beauty. These adverse environmental impacts cause harm to human health, injury to ecosystems essential to man's welfare, loss of economic values, and a decline in aesthetics and other aspects of life quality. Industrial nations have tried to devise a number of ways of holding these impacts to acceptable, or even tolerable levels in the face of their ever-increasing demands for energy. There is a question whether they will be able to do so. This chapter will briefly describe the environmental effects of energy-related activities, outline the methods by which these effects can be mitigated, discuss some of the problems which hinder environmental protection, and suggest some possible solutions. The focus will be on the United States and Canada, but much of the discussion is relevant to situations in other countries.

ENVIRONMENTAL IMPACTS
OF ENERGY-RELATED ACTIVITIES

North American energy is presently derived almost entirely from petroleum, coal, natural gas, hydroelectric power, and nuclear power. The adverse environmental consequences of each of these kinds of energy will be discussed separately.

Petroleum supplied 42 per cent of energy in the United States in 1970 and 55 per cent in Canada. Petroleum is produced both onshore and offshore, and increasing quantities are imported. Onshore petroleum production has some adverse impact on air and water quality and entails the use of considerable amounts of land. However, as compared with other methods of energy production, onshore

357

oil production has comparatively minor adverse environmental impacts, except in unusually fragile areas such as the Arctic.

Offshore oil production and transportation results in pollution of marine waters. This pollution comes about in three ways: oil spills due to equipment failure or human error which cause severe harm to aquatic life, birds, marine ecology, and the environment of adjacent shorelines; discharge into the ocean of brines, extracted with the oil, from which the oil has not been completely separated; and pollution from chemicals discharged into the water during well workovers and other operations.

Oil is transported primarily by marine tankers and offshore or overland pipe-lines. Petroleum transportation by tanker, which is increasing as overseas imports rise, can result in harmful oil spills in the event of casualties. The effect of such spills in inland waters or near shore is similar to that of spills from offshore operations.

Oil transportation by overland pipeline temporarily disturbs the land and can cause severe pollution of inland waters in the event of a pipeline rupture, but its environmental impacts are comparatively minor except in wilderness areas, the Arctic, wetlands, or other unusually fragile locations. The undersea portions of pipelines from the outer continental shelf pose severe environmental risks. An oil spill comparable in size to the well-known spill off Santa Barbara resulted in 1970 when a ship dragged anchor and broke an offshore pipeline in the Gulf of Mexico. Rupture of older offshore pipelines due to structural weakening is significant in offshore pollution.

Petroleum consumption in motor vehicles is a major cause of urban air pollution. The nitrogen oxides and hydrocarbons emitted from motor vehicles irritate the eyes and respiratory passages, produce visibility-reducing smog, and cause deterioration of the lungs. Carbon monoxide emissions in urban traffic can reach concentrations which reduce human mental and motor efficiency. Petroleum consumption in electric power plants releases to the air nitrogen oxides, sulfur dioxide, and particulates. Sulfur dioxide is harmful in itself, and converts in the air to other compounds, including sulfuric acids. These sulfur pollutants are very harmful to crops and other vegetation, cause corrosion and etching of building materials, and can severely damage human respiratory passages. Sulfur pollutants are considered mainly responsible for the 'killer smogs' which have caused many deaths. Particulates can become lodged in the lungs, causing respiratory problems. Particulates also soil the objects on which they land. The cost of cleaning up this soilage has been estimated at tens of billions of dollars per year.

Coal provided 19 per cent of United States energy in 1970 but only 6 per cent of Canadian energy. It is produced by both stripmining and deep mining. Stripmining is regarded as the most economical means of producing coal, and now accounts for more than half of all production. In areas with considerable rainfall, stripmining can cause 'acid mine drainage' and siltation. Acid mine drainage results from the exposure of mining rocks high in iron sulfides and their subsequent breakdown to acids. Siltation results from erosion of refuse sites and unreclaimed areas disturbed by mining. These effects can render waters unfit for plant and animal life or for human use.

Stripmining also has adverse effects on the land's surface. In areas with considerable rainfall, it can cause severe erosion which renders the soil unable to sustain plant life, as well as harming water quality. It can also cause severe environmental harm in arid regions. In these places, ecological conditions are fragile and disturbance of the land by stripmining again can render the land incapable of holding vegetation. A total of more than 1.5 million acres of land is thought to have been affected by coal stripmining. It remains to be seen whether in either wet or arid regions economically feasible reclamation measures can hold environmental damage to acceptable levels.

Deep mining of coal also causes acid drainage which harms water quality. Deep mining results in subsidence of the land over worked-out coal mines. In the United States about two million acres have already subsided, and another five million acres have been undermined. Deep mining produces refuse piles which may erode into waterways. Deep mining is harmful to the health of miners, primarily due to 'black lung' disease, and involves a comparatively high risk of serious accidents.

About 70 per cent of all coal is cleaned prior to combustion to reduce the content of inorganic sulfur and ash. This processing results in production of solid wastes. Waste water from the process and erosion of solid waste piles may pollute streams. Overall, more than 10,000 miles of streams and over 100,000 acres of lakes and reservoirs are estimated to have been adversely affected by coal extraction and processing.

Most coal is consumed at power plants to produce electricity or in industrial plants to produce heat. Combustion of coal results in emissions of large quantities of pollutants to the air. These consist mainly of sulfur oxides, nitrogen oxides, carbon monoxide, and particulates. The environmental impacts of the former three pollutants have already been described. Combustion of coal also produces solid wastes and causes thermal discharges to water.

Nuclear fission accounted for only 0.4 per cent of North American energy in 1970, but the proportion is increasing rapidly. In the United States the conversion of uranium to uranium fluoride for use in light water reactors creates radioactive tailings in the milling stage and some air radiation in both the milling and gaseous diffusion stages. The effects on human beings and other living things of continued exposure to low levels of radiation are not known but are thought by some to be seriously harmful.

Production of electricity in nuclear reactors involves the release of small amounts of radioactivity to air and water. Very large amounts of radioactivity could be released to the environment in the event of a reactor accident. Reprocessing of nuclear fuel after it leaves the reactor in order to recover uranium and plutonium results in release of more radiation than at any other stage of the fuel cycle.

Transportation of nuclear fuel and radioactive wastes involves danger of accidental release of radioactivity to the environment, and risk of deliberate release following a hijacking. The highly radioactive wastes which are a by-product of the nuclear fuel cycle must be segregated from the biological environment for periods ranging up to hundreds of thousands of years.

All types of power plants produce waste heat. Nuclear plants currently generate proportionally more than fossil-fueled plants because their thermal efficiency is lower. Water is commonly used as a coolant to dissipate waste heat. Nuclear plants must rely more heavily on water cooling than fossil-fueled plants, because the latter discharge considerable waste heat to the atmosphere through their stacks.

Water cooling is often accomplished by discharging waste heat directly into a body of natural water. About 10 per cent of the flowing fresh water in the United States is used in this 'once-through' cooling process, at least three-fourths of it in electric power plants. Once-through cooling raises the temperature of the receiving waters. The environmental effects of these temperature changes are not fully understood, but they are known to disrupt some aquatic ecosystems and to be lethal to some aquatic life. Alternatives include artificial ponds or 'wet-draft' towers which cool by evaporating water. These cooling methods consume considerable water and can cause atmospheric fogging and icing. 'Dry' towers which recycle water are considerably more expensive.

Most hydroelectric power is produced from dams. There is increasing reliance on pumped-storage plants, which pump water upwards to a reservoir during hours of non-peak electricity demand so that it may descend to produce electricity at times of peak demand. Dams and pumped-storage plants often destroy aesthetic and recreational values in rivers. Hydroelectric dams may prevent anadromous fish from spawning or kill them by supersaturating the water with nitrogen. Dams can alter the ecology of entire river valleys.

Transportation of electricity from hydroelectric plants, as from other types of power plants, is by transmission lines. Electric utilities in the USA presently operate some 3000 miles of overhead transmission lines, requiring four million acres of right of way.

It should be emphasized that the environmental impacts of the energy system are poorly understood. The known adverse effects of that system on human health or upon ecosystems important to mankind may be merely the tip of the iceberg. Such critical, long-term effects as the role of particular air pollutants in causing respiratory diseases and cancer, the extent to which sustained low-level radiation causes cancer and genetic defects, and the impact of low-level oil pollution on the marine environment are simply unknown. There are also large gaps in knowledge about the extent of energy-related pollution. For example, as recently as February 1973 the United States National Oceanographic and Atmospheric Administration could report the discovery of theretofore unknown, widespread oil pollution of the Atlantic Ocean off the east coast of the United States.

In sum, the 'system' of energy production, transportation, and consumption accounts for a majority of North American air pollution and has severe impacts on water quality, land, and aesthetic values. Although the harm caused by these impacts is not fully understood, in many cases it is obviously serious.

Trends within the energy system indicate that adverse environmental impacts may increase faster than energy consumption. Even with the recent and prospective price changes for energy, consumption of energy will likely grow at rates around the annual world increase in GNP. A greater proportion of North American oil seems destined to come from such environmentally fragile areas as the outer continental shelf and the Arctic, and from overseas. The perceived disadvantages of imported oil apparently will dictate that a considerable proportion of energy will continue to come from coal, which is relatively harmful to the environment at the points of production and consumption. There is a trend toward production of coal by stripmining, the most environmentally harmful method. Production of natural gas, the least environmentally harmful of the major fuel sources, is barely holding even. Therefore, increased energy demands will have to be met by more environmentally harmful fuel sources. Nuclear power is proposed to come from larger and larger reactors of less and less tested design, culminating in the liquid-metal fast-breeder reactors, each of which will contain enough highly toxic plutonium to induce cancer in every member of the human race.

METHODS OF PROTECTING THE ENVIRONMENT

It has been seen that most environmental impacts of the energy system are detrimental. These impacts are known to result in damage to human health and to ecosystems important to mankind. Many effects of energy production and transportation techniques used in the past are still inadequately understood. It will take years to understand these impacts, much less those of techniques just beginning to be used or still on the drawing boards.

In view of these facts, mankind must strive to minimize these impacts so far as this is consistent with other essential goals. There are a number of basic methods by which environmental impacts can be reduced. All of them involve government intervention in the energy system. Even the most ardent advocates of laissez-faire concede that an optimal level of environmental protection cannot be achieved through the free market alone, and whatever environmental protection measures would be taken by private participants in their own self-interest presumably are already in effect.

GOVERNMENT INSTRUMENTS TO CONTROL POLLUTION

One method of reducing environmental impacts is for government to enforce regulatory standards intended to reduce the output of pollution from existing energy technologies or bring about the use of feasible technologies with less environmental impact. This method has been widely used in both the United States and Canada, where most regulatory standards with significant effects on the energy system have been imposed at the federal level. Some environmental impacts of the energy system are not yet subject to any federal regulation, but federal standards have been proposed to deal with almost all impacts except those which are plainly local.

The American federal Clean Air Amendments of 1970 put into effect a scheme for cleaning up the air of the United States by the late 1970s. The basic approach is to establish standards for new stationary and mobile pollution sources and to require states to devise and implement plans for achieving air quality goals. The most severely affected parts of the energy system, because their air pollution effects are greatest, are fossil-fueled power plants and petroleum consumption in motor vehicles. Industry argues that there are no practicable techniques for controlling emissions from coal-fired power plants and automobiles, but federal officials assert that techniques do exist.

There are some gaps in this regulatory system. The Clean Air Amendments require that air pollution be reduced only to the extent practicable. One consequence is that the emission from power plants of small particulates remains largely uncontrolled because control is deemed impracticable, even though these emissions are harmful to health and to visibility.

In Canada the degree of federal involvement in pollution controls is limited by the constitutional division of power. The provinces have the right to control property and civil rights while federal authorities can control interprovincial or international trade and commerce. It is against this constitutional backdrop that Canadian policies must be discussed. The federal Clean Air Act empowers federal authorities to set national air quality standards and objectives. Since constitutionally the federal authorities cannot regulate or control property, these standards can be imposed only when there is a significant danger to health or where international agreements are involved. The act also empowers officials to regulate the composition of fuels produced or imported into Canada. This clause could be used to prevent the importation of oil or coal with high sulfur contents (for instance, Venezuelan crude or Pennsylvanian coal).

The provinces can, then, subject to the stated but legally ambiguous right of the federal authorities, set their own pollution standards. For example, the Ontario Environmental Protection Act of 1971, superseding the various regulations made under the Air Pollution Control Act 1967, set up an air management branch directed to upgrade air quality standards. Accordingly, emission standards for automobiles and industrial users and the sulfur content of fuels have been tightly regulated.

The Federal Water Pollution Control Act Amendments of 1972 established a somewhat similar scheme for cleaning up American waters by the mid-1980s. The amendments set up a comprehensive plan for controlling water pollution in inland waters and seaward to the three-mile limit, basically by establishing federal emission standards for pollution sources. The greatest energy impacts are likely to be on coal mining and processing, and on thermal discharges from power plants. It is proposed that thermal discharges be controlled primarily by requiring power plants to use cooling towers, described previously, which discharge waste heat to the atmosphere rather than to water.

A number of federal bills in Canada control water pollution. The Fisheries Act, giving the national government the power over waters in which fish spawn, enabled strict controls over a number of years. Under the National Housing Act nearly $400 million has been lent since 1960 to municipalities for the construction of sewage treatment plants and main sanitary sewers. If the project was completed before a certain date, 25 per cent of the loan was forgiven. The federal Canada Water Act was enacted in 1970 'to provide for the management of water resources of Canada ...' and has some significant provisions. With respect to water either where there is a 'national interest' (s. 4) or, in the case of interjurisdictional waters, where water quality has become a matter of 'urgent national concern' and where the province has refused to upgrade this quality of water (s. 11(1)), the minister may with the approval of the Governor-in-Council establish with the province (or on federal initiative alone) agencies to control the quality of specific water basins. In any federal waters, the government may also unilaterally establish such management agencies, with powers to define local quality standards, design and operate sewage treatment facilities, and prosecute offenders (who would be liable, on summary conviction, to fines of up to $5000 per day). Effluent fees are suggested as one means of ensuring the required water standard.

United States offshore oil drilling operations beyond the three-mile limit are regulated by the United States Geological Survey under the Outer Continental

Shelf Lands Act. In order to prevent oil spills, the survey controls both the type of technology and the methods of operation employed. The location of pipelines to shore from the outer continental shelf is governed by the Interior Department's Bureau of Land Management.

The main energy-related environmental impacts not covered by federal regulatory standards are those on the oceans and on land. There are as yet only limited controls over pollution from marine tanker operations. The United States does regulate near-shore tanker operations, and some states have imposed liability for pollution of their waters. International tanker operations are the subject of proposed international conventions. Failing adoption of effective conventions, the United States could impose its own standards on tankers which enter United States waters or operate under the United States flag. It appears that no federal agency has jurisdiction over proposed offshore ports to accommodate very large tankers. Construction of such ports on the outer continental shelf is probably forbidden by the Outer Continental Shelf Lands Act. Congress is now considering legislation which would allow construction subject to federal controls.

In Canada four federal acts – the Shipping Act, the Arctic Waters Pollution Prevention Act, the Northern Inland Waters Act, the Oil and Gas Protection and Conservation Act – extend federal jurisdiction over waters above and beyond the continental shelf, by limiting oil spillage by ships and controlling offshore exploration for oil and gas. Canada has incurred American wrath in attempting to devise 'shipping safety control zones' which extend up to 100 miles offshore in waters north of the 60th parallel. One country's pollution control is another country's threat to sovereignty.

All aspects of US nuclear fuel cycle and nuclear power production are subject to detailed federal regulation by the Atomic Energy Commission under the Atomic Energy Act of 1954. Virtually every nuclear-related activity must be licensed by the commission and some activities – including nuclear fuel enrichment – are carried on solely by the federal government. The original purpose of the Atomic Energy Act was the protection of human health and safety rather than the natural environment. Even after enactment in 1969 of the National Environmental Policy Act, the Atomic Energy Commission was slow to fulfill its environmental responsibilities. The United States Court of Appeals for the District of Columbia Circuit ordered the commission to reform in the case of *Calvert Cliffs' Coordinating Committee* v *Atomic Energy Commission.* The nuclear system is also subject to the federal statutes regulating air and water pollution.

A few energy-related land impacts are federally regulated. As noted the Atomic Energy Commission must license nuclear power plants and other nuclear facilities. Natural gas pipelines in interstate commerce must be licensed by the Federal Power

Commission. Some hydroelectric facilities are federally constructed and operated. Private hydroelectric projects must be licensed by the Federal Power Commission. The FPC must license transmission lines from hydroelectric facilities subject to FPC jurisdiction. Energy-related activities on federal lands are regulated by various agencies. These activities include construction of pipelines across federal lands, transmission lines across federal lands, and power plants or other facilities on federal lands.

Similarly, the Atomic Energy Control Board controls the development of all nuclear power plants in Canada. All interprovincial pipelines, oil, gas, products, or slurry must be approved by the National Energy Board. Detailed rigorous examination of the ecological effects of the proposed MacKenzie Valley pipeline is certain. All hydro projects are provincially owned. Two cases of ecological problems deserve discussion. Recently, natives living in the James Bay drainage basin have attempted to halt construction of the massive James Bay hydro project which entails the flooding of millions of acres of land. Quebec provincial authorities appear to minimize environmental consequences, feeling that the project controls that province's economic destiny. In Ontario a decision to construct a thermal plant hundreds of miles from the major market involves a large power corridor to transmit the energy. Provincial Ontario officials have spent a good deal of time and thought studying all possibilities.

The most important land use gaps in both countries are the lack of federal control over most stripmining of coal and over the location of fossil-fueled power plants, refineries, and other major energy facilities. State regulation of these land uses is inadequate, and legislation now pending before the American Congress would go far toward closing both gaps.

The regulatory standards approach to protecting the environment has the advantages of being relatively direct and swift. If the environmental quality goals mandated by the standards are attainable with existing technology, the degree to which pollution will be reduced can be determined quite accurately in advance. The approach also has disadvantages. In the real world, precise information commonly is not available about either the capabilities of technology or the effects of pollution. These uncertainties can be exploited by affected industries through the political process to produce delays and relaxation of standards. This has been demonstrated, for example, with respect to automobile and power-plant emission standards. These uncertainties also make it difficult to calculate the societal costs and benefits which will be derived from different standards.

A second general method of achieving environmental quality is for government to provide economic incentives for industry to reduce pollution. This can be accomplished through effluent charges, tax subsidies, or other devices. This approach, though widely favored by economists, has been little used in the United

States. A proposed tax on sulfur emissions has languished in the Congress for several years. The economic-incentives approach could be used either separately or in combination with the regulatory-standards approach. As already mentioned, the Canada Water Act includes provisions for enacting effluent charges. As yet, none have been introduced.

The economic-incentives approach has theoretical advantages. The presence of economic incentives should enlist industry on the side of government in the fight against pollution and allow each firm to develop and implement its own methods for reducing pollution to the extent dictated by its economics of production. By changing the level of incentives, any reasonable level of pollution reduction could be attained at a cost comparatively easy to calculate. In theory, economic incentives are the way to achieve the maximum reduction in pollution at the minimal cost.

The economic-incentives approach has disadvantages in practice, however. Uncertainties about the way firms will actually react to particular incentives makes it difficult to predict the level of pollution reduction which will result. Some such uncertainty is inevitable, and it is compounded by the fact that information about industry reactions is generally in the hands of industry itself. As in the case of regulatory standards, lack of information about environmental effects makes it difficult to determine what level of pollution reduction is desirable.

A third general method of reducing the environmental impacts of the energy system is government action to bring about the use of less polluting fuels. Government may intervene directly to forbid or penalize the use of particular fuels. For example, in New York City the burning of residual fuel oil containing more than a specified percentage of sulfur is forbidden. Or firms may convert to less polluting fuel sources in response to governmental regulatory standards or economic incentives limiting or penalizing pollution. The imposition of federal clean air standards has, for instance, caused many utilities to shift from coal to oil as a fuel for power plants. This method has the advantage of being comparatively simple to enforce and relatively efficacious so long as the connection between specific fuels and pollution is clear and sufficient quantities of 'clean' fuels are available. Disadvantages are that costs and benefits may be hard to calculate and that the method works only so long as sufficient quantities of clean fuels are available. The province of Ontario has established strict rules on sulfur content of fuels, rules neglected by other provinces.

A fourth general method of reducing environmental impacts is to make more efficient use of the environment's capacity to absorb pollution. Government may compel this directly, as through government regulations requiring tankers to discharge oil in mid-ocean rather than near shore (for example, the Canadian Shipping Act). This method of reducing pollution may be invoked through the 'clean fuels' approach just described, as well as by government requirements that power plants in regions with relatively clean air burn dirtier fuels to make clean fuels available in urban areas where the air is heavily polluted. Or its use may result from governmental imposition of pollution standards or economic incentives to reduce pollution. For example, air pollution restrictions around Los Angeles have caused power companies to supply electricity to that area by building 'dirty' coal-fired power plants in the Four Corners area of the Southwest and utilizing long-distance transmission lines.

This method may have few disadvantages in areas where the environment has substantial excess pollution-absorbing capacity. However, ecosystems generally have not evolved with this capacity, and the choice usually is between increased pollution in one place or another. If the 'rational' course is chosen of placing additional pollution where existing pollution is lowest, the result will be to degrade all areas to a relatively low level of environmental quality. This may reduce ecosystem diversity and conflict with the desires of those who wish to live in or visit a region with higher-than-minimal environmental quality. It also may reduce the incentives for local pollution reduction measures, since residents of localities may anticipate that in the long run the environment will be degraded anyway. Courts have interpreted the US federal Clean Air Amendments to forbid degradation below existing levels of air quality, and thus to prohibit this means of reducing air pollution.

A fifth general method of reducing environmental impacts is through government-sponsored research. Research can discover new techniques of energy production or transportation which do less harm to the environment. It can find ways of reducing the overall environmental impact of existing techniques, either by increasing their efficiency, and thus the amount of energy output for each unit of pollution, or by developing superior techniques for reducing the amount of pollution directly.

The American federal government now spends more than one billion dollars per year on energy-related research. Most of this research concerns more efficient methods of producing electricity by nuclear fission; more than $300 million is expended annually to develop the liquid-metal fast-breeder reactor. Smaller but increasing sums are devoted to research on ways of removing sulfur from coal and such 'clean' methods of energy production as solar power and the fusion of atoms. Environment Canada, the federal department responsible for environmental standards, has a direct research aim as well as sponsoring research at a number of universities in Canada.

The research method has many advantages. Given time, research can discover ways of reducing the environmental impact of almost any level of energy production and consumption. Ultimately, research may make available relatively cheap, almost nonpolluting energy sources, such as solar or fusion power. The chief drawback of the research method is the long lead time required to discover and develop new techniques. It is also difficult to estimate in advance the costs and benefits of specific research projects, in part because it is hard to determine the environmental impacts of proposed technologies.

A sixth method of reducing the environmental impact of the energy system is to reduce the rate of growth of energy consumption. This may occur without direct governmental intervention, because of a shift in societal values which leads to a less energy-intensive lifestyle or changes in resource or other costs which make energy relatively more expensive. Government actions also may reduce the rate of growth of energy consumption. Government may regulate directly the quantity of energy consumed by different classes of users. It may impose regulatory standards, effluent charges, taxes, or other measures which raise the cost of energy and thus reduce consumption. These actions may be undertaken primarily to discourage energy consumption or for some other reason, such as environmental protection or national security. Government may also disseminate information, impose regulations, or provide economic incentives to correct market deficiencies which result in higher-than-optimal energy consumption. Thus, government may disseminate information about the economic advantages of increased insulation in government-insured dwellings.

Because environmental and national security considerations both favor strenuous government efforts to hold down the rate of energy consumption growth, it seems certain that all of these growth-dampening techniques will be employed during the coming decade. However, the American federal government until late 1973 was timid about energy conservation. Federal action was limited to reductions in energy consumption by federal agencies, insulation standards for federally-insured housing, and encouragement of voluntary energy conservation. The constitutional question seems effectively to hamstring the Canadian federal government's attempts to curb consumption.

The advantages of conservation as a method of protecting the environment are obvious. However, government-compelled demand reduction does narrow the range of choices open to societies and individuals. And the costs and benefits of different techniques of reducing energy demand may be difficult to determine.

A seventh method of reducing the environmental impacts of energy consumption is for government carefully and systematically to assess the environmental impacts of its own energy-related actions. At the federal level in the United States, this was the objective of the National Environmental Policy Act of 1969. It requires that before any federal agency undertakes any major federal action significantly affecting the environment, including recommendation of legislation to Congress, the agency must systematically assess the environmental impacts of the action and the alternatives. This analysis must be summarized in a detailed statement available to the public. The act has been held judicially enforceable, and court injunctions based on findings of noncompliance have delayed federal licensing of nuclear plants, the issuance of federal permits for the Trans-Alaska Pipeline, the sale of federal oil and gas leases in the Gulf of Mexico, and other federal energy-related actions. Some states have enacted their own 'little NEPAs.' A statute which would impose somewhat similar requirements concerning the energy-consumption effects of federal actions and require preparation of a national energy plan is currently being considered by the Congress.

Careful consideration of the environmental impacts of proposed federal actions is highly desirable. Strict compliance with NEPA assures that federal agencies do consider these impacts, at least on paper. However, judicial enforcement is essential to ensure obedience, and judicial delays of energy-related actions on account of noncompliance impose some costs.

OBSTACLES AND WAYS OF OVERCOMING THEM

Immediate and vigorous implementation of these methods for reducing the environmental impacts of the energy system probably could hold to acceptable levels the irreparable, long-term damage to human health and to ecosystems on which man depends. Some progress has been made. The federal statutes in both countries intended to achieve nationwide reductions in air and water pollution prescribe generally workable schemes which, if carried out (or agreed to by Canadian provinces), could control most air and water impacts of the energy system. Legislation is being seriously considered to close other regulatory gaps, notably those involving land use. Spending for research on ways of reducing energy-related pollution has increased manyfold.

Public concern about environmental impacts of the energy system is strong. A number of private organizations have proved effective as 'private attorneys general,' using persuasion and lawsuits to compel government agencies to obey environmental protection laws. Many organizations and individuals are active as environmental lobbyists.

There are, nevertheless, serious obstacles to adequate environmental protection, at both the national and international levels. Perhaps the most serious obstacle is the continued rapid growth of energy consumption in North America and the world, and the apparent necessity of meeting much of this incremental demand from environmentally harmful sources. Stripmining and combustion of coal, offshore oil drilling, oceanic oil transportation, and nuclear power production all are likely to increase dramatically over the next few decades.

There are no proven techniques for controlling some energy-related environmental impacts which are known to be harmful. These include small particulate emissions from power plants and long-term radioactivity of high-level nuclear wastes. Other impacts may cause serious long-run damage but are tolerated because controls would be expensive. These include 'routine' discharges of oil from offshore drilling rigs and low-level emissions of radiation at various stages of the nuclear fuel cycle. Increased energy consumption will result in more of these types of pollution.

Even with respect to environmental impacts which can be controlled, an increase in energy consumption may create pressures to relax pollution control standards rather than incur additional costs. Such pressures are already being felt with regard to emissions from fossil-fueled power plants, thermal discharges from power plants, and emission of pollutants from automobiles. And the need to meet increased energy demand may similarly defeat or weaken efforts to control environmental impacts not adequately regulated, such as those of coal mining. A related obstacle to environmental protection is the thrust of the private enterprise economic system toward uncontrolled energy development and its often overlooked effect on political decision-making. In theory, industry maximizes profits within constraints established by government for public purposes, including environmental protection. In practice, it often is in industry's self-interest to spend a portion of the potential profits from proposed activities in efforts to minimize governmental environmental safeguards. By spending substantial sums to furnish government decision-makers with data and studies supporting their positions, engage in personal lobbying of decision-makers, place favorable advertisements in the media, and use grassroots techniques to influence decision-makers, private firms may overbalance the decision-making process in favor of development and against environmental protection.

These industry pressures are not illegitimate in themselves. The problem is that there usually is no equivalent pressure for a decision favoring environmental protection. Environmental protection activities are carried on by volunteers or organizations supported by donations. These organizations have won notable court victories in the United States under the National Environmental Policy Act and other federal statutes and have had some lobbying successes. However, their resources are pathetically small compared to those of industry. Tax-exempt environmental organizations are forbidden to engage in legislative lobbying by the Internal Revenue Code, with the consequence that most of the lobbying groups lead a hand-to-mouth existence. Only rarely can environmentalists afford to advertise in the mass media. As a result, there is a decided imbalance in the forces operating on decision-makers. For example, the recent action of Congress in overriding the National Environmental Policy Act and ratifying the Interior Department's decision to authorize the Trans-Alaska Pipeline followed an intensive lobbying campaign by the oil industry, including considerable media advertising, a campaign which environmentalists simply could not match.

The imbalance between industry and environmental forces is compounded by the fact that industry controls much of the information on which government must rely to make energy-related decisions. Much of this information is denied to government and public because it is 'proprietary.' Thus, industry can be selective about the information it disseminates to decision-makers and uses in advertising, relying on that favorable to its position and suppressing that which is harmful.

This imbalance could be rectified in several ways. Environmental protection statutes could be enacted which leave little discretion to agencies, as in the case of the acts regulating air and water pollution, and enforcement could be assigned to agencies with an environmental protection rather than a development orientation. Other agencies could assign staff members, perhaps on a permanent basis, to argue and assemble information supporting the environmental protection 'side' of important decisions. Receipts from effluent taxes could be used to support the activities of environmental advocates in or outside of government. Environmental advocates outside government could be granted preferential access to the media and restrictions on their lobbying activities could be removed. Government could develop more of the information needed for energy decision-making, rather than relying on industry data, and government and the public could be permitted greater access to industry data. Rules governing lobbying by corporations could be more strictly enforced. Courts could be directed to give less deference to agency 'discretion' in challenges to administrative decisions affecting the environment, and environmentalists could be given greater access to the courts by establishment of new judicial remedies and liberalized rules governing class actions.

There are other obstacles to environmental protection, such as the absence of governmental institutions to formulate and carry out protection measures. At the federal level in the United States, this deficiency has severely hampered energy-environment decision-making. Until very recently, there was no Executive branch institution charged with policy-making and coordination with respect to all federal energy-related activities. There was no agency with overall operational or regulatory responsibility. There was no agency with overall responsibility for energy-related research and development or for energy conservation. No agency was capable of or charged with assessing the environmental impacts of new energy technologies before their widespread introduction into commerce. In the Congress, these responsibilities were even more fragmented among committees. Federal policy-making and energy conservation institutions have recently been established. The repeated transmutations of the energy policy office and its lack of accessibility to Congress and the public leave doubt that it will be the last word. Legislation before the Congress would establish a more accessible Energy Policy Council. The Interior Department's Office of Energy Conservation has just begun operation; its location at a low level in a generally pro-development department gives little promise of strong federal action in that area.

A Department of Energy and Natural Resources has been proposed by President Nixon to assume most operational energy responsibilities. The proposal has languished in the Congress for several years. A more recent proposal for an Energy Research and Development Administration to assume overall R&D responsibility appears likely to be combined in Congress with the side-tracked departmental plan. By presidential direction, a one-year study of energy regulatory jurisdiction was begun in the summer of 1973.

The Congress is in worse shape organizationally than the Executive. Congressional committees too numerous to name jealously guard fragments of energy jurisdiction. Congress has taken the lead only in the area of technology assessment, with the establishment in 1972 of a congressional Office of Technology Assessment. No comparable institution has been proposed in the Executive branch. The Atomic Energy Commission is reviewing the projected environmental impacts of commercial fast-breeder reactors only because ordered to do so by a court, despite the fact that the breeder development program is a proclaimed national priority, is funded at a level of more than $300 million per year, and is expected to have enormous environmental impacts within twenty years.

The bright side of the picture is that fragmentation of federal energy jurisdiction is widely recognized to be a handicap, considerable progress has been made, and proposals exist for remedying many of the remaining problems. It is likely that the Executive branch will be effectively organized within a few years. Congressional reorganization will probably take considerably longer.

Even with its split in jurisdiction between federal and provincial authorities, the federal government in Canada has for two years had an agency (Environment Canada) which pulls together all federal acts and policies. Surely, while this department wields less power than any potential American counterpart, it is a useful example to Americans.

At the international level also institutions are inadequate to deal with energy-related environmental impacts. Many of these impacts, such as air pollution which crosses national boundaries, possible hijacking of nuclear materials, and pollution of the oceans, are international in scope. Although establishment of the new Environmental Office of the United Nations was a welcome development, there is no international machinery for dealing with most of these problems except the traditional bilateral and multilateral treaties. These mechanisms usually give nations an actual or effective veto over application of environmental protection measures to their activities. Thus, for example, nations with shipping interests may be able to block effective standards for design and operation of marine tankers.

An issue at the heart of this discussion is the example of the joint work of Canada and the United States to control the pollution which spills over the international boundary. Canada alone cannot clean up Lake Erie, if Detroit continues to pollute. Ambient air quality standards over the state of Washington would have little meaning if the province of British Columbia was a major air polluter, and the prevailing winds were southward. We have two countries who share the world's longest unmanned border, who have a common language, institutions, and similar culture. If these two countries together cannot agree on common international environment standards, what possibility is there for the United Nations to work out a common standard? The International Joint Commission was established in 1909 to supervise boundary waters between the two countries, and since 1912 the commission, though having no enforcement powers, has duly noted pollution. In 1969 the IJC noted that 80 per cent of the pollution discharged into the Great Lakes came from the American side. Under incessant Canadian pleas, the two countries in 1971 agreed on a series of joint programs to reclaim Lakes Erie and Ontario. Enforcement has been left to the various provincial and state authorities! World efforts to combat pollution will only work if some enforcement mechanism is set up. The experience of the United States and Canada shows that no country, no matter how good an ally or neighbor, is willing to give up some sovereignty to receive effective enforcement.

Another obstacle to environmental protection at the international level may be the expectations of the developing nations. These nations have watched the developed nations rise to affluence through ever-increasing energy consumption. They are not likely to forgo rapid energy-based development for themselves because of concern about the international environment. The problem is exacerbated because the developed nations, some of them already international examples of conspicuous consumption, are still rapidly expanding their own energy use. It is not reasonable to expect the developing nations to be content with a lesser ultimate level of affluence or postpone to the indefinite future their efforts to attain it. Yet should all nations attempt in the foreseeable future to reach the per capita level of energy consumption which the United States had reached by 1970, much less the twice-as-great level which the United States might attain by 1990, it is likely that the absorptive capacity of the world's environment would be exceeded.

A serious obstacle to effective environmental protection is the lack of information about many environmental impacts of the energy system. Many of these information gaps have been mentioned previously. Badly needed is a comprehensive program of research to identify and assess these impacts as rapidly as possible. When crucial information is in industry's possession, it should not automatically be exempt from public scrutiny. Instead, the claim that secrecy is required to protect competition should be weighed carefully against the need for disclosure to protect the environment. Unless information about environmental impacts is made available to decision-makers by these means, environmental protection measures will continue to be based on guesswork.

Still another obstacle is a lack of adequate analytical techniques for determining the optimal level and method of environmental protection. Economic methods based on a calculus of individual self-interest do not seem adequate for assessing long-term societal costs and benefits. For example, discount-rate techniques may be adequate to determine the best course of action for a private firm which wishes to maximize short- to middle-term profits. They seem inadequate, however, for deciding whether to introduce an atomic technology, the effects of which will be felt by generations many times removed from our own. Economics has largely ignored aesthetic and recreational values, which become ever more important with increasing affluence and leisure time. Present cost-benefit techniques also appear unable to deal with ecological uncertainties which can be resolved only after long periods of study. It may be necessary to rely on ecologically oriented methods of analysis which emphasize the fullest possible understanding of ecological systems and the effects of human activity on them, and which require that the *status quo* be adhered to until major uncertainties about ecological impact have been resolved.

PAUL W. MacAVOY

Paul W. MacAvoy provides a fitting conclusion to the book. His paper tries to convince us of the differences between short-run market disequilibria and long-run problems. In MacAvoy's view and ours, the present problems involve short-run disequilibria, not long-term shortages.

How did this short-run aberration occur? As our introductions suggest, and as MacAvoy details, American government control of markets is an important factor. Various federal and state agencies have operated to maintain a high delivered price of coal and oil but a low price for natural gas.

The natural gas case is the prime example of distortions created by control of energy markets. The Federal Power Commission maintained 1959-60 prices throughout the 1960s and into the 1970s while costs were escalating at 5 per cent a year. As a result, excess demand for natural gas was created since the price was kept below its commodity value. In the late 1960s, MacAvoy has found, the demand for gas reserves as discovered in the exploration-development process exceeded the supply of new gas reserves by more than 50 per cent. This shortage of natural gas now exceeds 10 per cent of *total* demand.

The policies controlling the wellhead price of natural gas kept the supply of gas down, shifting demand to oil and coal just as temporary shortages appeared in the oil market.

What can be done? It is clearly in the interest of neither producer nor consumer to keep wellhead prices of natural gas at an oil-equivalent price of $3 per barrel when oil is selling at $10 per barrel.

MacAvoy estimates the effects on demand and supply of deregulation of field prices for new gas at the rate of 3.0¢ per year until 1980. He estimates

375

that at a 1980 field price of 73.6¢ per
mcf, additions to reserves would be
38.3 tcf and production demand 35.6
tcf. The 'shortage' in natural gas would
be eliminated.

Alternative policies to eliminate the
'shortage' would be taxes on consumption or subsidies for producers to find
gas. Either of these policies would cost
consumers more than simply deregulat-
ing new contracts.

For comparison, read Starratt and
Spann, Hamilton, and Waverman in
this volume, and Homet and Barnett
in the first volume.

PAUL W. MacAVOY

Policy disharmonies: problems created by the organizations that control energy markets

One of the more remarkable aspects of treatment of energy problems in the United States is a rather general confusion between (*a*) short-run shortages and (*b*) long-run trends in supplies relative to demands for energy. This may occur because of Americans' delight with (or demand for) emergencies, and because of the proclivity of the American newspaper and magazine industry to confuse short-run and long-run crises, whatever the bases for doing so. The brown-out of electricity service or the rationing of natural gas are properly treated as indications of inability of supply to adjust to increasing costs or changing demands. But descriptions of emergencies are coupled with the statement that there is a stock of energy resources on the planet earth, implying that there is an inability of the system to adjust in the long run.

There is very little economic basis on which to move from the short- to the long-run crisis. We have been on a long-term trend of relative increases in energy: Barnett and Morse, albeit in a somewhat dated study,[1] have shown that additions to annual energy supplies over the last half century have been greater than those to annual energy demands, primarily as a result of technical progress and discovery of previously unknown reserves. Even in the last fifteen years, consumers have received direct benefits from relative ease of supply: while the US Consumer's Price Index increased by 2.54 points per annum over 1955-71, the CPI for fuel and utilities has increased by 1.91 points (with standard deviations of 1.77 in both indices). These long-term trends may have been reversed in the last two years, but it is impossible to tell the difference between vibrations from trend and a change from positive to negative in the slope of the trend line itself with just these few years' data. There is little doubt but that technical progress was not as rapid in coal, natural gas, and electric power in the 1960s as during the 1950s; and, at least in the United States, additions to reserves in the 1970s, particularly in natural gas, have been less each year than additions to consumption. But it is not possible at this time to extrapolate a few years' data points to long-term reductions of supply of energy resources, never mind to shortages of supply.

Whether this year's problems lead to more of the same over a decade, in fact, may still depend on national policies in a number of fuel industries. An important determinant will be the behavior of the organizations that control energy in the United States. These organizations, overwhelmingly government agencies, can accelerate the adjustment process or can be impediments to the elimination of emergencies. This essay will examine the recent behavior of these organizations controlling the primary energy resources of coal, refined petroleum and natural gas accounting for all but 5 per cent of the total primary BTU output in 1970. After that, there will be some speculation – admittedly by extrapolating a few data points – on their role in creating long-term out of short-term energy problems.

Coal production has declined over the last twenty years. Once providing 70 per cent of total BTU production in this country (in 1920), coal now provides less than 20 per cent primarily because of declining demand rather than declining supply. But coal supplies have been controlled in ways that limit the volume available to industry and electric utility companies. Production itself has been fairly free of control of supply, either by the larger coal companies (since the market is not concentrated) or by governmental agencies. The transport price for bulk shipment of coal has been controlled by the Interstate Commerce Commission and the price at which coal is sold to electric utilities has been controlled indirectly by the Federal Power Commission and state power regulatory commissions. These independent regulatory commissions all seem to have worked towards raising the price of coal. The Interstate Commerce Commission has held unit train rates on coal for most of the bulk shipments in the United States to levels above the long-term marginal costs of transport (so that the price of coal at the delivery point has been systematically 25 per cent greater than real mine and transport costs). The higher delivered price has restricted demands for this fuel.

The national and state regulatory commissions in electric power have not controlled coal prices directly, but rather have controlled the electric utilities' procedures for purchasing fuel. These companies are responsible for 60 per cent of coal demands. Most of the state commissions have required detailed current information on the prices paid for coal and have encouraged the signing of open and even highly publicized long-term contracts for coal purchased by their electric utilities. These conditions setting the frame of reference for transactions at times greatly narrow the market. As a result of market narrowing and of elimination of confidential contracts (many times with discounts), the stage has been set for higher and more stable prices of coal than would have occurred otherwise. This again reduced the quantity of coal demanded in domestic markets.

Petroleum products provide approximately 40 per cent of the BTUs utilized in this country. This output, from domestic crude, imports, and gas liquids, has been supplied under a complex set of 'control conditions' in regional markets. Some of these conditions may have involved the ability of private companies to control supply, but mostly there has been effective competition among producers in providing for regional needs. The overbearing control mechanism for setting prices has been the interlocking control by the federal government of crude oil imports with conservation commission control of production from domestic wells by the state governments. These output controls, ostensibly for the purpose of limiting supply from more productive wells so as to add to that from 'marginal' wells, has increased the reserve-production ratio, and as a matter of course has had the effect of stabilizing falling prices. Probably the reserve-to-production ratio was increased to such an extent in the late 1950s and early 1960s that further exploration no longer was worthwhile. The inventory of known in-ground reserves within the borders of the United States was stabilized. Supported prices and fixed inventories do not prepare an industry to meet short-term wide swings of demand – or to meet long-term demand increases for more production from domestic sources. In effect, demands, supplies, and market responses were all reduced by the control organizations.

Natural gas has provided approximately 33 per cent of BTU production in recent years. This resource has been produced in regional markets characterized by effectively competitive conditions on the supply side, and by power of pipelines in some regions to control the demand side. But the single important element of control has been provided by the Federal Power Commission: since 1961, the Power Commission has set area price ceilings on all production going into interstate pipelines. These ceilings were put on at 1959-60 transaction price levels and maintained throughout most of the decade, while development and production costs were increasing at more than 5 per cent per year, and demand was increasing at more than 7-8 per cent per year. With frozen prices and increasing costs leading to static supply, and with frozen prices leading to increasing demands, markets ceased to clear in the late 1960s and early 1970s (last year excess demands probably were as large as 10 per cent of total production demands). Production shortages were preceded by reserves shortages, in the sense that the 'demand for reserves' exceeded the 'supply of reserves,' as found in the exploration-development process, by more than 50 per cent in the late 1960s. Thus a small production and large reserve shortage at fixed prices makes the future look even worse.

Paul W. MacAvoy

This melange of controls in coal, oil, and natural gas might well appear to be an inconsistent set. Price controls over coal transportation and natural gas production are in opposite directions – coal prices being increased by ICC controls, gas prices being decreased by FPC controls. Output controls in crude oil occur without direct price controls in that industry, so that two of the sources are subject to price limits while the remaining source is subject to output limits. Moreover, these are not the only types of control. Coal production is affected by wage controls and safety legislation; refined petroleum production is affected by transportation price controls put on pipelines by the Interstate Commerce Commission; and natural gas production is affected by control of imports by the Federal Power Commission. The melange, when extended to include all controls, is so confusing in coverage that it might seem unlikely there would be an overall impact on energy supplies or demands.

Our view is that coal, oil, and gas regulation are systematically effective in the sense that there are strong net overall effects on the production of energy. During the most recent years, coal prices have been increased by ICC transport regulation, probably as much as 25 per cent; moreover, the movement towards long-term contracts has probably decreased the flexibility of market response so that less coal has been provided than would have been the case otherwise. Natural gas field price regulation has reduced supplies and increased demands for natural gas so as to create a disequilibrium equivalent to 10 per cent or more of total national production demands. Both together have reduced production of coal and natural gas, coal controls by increasing relative coal prices so as to shunt consumers off to other fuels, natural gas by decreasing gas prices so as to create a shortage and queue of demanders who have no choice but to go to other fuels. The 'other fuels' in this case would appear to have been refined petroleum. Oil production controls have until recently maintained prices or allowed them to decline slightly over time. (The wholesale price index of refined petroleum increased each year an average of .93 points from 1955 to 1971, with a standard deviation of 2.41 points and with some decline in six of these years). The feed-in from coal and natural gas together in 1970 could have been as much as 10 per cent of total refined petroleum demands (at least 1 trillion BTU from coal, assuming relative coal prices 25 per cent too high and an elasticity of demand of -.5, and at least 2 trillion BTU from natural gas from the shortage). This amount of additional demand is the present margin of supply stringency in petroleum markets. Of course, the slowness in expansion of domestic refinery capacity has contributed to the problems in petroleum markets as well. But the argument is that the extra 10 per cent of petroleum demand created by regulatory organizations has put too much pressure on petroleum markets, and has created the short-term emergencies in low sulfur fuel oil and gasoline that we have experienced in the last year of two. In all, the results of all the controls have probably been less energy, and less short-term responsiveness to changes in costs and demands for energy.

Then, given the results to date, it is not likely that producers have benefited more than consumers by regulation; prices of natural gas have been systematically too low and curtailed supplies of crude have also been too low for producers to make money in exploration and development in either industry. At the same time, there have been shortages in all of these markets not beneficial to producers, so that 'control to benefit producers' is not an altogether convincing description of the results. It would not seem possible to put together all these policies into a coherent plan to benefit a few producing companies. But the net effect so far has probably been to increase the demands on the refined petroleum products industry, while not adding to supplies. This probably increased the economic and political problems of this industry in the last few years in a way that would make it scarcely much better off than it would have been without regulation.

Since they offer difficulties for everyone and no clear gain for anyone, the energy regulatory organizations lack justification at this time. We could move back onto the trend line more rapidly by eliminating field price regulation of natural gas and Interstate Commerce Commission control of unit train rates on coal. Both policy changes are long-standing proposals, having been before Congress in many of the last few years. This year may well be the time to act on the proposals. Work can also begin to make the structure of supply of refined petroleum more flexible and responsive to year-to-year price changes – by eliminating national and state commission controls over crude oil production. In all, regulatory organizations have probably played a role in *creating* the energy crises of the last few years. They can probably be eased out of that role in the next few years so that markets can operate more flexibly along the long-term growth path (whatever direction that path may take).

NATURAL GAS: THE WORST CASE

The prime example of the distortions created by organizations in energy markets is the natural gas market.

The shortage of natural gas in the United States has grown rapidly in the last two or three years and is now to the level that it probably exceeds 10 per cent of total demands. This is not a result of the shifting of demands to natural gas from the Arab oil embargo. Rather, this is a continuous and systematic long-term shortage. There is every reason to believe that the shortage will not be eased appreciably over the remaining years of this decade under the Federal Power Commission price controls – even if the FPC were to continue its recent policies of raising price three or four cents on average on new contracts each year. Under conditions in which great pressure is put upon gas demands as a result of oil price increases beyond $6.00/bbl, excess demand under FPC regulation is likely to expand so as to make up more than one-fourth of total demands in the next few years.

These conditions need not continue, since it is in good part the result of US federal government policies controlling the levels of prices for natural gas at the wellhead. Any industry subject to price ceilings put into effect and frozen for a decade is likely to fall short of demands, as a result of factor cost increases and general price level increases on other goods. Policies of controlling a natural resource subject to rising cost of exploration are self-defeating – if prices are not allowed to rise, then society receives no signals indicating the relative scarcity of that resource. Energy resources have become relatively scarce in the last few years and the Federal Power Commission operating under the Natural Gas Act has not allowed the economy as a whole to obtain signals of the relative scarcity of this depleting natural resource. Changes in federal government policies on price controls – a relaxation or removal of these controls entirely – would reduce the shortage of natural gas which will otherwise continue to grow. In particular, policies which allow prices for gas purchase at wholesale to increase at roughly 7 to 8 per cent per annum would go a long way towards ameliorating the natural gas shortage. It is possible, in fact, that if all wellhead prices were raised by this amount each year the shortage could be eliminated entirely.[2]

Because of the control of prices by the FPC, supplies of reserves and production could deplete known stocks. With a change in price controls, significant new reserve finds might occur to forestall depletion. To examine the effects of a range of policy alternatives, we attempt to forecast supply with the MIT econometric gas model assuming two quite different policies on gas prices. Both are alternatives to the *status quo*, or to the practice of the FPC increasing prices by 3 or 4 cents on average per year on new contracts only.

One alternative is that policies would be directed towards a price freeze. This is likely to occur under restrictive regulation. Restrictive regulation is meant here to be similar to that implied by the Senate Commerce Committee bill s-2506 (the 'Stevenson bill') which calls for an expansion of regulatory jurisdiction for the Federal Power Commission to cover all of the sales at the wellhead (including intra-state sales). The bill requires that price ceilings be based upon historical average costs, so that this legislation seeks to stop the price increases now occurring under more 'relaxed' Federal Power Commission regulation. The price implication might well be to limit increases to approximately one cent per year where justified by changes in average costs of drilling and production. There are many possible variations on this price trend. But it is unlikely that price increases much greater than one cent per year are implied by the bill, since price increases of three cents a year are now being put into effect by the FPC and the bill specifically delineates costing standards which would not allow such three cent increases. The general thrust of this and similar legislation is thought to be to hold the line on present prices, so as to prevent gas sales from following the 'pricing spiral' now being realized in petroleum sales.

The most important alternative policy to strong controls is that of reducing current restrictions on field prices. The purpose would be to provide incentives for increasing reserves and production (by higher prices) and to eliminate low value uses for natural gas (by reducing demands through price increases). The use of market forces to add to supplies and reduce demands would have different effects depending on how rapidly and extensively prices were increased. Immediate and complete elimination of price controls would establish short-term equilibrium prices much greater than those that would persist over the long run – particularly under conditions of shortages in alternative fuels such as fuel oil. Phased decontrol, however, could be put into effect in a way that would gradually move prices over a five-year period into long-run equilibrium.[3] Let us now consider the effects of stronger controls.

Holding the price line implies that there will be little additional incentive to explore and develop new reserves, or to reduce demands for natural gas as the price of fuel oil increases. New contract field prices are assumed to rise from roughly 34¢ in 1973 to 41.5¢ in 1980 on average, at a rate of one cent per annum; as a result, wholesale prices throughout the United States are expected to rise on average to 49.6 cents by 1980. Assuming that wholesale prices as a whole rise at $3\frac{1}{2}$ per cent per annum, and population increases at 1 per cent per annum, the market for natural gas is expected to grow over this period. Given the 1973-4 conditions in world oil markets, it is assumed as well that crude oil prices will range from a low of $5.00 per barrel to $7.00 per barrel in the next 18 months – to a level which would maximize long-term profits for OPEC. These conditions in oil markets have strong implications for excess demands for natural gas. Rising oil prices lead to substantial increases in demands for natural gas which cannot be satisfied at the regulated or frozen level of prices for natural gas.

The effects of such price controls are shown in Table 1. The low levels of annual production (in the range of 23 to 30 Tcf) and high levels of demands (in the range of 26 Tcf in 1974 to 40 Tcf in 1980) result in significant excess demands. Excess demands, equal to the difference between these quantities of forecast production and demand, increase from 2 Tcf at the present time to 10 Tcf in 1980 – by that time, approximately 25 per cent of total demands. This simulation with the MIT model indicates that the application of comprehensive regulatory controls along lines of the Stevenson bill will result in substantial ex-

Paul W. MacAvoy

TABLE 1

Supply under a regime of strict controls

Year	Field prices on new contracts ¢/mcf	Additions to reserves Tcf	Production supply Tcf	Production demand Tcf
1972	30.1	9.8	19.4	23.4
1973	33.9	12.6	23.1	24.8
1974	35.0	14.4	23.7	26.6
1975	36.1	17.7	24.6	28.6
1976	37.2	20.8	25.6	30.7
1977	38.3	22.9	26.7	32.9
1978	39.4	24.7	27.8	35.1
1979	40.5	26.7	29.0	37.4
1980	41.6	28.9	30.3	40.0

cess demand. The shortage would be so great as to make it impossible for the pipelines to continue to supply all the needs of established consumers. Rationing undoubtedly would have to be put into effect to curtail these demands. This rationing would be permanent, since this is not a 'short-term' shortage. Most of the effects of rationing would be felt in the upper Midwest, where population and industrial growth are large and where the pipelines serving the region come from field-producing areas that are most depleted.

The alternative of relaxing price controls should allow significantly greater annual increases in gas production after a few years. It is assumed here that this is the purpose of the Administration Bill, s-2048, which, following from President Nixon's April 1973 Energy Message, proposes to deregulate prices on new contracts for gas sold to interstate pipelines. Again, this does not imply immediate deregulation – new contract price increases would be limited by the Federal Energy Administration for some years – presumably to keep the increases in line with general cost of living increases. (We translate the 'national guideline' into an average rolled-in wholesale price increase of 50 per cent over the period 1974-80.)[4] This much increase over that period implies a ceiling on new contract field prices of approximately 50¢ in 1974 (over a 35¢ average price in 1973). There would be a three cent per annum price increase each year thereafter. Of course, actual prices might vary from these, but it is believed that the price series posited here will be close enough to indicate the effect of introducing market pricing along lines proposed by the Administration. Field price increases would feed through as price increases charged by pipelines to wholesale buyers so that the immediate impact would be a 2¢ per mcf increase in wholesale gas prices across the country.

384

TABLE 2

Supply under phased price decontrol

Year	Field price on new contracts ¢/mcf	Additions to reserves Tcf	Production supply Tcf	Production demand Tcf
1972	30.1	9.8	19.4	23.5
1973	33.9	12.6	23.1	24.8
1974	49.1	14.4	25.7	26.4
1975	53.2	18.2	27.1	28.1
1976	57.3	22.9	28.5	29.7
1977	61.4	27.4	30.1	31.2
1978	65.4	31.0	31.6	32.7
1979	69.5	34.6	33.2	34.1
1980	73.6	38.3	35.0	35.6

By 1980, field prices on new contracts would have risen to more than 73¢ while wholesale prices increase to 64¢ per mcf. The effect of the price increases would be to substantially increase additions to reserves over a five-year period, and to increase production both because of the reserve additions and because of more intensive depletion of existing reserves. Production is expected to rise from 26 to 35 Tcf over the period 1974-80. At the same time, demands are restricted as consumers attempt to avoid the price increases; home consumers save on heating uses, while industrial consumers reduce process heat by reducing their outputs and by substituting other, relatively cheaper fuel sources. Excess demand starts out as 0.7 Tcf per annum in 1974, rises to 1.0 Tcf in 1975, but then declines to 0.4 Tcf by 1980. In effect, the use of market forces has the expectation of eliminating excess demand through a combination of (1) additional supplies, (2) output reductions by buyers faced with higher fuel costs, and (3) substitution effects away from this higher priced fuel.

The MIT model simulation results support the position that phased price increases (leading to a reliance on market forces over the long run) can be used to ameliorate the present and growing shortage of natural gas. As price incentives improve the profitability of additional drilling in the United States, more reserves are likely to be accumulated, and more production can then take place. Most geological estimates indicate that these reserves are indeed available inground, albeit at higher costs of discovery and extraction. A system of price incentives at least as great as those now prevailing in other industries may allow gas supplies to increase considerably. Higher prices to consumers will be more representative of the true value of this scarce resource, and consumer demand should respond accordingly.

TABLE 3

Taxes on consumption to eliminate the gas shortage

Year	Field price on new contracts ¢/mcf	Excise tax on new contracts ¢/mcf	Production supply Tcf	Production demand with taxes Tcf
	(table 1)		(table 1)	
1973	33.9	0.0	23.1	24.8
1974	35.0	13.1	23.7	26.4
1975	36.1	26.1	24.6	27.9
1976	37.2	39.2	25.6	29.2
1977	38.3	52.2	26.7	30.0
1978	39.4	65.2	27.8	30.5
1979	40.5	78.1	29.0	30.5
1980	41.6	91.1	30.3	30.3

TABLE 4

Subsidies to eliminate the gas shortage

Year	Field price on new contracts ¢/mcf	Subsidy new contracts ¢/mcf	Production supply with subsidy Tcf	Production demand Tcf
	(table 1)			(table 1)
1973	33.9	0.0	23.0	24.8
1974	35.0	12.1	25.3	26.6
1975	36.1	24.2	27.8	28.6
1976	37.2	36.2	30.2	30.7
1977	38.3	48.2	32.5	32.9
1978	39.4	60.2	34.8	35.1
1979	40.5	72.1	37.2	37.5
1980	41.0	84.0	40.0	40.0

As a matter of course, various fiscal measures could be taken to mitigate the current natural gas shortage. Taxes could be imposed either on sales at the well-head, or on wholesale transactions of the natural gas pipelines, so as to reduce wholesale demands. Holding field prices paid to the producer at levels in keeping with 'severe regulation,' these taxes in 1980 would have to be equivalent to 91¢ per mcf in order to reduce the demands shown in Table 1 to the 30 Tcf level of production. This is shown in Table 3, for each year from 1974 to 1980. This gives a much greater change in price to the gas consumer than is implied by relaxation of regulation along the lines of the Nixon bill.

Subsidies could be provided to increase exploratory and development activities, so as to increase the volume of supply forthcoming. Subsidies sufficient to eliminate the shortage, while price is maintained at the level implied by 'severe regulation' as in Table 1, would be extremely large. They are shown in Table 4. An amount equivalent to 84¢ per mcf for each additional thousand cubic feet of production would be required to bring forth 40 Tcf per annum, so as to clear demands in 1980. Since this would have to be provided under all *new contracts* for additional gas - there is no feasible way to distinguish between high and low cost gas before the fact - then the amount of the subsidy would be approximately 0.7 billion dollars in 1975, and would increase to 7.4 billion dollars in 1980.[5] This is a much higher level of increased payments to producers than could be expected to result from the simultaneous incentives to both demand and supply implied by phased deregulation of new contract prices.

Could imported liquefied natural gas fill the domestic supply demand gap? It would be in the interest of some of the pipeline companies to argue that it would.[6] Unfortunately, most of these ventures do not appear to be profitable in competition with gas produced from United States reservoirs when gas prices are decontrolled. The demands for LNG and the various domestic gas pricing schemes can be indicated along the following lines. Assuming phased deregulation as in Table 2, there is no demand for large-volume imports of liquefied natural gas from Algeria or the Soviet Union, since the market is cleared by domestic production before the end of the decade. Alternatively, the control of price increases to amounts equal to the average cost of drilling and production that year results in excess demand as large as 10 Tcf by 1980 (as in Table 1). Under these conditions, the demand for LNG would be quite extensive.

An attempt to assess the magnitude of the demand for LNG under the regulation-induced shortage of domestic production can be made as follows. Assuming that the prices are controlled as in Table 1, the demand for LNG at approximately 40¢ per mcf is as large as 10 Tcf (the difference between production demands and supplies under the Stevenson price controls as shown in Table 1). If the excess demand is equally distributed among all consumers, and the LNG price is 'rolled in' with all the domestic prices so as to result in a uniform average wholesale price for all consumers, then excess demands can be eliminated by combinations of *very high LNG prices* and very small additional quantities of gas provided in the form of liquefied natural gas. Table 5 shows the limits on the LNG price predicted for the rest of the decade from providing either 1 or 2 Tcf per annum of gas of this form. These additional supplies, at the prices indicated, clear the

Paul W. MacAvoy

TABLE 5

Demands for LNG, assuming a freeze on fuel prices

Year	New contract field prices ¢/mcf	LNG price, for sales per annum of	
		1.0 Tcf ¢/mcf	2.0 Tcf ¢/mcf
1977	38.4	2.51	2.43
1978	39.4	2.53	2.45
1979	40.5	2.55	2.48
1980	41.0	2.58	2.50

market of excess demand, because the quantities and prices significantly increase wholesale prices to all consumers so as to reduce demands of all these consumers to the level of available domestic plus LNG supply. These findings, from the MIT econometric model, agree with prices now being quoted informally by LNG affiliates of the larger interstate pipelines. These prices are conceivable – they can be gotten from final consumers seeking substantial supplies but unable to get them from domestic sources. The amounts involved exceed more than 3 billion dollars per annum, of which it would appear that more than one-half would constitute rate base for purposes of calculating profits of the pipelines.

The decade of price ceilings imposed by the Federal Power Commission created 1972-3 shortages of natural gas as great as 10 per cent of demand. This condition can be improved, and supply increased by as much as 50 per cent over the coming decade. The most effective long-term domestic policy for doing so would be to allow gas prices to increase through phased decontrol. This would add to domestic gas production and, as well, would eliminate more demanders, subsidized by price controls, from the market. There are many lessons to be learned in this example of the policy disharmonies in one market, lessons for the smooth operation of all markets, energy or non-energy. The first is that price controls create more problems than they solve.

NOTES

1 Cf. H. Barnett and C. Morse, *Scarcity and Growth*, Baltimore, Maryland, Resources for the Future, 1962
2 These conclusions follow from analyses of alternative policies carried out with a large-scale econometric model of natural gas field and wholesale markets.

This model and its application to policy analysis is described in P.W. MacAvoy and R.S. Pindyck's 'Alternative Regulatory Policies for Dealing with the Natural Gas Shortage,' *Bell Journal of Economics and Management Science* 4, 2 (Autumn 1973). It is here termed 'the MIT Econometric Gas Model.'

3 It is important to make clear that this policy option of field price increases does not imply complete deregulation. The econometric model is a model of a regulated industry, and we assume that that industry will continue to be regulated. We are *not* analysing the effects of deregulation on the natural gas industry; rather we are studying the impact on that industry of phased price increases.

4 This policy has the immediate effect of taking field prices from 34¢ to 49¢ per mcf on new contracts. This would be the average new contract price over the 18 production districts in 1974 as a result of freeing contract transactions from FPC regulation but subjecting them to FEA control to increases of no more than 15¢ per mcf.

5 One might ask what the impacts of specialized subsidies are likely to be. What might be the impact, for example, of a subsidy (or tax allowance) to producing companies based on all or some part of expenditures on new gas field exploration? Might such a subsidy result in greater exploratory activity than simple price additions (or subsidies) for new or total production? Unfortunately we can not provide answers to detailed questions like this at present, not because questions such as this have not been of interest to us, but rather because not enough is known at the present time about the economics of exploratory activity to make meaningful answers possible. We would in fact be suspicious of any estimate of exploration response to one or another 'particular' subsidy.

6 The inference requires some speculation on the motives of the pipelines. These pipelines carry large volumes of gas over long distances of the producing regions of the Southwest to, primarily, residential and commercial consumers receiving service from retail gas utilities in the larger population centers of the Northeast, North Central area, and California. A casual examination of the history of these lines indicates that many of them were built in the late 1950s or early 1960s, and have been providing services and charging prices for their services ever since under the jurisdiction of the Federal Power Commission. The Commission has followed the 'orthodox rate base/rate of return' regulation under which the company is allowed to earn a profit on its original capital investment minus depreciation. Many of the lines have experienced significant depreciation over the last fifteen years – given that most of them were supposed to be amortized over a thirty-year period. New ventures for these pipelines must involve critical consideration as to whether there is some way of obtaining more capital invest-

ment to replenish the losses of the original cost-rate base. Among the ventures most likely to be of interest to these lines, as a consequence of this concern for rate base, are those involving the construction of liquefaction and gasification facilities and the purchase of large-scale refrigerated tankers by the pipeline company or one of its subsidiaries.

Contributors

M.W. BUCOVETSKY University of Toronto
DUANE CHAPMAN Cornell University
J. DEBANNÉ University of Ottawa and Massachusetts Institute of Technology
DONALD N. DEWEES University of Toronto
EDWARD W. ERICKSON North Carolina State University
FRANKLIN M. FISHER Massachusetts Institute of Technology
RICHARD L. GORDON Pennsylvania State University
RICHARD E. HAMILTON York University
LARRETT HIGGINS Ontario Hydro
H.S. HOUTHAKKER Harvard University
R.M. HYNDMAN University of Toronto
JOHN HELLIWELL University of British Columbia
PAUL W. MacAVOY Massachusetts Institute of Technology
STEPHEN L. McDONALD University of Texas, Austin
S.W. MILLSAPS Appalachian State University
G.D. QUIRIN University of Toronto
ROBERT M. SPANN Virginia Polytechnic and State University
PATRICIA E. STARRATT Staff Member, United States Senate Interior Committee
TOM STOEL National Resources Defense Fund
LEONARD WAVERMAN University of Toronto